Issues *in* Travel Writing

PETER LANG
New York • Washington, D.C./Baltimore • Bern
Frankfurt am Main • Berlin • Brussels • Vienna • Oxford

Issues *in* Travel Writing

Empire, Spectacle, and Displacement

EDITED BY
Kristi Siegel

PETER LANG
New York • Washington, D.C./Baltimore • Bern
Frankfurt am Main • Berlin • Brussels • Vienna • Oxford

Library of Congress Cataloging-in-Publication Data

Issues in travel writing: empire, spectacle, and displacement /
edited by Kristi Siegel.
p. cm.
Includes bibliographical references (p.) and index.
1. Travel writing. 2. Travelers' writings—History and criticism.
I. Siegel, Kristi.
G151 .I8   808'.06691—dc21   2002023807
ISBN 0-8204-4580-0

Die Deutsche Bibliothek-CIP-Einheitsaufnahme

Issues in travel writing: empire, spectacle, and displacement /
ed. by: Kristi Siegel.
−New York; Washington, D.C./Baltimore; Bern;
Frankfurt am Main; Berlin; Brussels; Vienna; Oxford: Lang.
ISBN 0-8204-4580-0

Cover art: *The Sleeping Gypsy*, 1897, Henri Rousseau.
Digital Image © The Museum of Modern Art/ Licensed by SCALA/Art Resource, NY

Cover design by Joni Holst

The paper in this book meets the guidelines for permanence and durability
of the Committee on Production Guidelines for Book Longevity
of the Council of Library Resources.

Printed in the United States of America

✖ Table of Contents

Part Three
Displacement: Situating Identity, Home, and Diaspora

◈ Acknowledgments

Most of all, I would like to thank my contributors for their excellent essays, prompt responses, and congeniality during the long editing and production process. I would also like to thank Mount Mary College (Milwaukee, Wisconsin) for awarding a grant that provided course release time to complete this book and to the members of Mount Mary English department for the collegiality, good humor, and intellectual stimulation they provided. Sylvia Linton, Assistant Director of Mount Mary's Haggerty Library, helped in more ways than she might realize; I am in her debt. Throughout all of this book's stages, I have received excellent advice, support, and ongoing insights from Dr. Heidi Burns, the Senior Acquisitions' Editor at Peter Lang Publishing. I would also like to thank Sophie Appel, the Production Coordinator at Peter Lang, for patiently answering my endless questions.

As always, I would like to thank my family. My four children, Aaron, Adam, Ross, and Elizabeth and my husband, Ron, may have wished for more of my time. Nevertheless, they sustained me through a schedule that seemed only to get busier and busier. My gratitude to them is immeasurable.

Introduction

Travel Writing and Travel Theory

Kristi Siegel

Whether travel is a metaphor of exile, mobility, difference, modernity, or hybridity,it suggests the particular ways in which knowledge of a Self, society, and nation was, and is, within European and North American culture, to be understood and obtained.
—Inderpal Grewal, *Home and Harem*

Theorizing Travel

Despite the number of books now devoted to travel studies, a succinct response to the question, "What is travel theory?" would prove difficult. Entering "travel theory" as keywords on an Internet search engine would be likelier to yield references about physics than topics on travel literature and its study. At its simplest, travel theory examines travel writing and the process of travel itself. Even so, that definition falls short in the same way defining autobiographical theory as "the study of life writing" would also reduce its complexity. Like autobiography, still categorized as a sort of illegitimate and lesser offshoot of biography, travel writing—associated with guidebooks and other tourist apparatuses—struggles for its place as a distinct (and respected) genre, and the study of travel writing suffers a similar fate and confusion. The shift in focus from biography to autobiography in the mid to late twentieth century occurred in tandem with growing skepticism about any clear divide between fact and fiction, debate on the existence of a knowable self, and controversy on the way subjectivity is inflected by circumstances, gender, and race. Similarly, interest in travel and travel writing emerged as the result of an intellectual climate that is interrogating imperialism, colonialism/postcolonialism, ethnography, diaspora, visual culture, and spectacle.

One way to gauge whether a discipline is "taking hold" would be to note whether it has developed its own vocabulary. Those studying travel writing often use words from other disciplines, but give these terms a different "spin." Further, in theorizing travel, scholars have created their own set of terms and expressions, instantly recognizable to others investigating travel writing. Travel theory's lexicon includes words such as transculturation, metropolitan center, imperial eyes, contact zones, border crossing, tourist/traveler, imperial frontier, diaspora, road narrative, mapping, expatriation, repatriation, cosmopolitanism/localism, hybridity, margin, exoticism, pilgrim/pilgrimage, museology, displacement, migration, exile, nationalism, home/abroad, arrival/return, to name just a few. Even a cursory glance at these terms demonstrates that "travel theory" is broad in scope and timely in its concerns.

By necessity, travel writing treats both spectacle and culture. Travel may occur, in the specific sense that James Clifford uses the term (at one point in *Routes*), as the "volunteerist" practice of leaving one's home to visit another "place," or, more urgently, as the involuntary practices that occur, for example, when people flee to save their lives and seek asylum elsewhere. Travel, then—whether undertaken voluntarily or involuntarily—generally entails going to another culture, and travel writing is—in large measure—the record of what one *sees* on that journey.

Although many have noted, with surprise, the sudden burgeoning of travel writing and travel studies, its emergence is logical. Travel theory follows on the heels of critical interest in autobiography (a genre closely aligned to travel literature); commentary on multiculturalism, nationalism, colonialism, and postcolonialism; and interest in spectacle and visual culture. The essays collected here encompass an unusually rich and diverse range, focusing variously on issues of colonialism/postcolonialism, empire, subjectivity, identity, spectacle, tourism, spirituality, diaspora, and displacement.

Empire: Revisiting Imperialist Travel Writing

Richard Burton's comment, "See one promontory (said Socrates of old), one mountain, one sea, one river, and see all," might be the ultimate imperialist statement. Implicit in the statement is the idea that seeing one instance of any general category could stand in for them all. By this logic, seeing one Indian "native," meeting one Tibetan monk, or viewing one Norwegian fjord would be the same as seeing them all—difference and particularity are erased entirely. Put this way, the reification is obvious and ludicrous, yet it is just this type of sweeping generalization that typifies much of imperialist travel writing. Further, many imperialist travelers assumed they could understand a culture simply by "looking" at it and that, in fact, they could translate it—more articulately, more profoundly—than its inhabitants.

Two travel writers who might epitomize imperialist discourse are Ernest Hemingway and Theodore Roosevelt, both critiqued by Edward Whitley in "Race and Modernity in Theodore Roosevelt's and Ernest Hemingway's Travel Writing." Hemingway and Roosevelt saw Africa both as America's past (when it was still an unspoiled happy hunting ground) and as its Other (e.g., Africa's so-called "primitive" culture reassures them of America's superiority). Whitley contends that in creating an American imperialist subjectivity in their narratives, Roosevelt and Hemingway represent Africa as not so much a place as a time, a time of adventure untarnished by civilization.

The imperialism Melanie R. Hunter identifies is more submerged. In "British Travel Writing and Imperial Authority" Hunter focuses on travel writers such as Paul Fussell, Graham Greene, Joseph Conrad, Doris Lessing, and V. S. Naipaul. Hunter maintains that the journey's impulse is always closely aligned with the traveler's autobiography and his or her search for origins and identity. Constructing identity, however, is also a means of establishing authority. British writers struggling with these issues during the late nineteenth and early twentieth centuries were further confounded by the parallel struggle for identity and authority England faced as its empire and power declined. Additionally, "imperial" authority—whether desired or not—is, Hunter asserts, influenced by perspective, location, circumstance, and privilege. For example, what does it means to be English when you are yourself—as Doris Lessing was—a "colonial" as a white settler on colonial territory? In another instance, Hunter analyzes Joseph Conrad's dark and nuanced exploration of English identity after its treasured notion of "civilization" is set loose in the heart of a colonized country. Provocatively, Hunter shows how identity and authority are, to use her own words, "negotiated, repositioned, manipulated, and reconfigured to serve the various projects of the writer traveling, en route."

In "Travel Writing and the Imperial Subject in 1930s Prose: Waugh, Bowen, Smith, and Orwell," Adam Piette identifies a similar upheaval taking place in narratives of English selfhood and nationhood. Using works by Evelyn Waugh, Elizabeth Bowen, Stevie Smith, and George Orwell, Piette argues that although it may have been possible before and during the 1920s to "see travel as an epic journey into the mind and private relationships," by the 1930s the situation was far more complex. Travel writing serves as a particularly apt genre to study the changing political culture because, as Piette notes, travel writing has always been *about* culture. In examining colonial and postcolonial writing in the 1930s, Piette reveals how notions of English (imperial) selfhood were being attacked and reconfigured by the very "underclasses and subject territories that had underwritten their definition."

Germany's "construction" of Italy suggests that the dynamics of colonization may occur at the level of narrative and imagination as well. Cecilia Novero, in her essay, "Contemporary German Journeys to Italy" examines various representations of Italy in contemporary literary and popular accounts published in German for the past thirty years. Novero contends that the issues she raises would contribute to the discussion on postcolonial theory, in spite of the fact that neither Germany nor Italy is a postcolonial nation. Through the eyes of the German travel writers, Italy is constructed as different from Germany; it represents, Novero states, the "power of the earth, nature, and the other side of the 'Spirit.'" Consequently, Italy serves as Germany's Other, and represents this difference in an "absolute way." Germany's appropriation of Italy essentially colonizes Italy for, as Novero argues, postcolonial studies demonstrate that the "specificity and multidimensional, multifaceted character of any contemporary nation lies in the nation as hybrid."

Andrea Feeser, though also focusing on colonialism and postcolonialism, treats a far different locale in "Constance Fredericka Gordon Cumming's 'Picturesque' Vision: A Christian, Westernized Hawai'i." Feeser analyzes the British travel writer and illustrator Constance Fredericka Gordon Cumming and her various travel books written toward the end of the nineteenth century. In her desire for a country that is at once exotic and restrained, Cumming's describes and paints Hawai'i to conform to her own ideals of "picturesque exoticism." As Feeser demonstrates, Cumming's rather romanticized perceptions prefigure the "ideological and emotional investments many foreigners had (and continue to have) in Hawai'i: namely that it conform to the fantasy of a tropical paradise that both excites and seduces, but is tamed."

Spectacle: Mapping Cultural and Spiritual Landscapes

In an essay about pastoral poetry, Frank Kermode commented that the view of the country always implies the view from the city. Similarly, travel writing often implies the view from home. Travel implicitly calls the notion of "home" into question because that is typically the standard from which experiences are measured. By definition, then, exotic would be "other than home." In journeys outward—away from home—other landscapes, countries, and cultures are often viewed in terms of how they compare to one's home. In "Travel as Spectacle: The Illusion of Knowledge and Sight" Kristi Siegel and Toni B. Wulff question the often assumed relationship between vision and knowledge. Siegel and Wulff trace the history of vision and knowledge and interrogate the notion that travel (i.e., "seeing" other cultures) inevitably results in knowledge. Further, the way industrialized cultures (in particular) perceive "reality" may have altered, and western culture's dominant mode of seeing shifted, in response to what Guy Debord termed the "society of the spectacle." If vision has been reduced to "scanning"—a rapid skimming of surfaces—what does the traveler actually see and recollect? More to the point, what has a traveler ever been able to see? In contrast to "gazing," or surveying culture through "imperial eyes," scanning is innately humble in its lack of mastery, a gesture that may—as Walter Benjamin might assert—be recollection in its most honest form.

Marco Diani and Gary Totten both treat views of America through the lens of France. Marco Diani, in "Baudrillard's Explorations of Tocqueville's America: Wandering in Hyperdemocracy," sees the "relentless seriousness" Jean Baudrillard evinces stemming from his concern that America forecasts Europe's future. In Baudrillard's view, America is symbolized by its desert, a place, Diani writes, "whose history has been forgotten, leveled, made an object of preservation, and whose meaning has vanished in its own heat." Similarly, well over a century earlier, Tocqueville explored America "so at least to know what we have to fear or hope therefrom" (*Democracy* 19). What Baudrillard and Tocqueville ultimately see in America, however, differs completely. Baudrillard seeks out "*astral* America," the America he perceives in its literal and metaphoric deserts (*America* 5) while Tocqueville, in contrast, performs a systematic study of America's customs and democracy and then makes the remarkable assertion that he sees "more in America than America" (*Democracy* 19).

Gary Totten, in "Simone de Beauvoir's *America Day by Day*: Reel to Real," examines Beauvoir's 1947 four-month speaking tour of the United States which she chronicles in *America Day by Day*. Totten notes that, similar to previous and even future texts (e.g., Alexis de Tocqueville's *Democracy in America* or Jean Baudrillard's *America*), Beauvoir's account of her American trip "casts a critical gaze on American culture." In searching for an "American essence," Beauvoir's observations often seem similar to those made by Baudrillard nearly four decades later. Like Baudrillard, Beauvoir comments on America's materialism and superabundance. Often, Beauvoir's perceptions are shaped by a complex blend of scenes from her American tour and scenes from the many American movies she obsessively watches. Ultimately, Totten writes, Beauvoir "weaves an adventure tale—both 'reel' and real—of her search for an American essence."

Alexis de Tocqueville, Jean Baudrillard, and Simone de Beauvoir all surveyed the American spectacle in hopes of defining its essence. The "essence" of medieval Rome is no less challenging. In "St. Lawrence and the Pagans in *The Marvels of Rome*," Cynthia Ho questions the agenda of a medieval guidebook, i.e., *The Marvels of Rome,* the conventional title for *Mirabilia urbis Romae,* a manuscript written around 1143. Ostensibly, the work is merely a guidebook, a medieval Baedeker, designed to guide early travelers to Rome. More complexly, Ho argues, *The Marvels of Rome* really seeks to retain and acknowledge Rome's significant other—its pagan past—into "the aesthetics of Christianity." Ho uses map theory to demonstrate how the story of St. Lawrence, whose story is strategically placed in the book's center, marks "the intersection of the two meanings of the name 'Rome': Christian universal church and pagan empire."

The first four essays in this section focused more on travel's spectacle than its journey. However, travel—the road, the path, the quest—has also served as a metaphor for religious and spiritual journeys. In these journeys, the eye turns inward. In the essays of Theodore C. Humphrey, Heidi N. Sjostrom, Donna Foran, and María Francisca Llantada Díaz, the authors and their characters become pilgrims on a journey. For John McPhee, one's spirituality and the land itself are inextricably linked. In "John McPhee's Spiritual Journeys: The Authenticating Eye," Theodore C. Humphrey portrays McPhee as a mind reading the world from the unexpectedly spiritual perspective afforded his travels by the "deep time" of contemporary geological theory. McPhee's grasp of plate tectonics, glaciation, volcanism, his understanding of the forces of fire, water, and landforms in Southern California or his celebrations of environments as disparate as Atlantic City and the Pine Barrens all contribute to the conclusion that he is a profoundly spiritual writer whose artistically crafted reports evoke the sense of the complexity and wonder of the earth as our physical home. Humphrey explores some of the contexts in which McPhee's spiritual (and joyous) journeys take place and the elements of his writing—his authenticating eye—that "create the special persona of the spiritually motivated yet scientific voyager."

Similarly, the focus on spirituality, land, and journey is also evident in the work of Willa Cather. As Heidi N. Sjostrom points out in "Willa Cather's Nebraska Prairie: Remembering the Spirit of Its Land and People," the land itself provides the spiritual soil for Cather and many of her characters. Much of what Cather found "good" and "true" was embodied in the Nebraskan landscape. Though Cather does not require that people remain on or return to the prairie, she does celebrate the "prairie values that enriched" their lives. Cather's life on the prairie consisted of its many natural elements—both good and bad—and most importantly, the people she met there. Throughout, Sjostrom shows how Cather and many of her characters learned to value the prairie more in retrospect, when it was contrasted to the city to which many of them later traveled.

Ostensibly, the often wildly fantastic travels evident in Kurt Vonnegut's fiction appear whimsical rather than spiritual. However, in "Kurt Vonnegut's Search for Soul," Donna Foran maintains that Vonnegut journeys inward in an attempt to get at truth itself. Critics have posited that Vonnegut's writings all hinge on the February 13, 1945, fire bombing of Dresden by American and British bombers. Foran agrees in part but wonders, then, how his other journeys to "Tralfamadore, Vonnegut's fictional planet, or to the center of Kurt Vonnegut himself" might be explained. These journeys do not pivot on a single event; rather, Foran contends, his travels reach into both "Vonnegut's genealogy" and the philosophies that drive America. Further, though his fiction is often funny, it is also serious, and despite its postmodern form, Vonnegut's journey is ultimately more sacred than playful.

María Francisca Llantada Díaz, in "Dorothy Richardson's *Pilgrimage* as Journey Down to the Center of Being," demonstrates how Dorothy Richardson, by titling her multivolume work, *Pilgrimage,* endows it with all the "mythical and religious references" and multiple allusions the word *pilgrimage* implies. Further, as Díaz demonstrates, the goal-directed nature of pilgrimage closely aligns it to *Bildungsroman,* where protagonists become educated in the process of a life journey that takes them "from innocence to maturity" in order to achieve "self-knowledge and understanding of the world." In some sense, Díaz argues, Dorothy Richardson becomes a mystic, as she travels down into herself to the "heart of reality."

Displacement: Representing Diaspora and Fixing Identity

The final group of essays treats displacements in travel writing: literal diasporas, attempts to situate or create identity, and the narrative tug between circling and linearity that can take place in travel writing itself. The first two essays question what happens when there is no home: situations where there never was a home—because of its shifting, destabilized nature—or where the home has evaporated, evacuated by a sudden diaspora. Joseph Pugliese's reflective essay, "In the Ruins of Diaspora: A Southern Italian Perspective," meditates on what is entailed, in conceptual and affective terms, in the exile's journey back "home." For Pugliese, this home is Spilinga, which—after his twenty-year absence—he sees largely in ruins, due to the effects of mass migration during the post–World War II years. Pugliese theorizes on the complex temporal relations that the exile must negotiate in the context of multiple displacements and draws on the work of the Jewish-French philosopher Emmanuel Levinas in an attempt to come to terms with the sense of loss and otherness that haunts the exile on their return "home." In mapping the devastation to the village by mass migration, Pugliese uses Walter Benjamin's "angel of history" in order to make sense of the complex layers of historical forces that constitute, and continue to operate on, the socio-physical fabric of the village.

In contrast to the strong sense of place—even in the face of loss—that permeates Pugliese's essay, Andrew Palmer explores what happens when one's place or home may never have existed at all. The meandering title of Palmer's essay, "(Re)-Visiting *Der Heim:* The Amazing Return to the Place You've Never Been Which Isn't There" aptly fits the topic of Jewish placelessness, uncategorizability, and alterity. Palmer explains how Jewishness disrupts "normal" categories of identity and creates apprehension because it is "not national, not genealogical, not religious, but all of these in dialectical tension with one another" (Boyarin and Boyarin 721).

The desire to stabilize identity may also be observed in Katy Nebhan's essay, "Australian Muslim Experiences of Meccan Pilgrimage or *Hajj,*" where she describes the struggle for identity experienced by Australian Muslims. Nebhan remarks that although efforts have been made to overcome internal differences such as ethnic, sectarian, and cultural divisions, a cohesive identity which is both "Australian" and "Muslim" has yet to be fully realized. However, the pilgrimage to Mecca, Nebhan contends, serves as a potent metaphor for Australian Muslims, an experience that is both structured around an "ideal" memory and that communicates the socio-religious world through which Australian Muslims filter what they see.

V. S. Naipaul also struggles to "locate" his identity. In "A Million Enigmas Now: V. S. Naipaul's Use of Landscape in the Construction of the 'English' Self," Pallavi Rastogi shows how Naipaul—who straddles the identities of colonized and would-be colonizer—deliberately recreates himself into an Englishman. In *A Million Mutinies Now* and *The Enigma of Arrival,* Naipaul's creation of an English self is strongly tied to his perceptions of landscape "where, in one work, landscape is idealized and, in the other, orientalized." Rastogi shows how, in both *A Million Mutinies Now* and *The Enigma of Arrival,* Naipaul fashions his English self at the expense of his own origins and the "orientalized" landscapes he rejects.

The narrative expectations built into a genre—such as travel writing—may impose a different type of constraint. In "Jonathan Raban's *Coasting* and Literary Strategies in Contemporary British Travel Writing," Jan Borm focuses on England's travel writing and begins by analyzing the notion of "circling" that lies at the heart of Jonathan Raban's *Coasting.* Borm then shows how this literary strategy of circling the center—a type of discontinuity at odds with more linear travel narrative—characterizes a number of contemporary British travel books. British travel writers such as Bruce Chatwin or Redmond O'Hanlon and Jonathan Raban, in particular, Borm argues, confound travel's usual arrival/return, chronological pattern by using narrative strategies that allow "contemporary authors to leave the circle of the conventional."

In an excellent review essay on recent travel literature, Nicholas Howe posits that as "scholars started to write books about travel books…the genre came to seem yet again on the edge of exhaustion." Here, however, Howe is premature. The depth and diversity of the essays in this collection demonstrate energy rather than exhaustion. What Howe may really be pondering is the importance of this critical endeavor. Why bother to study travel writing at all? Travel writing warrants our attention because it foregrounds many of the cultural and historical issues that currently dot our critical landscape. By its very nature, travel writing crosses literal and figurative boundaries and works to expose our cultural preconceptions. The essays here focus on empire, spectacle, and displacement, topics that are central both to our understanding of travel writing and to our understanding of an increasingly interconnected world.

Works Cited

Baudrillard, Jean. *America.* London: Verso. 1986.

Beauvoir, Simone de. *America Day by Day.* 1952. Trans. Carol Cosman. Berkeley: U of California P, 1999.

Benjamin, Walter. *Illuminations.* Trans. Harry Zohn. Ed. Hanna Arendt. New York: Schocken Books, 1989.

———. *The Origin of German Tragic Drama.* Trans. John Osborne. London: NLB, 1977.

Boyarin, Daniel, and Jonathan Boyarin. "Diaspora: Generation and the Ground of Jewish Identity." *Critical Identity* 19 (1993): 693–725.

Chatwin, Bruce. *In Patagonia.* 1977. London: Picador, 1979.

Clifford, James. *Routes: Travel and Translation in the Late Twentieth Century.* Cambridge: Harvard UP, 1997.

Debord, Guy. *The Society of the Spectacle.* Trans. Donald Nicholson-Smith. New York: Zone Books, 1995.

Fussell, Paul. *Abroad: British Literary Traveling Between the Wars.* Oxford: Oxford UP, 1980.

Grewal, Inderpal. *Home and Harem: Nation, Gender, Empire, and the Cultures of Travel.* Durham and London: Duke UP, 1996.

Howe, Nicholas. "How We Travel Now." Review article. *The New Republic Online.* http://www.tnr.com/080601/howe080601.html.

Kermode, Frank. *English Pastoral Poetry.* New York: Barnes & Noble, 1952.

The Marvels of Rome. Mirabilia Urbis Romae. Ed. and Trans. Francis Morgan Nichols. 2nd ed. New York: Italica Press, 1986.

Naipaul, V.S. *The Enigma of Arrival.* New York: Vintage Books, 1988.

———. *India: A Million Mutinies Now.* London: Minerva, 1990.

O'Hanlon, Redmond. *Into the Heart of Borneo: An Account of a Journey Made in 1983 to the Mountains of Batu Tiban with James Fenton.* 1984. London: Penguin, 1985.

Pratt, Mary Louise. *Imperial Eyes: Travel Writing and Transculturation.* Routledge: London and New York, 1992.

Raban, Jonathan. *Coasting.* 1986. London: Picador, 1987.

Richardson, Dorothy. *Pilgrimage.* Vol. I. *Pointed Roofs,* 1915. *Backwater,* 1916. *Honeycomb,* 1917. London: Virago, 1995.

———. *Pilgrimage.* Vol. II. *The Tunnel,* Feb 1919. *Interim,* Dec 1919. London: Virago, 1992.

———. *Pilgrimage.* Vol. III. *Deadlock.* 1921, *Revolving Lights,* 1923. *The Trap,* 1925. London: Dent, 1967.

———. *Pilgrimage.* Vol. IV. *Oberland,* 1927. *Dawn's Left Hand,* 1931. *Clear Horizon,* 1935. *Dimple Hill,* 1938. *March Moonlight,* 1967. London: Virago, 1979.

Tocqueville, Alexis de. *Democracy in America.* Ed. J. P. Mayer. New York: Harper & Row, 1969.

Part One

Empire:

Reassessing Imperialist

Travel Writing

✖ Chapter 1

Race and Modernity in Theodore Roosevelt's and Ernest Hemingway's African Travel Writing

Edward Whitley

Coming on the heels of Theodore Roosevelt's return from his 1909 East African hunting safari, the Pittsburgh *Gazette-Times* ran an editorial cartoon showing how both the people and animals of Africa had been forever changed by their encounter with the former president. Lions, snakes, birds, tigers, monkeys, and Africans in caricature all wear wire-rim glasses and big, toothy, Rooseveltian grins. "Gone, but not forgotten," reads the caption, while a bow-tied raccoon in the lower corner—spokesman for *Gazette-Times* cartoonist "Ole May"—says respectfully of T. R.'s influence, "Some men always leave their impress" (Gros 307). The impression this American cartoonist depicts Roosevelt as leaving on Africa is nothing compared to the impression Africa made on American readers in *African Game Trails,* Roosevelt's two-volume travel/hunting narrative depicting an exotic Africa full of primitive people and animals. By reading *African Game Trails,* Americans saw more than T. R.'s famous grin in the faces of Africa's prehistoric people and animals; they saw the negative reflection of their own modernity, a reflection that formed a stunning chiaroscuro of perceived black primitivism and white so-called modernity, color-coded in the racialized language of early twentieth-century America. As Roosevelt writes primitivism onto Africa in *African Game Trails,* he impresses on Americans the notion that if Africa is to come out of the past and into the modern world, it will be through the intervention of whites. This racialized and temporalized image of Africa aligns itself well with the imperial expectations of a self-defined "modern" nation eager not only to justify claims in Africa, but also to find a rationale for further expansion across the globe.

African Game Trails by Theodore Roosevelt was released in 1909 to huge commercial success. It was so popular among adult readers that it went through

Figure 1.1: Artwork from page 307 of Gros, Raymond. *T.R. in Cartoon.* New York: Saalfield, 1910. Copyright, Ole Miss, *Pittsburgh Post-Gazette,* 2000, all rights reserved. Reprinted with permission.

several editions and was quickly adapted by Marsall Everett into a juvenile picture-book, *Roosevelt's Thrilling Experiences in the Wilds of Africa*. While immensely popular, neither Roosevelt's *African Game Trails* nor the juvenile adaptation was anything new to the American reading public. That very lack of originality is probably what made the books so popular, however. Both texts fit into the well-established genre that Richard Phillips calls "adventure stories," defined as "the narratives of explorers, surveyors, geographers, [hunters] and other storytellers who describe journeys 'into the unknown'" (1). The popularity of Roosevelt's narrative was not out of the ordinary. Phillips says, "Adventure was perhaps the most popular literature…of the modern period.…[A]dventures were printed in large quantities and read by mass audiences…around the world" (10, 46). The "plots and characters" of these adventure stories—both fictional and nonfictional—were "so formulaic and familiar" that audiences demanded conformity, not creativity, in the tales (46). Roosevelt's book, true to its genre, plods through a predictable narrative strain of hunting, avoiding danger, succeeding under great odds, and so on. The publisher's preface to the juvenile adaptation reads,

> [In this book you will read of] the thrilling incidents and narrow escapes [Roosevelt] passes through, the tropical natural scenery in which he dwells, the many unknown and strange quadrupeds, bipeds and quadrumana he meets, the fabulous wealth of the African fauna and flora, which baffles the eyes, and you will see enacted before your wondering and admiring eyes a drama so unique, so exceptional and so extraordinary as to surpass anything you have either seen or heard of before. (Everett 33)

Despite claims to uniqueness ("drama so unique…as to surpass anything you have either seen or heard of before"), the Roosevelt texts were very much like other adventure stories of the day. In fact, it would be no stretch of the imagination to assume that J. H. Moss, the publishing company, used this as the preface to all of its adventure stories, modifying only the name of the particular hero to fit the particular text. Underneath this veneer of conformity in adventure stories, however, is a subtext that, Phillips tells us, was "motivated by a clear political agenda: broadly speaking, imperialism" (12). Indeed, the imperial rhetoric in Roosevelt's narratives can hardly even be called subtextual. The publisher's preface to the adolescent adaptation of Roosevelt's narrative begins by telling young boys that they should learn from the ex-president all the manly virtues embodied by hunting, and then goes on to say,

> But our book will not only serve as an entertainment on leisure hours or an instruction for the young.…Might it not even be possible, Mr. Businessman, that you will discover in these fascinating pages new fields for your enterprising mind, new fields for American trade and industry? The old world is soon covered by competing concerns.…But Africa's virgin soil and barbarian population will for

decades and perhaps centuries to come be in need of our products and our commerce. (Everett 34)

This open invitation to the "Mr. Businessman" of early twentieth-century America to make Africa an easy commodity for consumption establishes both Roosevelt texts as stories of American imperialism. As stories of imperialism, Roosevelt's texts, like most travel writing, "affirm a particular vision of reality for a community of readers" (Kaplan 42). As Phillips says, "the world of adventure" is a space for readers to "find their world views reaffirmed in its bold images and uncomplicated terms" (89). The "particular vision of reality" found in "the world of adventure"—that America was an imperial power in Africa—fed the imagination of millions of Americans.

One particular American imagination that these Roosevelt narratives fed was that of a young Midwesterner named Ernest Hemingway. Hemingway, biographer John Raeburn tells us, was so taken with Roosevelt's tales of imperial adventure that he "modeled himself on the hero of San Jan Hill" (3). From the day Hemingway, as a young boy, met Roosevelt—"who greeted [him] with a hearty handclasp and a high squeaky voice" (3)—to the day in 1933 when he arrived in Kenya for his own African safari, recorded in his 1935 *Green Hills of Africa,* he longed to be like the great T. R. Raeburn writes of Hemingway's success in becoming his boyhood hero:

> Both men had tremendous energy, personal magnetism, boastful self-confidence and a boyish joy in ordinary experience. Both advocated the strenuous life, and placed great emphasis on bodily fitness and physical strength. Both were pugnacious and belligerent, and became experienced boxers. Both were keen naturalists who hunted big game in the American West and in East Africa. Both were men of letters who became men of action, and heroes who generated considerable publicity. (3–4)

As public heroes, what Hemingway and Roosevelt most had in common was that both believed the myths the public constructed around them. Raeburn continues, "If Mark Twain was the Lincoln of American literature,...then Hemingway was the Theodore Roosevelt...[People] loved them more for the legend of their lives than for their objective achievements" (11). Indeed, in one of his few poetic endeavors, Hemingway wrote a homage to Roosevelt in which he praised that "all the legends that he started in his life / Live on and prosper, / Unhampered now by his existence" (*Three Stories and Ten Poems* 52). One of the Roosveltian legends that loomed largest in Hemingway's mind, both as a boy and as a man, was the image of Roosevelt as the great white hunter in Africa. Biographer Michael Reynolds concurs that "[it was] Theodore Roosevelt's epic 1909 safari, which young Hemingway followed in magazines, and in Oak Park watched the jerky moving pictures of the Colonel's expedition on the silent screen [which] more than any[thing] else...was responsible for opening East Africa to Hemingway's imagination" (*Hemingway: The 1930s* 156).

It was Roosevelt and the legend of the great white hunter in Africa that he had come to represent that ultimately led Hemingway to Africa from 1933 to 1934, the scene for his nonfiction novel, *Green Hills of Africa*. While Hemingway had ostensibly set out to write *Green Hills of Africa* as a new kind of nonfiction novel—"an absolutely true book to see whether the shape of a country and the pattern of a month's action can, if truly presented, compete with a work of the imagination," as he states in the foreword of the book—his influences for writing about Africa were firmly set in the genre of the adventure story. Despite his desire to capture "the shape of a country," Hemingway did not actually write *Green Hills* while in Africa; he wrote it *after* the trip while living in Key West (Meyers 264). What informed his writing about Africa, then, was not the continent itself, but the pages and pages he read from adventure narratives about Africa while in America. During his stay in Key West, Hemingway compiled a list of all the books in his personal library. The list is very telling in the large number of books—forty-one, to be precise—devoted to hunting and adventure in Africa. His list includes such titles as *African Adventures, Hunters' Wanderings in Africa, African Hunting, African Hunter, In Wildest Africa* (two volumes), *Game Ranger on Safari* (written by Philip Percival, the British hunting guide who accompanied first Roosevelt, then Hemingway in Africa), *Big Game Hunting and Adventure, In Brightest Africa, The Man-Eaters of Tsavo, Savage Sudan,* and, of course, Theodore Roosevelt's *African Game Trails* (Reynolds, *Hemingway's Reading* 46–70). Only twenty-one of these African books from the Key West catalogue were recent purchases (bought in Paris after the trip to Africa [27]); the other twenty had been in Hemingway's possession for who knows how long—since boyhood, perhaps?

Apart from the Key West list, Reynolds, the compiler of an awesome list of what Hemingway probably read between 1910 and 1940, records that Hemingway had at least an additional twenty books about Africa at his disposal (*Hemingway's Reading* 205). A grand total of sixty books on Africa, fully three times as many books as he had on Italy (208), and an almost equal number of the books he had on bullfighting (206). Reynolds comments on Hemingway's reading of the Africa books: "Hemingway read the books, including, I'm sure, Theodore Roosevelt's African adventures. Look at the pictures: Ernest with his Teddy mustache posed next to the trophies. His guide is Percival, the hunter who had led Roosevelt on to the Serengeti Plain thirty years earlier. Hardly a coincidence" (27). The "hardly coincidental" thread connecting Roosevelt and Hemingway's travel/hunting writing that I would like to tug on is the image of a temporally primitive and racialized Africa that offers itself up for American consumption. The continuation of this image through the writing of two such prominent Americans—both of them Nobel Prize winners whose exploits fascinated the American public—suggests more than just a similarity in style and personality. It suggests a larger national consciousness, articulated through the boldness of a Roosevelt and the brashness of a Hemingway.

In order to depict Africa as temporally primitive, Roosevelt and Hemingway first must have a sense of themselves as temporally modern. To have a sense of oneself as "modern" implies that identity is not defined with regards to physical characteristic, but to a perceived sense of time. Matei Calinescu says, "The idea of modernity could be conceived only within a framework of a specific time awareness, namely, that of *historical time*, linear and irreversible, flowing irresistibly onwards" (13). To be modern is to imagine oneself within what Johannes Fabian calls "a scheme in terms of which not only past cultures, but all living societies were irrevocably placed on a temporal slope, a stream of Time—some upstream, others downstream" (17). To be modern is to imagine the world in terms of linear history with "modern" people at the most recent point and "primitive" people faltering far behind. Building upon Enlightenment theories of modernity and progress as far back as Rousseau—who, incidentally, defined human perfectibility in terms of the progress one had made from "a primitive state" (Montag 290)—Roosevelt and Hemingway define themselves as "modern," and, as such, view themselves as having traversed further along the scale of history than the Africans they encounter.

Within this context of modern temporality, then, Roosevelt and Hemingway do not experience Africa as a place but as a time, a tendency common among modern travelers, who, Caren Kaplan says, "look for an escape from modernity" (78). Because modernity, as I am using the term here, is a sense of being at the forefront of, and saturated with, time, in order for Roosevelt and Hemingway to "escape from modernity," they have to make the earth an ontological clock with America at the forefront of time and Africa in the distant past. Africa, then, becomes not a place on the map, but a moment in time—a moment in the static, primitive past to which these modern men can travel and write about for a modern audience at home. The travel to foreign places in modern adventure stories is not an experience with geographic spaces, but with moments in premodern history. Kaplan writes, "When the past is displaced, often to another location, the modern subject must travel to it...a 'place on a map' can be seen to be a 'place in history'" (35, 25). Fabian concurs, writing that, "Travel itself...is instituted as a temporalizing practice" and through this temporalizing practice, "the philosophical traveler, sailing to the ends of the earth, is in fact traveling in time; he is exploring the past; every step he makes is the passage of an age" (7). Roosevelt himself says in *African Game Trails*, that riding through Africa is "like retracing the steps of time" (66). At one moment in the book, when Roosevelt and fellow hunting companion, son Kermit, come across a rhinoceros, they marvel at how such a "prehistoric" creature could exist in the modern world they inhabit. Roosevelt points out the animal to his son as he sees it "deep in prehistoric thought" (214). The temporarily displaced rhinoceros, for Roosevelt, stands as "the survival from the elder world that has vanished: ...he would have been out of place in the miocene; but nowadays he can only exist at all in regions that have lagged behind" (214).

From the outset of *African Game Trails,* Roosevelt's description of Africa— the "region that [has] lagged behind"—is in decidedly temporal terms. The name of the opening chapter of the narrative, "A Railroad through the Pleistocene," shows Roosevelt's vision of Africa as a space better described by its relationship to history than to geography. He ·says in the opening paragraph that Africa is a "phase of the world's life history," not a place on a map (1). He then goes on to say that the manner in which a place in history can become a space of modernity, without having to wade through "centuries of slow development" (1), is through the intervention of whites, the first hint he gives of temporality providing a way for Africa to become a commodity for American imperialism: "Again and again, in the continents new to peoples of European stock, we have seen...high civilization all at once thrust into and superimposed upon a wilderness of savage men and savage beasts" (1).

The continent of "savage men and savage beasts" to which Roosevelt refers in the opening paragraph of his narrative is not a place on a geographic map, but a "phase of the world's life history." Africa, for Roosevelt, will remain a moment in time, not a place on a map, until "peoples of European stock"—not necessarily Europeans themselves, he makes sure to clarify, but "peoples of European stock," allowing for the imperial intervention of white Americans— make it a place by "thrusting civilization" onto it. It takes a "person of European stock," invested with modernity, to create a "high civilization" of a moment in the world's life history. The image of the railroad as an authenticating force for whites in Africa, then, is startling. Roosevelt says, "This railroad [is] the embodiment of the eager, masterful...civilization of today" (3). As such, the railroad cuts through time, not geographic space. It is "A Railroad through the Pleistocene," not "A Railroad through Africa." Right from the outset Roosevelt temporally codes Africa and then provides the means by which primitive Africa can become modern—namely, through white intervention. The railroad, emblematic of whiteness and modernity, injects history into timeless Africa.

In the narratives of both Roosevelt and Hemingway, whiteness and modernity are inseparably connected. This is nothing new in American discourse; as Toni Morrison asserts, white American writers have consistently used temporally coded figures of blackness to establish their identity as (white) Americans. She says that Americans use temporally coded figures of blackness as "the vehicle by which the American self knows itself as...not history-less, but historical;...not a blind accident of evolution, but a progressive fulfillment of destiny" (52). A sense of being "white" in America is intimately tied to notions of progress and history. Because, as Morrison argues, whiteness is inextricable from a presence of blackness, whiteness-as-modern can only arise within the context of blackness-as-primitive. As "an Africanist idiom is used to establish difference or...signal modernity," she writes, images of blackness "are appropriated for the associative value they lend to modernism" (52). Thomas G. Dyer, in a comprehensive study of Roosevelt's ideas on race, found a fascinating link in Roosevelt's thought between the notion of modern progress and race, similar to what Morrison says about whiteness equating modernity and blackness equating primitivism. Roosevelt, a Lamarckian, followed the belief that evolution was the result of one generation acquiring the characteristics which would make their species more likely to survive—French evolutionist Jean Lamarck's classic example is that of the giraffes who passed on the trait of long necks to their posterity by earning those necks through the hard labor of stretching towards edible leaves. Roosevelt believed that only those "races" or "species" (terms ambiguously related for Roosevelt and other nineteenth-century race thinkers) which put forth the requisite effort would progress. Dyer writes, "Roosevelt took the general stand that evolution did not necessarily ensure steady progress...he adhered to the belief that progress was not foreordained and found it a 'rather irritating delusion' that 'somehow or other we are all necessarily going to move forward in the long run.' He admitted, however, a 'very firm faith in this general forward movement, considering only men of our own race'" (33). Whereas Roosevelt doubts the universal progression of the entire human species, he is quite positive that whites ("men of our own race") are progressing. In the temporally bankrupt land of Africa, that progression is through time as well as space.

Whiteness and modernity, linked in Roosevelt's narrative, move the former president to say that not only is Africa a phase in the "world's life history," but that it is a phase in white racial history. Roosevelt says that Africa is "a region in which nature, both as regards wild man and wild beast, did not and does not differ materially from what it was in Europe in the late Pleistocene" and that the savagery of both the African animals and peoples "reproduces the conditions of life in Europe as it was led by our ancestors ages before the dawn of anything that could be called civilization....African man, absolutely naked, and armed as our early ancestors were armed, lives...[as the prehistoric European] men to whom the cave lion was a nightmare of terror" (3). In several instances Roosevelt invokes the notion that Africans live as Europeans did centuries ago as a way to both differentiate himself (and his audience) from the primitive Africans and to be similar to them. James Clifford, paraphrasing Fabian, says, "there has been a pervasive tendency to prefigure others in a temporally distinct, but locatable, space (earlier) within an assumed progress of Western history" (101–2). In passing, Roosevelt says of a tribe of Africans he encounters, "they were living just as paleolithic man lived in Europe, ages ago" (442). When he encounters a group of Africans whom he describes as living in constant terror of being eaten by the wild animals which roam the plains, Roosevelt reflects on the relative safety of the modern world and the "intensity of terror felt by his ancestors" who, ages ago, experienced a similar time: "It is only in nightmares that the average dweller in civilized countries now undergoes the hideous horror which was the regular and frequent portion of his ages-vanished forefathers, and which is still an everyday incident in the lives of most wild creatures [and in Roosevelt's this would include Africans themselves]" (244–45). In this passage, Roosevelt makes the rhetorical double move of identifying himself with Africans who represent his past ("terror felt by his *ancestors,*" "hideous horror…of his ages-vanished *forefathers*") while rushing to say that he is completely different from them (what is a "regular and frequent" occurrence in their lives could only possibly be a "nightmare" for him). Roosevelt's need to explain how whites and Africans are different, even though they share a similar temporal origin, is significant. It validates and reinforces his position at the forefront of human progress while at the same time claiming a historical right to own Africa. Nevertheless, he concedes, "The savage of today shows us what the…[age] of our ancestors was really like…[they are] the existing representatives of [our] 'vigorous, primitive' ancestors" (246). Roosevelt succeeds in highlighting his modernity while staking a claim to possessing the continent given his historical link to it. The common temporal origin of whites and Africans is balanced out by the racial differences, thus making temporality a rationale for claiming ownership of the African land and race a rationale for distancing oneself from African people.

Depicting Africa as a moment in the white racial past allows Roosevelt to create an image of Africa as primed for American consumption. This move to consume an exotic culture within a temporal and racial framework is part of what Kaplan calls "the conquering spirit of modernity" (35). Caren Kaplan writes, "Within the structure of imperialist nostalgia, then, the Euro-American past is most clearly perceived or narrativized as another country or culture" (34). Roosevelt is able to take possession of Africa after "narrativizing" it as part of his racial past. He deduces that by virtue of his modernity, which makes him possessor of the history of the world, he must also possess those global spaces stuck somewhere in the time that his race has already experienced. In other words, since he owns "primitive" time by virtue of having already experienced it in his racial past, he also owns the physical space on the globe that he defines as "primitive." The capstone moment in this opening chapter is when Roosevelt says, "This region, this great fragment of the long-buried past of our race, is now accessible by railroad to all who care to go thither" (3–4). Here Roosevelt uses his sense of himself as white and modern to open the door for the American consumption of Africa. First, the African space is turned into a time: "This region" becomes a "fragment of the long buried past." Second, that moment in time becomes a moment in white racial history: "the long buried past *of our race.*" Third, once it is established that the time which Africa represents belongs to white racial history, physical possession of Africa soon follows: "[Africa] is now accessible by railroad to all who care to go thither." As the nineteenth century's preeminent metaphor for progress, the railroad possesses Africa for white America.

This racialized and temporalized image of Africans which Roosevelt presented to Americans was by no means new or original. What he did in *African*

Game Trails was put his stamp of approval on it and preserve it for a future generation of readers. Hemingway, as part of that generation, continues to talk about Africa in terms of race and temporality where fellow Noble Prize winner Roosevelt leaves off. Despite their differing attitudes toward Africa, these two men use a surprisingly similar rhetoric. Whereas Roosevelt is overtly imperialistic, calling for the settlement of Africa as a "white man's country" and encouraging American businessmen to take advantage of African resources, Hemingway is less so. His desire is that Africa remain settled enough so that there would be somewhere he could stay when he came to hunt, but not so much so that all the good hunting grounds vanish. Hemingway's concern is more literary, to "see whether the shape of a country and the pattern of a month's action can, if truly presented, compete with a work of the imagination." Though Hemingway is not overtly imperialistic, the genre he writes in is shot through with the traces of American imperialism. As Richard Phillips tells us, "some adventure writers and stories were directly and explicitly imperial, others indirectly and implicitly [imperial,]" and traces of imperial discourse are always present (68). Whereas Hemingway at moments expresses disgust at the fruits of African colonization, David Spurr locates in the language of *Green Hills of Africa* a longing to go back to the security of Rooseveltian, or even pre-Rooseveltian, imperial certainty: "There may be, for a man of Hemingway's sensibility, arriving late on the colonial scene, a nostalgia for the moral certainty of a Stanley" (24).

Roosevelt's picture of Africa as a primitive state is the language of imperial certainty permeating Hemingway's *Green Hills of Africa*. We see this, for example, when Hemingway, similar to Roosevelt, describes a rhinoceros as "prehistoric looking" (79), suggesting that the continent and its animals belong to another era in the world's history. In another instance, he notices "tracks graded down through the pleasant forest" and suggests that these are the tracks of woolly mammoths, a species which has been extinct for ages (250). It is possible to imagine, he seems to imply, that such ancient animals still exist in this primitive country. He then compares primitive Africa to modern America: "[W]e had the mammoths too, a long time ago...It was just that we were an older country" (250). America, a modern country saturated with history, differs from primitive Africa, which is still roamed by prehistoric (extinct) animals. Hemingway, like Roosevelt, articulates Africa as a temporal moment in white racial history. The entire quote, in context, is as follows:

> I was thinking all the country in the world is the same country and all hunters are the same people....Looking at the way the tracks graded down through the pleasant forest I thought that we had the mammoths too, a long time ago, and when they traveled through the hills in southern Illinois they made these same tracks. It was just that we were an older country in America and the biggest game was gone. (249–50)

In this passage, Hemingway marks the sameness between Africa and America as continents, and the sameness between African and white American hunters. He then goes on to mark the difference between the two in terms of temporality: Africa and America may be the same ("all the country in the world is the same country"), but America is more saturated with time than Africa ("we were an older country in America"). America, an "older country," no longer has the primitive animals (i.e., "mammoths") of Africa. America is historical and progressive (the "biggest game was gone" possibly, though he doesn't say why specifically, because of the industrialization and progress which has taken place in modern America), but Africa is ahistorical and primitive, a place devoid of temporal substance. Fabian calls this move the tendency to "assign to the conquered populations a *different* Time" (30). In Hemingway's insistence that America is "an older country" than Africa he is not saying that America has been on the earth longer nor has it been inhabited by people longer than Africa has. What he insists on is that while Africa has remained primitive in the possession of Africans, America has aged in the possession of temporally saturated whites. From this perspective, then, America, as an older country, and Americans, as a people who possess history, have the right to own the past that is Africa.

Working within the modern framework where places on the globe become moments in time, the question arises, whose experience with time is made the reference point for the march of history? Who, in other words, *really* experiences time? Who carries with them, as an essence, almost, the experience of time? Kaplan answers this by arguing that "the tourist [or travel writer who can tell stories about the world from the vantage point of having been there] becomes the key to social structure in the modern era" (5). Hemingway marks the difference between African primitivism and modern white temporality through a bodily experience of time. On several occasions, he remarks that the continent is without history until he, a modern white man saturated with history, physically experiences it. Hemingway's modernity, then, his saturation with history, validates Africa as a geographic space. Hemingway, in viewing history and memory as essential to himself, comes to see history as an essence he carries in his body. The Africans who live there, however, do not experience time, so the ahistorical continent does not change in their presence. He writes in *Green Hills,* "A continent ages quickly when we come" (284), suggesting that the African country shapes itself in the presence of a modernized person just as nature shapes itself around Wallace Steven's jar. Hemingway's body, just like Roosevelt's railroad, paves the way for making Africa more than just a timeless matrix of human primitiveness.

Hemingway and his hunting party come across a "white rest house and a general store" in the little African village of Kibaya where "Dan [a friend of Hemingway's who had been in Africa years earlier] had sat on a haystack one time waiting for a kudu to feed out into the edge of a patch of mealy-corn and a lion had stalked Dan while he sat and nearly gotten him" (159). While sitting in this spot in Africa where their white friend had earlier had a hunting experience, Hemingway remarks, "this gave us a strong historical feeling for the village of Kibaya" (159). Nowhere else in the narrative does Hemingway remark on having a "historical feeling" for Africa because nowhere else (to his knowledge) had whites validated African space with their temporal presence. However, once Hemingway experiences a place in Africa which a white person has injected with temporality, he becomes "full of historical admiration" for the place (159). As soon as Hemingway leaves this temporally validated place, however, the rest of the continent reverts to blankness. In the following paragraph, right after they leave the village of Kibaya, he describes the country in less flattering terms: "[We headed out through] a million miles of bloody Africa, brush close to the road that was impenetrable, solid, scrubby-looking undergrowth" (160). Hemingway sees that part of Africa which has not been injected with history at the hand of whites, what he calls in the next paragraph "the million-mile country," as an endless, ahistorical spot of land which looks the same for millions of miles and has been the same for millions of years.

For Hemingway, African bodies contrast with his own temporally saturated body in that they experience time in an animal-like fashion, understanding only the immediate world around them. Hemingway says of his guide M'Cola, "I believe his working estimations were only from day to day and required an unbroken series of events to have any meaning" (44). In another instance he says, "M'Cola was an old man asleep, without history and without mystery" (73). The depiction of M'Cola as a man in perpetual slumber resonates with the rhetoric of race and temporality. His sleepy state, for Hemingway, becomes a timeless state—he is "without history"—and his lack of temporality becomes ontological, when Hemingway defines the African as "without mystery," without thoughts, without secrets, without being. The African body's lack of any internal sense of history, for Hemingway, defines African primitivism and reinforces white modernity. As Spurr says, "The body, rather than speech, law, or history, is the essential defining characteristic of primitive peoples. They live, according to this view, in their bodies and in natural space, but not in a body politic worthy of the name nor in meaningful historical time" (22). Even though the African country itself might resemble modern countries, as Hemingway remarks on certain occasions, it is the lack of history *in the bodies of African people* which makes the country primitive. He writes on one occasion, "The country was so much like Aragon that I could not believe that we were not in Spain until, instead of mules with saddle bags, we met a dozen natives bare-legged and bareheaded dressed in white cotton cloth they wore gathered over the shoulder like a toga; but when they were past, the high trees beside the track over those rocks was Spain" (146). Just as the white body possesses history such that "a continent ages quickly when we arrive," so does the African body's *lack* of history revert the African space to a primitive time. Without Africans on it, the land begins to modernize, to look like modern Europe to white eyes ("The country was so much like Aragon that I could not believe that we were not in Spain"). When Africans come onto the scene, though, the continent reverts back to its primitive state ("until...we met a dozen natives"). When the African bodies leave, Hemingway reports that the continent modernizes ("but when they were past, the high trees beside the track over those rocks was Spain"). Note also that it is the bareness of the African body which most signals primitivism: "[W]e met a dozen natives *bare-legged* and *bare-headed.*" The African body, with nakedness as the telltale sign of primitivism, is so void of history that it has the power to extract modernity (Spain-the-place articulated as Spain-the-moment-in-modern-time) from the landscape.

Roosevelt also remarks on the Africans' nakedness as an indicator of their primitive state. He writes, "They are in most ways primitive savages, with an imperfect and feeble social, and therefore military organization" (as compared to the thriving military of turn-of-the-century America); "they live in small communities under their local chiefs" (as compared to the huge metropolises of America and Europe); "they file their teeth, and though they wear blankets in the neighborhood of the whites, these blankets are often cast aside; even when the blanket is worn, it is often in such fashion as merely to accentuate the otherwise absolute nakedness of both sexes" (in the manner of animals with sharp teeth and no need for clothing) (44). Despite the "primitive" economic and social order of the Africans, it is their "absolute nakedness" which reifies their primitivism. He writes that the Kikuyu were "real savages, naked save for a dingy blanket....[When it rained] they had to be driven to make bough shelters for themselves. Once these shelters were up, and a little fire kindled at the entrance of each, the moping, spiritless wretches would speedily become transformed into beings who had lost all remembrance of ever having been wet or cold" (330). What first defines the Kikuyu as primitive "savages" is their nakedness, but what supports that claim to primitivism is their inability to experience time (at one moment they are cold and wet, at the next, they lose "all remembrance of ever having been wet or cold"). In one very telling moment in *African Game Trails,* Roosevelt's description of the nakedness of a group of Africans betrays his belief that nudity equals primitive savagery. He says that the Kavirondo people, "both men and women, as a rule go absolutely naked, although they are peaceable and industrious" (451). Roosevelt's "although" signals his belief that naked bodies are inherently primitive and that those Africans who walk around naked and are also "peaceable and industrious" are the exception to the rule.

Temporality and a bodily sense of history are defined by the naked baring of African skin, but more than anything else it is the *color* of that naked skin which signals primitivism as primitive temporality is color-coded as black. At one point in *African Game Trails,* Roosevelt encounters what he describes as the remnants of an "advanced" tribe of Africans, but he quickly covers their "progressive" attributes by hinting that the blackness of the continent itself dragged them back to a primitive state. He opines that this tribe must have been "in some respects more advanced than the savage tribes who now dwell in the land....Barbarians they doubtless were; but they have been engulfed in the black oblivion of a lower barbarism" (429). The continent itself, marked as "black," is so primitive that it can destroy any possible attempts at progress; it can literally engulf progress into a "black oblivion." This depiction of Africa not only reinforces that the continent is a space of primitive time, but also that "blackness" is a color-coded shorthand for a primitive temporality. The primitive oblivion that this progressive race vanished into is a "black oblivion." Blackness and temporality, Roosevelt indicates, are always interrelated. Marshall Everett, the author of the juvenile adaptation of Roosevelt's *African Game Trails,* writes in his preface to *Roosevelt's Thrilling Experiences in the Wilds of Africa* a startling depiction of the African indigenes which also links temporality with skin color:

> [This book] introduces you to the primitive inhabitants of this mysterious continent, the brown and black savages, to whom civilization is a question mark and culture is as little known as snow in August. It makes you acquainted with the strange habits, superstitious rites and religious ceremonies of these darkened cousins of the apes and monkeys, whose only right to bear the human name seems to be their poor and infantile jabbering. (Everett 36)

The Africans are "primitive," their continent "mysterious," their relationship with civilization "questionable," and their progressive distance from (white) humans so distant that they are best grouped with animals. African nakedness is not so much a sign of primitivism here as is African *blackness* ("*brown and black* savages"; "*darkened* cousins of the apes"). The most disturbing thing about race and temporality in the adaptation of Roosevelt's narrative is that the book was aimed at children. So profound was the impress that Roosevelt's image of Africa left on America that it not only affected Hemingway, one of the major authors of the twentieth century, but it also presented to young Americans a basis for imperialism which lasted long into his and the next century.

Roosevelt and Hemingway write primitivism onto Africa for white Americans to read and feel assured that they are the people entitled to colonize the world, as imperialism becomes a mechanism not of a particular nation, but the historical march of time itself. From the perspective of Roosevelt's and Hemingway's white American modernism, images of a timeless Africa reinforce the exigence of American imperialism.

Works Cited

Calinescu, Matei. *Five Faces of Modernity: Modernism, Avant-Garde, Decadence, Kitsch, Postmodernism.* Durham: Duke UP, 1987.

Clifford, James. "On Ethnographic Allegory." Ed. James Clifford and George E. Marcus. *Writing Culture: The Poetics and Politics of Ethnography.* Berkeley: U of California P, 1986. 98–121.

Dyer, Thomas G. *Theodore Roosevelt and the Idea of Race.* Baton Rouge: Louisiana State UP, 1980.

Everett, Marshall [pseudonym]. Neil, Henry. *Roosevelt's Thrilling Experiences in the Wilds of Africa and Triumphal Tour of Europe.* New York: J. H. Moss, 1909.

Fabian, Johannes. *Time and the Other: How Anthropology Makes Its Object.* New York: Columbia UP, 1983.

Gros, Raymond. *T. R. in Cartoon.* New York: Saalfield, 1910.

Hemingway, Ernest. *Green Hills of Africa.* 1935. New York: Touchstone, 1996.

———. *Three Stories and Ten Poems.* Paris: Contact, 1923.

Kaplan, Caren. *Questions of Travel: Postmodern Discourses of Displacement.* Durham: Duke UP, 1996.

Meyers, Jeffrey. *Hemingway: A Biography.* New York: Harper and Row, 1985.

Montag, Warren. "The Universalization of Whiteness: Racism and Enlightenment." Ed. Mike Hill. *Whiteness: A Critical Reader.* New York: New York UP, 1997. 281–93.

Morrison, Toni. *Playing in the Dark: Whiteness and the Literary Imagination.* New York: Vintage Books, 1994.

Phillips, Richard. *Mapping Men and Empire: Geography of Adventure.* New York: Routledge, 1997.

Raeburn, John. *Fame Became of Him: Hemingway as Public Writer.* Bloomington: Indiana UP, 1984.

Reynolds, Michael. *Hemingway: The 1930s.* New York: Norton, 1997.

———. *Hemingway's Reading 1910–1940: An Inventory.* Princeton: Princeton UP, 1981.

Roosevelt, Theodore. *African Game Trails.* Vols. I and II. New York: Scribner, 1909.

Spurr, David. *The Rhetoric of Empire: Colonial Discourse in Journalism, Travel Writing, and Imperial Administration.* Durham: Duke UP, 1993.

Chapter 2

British Travel Writing and Imperial Authority

Melanie R. Hunter

Twenty-nine train trips turn the most intrepid writer into Willy Loman. But: all journeys were return journeys. The farther one traveled, the nakeder one got, until, towards the end, ceasing to be animated by any scene, one was most oneself, a man in a bed surrounded by empty bottles....But he does not know—how could he?—that the scenes changing in the train window from Victoria Station to Tokyo Central are nothing compared to the change in himself; and travel writing, which cannot but be droll at the outset, moves from journalism to fiction, arriving as promptly as the Kodama Echo at autobiography. From there any further travel makes a beeline to confession, the embarrassed monologue in a deserted bazaar.
—Paul Theroux, *The Great Railway Bazaar*

The enigma of the journey—the underlying, often unacknowledged impulse for travel abroad—is transformed into, or transposed as, the autobiography of the traveler, the search for origins and identity, the revealing of the various attempts to construct and confirm *authority,* in terms of both authorship and ownership. The ever-confounded "genre" of travel writing, when viewed through the lens of post- or neoimperialism and post- or neocolonialism, becomes intimately bound up with the struggle between the metropolitan centers of power (in this case, Great Britain) and the (post-)colonial margins. "Self" and "Other" become highly contested sites of meaning and/or authority, and the way travel is represented between "here" and "there," between "home" and "abroad," depends on from where you are coming and to where you are going and *why.* As James Clifford acknowledges, in his essay "Traveling Cultures," "travelers move about under strong cultural, political, and economic compulsions....These different circumstances are crucial determinations of the travel at issue—movements in specific colonial, neo-colonial, and postcolonial circuits, different diasporas, borderlands, exiles, detours and returns" (108). In other words, when one is considering the subject of travel and of travel writing, one must also consider the matter of perspective, of location, of circumstance, of privilege.

Specifically, I am interested in following the shifting constructions and perceptions of authority in a travel writing that concerns itself, implicitly or explicitly, with the formations, formulations, and/or declining powers of Empire.[1] This occurs, in part, as the result of the changing perspectives growing out of post- or neocolonialism: Great Britain, or Europe—the "West," in a broader sense—formerly seen as the imperial center, as the intellectual and literal point of origin, becomes "marginalized" by the encroaching Other, as it becomes destination and thus the object of the travel writing eye/I. Essentially, the continuing moment of colonialism and imperialism (the "post" does not denote finality) creates an anxiety over the complex reworkings of identity: That is, what does it mean to be "English," in a national and personal sense, in the face of both the encroaching world and the far-flung empire, a question which deeply concerns both Paul Fussell and one of his subjects in *Abroad,* Graham Greene? From quite another perspective, Paul Theroux also addresses these concerns; although Theroux is, nationally speaking, an American, he begins his journeys from the imperial center of London, and both follows and distances himself from a British travel writing tradition. What does it mean to be an imperial authority in the colonial margins, as Joseph Conrad asks? What does it mean to be "English" (citizen and writer) when you are, in fact, a "colonial," as white settler on colonial territory, in the case of Doris Lessing, or as displaced native inhabitant of colonial territory, in the case of V.S. Naipaul? Furthermore, how does one construct, re-construct, and represent authority in writing out of and to these different situations? That authority—imperial in nature, whether as disseminating subject or dominated object—is negotiated, repositioned, manipulated, and reconfigured to serve the various projects of the writer traveling, en route.

Paul Fussell and Graham Greene Go *Abroad:* Imperial Longing

First, it is important to acknowledge that Paul Fussell's *Abroad,* while it does not exactly admit this as its focus, is quite dependent on the implicit acknowledgment of the very substantial presence of the British empire—in the same way the empire is quite dependent on the presence of the colonies for its conception of itself; or to put it another way, the center is quite dependent on the margins in its formulations of itself, its identity. Thus, what at first appears rather marginal to Fussell's account actually becomes quite crucial to understanding its central narrative, "British Literary Traveling between the Wars." It is also important to remember, I think, that Great Britain's situation between the wars—or, to extend it a bit, from the high Victorian period until World War II—was one in which national prosperity and imperial dominance figured prominently. Before World War II, in fact, Britain had only lost three of her commonwealth nations to "dominion status" (Canada, Australia, and New Zealand), where the king remains an ex-officio "head of state," but the territories are essentially self-governing. Therefore, keeping this historical moment in mind, I would argue that Fussell's account of British travel writing between the wars is, at least psychologically, also an account of the anxiety over attempts at self- and national definition after participating in World War I and during the height of imperial power, leading to the looming question of how to define oneself over and against the rest of the (uncivilized) world. In addition, Fussell's very account of this anxiety produces its own troubled response; that is, his narrative deals in nostalgia, mourning the passing of the relationship between empire and colony, between home and abroad. Paul Fussell's *Abroad* supports, bolsters, and reinscribes the legitimacy of the imperial project through the investigations of such English travel writers as Graham Greene.

In the section "I Hate It Here," Fussell recounts the many reasons why British writers felt the need to go abroad: "[D]eparture is attended by the conviction that England is uninhabitable because it is not like abroad," and thus to travel is "to escape something hateful at home" (15). He gives us lots of reasons, in his humorously indulgent and sometimes defensive style, of what might be considered "hateful" about England: the weather, the industrial pollution, the overly regulative British sensibility which governs pub closing-times and sexual orientation, among other things. However, what stands out, for me at least, in this catalogue of defects is the discomfort Fussell's subjects seem to feel concerning the state of civilization, which, in fact, is a concern about the state of *English* or *European* civilization: Britain is ruined; it is a "'dying civilization'" as Cyril Connolly puts it (qtd. in Fussell 16); it breeds awkwardness, according to Fussell's interpretations of E.M. Forster's work; and, it has indeed allowed the barbarians to break in, to paraphrase the historian A.J.P. Taylor (qtd. in Fussell 23). All this, then, facilitates the rapid decline of civilization, the end of authenticity—"'our towns are *false* towns,'" says D. H. Lawrence (qtd. in Fussell 17)—and exclusivity, as the intrusion of the "barbarians" contaminates the national and ethnic isolation of the British isles. So, then, what is a beleaguered British writer to do in the face of such overwhelming change? "'Lament and withdraw,'" again according to Taylor (qtd. in Fussell 23)—yet, this "withdrawal" is not as passive or as genuine as it might at first sound. This "withdrawal" is, actually, a departure from England, an active escape out into the world, where many territories are seen as the "lawful" property of the Empire. This active escape becomes, I would argue, active "conquest," a version of the anti-conquest detailed by Mary Louise Pratt in *Imperial Eyes:* "the strategies of representation by which European bourgeois subjects seek to secure their innocence in the same moment as they assert European hegemony....The main protagonist of the anti-conquest is a figure I sometimes call the 'seeing-man,' an admittedly unfriendly label for the European male subject of European landscape discourse—he whose imperial eyes passively look out and possess" (7). The conquest need not be a literal "taking over" of land or peoples; it can also be the falsely innocent intention to possess, scientifically, psychologically, linguistically, an Other place. This possession, as I would like to show with the case of Graham Greene and Africa, entails in part an appropriation of the identities of the Other—the landscape, the culture, the history—in order to shore up, redefine, or rejuvenate the identities and authorities of the Self. Indeed, while the "barbarians" must be held firmly at the gates, the allure of the "primitive"—*away* from home, in the wilds of abroad— beckons the intrepid travel writer.

When Fussell talks about the fiercely antiforeign writers of the time, Kingsley Amis among them, he claims that "such poets were extremely conscious of the Englishness of their work" (20), and also, we can then presume, of the Englishness of their identity. In fact, this is even more significantly the case for those writers going abroad: As in Greene's African travels, detailed in *Journey Without Maps*, the search for the "primitive" out in the "wilds" of abroad is, in the end, a search for self and a search for home. Greene's conclusion about England and Europe, extrapolated from the experiences of living "at home," reveals a fundamental despair about the state of civilization (which, again, emanates from the West): "[W]hen one sees to what unhappiness, to what peril of extinction centuries of cerebration have brought us, one sometimes has a curiosity to discover if one can from what we have come, to recall at what point we went astray" (21). Greene's journey "back" to Africa becomes a retreat into the past, into history, as well as into the "backwardness" of precivilization; it is a salvific journey, a return to darkness in order to rediscover the light of civilization. He writes, later in the book, that "the method of psychoanalysis is to bring the patient back to the idea which he is repressing: a long journey backwards without maps" (96–97). Essentially, Greene constructs primitive Africa as the childhood memory European civilization, in its adulthood, is repressing; thus, it is also a journey "back" in terms of intellectual or social development, a westerner's assessment of what forms cultural maturity in the West as opposed to the psychological innocence of Africa. As he comes to the end of his dangerous and arduous journey, Greene admits, "what had astonished me about Africa was that it had never really been strange....The 'heart of darkness' was common to us [Europeans and Africans] both" (248). Ultimately, the journey out of England, the "withdrawal," becomes, not so ironically, the search for national memory, for civilization's "roots," the Englishman's psychologically innermost identity. Greene's "metaphysics of perception," in Fussell's words (70), can easily be translated as Pratt's "imperial eyes." Greene actively rewrites European history and development into and onto the African landscape and people, effectively erasing or at least covering over African history and culture in order to "satisfy, temporarily, the sense of nostalgia for something lost" (Greene 19), an imperial longing for the lost (mythic) edenic innocence.

To return to an earlier section in Fussell's book, the "passport nuisance" participates in this imperial vision, as well, the neurotic underbelly of the search for national and self-identity. As Fussell records C. E. Montague's words, before the degenerate days of the passport, "'you wandered freely about the Continent as if it were your own country'" (24)—and, certainly, Fussell's tone implies, what could be wrong with that? Passports limit the implicit ownership rightfully assigned to the imperial subject of Other Places—and turns this back on the traveler himself: "[I]t [the presenting of the passport] is a moment of humiliation, a reminder that he [the traveler] is merely the state's creature, one of his realm's replaceable parts. And returning is worse" (30). The moment of presenting the passport represents a loss of authority in the traveler, the loss of the ability to write the journey, to travel abroad *without restriction*. Not only is the passport despised for its ability to humiliate—to put one in one's proper isle-bound place—it is also feared for its ability to create anxiety, or the "modern neurosis," to use Fussell's terms (26). Fussell's comparison of the anxiety generated by the passport to the closing scenes of Virginia Woolf's *Between the Acts* is representative, although I see its representative potential quite differently from how Fussell does: Miss La Trobe's amateur pageant has been a retelling of British history, and, as the audience members reach the Present Time, coming close on the heels of Victorian arrogance and self-assuredness, they are shown themselves, reflected in mirrors—what Britain has been metamorphosed through mirrors into what Britain now is. The passport, in this comparison, functions as a kind of national mirror: reflecting an anxiety over the Present Time, the current configuration of British identity in the midst of an ever-expanding and encroaching world. That is, the passport is not only an indication of the loss of authority of the traveler, the imposition of the authority of the state, but it is also, in part, the celebration of nationalism and imperialism, a kind of declaration of national and imperial origins. This is the paradox revealed in both Greene's travel writing and Fussell's account of that travel writing: These forays into Africa and the subsequent nostalgia surrounding the postimperial return to those journeys would not have been possible if there had not been a British empire (and, indeed, the passport issued by that empire). The acknowledgment of the privilege granted by the presence of empire is elided in the search for authenticity and origin, in Greene's case, and in the nostalgia for lost imperial power, in Fussell's case.

Certainly, I must also add, the "nasty dehumanization" (Fussell 31) of the passport seems rather trivial when compared to the identity cards that were required to be carried by Africans and Indians in South Africa, for example, or to the patches worn by Jews and others in Nazi Germany. The "smallness" of Britain, in Fussell's view of it—spatially, psychologically—is revealed by the passport, symbolic of fears of cultural contamination from abroad and catalyst of anxiety over national and self-identity. The imperial project, carried on through the writing which takes place "abroad," guides Fussell's critical explanations of

British travel writing between the wars and, concomitantly, Greene's search for authority and identity in the African landscape.

Paul Theroux in Great Britain and Asia: Approaching Full Circle

Paul Theroux begins his travel book on Great Britain, *The Kingdom by the Sea,* by discussing what he sees as the particularly "British" practice of travel writing:

> The British had invented their own solution to travel writing. They went to places like Gabon and Paraguay and joked about the discomforts, the natives, the weather, the food, the entertainments. It was necessary to be an outsider, which was why they had never written about Britain in this way. But it was a mystery to me why no one had ever come to Britain and written about its discomforts and natives and entertainments and unintelligible dialects. The British, who had devised a kind of envious mockery of other cultures, and who had virtually invented the concept of funny foreigners, had never regarded themselves as fair game for the travel writer. They did not encourage aliens to observe them closely. (16)

Theroux, naturally, will change all this, as he delves deep into the national—and imperial—psyche of Great Britain. Indeed, he takes possession of the country in much the same way other British travel writers, such as Graham Greene, have taken possession of and claimed authority in other countries: "I sometimes felt like the prince in the old story," Theroux writes, "who because he distrusts everything he has been told and everything he has read, disguises himself in old clothes and, with a bag slung over his back, hikes the muddy roads talking to everyone and looking closely at things, to find out what his kingdom is really like" (18). Theroux deems himself the sovereign of his journey, the monarch of all he surveys, like the imperial eye actively possessing all he sees—because he presents himself as the prince, it is then *rightfully* his to possess. Theroux's purposes in traveling, in writing about travel, are similar in other ways to Greene: He travels, and writes about travel, in order to *know himself,* in order to tell his own story; as in the example with the prince, knowing his kingdom is a form of discovering himself. "Because," he admits in *Riding the Iron Rooster,* "travel writing is a minor form of autobiography" (68). Theroux, the sovereign, seeks out authority—authorship, in the guise of autobiography, and ownership—in and through his travels.

At the same time, however, Theroux is different from Greene, his writing—in an allegedly postcolonial moment—distinct from Greene's experiences abroad. To use the most obvious example, Theroux does something Greene cannot: He writes a travel book about Great Britain; as an American expatriate he has access to Britain, to England, to "Englishness" in a way that Greene does not. That is, Theroux constructs his authority to exist both *inside* the place to which he is traveling, about which he is writing—in Britain, he is an insider as resident, as English-speaker—and *outside* that place, which gives him the distance needed to critique "objectively" with those "seeing" (knowing, apprehending) eyes. This rhetorical positioning is not unusual, and it surfaces in different ways and to differing degrees in the work of Joseph Conrad, Doris Lessing, and V. S. Naipaul. As in the lengthy quotation above, "it was necessary to be an outsider" when attempting to write the journey (16). For example, Theroux claims, "writing about a country in its own language was a great advantage...language grew out of the landscape—English out of England" (16). In this statement, he asserts his claim, linguistic and implicitly literary, to this land; he also "naturalizes" that claim, that language—naturally, an English-speaker claims England—by organically linking the language to the land, the former "growing" out of the latter. However, "the problem was one of perspective...I was an alien" (16). In the very next moment, after claiming access to England, he distances himself as "an alien"; in this way, he remains a "privileged" observer, someone with "natural" access and legitimate claims of ownership, while at the same time he manages to avoid implicating himself in the "[English] perspective"—his authority and authorship exist "safely" outside the national perspective, and Theroux is therefore an observer, the "seeing-man," *not* a tainted participant.

However, Theroux does not limit his travels to England; he also goes "abroad," into Asia, for one example: how does this—or does this—alter his constructions of authority and access? To get at this question, I want to return to Fussell and his discussion of what it means to be a traveler, what it means to create and cross frontiers. In the section "Exploration to Travel to Tourism," Fussell sets up, in declining order of degree of authenticity, the differences between these three ways of, or ideological impulses for, going abroad. His categories themselves have everything to do not only with the necessary and anxious construction of authenticity and authority in British travel writing but also with the continuing insistence of the legitimacy of the imperial mission and presence. If, as according to Fussell's schema, to explore—to seek the undiscovered, in *European* terms—is the ultimate because most authentic experience of Abroad, and tourism is the least authentic because it aims for the "known" and the safe, or the familiar, then travel exists somewhere in between the two extremes; more legitimate than tourism, on the one hand, and the inheritor of the legacy of exploration (which, of course, is no longer possible) on the other. One can extrapolate from this hierarchy that this legitimation of exploration—travel plus adventure and discovery plus writing as witness—sanctions the conquest, or anticonquest, of the imperial eye. Thus, this legitimacy claimed by exploration bleeds or trickles down into the category of travel: Etymologically, travel is linked to travail—the more difficult the journey the more authentically it is read—which, in turn, also links travel to the trials of exploration, the "originary moment" of travel, of the difficulty of discovery. Furthermore, as Fussell writes, "travel was conceived to be like study" (39), the study of abroad, the anthropological impulse. In this case, then, if we are to follow Fussell's categorizations, no travel or, in turn, travel writing is politically innocuous or emptied of imperial purpose. I would like to suggest that Theroux is operating, writing, under these kinds of assumptions: The closer to exploration one gets, the more legitimate is one's travel, and the connections between exploration and conquest are inherited by travel; therefore, his work is open to the same critique of his implicitly imperialist project in traveling and writing about travel.

To use a representative example, I want to explicate the section in *Riding the Iron Rooster* in which Theroux describes his travels to and through Tibet. I use this example as it seems to bring to the fore Theroux's underlying assumptions (thematic, tropic, generic) about travel writing, and his experience of travel in a broader sense; that is, the occasion of Tibet, for Theroux, seems to provoke the employment of most, if not all, generic and authorial conventions, *as he understands and perpetuates them.* As Theroux embarks upon the last stretch of his journey through Chinese territory, headed into the strange and wonderful Tibet, he writes, "So I had nothing to fear: I was already in exile" (410). The travel writer—the explorer—is necessarily an *outsider,* as I have already argued, an exile from home, thrust into the "wilds" of the Other Country or Countries, beyond the "frontier." The solitariness of the traveler[2] is also crucial to the construction of his authority: Theroux figures himself as the lone exilic (expatriate) writer, the inheritor of the explorer's legacy, whose ability to "see" is inherent to that status of outsider, of exile, of European male seeing subject. He then continues to describe Tibet as "a world I had never seen before" (421); it was "emptiness" incarnate (421, 435); it "was beyond a moonscape—it was another universe entirely" (425); it was "vast and inaccessible and strange" (440). Tibet is unexplored country—a strange, new world—and Theroux is then the explorer, embarking on the mission not only to see, to witness the strangeness of the unexplored place, but also to access it, to attempt to understand it, to *know* his subject. As he admits, "You have to see Tibet to understand China" (449). This is another example of the impulse of the anti-conquest: Whereas Theroux does not openly appropriate Tibet for the reconstruction of European identity, as does Greene with Africa, he does, in fact, *read* and *interpret* the landscape of Tibet—simply another manner of possessing, of owning, of inscribing authority onto the other place. As Pratt argues, "the *discourse* of travel [in the anticonquest]...turns on a great longing: for a way of taking possession without subjugation and violence" (57). Theroux crosses the "final frontier"—"we were over the edge, way past the Chinese frontier, four days from civilization" (408)—and becomes the representative of western knowledge and authority in the "uncivilized" world beyond the reaches of the tourist.

Fussell also investigates the significance of frontiers, borders, boundaries, in a conceptual as well as physical sense. His discussion of frontiers supports the position detailed above: As exploration is encoded as the most authentic form of going abroad, so England's national boundaries are seen as the most authentic because they are "'defined by nature'" (34) (except, as Fussell fussily admits, the

"embarrassing line" separating Ulster, or Northern Ireland, from Ireland; ultimately, the admission is quickly forgotten, buried in the text). Thus, one could
argue, England's lack of frontiers legitimates its expansive imperialism—there
are no moral or physical boundaries—while its expansive imperialism legitimates
its claim of lacking frontiers: We don't have the nuisance of frontiers; there are
no boundaries to disturb our unified imperial front, but there are also no
boundaries between us and our property claims out in the world. Instead of fos-
tering isolation, this view facilitates a feeling of ownership and authorship in the
sense of "writing" the imperial boundaries. England's national boundaries are
"naturalized" in this trope, which functions in turn to "naturalize" both the imperial mission and its attendant form, exploration. It is natural to venture out in
the world, to go abroad, because frontiers are merely momentary constructions,
when they are drawn abroad, or naturally occurring borders, when they encompass—and protect—the island empire. This unique conception of frontiers is an
enclosed circular construction (shaped like an isle?): England's naturalized frontiers keep the Other out, while at the same time they legitimate the center's
claims on the margins, as in "our Empire knows no bounds." Again, it is clear to
me that Theroux undergirds the structure of his journeys, of his writing about
those journeys, with these hidden assumptions.

Pratt writes of Theroux, in a section entitled "The White Man's Lament,"
"What [he] see[s] is what there is" (217); or, to put it another way, what he sees
is naturalized, *naturally there,* because what he sees is what is (there, or the only
thing that is there). What he sees is passively presented to him; he merely observes and records, as opposed to creates and judges. Again according to Pratt,
what he sees is mostly unpleasant and depopulated.[3] She also writes that Theroux's travel narratives exemplify "a discourse of negation, domination, devalua-
tion, and fear...the official metropolitan code of the 'third world,' its rhetoric of
triviality, dehumanization, and rejection coinciding with the end of colonial rule
in much of Africa and Asia" (219–20). The realm of the "seeing-man" is shrinking and becoming violent (a result of the rise of nationalism, for one example),
thus producing anxiety in the neoimperial authorial voice. To give one example
of this anxiety, Theroux is positively obsessed with the possibility that *he,* rather
than the Other, is being observed: "I hated being observed. One of the pleasures
of travel is being anonymous" (*Iron Rooster* 10). Theroux does not see himself,
as he accuses the British of not seeing themselves, as the "proper" object of
study; he is the "seeing-man," not the anthropological subject. In addition, the
author seems to fear the (contamination of the) other; he desires to keep his distance, literarily and literally:

> The bigger the train, the longer the journey, the happier I was—none of the tem-
> porary suspense produced by the annoying awareness of the local train's spots of
> time. On the long trips I seldom watched the stations pass—the progress of the
> train didn't interest me very much. I had learned to become a resident of the ex-

press, and I preferred to travel for two or three days, reading, eating in the dining car, sleeping after lunch, and bringing my journal up to date in the early evening before having my first drink and deciding where we were on the map. Train travel animated my imagination and usually gave me the *solitude* to order and write my thoughts: I traveled easily in two directions, along the level rails while Asia flashed changes at the window, and at the interior rim of a *private* world of memory and language. I cannot imagine a luckier combination. (emphasis added, 166)

Again, one must ask the purpose for Theroux's journey; here it seems he admits that the journey is a profoundly self-centered thing—Asia is merely the passing backdrop upon which the lone writer paints his own image, over and over. To "become a resident of the express" is to denationalize oneself, to deracinate oneself even: Theroux is happiest when he is alone on a transport, speeding through (rather than slowly ambling through, as in England) the unremarkable and depopulated countryside. In the conclusion to *The Great Railway Bazaar,* as he ends the long and rather grueling journey, he writes, "The trip is finished and so is the book, and in a moment I will turn to the first page, and to amuse myself on the way to London will read with some satisfaction the trip that begins..." (342). He then proceeds to rewrite the first few lines of the book; thus, we have come full circle—"all travel," says Theroux, "is circular" (342)—trapped within this never-ending, self-perpetuating space; like the loop of the isle itself, described in Fussell's discussion of frontiers, Theroux's journeys *naturally* complete themselves, are justifications in themselves, are revelations of the authority that guide them.

Finding Conrad's Heart of Darkness: The Absenting of Imperial Authority

Conrad's *Heart of Darkness* (1899), in contrast to the works discussed above, reveals the emptiness of colonial authority, the hollowness of that illusory, momentary power; his short novel prefigures the postcolonial age as it acknowledges the impossibility of transplanting European ideas into Africa (and, indeed, the danger—to both Europe and Africa—of doing such a thing). This much examined text reveals a way *out of* the vision of imperial authority proposed by Fussell, Greene, and Theroux: Conrad, in the midst of the frenzy of imperial expansion and acquisition, anticipates the breakdown of such an anxious—repetitious, uncertain, overwhelming—representation of authority. In the end, the colonial impetus is implicated not in the enlightening of African civilization, of "the dark places of the earth," but in the revealing of the constructedness of civilization itself; only a thin veneer of so-called civilization separates the Europeans from the Africans, and, ultimately, that veneer is stripped away. Edward Said's arguments about *Heart of Darkness,* in his book *Culture and Imperialism,* suggest that Conrad is both implicated in the system of imperialism—it is so pervasive culturally that Conrad cannot but see it as *the only alternative*—and critical of that system: "Conrad's realization is that if, like narrative, imperialism has mon-opolized the entire system of representation...your self-consciousness as an out-sider can allow you actively to comprehend how the machine works, given that you and it are fundamentally not in perfect synchrony or correspondence" (25). Thus, Conrad—immigrant, nonnative English speaker—is able to glimpse, from his privileged position as *outsider* with access to the inside, something disruptive in the complex workings of the seemingly coherent project of imperialism itself. In contrast to Theroux, Conrad uses this outsider/insider, liminal position in order to critique the system, the assumptions of that system, rather than to con-struct objectivity in the witnessing of the Other. Kurtz, the complicated figure of colonial authority and atavistic impulse, is the representative of this tension be-tween the imperial project and its attendant atrocities: He glimpses "the horror" of the imperial project and then dies, leaving behind the legacy of Marlow's tale—and Marlow's deception. Colonialism corrupts. When read through the ubiquitous figure of Kurtz, a figure both centrally placed, in terms of narrative utility, and ultimately displaced, in terms of symbolic import, this novel begins to pose a series of intriguing, and colonially disruptive, questions.

How Kurtz is presented, or represented, in this novel becomes crucial, as he becomes the manifestation both of imperial authority, its ruling power, and of the thing imperialism most dreads, its loss of such power: Thus, how is Kurtz understood, from the colonial perspective, from Marlow's point of view? Indeed, *is* he understood in the role given to him by faraway European bureaucracy; that is, can he be fully present, fully realized as imperial authority when placed in the heart of African difference? This then begs another set of questions of perspective; where, finally, is the heart of darkness, when considered not from the perspective of Marlow (or of Europe), but from the displaced point of Kurtz's view? Indeed, what is "the horror" to which Kurtz refers? What does Marlow make of it, from his European position, as he retells his story to other Europeans who glide with him down the Thames—in the heart of civilization, as it were? In answer to some of the questions posed here, the heart of darkness is located not in the center of Africa but rather in the displaced civilization of Europe, represented in the novel by Kurtz, and Conrad prefigures the demise of colonial authority, revealing the fundamental absence of that illusory power. As Tzetvan Todorov argues, "'Kurtz is certainly the centre of the narrative, and his knowledge [is] the driving force of the plot...Kurtz is the heart of darkness, but this heart is empty'" (qtd. in Lothe 22).

Kurtz provides the connective tissue for Marlow's tale, as he first appears in the book as a rumor, as an enigma, and becomes a kind of psychological impetus for Marlow's journey deeper into Africa: "that was exactly what I had been look-ing forward to—a talk with Kurtz," Marlow admits (119). Kurtz's status as a rumor persists throughout the novel, and, even when Marlow finally meets the man behind the epithets ("Kurtz the remarkable, the extraordinary"), that sense of Kurtz as imperfect presence is reinforced. Kurtz is not really or wholly "there." He is simply not present in the story, in the colonial system; he is a gap, a significant absence, a hole in the colonial web of ideology, knowledge, and power. He wields no true authority over the natives, just as the colonial bureaucracy wields no real power over him (as long as he produces capital, he is left to his own devices). He is a mere shadow, a rumor, an extraordinary element within the very ordinary bureaucratic tangle of imperialism, as represented by the rather faceless and "colorless" managers and accountants who populate the story.

Even after he is found by Marlow, he remains a nonpresence; indeed, he is marked by his "holeyness" (with an obvious play on "holiness"). For examples: Kurtz's faithful manager, the harlequin figure, remarks that Kurtz would "forget himself amongst these peoples—forget himself" (131). As Marlow looks upon Kurtz's African dwelling for the first time, he notes that "there were no signs of life," but he points out "three little square window-holes," indicating the "holeyness" at the center of Kurtz's (non)existence (132). The shrunken heads which ghoulishly surround Kurtz's abode are turned inward—not outward, as a warning to invaders or outsiders, but looking toward the house enclosing this empty space within a grim circle of ritualized death/absence. In his razor-sharp analysis of Kurtz, Marlow comments that "the wilderness...had whispered things to him, things about himself which he did not know, things of which he had no conception till he took counsel with this great solitude—and the whisper had proved irresistibly fascinating. It echoed loudly within him because he was hollow at the core" (133). Following both Todorov's earlier comments and my own arguments, this hollowness leads one directly to the heart of darkness: the emptiness within Kurtz, the lack of "soul" or of adequate civilization, the hollow core created by "all Europe": Kurtz is corrupt before ever arriving in Africa. The heart of darkness represents the ultimate terror, the fear against which colonialism's authority struggles to assert itself: that a "dynamic of powerlessness [resides] at the heart of the imperial configuration," in Sara Suleri's words (112). This powerlessness is also the emptiness of colonial power, of a singular authority: A power wholly dependent on the idea of "other," of uncivilized jungle and primitive peoples, to uphold its own ideas of its falsely autonomous self—self versus other; civilization versus savagery—is ultimately not a power at all.

It is the accountant who first mentions, while Marlow is waiting for his steamer, "'In the interior you will no doubt meet Mr. Kurtz.' On my asking who Mr. Kurtz was, he said he was a first-class agent...and...added slowly, laying down his pen, 'He is a very remarkable person'" (84). Remarkable, yet the manager (and everybody else who speaks of Kurtz) has nothing further to remark, only that Kurtz is "out there" somewhere. Here, Kurtz appears as an inevitability—"'you will *no doubt* meet Mr. Kurtz'"—notable for two reasons: one, as we discover in the final section of the book, Kurtz's condition is far from ideal, unacceptable really, in European or colonial terms; two, the allusion to his inevitability is also perhaps an allusion to the inevitability of colonial decline. As Marlow aptly notes, "All Europe contributed to the making of Kurtz" (123); conversely, Kurtz contributes to the "unmaking" of all Europe, considering his status as colonial "representative" of European civilization. Furthermore, although Kurtz "sends in as much ivory as all the others put together" (84), thus fulfilling the capitalist impulse of empire, he does not finally fulfill the claims to power made by colonialism from the bureaucratic center, or fall himself within the control of that same colonial power. Ultimately, Kurtz neither wields any significant power—even for all his ivory, Kurtz's power is merely appropriated from the natives; he is doomed to die, in any event—nor does he work within the confines of the colonial system of power—he does not play by European rules. His attempt to sneak back into the jungle is thwarted by Marlow, reluctant bearer of imperial propriety, but in the horror of his death, Kurtz once again slips out of the grasp of his "masters": Now, we will never know the "real" story of Mr. Kurtz in the jungle, only Marlow's retelling of it. In addition, the inevitability of meeting Kurtz already implicates Marlow in the colonial situation, in the hollowness of the imperial enterprise; after all, it is through Marlow's narrative that we discover Kurtz and the heart of darkness. As Suleri suggests, "narration occurs [in colonial situations] to confirm the precariousness of power" (113): Marlow tells the tale, as he cannot escape his failure, the lies he is compelled to tell about the colonial experience. Indeed, Marlow admits he lies to Kurtz's intended: Ashen, pale, and shrouded in black, the mourning fiancée seems to embody the frailty of European civilization itself; Marlow's claim, that Kurtz's last words were her name, inextricably links her, even names her, as "the horror."

As Homi Bhabha writes, in his article "Signs Taken for Wonders," "What is 'English' [read: authoritative] in these discourses of colonial powers cannot be represented as a plenitudinous presence...the colonial presence is always ambivalent, split between its appearance as original and authoritative and its articulation as repetition and difference" (107). In other words, that colonial power, here represented by Kurtz, is at once attempting to claim original authority—we belong here; we must bring light into these dark forests, as we are the more civilized—and struggling to distance itself from what it sees as different and dangerous—we do not belong here, as only primitive savages and animals could exist in these "dark places." Kurtz, placed exactly at the boundary between the attempts to belong and to distance, between what is civilized and what is not, reveals the constructedness of all of these dichotomies (civilized/uncivilized; self/other; authority/silence) and of the idea of civilization itself. Thus, the very attempt at colonial control is a self-divisive, self-destructive move; colonial authority is profoundly ambivalent, at odds with itself, not fully present, and, indeed, hollow at its core.

Doris Lessing Out of Africa, Pursuing the English: Postcolonialism Comes Home

Doris Lessing, in this series of writers, represents a response not only to Graham Greene's writing on Africa but also to Theroux's portraits of the English and to Conrad's analysis of imperial authority in Africa. That is, when Lessing, as a white settler in the British colony of Southern Rhodesia (now Zimbabwe), travels to England in *In Pursuit of the English* and returns to Africa in *Coming Home,* she complicates the notion of what it means to be "English," what it means to represent—if only by proxy—imperial authority, what it means to construct an authorial and authoritative voice in the realm of the other. Her work reveals the possibilities for the *re*construction of authority in postcolonial terms; Lessing constructs her authority from an unstable but privileged interstitial or liminal position. She is English, nationally and ethnically speaking, but she has been raised in Africa (born in Persia) and is thus a kind of "colonial" outsider. As Edward Said explains of the postcolonial moment, "Only now instead of being *out there,* they [the former colonists and subjugated natives] are *here*" (188). Thus, Lessing's anthropological investigations of the English and her travels to and within Africa represent not only a disruption in the carefully enclosed, circular loop described by Fussell and, implicitly, by Theroux, but also a dissolution in the underlying imperial and colonial projects themselves.

In order to get at the significance of Lessing's work in this context, I want to use a term from Pratt's *Imperial Eyes, transculturation.* Pratt uses this term "to describe how subordinated or marginal groups select and invent materials transmitted to them by a dominant or metropolitan culture. Whereas subjugated peoples cannot readily control what emanates from the dominant culture, they do determine to varying extents what they absorb into their own, and what they use it for" (6). In other words, transculturation is a kind of *writing back* from the margins to the centers; although Pratt uses the term in relation to "subjugated peoples," which generally refers to non-European subjects of empire, it can also be useful to reveal the complex interactions between the colonies, the colonist settlers, and the metropolitan centers. As Pratt acknowledges, "with respect to representation, how does one speak of transculturation from the colonies to the metropolis?...Borders and all, the entity called Europe was constructed from the outside in as much as from the inside out" (6). Therefore, Lessing is both caught up in this project of constructing the center, as her longing for England affirms, and critical of this project, as her playful satire on the notion of "Englishness" reinforces.

For example, Lessing writes, "I did learn early on that while the word *English* is tricky and elusive enough in England, this is nothing to the variety of meanings it might bear in a Colony, self-governing or otherwise" (*In Pursuit* 2). Implicitly, the acknowledgment here is that the notion of Englishness becomes destabilized in the colonial setting, in the context of the other and the other place; therefore, in this situation, the Englishman or woman must define and redefine, anxiously and sometimes obsessively (as we noticed with Conrad), what being English means, over and against what being other means. This destabilization of identity and authority is, in fact, transported from the colonial margins back to the imperial center: It becomes not only a colonial question or problem but a national one, as well (Fussell's *Abroad* is very revealing in this sense). This problem, or question, or obsession of what it means to be English can be tracked throughout the history of the English novel and in British travel writing from *Robinson Crusoe* forward. In Lessing's case, the problem is ironized and complicated, as what does it mean to be English *when you live and grow up in (colonial) Africa*.

First and foremost, it seems to mean nostalgia, a longing for the home one has never seen or visited. As Lessing acknowledges, "I can't remember a time when I didn't want to come to England. This was because, to use the word in an entirely different sense, I was English" (8). She then continues by describing what it means to call herself English in the colonial setting: "In the colonies or Dominions, people are English when they are sorry they ever emigrated in the first place; when they are thoroughly assimilated into the local scene and would hate to ever set foot in England again; and even when they are born colonial but have an English grandparent" (8). In this way, then, Lessing establishes her own authority and, in part, reaffirms colonial authority: She is an insider, born English, after all, if not born in England; but she is also an outsider, a "colonial." To repeat Bhabha's points: "[T]he colonial presence is always ambivalent, split between its appearance as original and authoritative and its articulation as repetition and difference" (107). Lessing both belongs in Africa, the heir of colonial property and authority, and does not belong in Africa, the foreign presence in a very "foreign" land; her position is repeated in the case of England, as she both belongs to England because of her birthright and does not belong to England because she is a colonial exile. Like Theroux and Conrad, Lessing occupies a privileged liminal space, moving (un)comfortably between the margins and the centers. This status both defines her authorial voice because she can, like Theroux, write funny and insulting things about the English, who are "different" from her. She explains her privilege: Unlike the native Africans, those "Other" imperial subjects, she lays claim not only to Africa, as colonial property, but also to England, as imperial authority. She uses this position in order to critique it, to critique both her status as an "Englishperson" and as a white colonial in Africa.

For example, when she returns to Africa for the first time after immigrating to London, she writes, "On that morning over Africa I learned that I had turned myself inwards, had become a curtain-drawer, a fire-hugger, the inhabitant of a cocoon [in London]. Easy enough to turn outwards again: I felt I had never left [Africa] at all. This was my air, my landscape, and above all, my sun" (*Going Home* 8). Lessing claims and takes possession of this other place, Africa; yet, it is a possession of home—note the title of the book: *Going Home*—which, for her, as the direct result of imperialism and the colonial project, is Africa. She is therefore implicated in that imperial system; she exists as one of its legacies. Still, in the very next moment, she also writes, "Africa belongs to the Africans; the sooner they take it back the better. But—a country also belongs to those who feel at home in it...Perhaps" (8). Lessing realizes and displays, examines and puzzles over her paradoxical position; she embodies, to follow Edward Said's work in *Culture and Imperialism,* the postmodern and postcolonial exile, the not uncommon condition of postimperial migrancy. As she herself mentions, "The fact is, I don't live anywhere. I never have since I left that first house on the kopje. I suspect more people are in this predicament than they know" (*Going Home* 30). She is quite careful in her claims to *anywhere* in the world.

Returning to *In Pursuit of the English,* Lessing is also careful in her claims to Englishness, to English identity; she is critical of the practice by which the English define themselves over and against the other. She explains, "I came into contact with the English very early in life, because as it turns out, my father was an Englishman" (1). At once, she succeeds in distancing herself from the notion of this "essentializing" identity; she is not, it would seem, "English," just because it is her national or racial birthright, but rather she is a colonial, white settler, African. After displacing herself from the "center" of this narrative, which is, if we are to follow the title, about the English, of whom she is *not* one, she details the project of her book, why she has undertaken such a topic: "It is, then, because of my early and thorough grounding in the subject of the English character that I have undertaken to write about this business of being an exile [in England]. First one has to understand what one is an exile from. And unfortunately I have not again succeeded in getting to know an Englishman. That is not because, as the canard goes, they are hard to know, but because they are hard to meet" (2–3). In other words, Lessing is getting to know the self, the Englishman/person, in order to understand the exiled other, the colonial subject: She thus reverses the process by which both Greene and Theroux attempt to write themselves through travel. She is the other, in this book, and her suspiciously anthropological-sounding project is to uncover what it means to be English; but the anthropological move, to search for the dying breed of Englishperson, is, at least in part, ironic because it is also self-referential.

More precisely, if Lessing is the exile in this project, she is also the Englishperson; she projects an authority that is profoundly unstable, shifting between identities with multiple meanings in different situations: It is quite different to be English, as she admits, in the colonial setting, than at home in England. She also teases her readers here while making a more significant political point about the postcolonial world: Why are Englishmen hard to meet? Because "London is full of foreigners" (3), a statement which works to reinforce the notion of exile *within* one's own country, *within* the shifting meanings of one's own multiple identities.

It also serves to address the anxiety over self- and national definition in the post-colonial moment: If London is full of foreigners and if Lessing herself is one of those foreigners, then we must assume that many of these foreigners are former imperial subjects, either settlers or colonized peoples. That is, London is full of foreigners as the direct result of empire; the Englishman is a "dying breed" because he is now one among many permutations of that very thing. The explanation of what it means to be a foreigner versus what it means to be an Englishman is profoundly destabilized; the postcolonial comes home. "The sad truth is that the English are the most persecuted minority on earth" (3), a statement that reveals through its irony Lessing's critique of the very notion of searching for or believing in an essential or racial notion of Englishness: "[L]ike Bushmen in the Kalahari, that doomed race, they vanish into camouflage at the first sign of a stranger" (3). Indeed, as it is revealed throughout the course of the book, this is not because the English are essentially elusive or aloof or unknowable; rather, it is because there does not exist, in fact, "the English," a single, nationally and/or ethnically unified race or identity of people.

Throughout the rest of the novel, Lessing details the lives of the working-class residents of the boardinghouse in which she lives and investigates the psyches of the people she randomly meets in London; these people are so unique, diverse, and unclassifiable as a group that the only conclusion at which the reader can arrive is that the English, as a species, do not exist. The novel—or documentary, as the work is subtitled—comes to an end with a conversation between the protagonist/writer and Rose, the young working-class woman who yearns for marriage and security. The landlady of the house exhorts them, as they are moving on to different places, not to forget their friendships, their relationships made in the house: "'If we was all kind to each other all over the world it would be different wouldn't it now?'" (228). While the Lessing character demurely agrees with this proposition, Rose, in the concluding sentence of the novel, retorts, "'A likely story'" (228). When considered from the larger perspective of the work as a whole, one can propose that this is not merely a response to the false idealism of the landlady, but that it is also a response to the project of "pursuing the English," in general. Ultimately, Lessing rejects the certain conclusion to such a project, casting doubt on any assertions she may have succeeded in making, as it is only "a likely story," suspicious and ambiguous. As Said impels his readers to recognize, "no identity can ever exist by itself and without an array of opposites, negatives, oppositions" (52). Lessing recognizes, embodies, and portrays this tension as the colonial African Englishperson.

V. S. Naipaul Rents a Cottage in Wiltshire: Re-presenting Authority

V. S. Naipaul interprets a painting by Giorgio de Chirico, entitled "The Enigma of Arrival," in his novel/memoir of the same name:

He would arrive—for a reason I had yet to work out—at that classical port with the walls and gateways like cutouts....He would enter there and be swallowed by the life and noise of a crowded city....Gradually there would come to him a feeling that he was getting nowhere; he would lose his sense of mission; he would begin to know only that he was lost....He would want to escape, to get back to the quayside and his ship. But he wouldn't know how....At the moment of crisis he would come upon a door, open it, and find himself back on the quayside of arrival. He has been saved; the world is as he remembered it. Only one thing is missing now. Above the cutout walls and buildings there is no mast, no sail. The antique ship had gone. The traveler has lived out his life. (*Enigma* 98–99)

Naipaul's own journeys—from Trinidad to England, from England to India and back, from naive, West Indian boy to seasoned "nation-less" writer—mirror the surrealistic world of the traveler in his unfinished story above (or perhaps it is finished as the completed and partially fictionalized memoir *The Enigma of Arrival*): The traveler appears to arrive, at first, and he explores his strange, new destination only to discover that it is not quite the right place, the expectations do not coincide with the actuality, and he must try to return, in a state of confusion and panic, to his ship, or point of origin. The ship, of course, is also not there, and the traveler has then spent his entire life seeking the moment of arrival; even so, the moment of arrival, because it exists as a specific time and place, can never be found in quite the same way again. The moment of arrival passes as soon as the traveler disembarks; the very moment the traveler arrives is the same moment he is already there, irrevocably removed from origin. The problem of arrival, or the struggle to arrive, is relevant both to the act of travel and of travel writing and to the autobiographical impulse within that travel writing: To travel is expressly *not* to arrive, in the sense that travel denotes movement; it is also to experience the disjunction between the expectation, literarily or psychologically formed, and the reality of the experience of the destination. Thus, the arrival is, at once, presence and absence, sense and nonsense: One does arrive, but not precisely to where one thought one was going. In the same way, the problem of arrival can be applied to the autobiographical impulse because the self one writes about is not precisely the self one is or is not.

As Judith Levy elaborates in her book *V. S. Naipaul: Displacement and Autobiography,* "a fundamental impetus of Naipaul's writing is to create a self, which, in textual terms, is to write autobiography; [and]...the writing of an autobiography is for Naipaul conditional on the acquisition of a myth of origin" (xi). She goes on to acknowledge that this "acquisition of a myth of origin" is "thwarted" by "cultural dislocation," Naipaul's paradoxical position—an impossibly divided one, to be sure—as East Indian West Indian, residing (and knighted, no less!) in Britain. Thus, the purely biographical attempt is futile, in these terms; it is a convenient fiction to envision a life story of closure and completeness, so what we end up with is a hybrid genre, greater than the sum of its parts, of the novelistic memoir or quasi-autobiographical fiction. The disjunction between the authorial voice—exuding certainty and completeness, mastery and control—and the author himself is constantly, anxiously displayed in Naipaul's works: He can often "force" a novel or a travel narrative to arrive, to mimic completeness, but his endless subject is the uncertainty and incompleteness of his own arrival, experience, and sense of belonging.

Naipaul illustrates the problem of arrival in *The Enigma of Arrival* (1987), subtitled "A Novel" but composed of verifiable biographical detail about his experience living in the English countryside. To link Naipaul's project to both Lessing and Conrad, the problem of arrival is inextricably bound up with the problem of the colonial, the eternal migrant. More precisely, this exiled figure floats adrift in a world without home, no longer ordered by dying Empire, while still being influenced, dominated, and acculturated by the decaying remains of that alien order, the language of that other world. Naipaul, as West Indian writer of East Indian ancestry and renter of a cottage on aristocratic British domain, represents and portrays the problem of the colonial and his inability to arrive, this conditional state of exile that is borne through the current plight of empire, precarious in its decay. His status as writer, as authority, is symptomatic of the postcolonial moment; his presence there, in the English countryside as in the canon of British literature, is always an anxious one: Where does he "fit"? How can he belong? Similar to Conrad's displaced colonial authority and Lessing's unstable colonial/English identity, Naipaul's authority is not easy to pin down, to place; his constantly shifting and emerging sense of identity, of authorship and ownership, provides a glimpse of what the postcolonial moment might look like, with the absolute and absolutely anxious construction of boundaries between center and colony, self and other, whiteness and shades of blackness transgressed and irreparably blurred. These works themselves—*Heart of Darkness, In Pursuit of the English,* and *Going Home, The Enigma of Arrival*—are problematic in the same way: To classify them, to place them, to force them to "arrive," is difficult at best, for they are a messy combination, in different degrees, of novel and social history and travel narrative and memoir and "meditation" (the last a Naipaulian designation). Indeed, particularly in the case of Naipaul's work, its very (non)structure mirrors its equally messy material: If the cohesive "life story" becomes the fluid, shifting, and numerous perceptions of "life's stories," then the forum for these stories also becomes unfixed, losing the rigid boundaries of genre. The colonial does not arrive because, ultimately, he or she sees the world as endless, boundless, and constantly in a state of flux—there is no home, only homes; there is no culture, only cultures; there is no single and stable authority, only a conglomeration of various and ever-shifting conceptions of authority, authorship, and ownership.

Colonially speaking, this lack of certainty in arrival echoes the emptiness in imperial rule, as both moments counter the idea of wholeness, of full presence, of complete authority. This moment of illusory arrival is a disconcerting moment for Marlow, as well. He never quite arrives into the heart of darkness—or, at least, not into the heart of primitive darkness, of African darkness, as the dichotomies set up against the European ideal are collapsed—and never quite meets the Kurtz he expects to meet. Marlow reacts to Kurtz's death by thinking, "the voice was gone. What else had been there?" remembering also that Kurtz's "was an impenetrable darkness" (148, 147). He also notes that "of course I am aware that next day the pilgrims buried something"—Marlow does not pretend to have met the Kurtz of his expectations—"in a muddy hole" (148). Therefore Kurtz, hollow at his core, comes to a fitting end, buried in emptiness. All of this lack of certainty, this acknowledging of absence, points again to the inability to account for what is, ultimately, not at the "center" of the book: Kurtz himself, the heart of darkness. Indeed, if Marlow arrives to anything at all, it is back into the places of civilization (which he now knows to be constructed), where he must hide the truth of "the horror" from Kurtz's intended. While Conrad's tale ends with Marlow's lie and the drifting down the Thames "into the heart of an immense darkness" (158), leaving us with a sense of hopelessness, he also leaves us Marlow's tale, the reassertion of a kind of textual presence that may be the hope for overcoming the horror and the darkness. Naipaul, in the postcolonial moment, sees even more for which one may hope.

Naipaul's struggle to insert himself into the English landscape is quite distinct from either Theroux's investigations of Great Britain and Englishness or Lessing's participation in and critique of the search for national identity. As Levy writes of *Enigma,* "it is a work of highly sophisticated artifice, the *record* of the creation of a myth of origin, i.e., a creation in language, and the resolution in terms of genre of the problem of writing autobiography" (97). Naipaul still sees with the colonial's eye and acknowledges the irony of the situation whereby he, a transplanted Indian and Trinidadian native, rents a traditional English cottage from an English aristocrat. In the section aptly titled "The Journey," Naipaul writes that "I discovered that to be a writer was not (as I had imagined) a state—of competence, or achievement, or fame, or content—at which one arrived and where one stayed" (*Enigma* 100–1). His journey in *Enigma* is to becoming a writer, and we know immediately that Naipaul has shed some of his illusions concerning the problem of arrival: He does not expect, any longer, to arrive or to stay put, to become somehow secure in his sense of self. A writer—the colonial-traveler—must continually be on the move.

He records his first attempts at being a writer: "The separation of man from writer which had begun on the long airplane flight from Trinidad to New York [and on to England] became complete. Man and writer both dwindled," as a result of that separation (147). This novel chronicles the reintegration of man and writer, the autobiographical description of the creation of authorial self. "I had given myself a past, and a romance of the past," he admits, and "both time and space separated me from my past at the end of that day [of that first journey]; and the writer's journey that had begun that day had not ended"—still has not ended (165). His self-proclaimed position as a colonial in England, with his "raw colonial's nerves," forces him into this recreation of a mythical past: In order to become the kind of writer he imagines a proper British writer to be, he must bury his colonial improprieties and focus on the "great subject" suited to great literature, as in his first (unsuccessful) short story "Gala Night" (142). This focus creates a false sense of self, a self divided from the realities of colonialism, a schizophrenic person hiding behind a mask of Englishness—the same accusation Naipaul himself hurls at the colonial Indians, calling themselves Bunty and Freddy, instead of Chandrashekhar and Firdaus, in *An Area of Darkness* (58). Levy points out that "Naipaul himself has stated at various points in his life, the reality of being an outsider in England, in contrast to the nurtured fantasy of England, forced him to turn to the past for his materials, even while denying its validity as a myth of origin. At the same time, the form he used was that of the English novel for which he knew no alternative" (xv)—until now, perhaps. Naipaul must reconcile these selves and generic forms—or, at the least, give equal space to these competing visions of self and of form, a space for a new vision of authority created through the course of *The Enigma of Arrival.*

Apart from his initial attempts at writing and traveling which have always been intimately bound together in his work, Naipaul finds a kind of reconciliation, an acknowledgment of his colonial self, in his experience of renting the cottage in England; this comes much later, of course, after his original journey to England and his first, tentative attempts to become a writer, but it is here, in the cottage and amidst a positively pastoral setting of English tradition and aristocracy, that Naipaul investigates and comes to terms with his paradoxical position as the colonial. Ruminating about his mysterious landlord, Naipaul writes, "I was his opposite in every way, social, artistic, sexual...it might be said that an empire lay between us. This empire at the same time linked us. The empire explained my birth in the New World, the language I used, the vocation and ambition I had; this empire in the end explained my presence there in the valley" (191). Naipaul's experiences—as a Trinidadian, as a writer, as a renter (in England, no less)—can only be explained by the phenomenon of empire; he is a colonial product, from birth to profession to the present. His very appearance there in the valley signifies a transformation, however, the decline of empire—in the same way this "novel" itself signifies a transformation in the conception of what a memoir might be—a transformation, even, in what the British canon of literature might become. He cannot help but be faced with the fact of his colonial status continually.

Naipaul does not see his presence in the valley as he saw the British presence in India; he is not the harbinger of corruption or doom—or of a kind of false consciousness that will inevitably infect the British countryside—rather, he becomes a symbol of that change, of a different sort of awareness, of a world beginning to move from colonial to postcolonial. Like Lessing's London full of foreigners, Naipaul's English cottage signifies a necessary revision in the conception of what it means to be foreign, or what it means to be—or to have access to—Englishness. In *After Empire: Scott, Naipaul, Rushdie,* Michael Gorra asks rhetorically, "does Naipaul's building himself a house on Salisbury Plain stand as a betrayal of Trinidad [of the colonial past], or does it rather alter one's conception of the English countryside? He himself sees his presence there as a perpetual novelty, an alteration of its human community" (92). To read Naipaul in this way—constructed as "the colonial" residing in the English countryside and as "the author" proclaiming a place within the British tradition of literature—would be to make him effective in establishing an authoritative position within the English countryside and, ultimately, the British canon. To draw an analogy from the Gandhi chapter in *An Area of Darkness,* Naipaul feels he is unable to reclaim Gandhi's original, reformist politics from the static heights of his status as Mahatma (and note that Naipaul implicitly links himself and his colonial status to Gandhi): "So it is when legends are complete. Nothing can add to them or take away from them. The image is fixed, unalterable" (82). However, the very act of writing about Gandhi in this way—a decidedly controversial interpretation of Gandhi's historical importance (i.e., that his importance is negligible, at best, in India)—does, in fact, reclaim this original Gandhi who, for Naipaul, represents the postcolonial possibilities for change. To push this idea one step further, Gandhi (and thus, by identification, Naipaul) does not need to be rehabilitated, for the Naipaulian version of Gandhi exists simultaneously with the Hindu version of the Mahatma, because the colonial never arrives at any singular point in history or in culture, nor can he return to the exact moment of his inception, his historical and cultural origins. The memoir is then transformed from the fixity of the generically constructed autobiographical "life story" into the generically unstable conception of the biographically verifiable novel—the self-as-author remains not "in reality" but "in process." In the same way, the act of acknowledging his own status as a colonial-traveler leads Naipaul to the acceptance of the uncertainty of arrival, the reclamation of that cultural anxiety which renders him, as displaced author and autobiographical subject, the outsider with piercing insider vision.

Naipaul writes of his attempt at autobiography, in his foreword to *Finding the Center,* "I would have liked to begin at the very beginning, with the blankness and anxiety of arrival. But it didn't work as narrative" (xi). Indeed, in writing this essay, I felt much the same way; if only I could have started at the beginning...but the narrative of this essay, as the narrative of these generically mixed works, grew out of the tangled impulses to understand the (post)colonial world(s), the authorial selves, the imperial footnotes as constructed by these various writers and their various projects, and, on the other hand, to tell a coherent story. In a 1994 interview with Stephen Schiff, Naipaul himself says of writing that "it's all narrative. It's a matter of choosing. It's when you're doing the other kind of writing—you start looking for a thing called plot and you get into trouble, you know? Narrative is something large going on around you all the time. Plot is something trivial—people want it for television plays. Plot assumes that the world has been explored and now this thing, plot, has to be added on. Whereas I am still exploring the world. And there is narrative there, in every exploration" (148). Perhaps this comment, its improvised quality, can lead us to a new vision of exploration and travel and, thus, the writing about travel: Exploration is not necessarily discovery—of a particular "foreign" or "exotic" place or "uncivilized" peoples—rather, it is narrative, the telling of *stories,* in the poly-vocal writing and rewriting of the postcolonial moment.

Notes

1   A complex notion itself—the "formations" or "formulations" of empire versus the "decline" or "end" of empire: I do not mean to imply that these are mutually exclusive or temporally contingent terms; indeed, they are both continually active notions of the ongoing processes of imperial interactions. That is, as we might see the empire at an end (in terms of "official" administration and/or lawful authority), we might also see the reformulating of imperial ideas in the international transmissions of cultural authority (e.g., the international prominence, indeed dominance, of the English language in terms of literary publishing)—just as the term postcolonial, in fact, contains and represents or re-presents the colonial.

2   See, for example, any number of travel books by Graham Greene (*Journey Without Maps; The Lawless Roads*), George Orwell's *Burmese Days,* any number of novels dealing with colonialism, such as E.M. Forster's *A Passage to India* and Joseph Conrad's *Almayer's Folly, Lord Jim,* or "Outpost of Progress." Most particularly, see Lawrence Durrell's *Bitter Lemons,* where he uses the phrase "loneliness and time" to suggest the ideal condition of the traveler, and Mark Cocker's critical work, *Loneliness and Time,* on British travel writing.

3   The "depopulated" landscape is a familiar trope in travel writing (according to Pratt in *Imperial Eyes;* for example, see Part I: Science and Sentiment, 1750–1800), beginning with the scientific, natural history travel narratives in the eighteenth and nineteenth centuries. Basically, to privilege the landscape, the scenery, the natural features above and at the expense of the people inhabiting this landscape is to sanction the imperial conquest of the place: If such beautiful or resourceful lands are uninhabited, depopulated, then we—imperial companies, scientific communities, colonial enterprises—claim it, should use it, should "civilize" it.

Works Cited

Bhabha, Homi. "Signs Taken for Wonders: Questions of Ambivalence and Authority under a Tree outside Delhi, May 1817." *The Location of Culture.* New York: Routledge, 1994. 102–22.

Clifford, James. "Traveling Cultures." *Cultural Studies*. Eds. Lawrence Grossberg, Cary Nelson, and Paula Treichler. New York: Routledge, 1992.

Cocker, Mark. *Loneliness and Time: The Story of British Travel Writing*. New York: Pantheon, 1992.

Conrad, Joseph. *Almayer's Folly and Other Stories*. New York: Signet, 1992.

———. *Heart of Darkness*. With *The Secret Sharer*. New York: Signet, 1950.

———. *Lord Jim*. Toronto: Bantam, 1981.

———. "Outpost of Progress." *The Portable Conrad*. Ed. Morton Dauwen Zabel. New York: Penguin, 1976. 459–89.

Durrell, Lawrence. *Bitter Lemons*. New York: E. P. Dutton, 1957.

Forster, E. M. *A Passage to India*. New York: Harcourt, 1952.

Fussell, Paul. *Abroad*. Oxford and New York: Oxford UP, 1980.

Gorra, Michael. *After Empire: Scott, Naipaul, Rushdie*. Chicago: U of Chicago P, 1997.

Greene, Graham. *Journey without Maps*. 1936. London: Penguin, 1971.

———. *The Lawless Roads*. London: Heinemann, 1978.

Lessing, Doris. *Going Home*. 1957, 1968. New York: Harper Perennial, 1996.

———. *In Pursuit of the English*. 1960. New York: Harper Perennial, 1996.

Levy, Judith. *V.S. Naipaul: Displacement and Autobiography*. New York: Garland, 1995.

Lothe, Jakob. *Conrad's Narrative Method*. Oxford: Clarendon Press, 1989.

Naipaul, V.S. *An Area of Darkness*. London: Penguin, 1964.

———. *The Enigma of Arrival*. New York: Vintage Books, 1988.

———. "The Ultimate Exile." Interview with Stephen Schiff. *Conversations with V. S. Naipaul*. Ed. Feroza Jussawalla. Jackson: UP of Mississippi, 1997.

Orwell, George. *Burmese Days*. Introd. Malcom Muggeridge. New York: Time, Inc., 1962.

Pratt, Mary Louise. *Imperial Eyes: Travel Writing and Transculturation*. London: Routledge, 1992.

Said, Edward. *Culture and Imperialism*. New York: Vintage Books, 1993.

Suleri, Sara. "The Rhetoric of English India." *The Postcolonial Studies Reader*. Eds. Bill Ashcroft, Gareth Griffiths, and Helen Tiffin. London: Routledge, 1995.

Theroux, Paul. *The Great Railway Bazaar*. New York and London: Pocket Books, 1975.

———. *The Kingdom by the Sea*. London and New York: Penguin, 1983.

———. *Riding the Iron Rooster*. New York: Ballantine Books, 1988.

Chapter 3

Travel Writing and the Imperial Subject in 1930s Prose: Waugh, Bowen, Smith, and Orwell

Adam Piette

Andrew Gurr, in his *Writers in Exile,* argues that exilic travel really defines the role of the writer in the twentieth century: "The normal role for the modern creative writer is to be an exile...a lone traveler in the countries of the mind, always threatened by hostile natives" (13). My contention is that this writerly deracination is a direct result of cultural, technological, and political changes in the 1930s which made it impossible for writers to look upon the world as a set of "countries of the mind," to use Gurr's breezy phrase. Though it may very well have been possible for intellectuals in the 1910s and 1920s to see travel as an epic journey into the mind and private relationships (as it is in Woolf's *The Voyage Out*),[1] by the 1930s mobility through acts of expatriation, exploration, and repatriation had become definitively politicized. As Tom Paulin argued in his reading of W. H. Auden and Louis MacNeice's *Letters from Iceland,* "While Auden and MacNeice may at times present their voyage to Iceland as being possibly escapist and solipsistic they are actually raising that criticism in order to insist on their political subject. They are not writing a travel book—they are writing about European culture" (70). Travel books, though, have always been about culture. The 1930s only made it inescapably obvious that this had to be the case. As Wyndham Lewis argued vociferously to the editor of his 1932 Moroccan travel book, *Filibusters in Barbary,* the book was not a mere entertainment or picturesque satire, but a cultural document revealing "the existence of a conflict between the colonizing, the Roman, impulses of the French nation...and the irresponsible, commercial and capitalistic, interests" (xvi). Travel writing in the 1930s sets out to demonstrate the close ideological parallels between the ways the private self relates to its environments and the ways a nation relates to supposedly alien cultural forces within and without its world.

In this article, I will be examining the idea of the foreign in 1930s writing—examining representations of imperial, colonial foreign cultures, the foreign culture of the working class within Britain, and the idea of Europe as sinister site of threat and apocalypse. By looking at these different senses of the foreign, the other, as it were, for the intellectual English middle class, I demonstrate that colonial and imperial discourses still shaped the ways in which culture could and was articulated in writing, but that the decade saw a radical breakdown in the ease and confidence with which these discourses served as a ground for prose writing. I examine how the ideas of England, Englishness, and English writing started to come under corrosive pressure from the underclasses and subject territories that had underwritten their definition. The sudden rise to dangerous power of the states, peoples, and classes that had hitherto acted as inferior foils to English selfhood and nationhood was traumatic and had long-lasting effects, not least on the myth of the mobile, modern, imperial subject.[2]

In his 1945 preface for an anthology of extracts from his 1930s travel writing, *When the Going was Good,* Evelyn Waugh bemoans the passing of the heyday of traveling:

> My own traveling days are over, and I do not expect to see many travel books in the near future. When I was a reviewer, they used, I remember, to appear in batches of four or five a week, cram-full of charm and wit and enlarged Leica snapshots. There is no room for tourists in a world of "displaced persons." ...others, not I, gifted with the art of pleasing public authorities may get themselves dispatched abroad to promote "Cultural Relations"; the very young, perhaps, may set out like the *Wandervogels* of the Weimar period; lean, lawless, aimless couples with rucksacks, joining the great army of men and women without papers, without official existence, the refugees and the deserters, who drift everywhere today between the barbed wire. I shall not, by my own wish, be among them. (xi)

For Waugh, the freedom of the young 1920s and 1930s traveler intellectual, immensely expanded by the extraordinary development of international communication (air travel, comfortable, speedy cruises, mechanized transport), has been eclipsed by the great cloud of officialdom and grim public authorities, by the desolation of culture in Europe, by the equally desolate spectacle of the lawless, aimless, refugee generation of the war. The fearsome events of the 1940s have replaced the heroic travelers with the ghoulish figure of the displaced person—charm, wit, and free opportunity replaced by stunned, bleak, and mindless mobility. The only option now is to stay at home, a brooding, broken attitude we find again and again in the queasy xenophobia of writers in the 1950s such as Kingsley Amis and Philip Larkin. The going was good because the world in the 1920s was up for grabs. Now by the 1940s it was the world that was doing the grabbing—moving and displacing *us*—and the writer had to retreat into the gloomy fortress of the beleaguered English home.[3]

Waugh attempts to explain the extraordinary globe-trotting mania of his generation between the wars: Peter Fleming to the Gobi Desert, Graham Greene to the Liberian hinterland, Robert Byron to the deserts of Persia, himself to Ethiopia, Mexico, Zanzibar. Europe, he remembers, could wait. Old age was the time for soft breezes and mellow sunshine. While he had the strength, "[he] would go to the wild lands where man had deserted his post and the jungle was creeping back to its old strongholds," in search of "barbarism":

> We turned our backs on civilization. Had we known, we might have lingered with "Palinurus"; had we known that all the seeming-solid, patiently-built, gorgeously ornamented structure of Western life was to melt overnight like an ice-castle, leaving only a puddle of mud; had we known man was even then leaving his post. Instead, we set off on our various stern roads....At that time it seemed an ordeal, an initiation to manhood. (*When the Going Was Good* x)

Here we have some intimations of the cultural rationale behind the sheer hedonism of travel. Travel was for Waugh an initiation into the imperial ideal, the imperial body and subject. This training is defined as both colonial appropriation, through experience, of the barbarian other—"the world wide open before us" in search of "barbarism"—and bodily transformation into the tough, fit colonial adventurer—"an ordeal, an initiation to manhood." But it is simultaneously an exploration of the *end* of empire at the outflung reaches of empire, where the white man has deserted his post.[4]

Paradoxically, Waugh's travel writing is at once imperial and postcolonial. It is imperial because it mimes the appropriating expansion and geographical movements of the imperial story. It is postcolonial because Waugh is interested in territories in the world in the process of being abandoned by empire; he records the hybrid and absurd mixed cultures produced and left behind by the retreat of imperial interests. As he put it in his 1934 *Ninety-Two Days:*

> One does not travel, any more than one falls in love, to collect material. It is simply a part of one's life. For myself and many better than me, there is a fascination in distant and barbarous places, and particularly in the borderlands of conflicting cultures and states of development, where ideas, uprooted from their traditions, become oddly changed in transplantation. (qtd. in the collection *When the Going Was Good* 197)

This fascination with the exotic, with borderland cultures, with transplanted, uprooted, and transformed ideas is clearly an immense resource for a writer with the comic genius of Waugh. This fascination, though, is in fact testing the very possibility of the imperial subject. Waugh relishes barbarism because it gives him richly comic experience that reflects back favorably on his own pseudo-imperial authority and gaze. He is also goring the bull of the imperial subject by simply giving the mad colonial subjects he meets on his travels the chance to air their crazy, preposterous, and warped points of view. Writers who feel compelled to travel, he argued in a *Spectator* review in 1934, "find in stunted forms and exotic overgrowths types which lead them to a new understanding of the forms of their own civilization" ("Desert and Frost" 139).

Just one instance of this should suffice. On an epic journey from British Guiana into Brazil in 1932, he meets an English rancher named Christie, who, left to his own devices in the savannah, has turned into a religious maniac, racked by visions and mystic numbers in the sky:

> "I always know the character of any visitors by the visions I have of them. Sometimes I see a pig of a jackal; often a ravaging tiger."
> I could not resist asking, "And how did you see me?"
> "As a sweetly toned harmonium," said Mr. Christie politely. (*When the Going Was Good* 230)

Christie vainly preaches to the natives, but they all have the devil in them. In thirty years he has not made one convert. He has children by his Indian mistress, but they too are lost to the devil. His visions tell him of the end of the world, and of how many of the elect are in heaven. He has absurd superstitions about rival faiths. Divorced from the tap-root of European civilization, the colonial subject goes quite simply mad through constant contact with the alien people. The fierce Calvinist ideology underpinning English imperialism (economic interests backed up by, and screened behind, evangelical motives) turns sour and strange in the alien environment abandoned by the imperial center. Waugh himself, as amused and bemused imperial traveler, finds Englishness warped beyond recognition. Even he is transformed into a sweetly toned harmonium, a grotesque reification of his civilizing presence (the pigs, jackals, and tigers are presumably Mr. Christie's visions of the wild and diabolical barbarians amongst whom he lives). Christian culture is under judgment at this absurd and abandoned outpost of Empire, as Mr. Christie's name implies in Waugh's narrative.[5]

Waugh's rich bemusement is savored once he returns to London, the imperial center. At the end of a trip to Zanzibar in 1930 and 1931, narrated in *Remote People*, he comes back to London and discovers that the new nightclubs of the elite are jazz dives with black waiters, rowdy and boiling hot like the African scene he has just left:

> I was back in the centre of the Empire, and in the spot where, at the moment, "everyone" was going. Next day the gossip-writers would chronicle who were assembled in that rowdy cellar, hotter than Zanzibar, noisier than the market at Harar, more reckless of the decencies of hospitality than the taverns of Kabalo or Tabora. (*When the Going Was Good* 196)

The outflung barbarianized colonies have occupied the imperial center, turning the imperial power structures upside down: "I paid the bill in yellow African gold. It seemed just tribute from the weaker races to their mentors" (196). The white supremacist ideology written into the imperialist project has been inverted, the center turning into a culture subject to the alien cultures of the "weaker races." Waugh's own racism is expressed in this sour articulation of the end of empire. The members of the elite at the center of the Empire have become slaves to the African peoples it once ruled at such effortless distance.[6]

One of the abiding topics of modernism is the replacement of English faiths and dogmas by global pluralistic cultures. The move to global culture is through the demise of the imperial idea. The center collapses under the weight of the influences of the peripheral colonies it can no longer satisfactorily govern, due to the prevailing skepticism of imperialism at the center, and is itself colonized by the host of alien faiths and practices. We see this in the admiration for totemic African art in Lawrence's *Women in Love;* in the respect for Eastern mysticism in the fragmented London of Eliot's *The Waste Land;* in Pound's adoption of Chinese poetic techniques in the *Cantos;* in Yeats's uses of Japanese *Noh* drama; in Conrad's representations of the South Seas.[7] Thinking about the primitive was not merely an atavistic search for lost faiths and civilizations, but also a way of exploring the consequences of the breakup of empire, of the invasion of the barbarian into the imperial center.

Even so it was also a demonstration of the single most alarming and extraordinary fact about twentieth-century culture, which was the shrinking of the world through the new technologies of the telephone, the telegraph, the aeroplane, fast trains, the automobile, the internet. As Randall Stevenson has shown, many modernists saw the instituting of the Greenwich mean time, in its imposition of a standardized clock time around the entire globe, as an image of the advent of the new world culture. The effects of this shrinking were thought less to be a sign of the triumph of western culture in imposing its chronology and technology on the world than an inauguration of a new era of ceaseless mobility, of uprootedness, a culture characterized by deracination, speed for speed's sake, and mere aimless movement through space, like Waugh's racing cars in *Vile Bodies.*[8]

The consequences of this valueless mobility on personal relationships is analyzed with extraordinary skill by Elizabeth Bowen in *To the North,* a novel which tells the story of the tragic death in a car accident of a young woman whose job it is, significantly, to run a travel agency. Emmeline is an orphan in the world, working as a single woman with her half-cousin, and she is portrayed by Bowen as a victim of the new psychic circumstances generated by the effects of communication technology on the deracinated mind. She spends a dirty weekend with her lover in Paris, but the experience fails to materialize into a real relationship, most importantly because Emmeline and Markie never stay still long enough to root themselves into themselves.

In the Bois de Boulogne, Emmeline reflects on the fact they got so easily and unpreparedly to Paris by plane. She has a dizzyingly fractured vision of images of Paris and London, and wonders how she came to think this way:

> Emmeline asked herself if this distended present, this oppressive contraction of
> space would be properties of airmindedness....She longed suddenly to be fixed, to
> enjoy an apparent stillness, to watch even an hour complete round one object its
> little changes of light, to see out the little and greater cycles of day and season in
> one place, beloved, familiar, to watch shadows move round one garden, to know
> the same trees in spring and autumn and in their winter forms.
>
> "This is frightful," said Markie, "let's go on somewhere else." (195)

Markie is extremely dangerous for Emmeline because he has adopted wholesale
the provisionality of this new culture of ceaseless mobility and change. Bowen
argues that the new speed and travel opportunities sponsored by technology will
lead to the destruction of the possibility of the marriage of true minds. This may
strike one as rather extreme, but what is under judgment here is futurist modernism as a cultural paradigm.

When Emmeline desperately asks Markie why he has cruelly rejected her, he
shrinks from her in horror—his horror is really an internal disgust at the idea of
marriage as a fixed and abiding bond between men and women. They are in the
Sacré Cœur when this frightening exchange takes place:

> [T]he church—for Markie an oppressive monument of futility—towered up high
> and frosty....The edge of his mind was restless with superstition: like natives be-
> fore the solid advance of imperial forces, aspiration, feeling, all sense of the imma-
> terial had retreated in him before reason to some craggy hinterland where,
> having made no terms with the conqueror, they were submitted to no control and
> remained a menace. Like savages coming to town on a fair day to skip and
> chaffer, travestying their character in strange antics, creating by their very pres-
> ence a saturnalia in which the conqueror may unbend, feeling crept out in him
> from some unmapped region. His brain held his smallish, over-clear view of life in
> its rigid circle. (204)

In this very bizarre, baroque passage, Bowen sets up a high analogy between
anti-imperial discourse and primitive, superstitious fear of fixity. The only way to
get to grips with Bowen's representation of Markie's consciousness here is to try
and track down the solid foundations such an analogy might have.

Specifically, futurist modernism, for Bowen, though championing technological culture, was leading to a globalization of imperialism whose main effect
was to allow the "savage" cultures under its government to occupy the central
emotional consciousness of the imperial subject. Because communications technology effectively contracted global space down to a travelable environment,
half-colonized cultures were being internalized by the imperial subject at the
center. Savage hinterland cultures could be so easily internalized because the
imperial center had been dissociated from its traditional loyalties and

home-grown, durable affections by the mobility, deracination, and fractured experiences engendered by the speed and scope of the same new technologies.[9]

Markie's terror of marriage and the church are symptoms of the anti-Victorian backlash of high modernism—though this is certainly being colored by more traditional anti-Catholic prejudice. By rejecting nineteenth-century values of fixed, enduring bond and faith, Markie retreats into the irrational arena of the mind. The resistance of his feelings to Reason, the imperial conqueror, crosses the id's struggle against the repressive ego with anti-imperial resistance and saturnalia. Bowen's fears about the futurist primitivism produced by technological contractions of space-time ratios is paradoxically proimperialist, like Waugh's disgust at the jazz age invasion of the center of the Empire.

More sensitively, perhaps, she feared that futurist speed and mobility would seriously affect the individual mind's perceptions of others, even its perception of objects, since the attention necessary for the vision of another consciousness and its associated contexts could not operate properly in lifestyles of constant change and throwaway experience. The foreignness engendered by the globalization and technologization of imperial economies was deep within the subject, the strangeness of the mind's relation to itself, its lover, and the outside world:

> this touch of strangeness upon [Emmeline's] nerves was becoming familiar; an isolation from life she felt bound her up more closely than life itself....Intense experience interposed like a veil between herself and these objects [in Markie's room]. When [Markie] spoke or approached it was for an instant as though the veil parted: something unknown came through—though he was all the time formlessly near her like heat or light. His being was written all over her; if he was not, she was not: then they both dissipated and hung in the air. But still something restlessly ate up the air, like a flame burning. (242)

The formless insecurity of her bond with Markie, the muffling isolation of the self from its contexts in an accelerated, high-consumption diet of intense experience, the lack of clarity of any bond based on sexual desire and satisfaction, the abandonment of the self to the other being shaping the changing days, all these are the essential features of the new heterosexual relationships of sexual companionship of the interwar years.[10] Sexual companionship is feared by Bowen because it is so emptily being shaped by the "airmindedness" of the new technologies, air-minds that are being restlessly consumed by the flame of vacant desire.

As the thirties progressed, this fear of technology and of the estranging effects of the internalization of alien cultures as part of the globalization of imperial relations was transformed into an abjectly political neurosis. The technological and imperial barbarians had come out of the woodwork for the 1930s intellectuals in the shape of German and Italian fascism. In her extraordinary novel *Over the Frontier,* Stevie Smith gave voice to this deep-seated neurosis. Smith's alter ego, Pompey Casmilus, lives in London with her aunt, who functions in the novel as an embodiment of the ethical imperialism of the British Empire—she is Aunty Lion, and knows all there is to know about India and the Raj. Pompey suffers a nervous breakdown at a party where she enters into a frenetic, savage dance that anaesthetizes her mind from the prevalent evil atmosphere of fascist militarism. She goes for a rest cure at the Schloss Tilssen on the northern border of Germany where, to all intents and purposes, she goes mad, imagining herself as a heroic resistance fighter struggling against the evil regime.

This is a deliberately melodramatic novel because it is about the melodramatizing of the unquiet self in urgent and evil times.[11] The melodrama is about travel, travel as an urge to escape the "bitter commotion of feeling" (35) infecting the imagination that cannot remain contented, like a sleeping lion, within its fictional empire. As Alison Light has argued, Smith's Englishness is always "haunted by its opposite," the "small empire of home" always dangerously open to its dark other across the frontier (Light, 245–46). Pompey is also leaving a dull lover behind, Freddy: "[T]he rhythm of good-bye is in my blood and I am set again for foreign parts" (Smith 42). However, the reckless travel to foreign parts is itself driven by the restlessness of a mind unruly, "a rushing tearing quality of unquietness that drives to death" (28). More precisely, at the heart of the unquiet mind is a fascist power of cruelty, hatred, and murderous mobility.

As Pompey dances at the fancy dress party, appropriately dressed "in khaki shorts and shirt, solar topee and sandals and representing the bounds—limit to you—of Empire" (71), she enters into the music's fascist rhythms, "faster, more slave-driving, more compelling":

> There is no rest, no pause. There are so many evolutions to be performed, evolutions, revolutions, and so little time. Quickly, quickly, correctly and meticulously, I turn, I chassée, I curtsey, dipping, turning, straining straining upwards and backwards....And within the music there is moving now a more insistent clamour, a harsh grating sound, a clashing of steel on steel. It is very menacing, very military, this rapidly increasing metallic clamour, thrusting, driving, marching. (Smith 49–50)

The music eventually leads her to the hellishly cold, bitter, and solitary sea of death.

Pompey's *danse macabre*[12] is a desperate attempt to travel away from the outside world with its vicious politics of cruelty and sadism, but her dance is motivated by the very same forces of military speed, power, and destructive movement. One of the nightmares of her book is that the inner imagination has been recruited into the imaginary *maelstrom* of fascist ideology; the writer carefully receptive to her own thoughts finds that her interiority has been politicized. Smith's characteristic charming little-girl voice, the voice of Alice in the nursery, itself becomes slightly sinister in this militarized atmosphere, the rhythms and music of the little dancing girl, curtseying and chasséing, thrusting, driving, marching to the music of the time.

Pompey narrates a private dream she has at the Schloss, in Woolf's room of one's own: "My room is secure and private. I lock the door. It is quiet as the grave, as secure and silent. The grave's a fine and private place. But none, I think, do there embrace" (134). The private, silent room of women's writing has been infected by the fascist death wish, and this is confirmed by the nature of the dream. Pompey's dream is one of herself in uniform, denying to her lover Freddy that she's been recruited by "some higher command." The private dream space has been militarized, enforcing a radical propagandizing of the emotions, instituting an economy of lies and secret political manipulation in the most private of relationships.

The whole journey to Germany is a dream journey, of course, a journey into madness. The privacy of madness, though, has become an anachronism. The mind is driven to radical flight by the menace of war, but the features of the imaginative escape are themselves driven by the same dark forces of military mobility, speed, and destructive power implicit in the rhythm of good-bye in the blood.[13]

Smith's novel is at once an intensely private account of the melodramatizing speed and restlessness suffered by the mind in intensely political times, and an allegory of Empire. The somber, ferocious, quiet, and aloof lion of empire has been infected by the death wish and mind sickness instituted by the fascist rhythms of cruel, destructive expansion and appropriation. The idea of the foreign has become Hitler's Germany. This blunt fact exposes the dark forces of a military technology of rapid mobility and destruction underlying the 1920s myth of the free-traveling mind of the intellectual. The nightmare possibility that the British Empire might have made the world easier prey to fascist ideology is explored in this allegory of the mobile imperial subject transformed into a fascist dancer mad with guilt.

If the 1930s was the decade in which German fascism infected and inflected dreams of imperial travel, it is also the decade when socialism instituted a new definition of empire as oppression of the working classes of the world. Orwell's *The Road to Wigan Pier* is an essay on the resemblances between the great subject peoples of the Empire and the working-class population in the England of the Depression. Orwell had worked as a policeman in colonial Burma and knew what he was talking about. As Richard Hoggart has remarked, "Orwell most obviously was reacting against imperialism and his own guilt as a former agent of imperialism" (74): "I now realized that there was no need to go as far as Burma to find tyranny and exploitation. Here in England, down under one's feet, were the submerged working class, suffering miseries which in their different way were as bad as any an oriental ever knows" (Orwell, *Road to Wigan Pier* 139).

Orwell's text is a travel book too, entering the "strange country" of the industrial North (101). The working classes are a "race of enemies" (117), enemies of the middle classes who exploit them, treat them with prejudice as powerful as racism: "The smell of their sweat, the very texture of their skins, were mysteriously different from yours" (120). For the squeamish middle class, the working classes represent "a sinister flood creeping upwards to engulf himself and his friends" (123), "alien and dangerous" (141). Orwell lives among them like Waugh among the alien natives: "I went among them as a foreigner" (145). Class difference is "comparable to race-difference" (213), and produces exactly the same set of prejudices.

With Orwell too, travel writing has become a journey to the heart of Empire, a gauging of the effects of the mechanization of capitalism on the class racism built into English culture. With an urgency as anxious and depressed as Smith's, he foresees the possible transformation of middle-class prejudice into fascist ideology if the journey towards the foreign at the heart of Empire is not somehow successful in internalizing and absorbing the enemy race of the working class. His pessimism was confirmed during the Spanish Civil War. Returning from Catalonia to southern England, the landscape he saw, after the tragic mess and ideological confusion of his experience in Spain, lay before him as a material trope for the self-appeasing deep sleep of little middle imperial England:

> And then England—southern England, probably the sleekest landscape in the world....The industrial towns were far away, a smudge of smoke and misery hidden by the curve of the earth's surface. Down here it was still the England I had known in my childhood: the railway-cuttings smothered in wild flower, the deep meadows where the great shining horses browse and meditate, and the slow-moving streams bordered by willows, the green bosoms of the elms, the larkspurs in the cottage gardens; and then the huge peaceful wilderness of outer London, the barges on the miry river, the familiar streets, the posters telling of cricket matches and Royal weddings, the men in bowler hats, the pigeons in Trafalgar Square, and the red buses, the blue policemen—all sleeping the deep, deep sleep of England, from which I sometimes fear we shall never wake till we are jerked out of it by the roar of bombs. ("Homage" 186–87)

The landscape *is* the sleep, pastoral and nostalgic surfaces smothering the mind, lulling it with their slow-moving, familiar traditions into browsing, meditating "deep, deep sleep." It is a seductive surface ("The curve of the earth's surface") that gives southerners the illusion of depth ("deep meadows...deep, deep sleep") only by concealing beneath and beyond its maternal curves and bosoms the far away, fairy-tale rumor of all that is alien to the sleepy imperial dream of home. The foreign "far away," though, a compound of the smoke and misery of the industrial towns and the urgencies of the Spanish Civil War, is brought home to the imperial center by the ultimate act of political travel writing, a proleptic imagining of the Second World War. Orwell brought it all back home too with his twin "travel" books, *Road to Wigan Pier* and *Homage to Catalonia*.

In all four cases of travel writing, Waugh's vision of an Africanized imperial center, Bowen's appalled exploration of the effects of communication technology on sexual relations, Smith's neurotic portrait of a fascist wanderlust in the imperial mind, and Orwell's quest for the alien people of the working class in England, the idea of the foreign is inverted and internalized to become a subversive and dangerous political power within the interiority of the free, mobile imperial subject. That subject, in the 1930s, turned into Auden's mad airman, corrupted to the very heart of the imagination by paranoid fear of the enemy:

> The aero plane has only recently become necessary, owing to the progress of enemy propaganda, and even now not for flying itself, but as a guarantee of good faith to the people, frightened by ghost stories, the enemy's distorted vision of the airman's activities. (Auden 76)

Travel writing is always about the relations between the mobile subject (the "airman") and the foreign country being traversed (the "enemy"). During the 1930s this relationship became doubly inverted: as neurotic symptom within the mind, and as political allegory of the struggle among imperial, class, and state powers. Travel writing became a distorted vision of war reportage written at the shifting borders between the political unconscious and a culture gearing itself up for total war.

Notes

1   Karen Lawrence has shown how travel in Woolf's *The Voyage Out* is a psychological rather than a political figure, the voyage exposing the self to its environment: "The myth of control over her environment quickly gives way to the feeling that [Rachel] moves through it at its mercy. The adventure of consciousness is tinged with the danger that, in expanding to include the world, the self will lose the sense of its own boundaries" (168). Lawrence's thesis is feminist, and concentrates on the construction of gender identity, but she does acknowledge in a footnote that imperial and political considerations are important (19).

2   For a proper background to the relations between modernist writing and imperialism, cf. Jameson and Brantlinger.

3   For a caustic account of the demise of Waugh's own talent for travel writing as a result of the harsh political cultural contexts of the late 1930s, see Paul Fussell's Waugh chapter in *Abroad*.

4   Travel for Waugh unweaves imperial fictions complacently believed in by those who remain happily ignorant at the metropolitan center. As he put it in a 1933 article about travel: "[T]he stay-at-home vaguely imagines the world as being under calm European domination, peopled with peppery colonels and astute officials" ("Travel—and Escape from Your Friends," *Daily Mail* 16 January 1933, Gallagher 134).

5   Waugh really did meet a Mr. Christie, and most of his peculiarities are substantially true, as Waugh's diary entries show. Cf. entry for 20 January 1933 (Davie 366–67). Christie was also the inspiration for the odious and nightmarish Mr. Todd in *A Handful of Dust.*

6   For a Lacanian reading of Waugh's concern with occupation of the center by fantasy others, cf. R. Neill Johnson.

7   Fussell's argument that one of the main signs of high modernism is its topographical travel dimension is most clearly signaled in what he terms "the British Literary Diaspora": "[W]hat a geographical work *The Waste Land* is, how it is the work of an imagination stimulated by great presiding motifs of movements between Germany, Russia, Greece, India, Switzerland, Smyrna, Carthage, Phoenicia, Jerusalem, Egypt, and Austria, as well as by shifts of perceived landscape and setting" (52).

8   Clearly a satire on Futurist dogmas. For an exploration of *Vile Bodies* as influenced by futurist manifestoes, cf. Brooke Allen.

9   For a discussion of this topic of invasion of the mind by "barbarians" in an Irish political context, i.e., in Bowen's analysis of the "Big House" state of mind, cf. Williams. Images of invasion, infection, and permeation by culture in her war stories are ably discussed by Jeslynn Medoff. Hermione Lee writes beautifully about deracination in *To the North.*

10   For a feminist interpretation of the reasons a veil might fall between modernist women and objects in Bowen's fiction, cf. Sandra Kemp.

11   The journey is partly based on two trips Smith made to Germany in 1929 and 1931 during her affair with Karl Eckinger. Smith has deliberately darkened and Nazified her memories of these holidays. Cf. Spalding 80–85.

12   For the *danse macabre* theme in Smith's poetry, cf. Storey and Thaddeus.

13   Catherine Civello gives a powerful Lacanian and Laing-inspired reading of Pompey's move to Germany, reading it as a quest for ambivalent womanhood.

Works Cited

Allen, Brooke. "Vile Bodies: A Futurist Fantasy." *Twentieth Century Literature* 40.3 (1994): 318–28.

Auden, W.H. "Journal of an Airman." *The English Auden: Poems, Essays and Dramatic Writings, 1927–1939.* Ed. Edward Mendelson. London: Faber, 1977: 73–94.

Bowen, Elizabeth. *To The North.* 1932. London: Jonathan Cape, 1950.

Brantlinger, Patrick. *Rule of Darkness: British Literature and Imperialism, 1830–1914.* Ithaca: Cornell UP, 1988.

Civello, Catherine A. *Patterns of Ambivalence: The Fiction and Poetry of Stevie Smith.* Drawer, Columbia, SC: Camden House, 1997.

Davie, Michael, ed. *The Diaries of Evelyn Waugh.* London: Weidenfeld & Nicolson, 1976.

Fussell, Paul. *Abroad: British Literary Travelling Between the Wars.* Oxford: Oxford UP, 1980.

Gallagher, Donat, ed. *The Essays, Articles and Reviews of Evelyn Waugh.* London: Methuen, 1983.

Gurr, Andrew. *Writers in Exile: The Identity of Home in Modern Literature.* Brighton, Sussex: Harvester Press, 1981.

Hoggart, Richard. "George Orwell and *The Road to Wigan Pier.*" *Critical Quarterly* 7 (1965): 72–85.

Jameson, Fredric. *The Political Unconscious: Narrative as a Socially Symbolic Act.* Ithaca: Cornell UP, 1981.

Johnson, R. Neill. "Shadowed by the Gaze: Evelyn Waugh's *Vile Bodies* and *The Ordeal of Gilbert Pinfold.*" *Modern Language Review* 91.1 (1996): 9–19.

Kemp, Sandra. "'But How Describe a World Seen without a Self?' *Feminism, Fiction and Modernism.*" *Critical Quarterly* 32. 1 (1990): 99–118.

Lawrence, D. H. *Women in Love.* 1920. New York : Barnes & Noble, 1996.

Lawrence, Karen R. *Penelope Voyages: Women and Travel in the British Literary Tradition.* Ithaca: Cornell University Press, 1994.

Lee, Hermione. "The Placing of Loss: Elizabeth Bowen's *To the North.*" *Essays in Criticism* 28 (1978): 129–42.

Lewis, Wyndham. *Journey into Barbary: Morocco Writings and Drawings.* Ed. C.J. Cox. Santa Barbara: Black Sparrow Press, 1983.

Light, Alison. "Outside History? Stevie Smith, Women Poets and the National Voice." *English* 43. 177 (1994): 237–59.

Medoff, Jeslynn. "'There is no Elsewhere': Elizabeth Bowen's Perceptions of War." *Modern Fiction Studies* 30.1 (1984): 73–81.

Orwell, George. *Homage to Catalonia.* 1938. Harmondsworth, Middlesex: Penguin, 1989.

———. *The Road to Wigan Pier.* 1937. Harmondsworth, Middlesex: Penguin, 1989.

Paulin, Tom. "'Letters from Iceland': Going North." *The 1930s: A Challenge to Orthodoxy.* Ed. John Lucas. Brighton, Sussex: Harvester Press, 1978: 59–77.

Pound, Ezra. *The Cantos of Ezra Pound.* 1932. New York: W.W. Norton & Company, 1972.

Smith, Stevie. *Over the Frontier.* 1938. London: Virago, 1980.

Spalding, Frances. *Stevie Smith: A Critical Biography.* London: Faber & Faber, 1988.

Stevenson, Randall W. *Modernist Fiction: An Introduction.* London: Harvester Wheatsheaf, 1992.

Storey, Mark. "Why Stevie Smith Matters." *Critical Quarterly* 21. 2 (1979): 41–55.

Thaddeus, Janice. "Stevie Smith and the Gleeful Macabre." *Contemporary Poetry* 3. 4 (1978): 36–49.

Waugh, Evelyn. "Desert and Frost." *The Essays, Articles and Reviews of Evelyn Waugh.* Ed. Donat Gallagher. London: Methuen, 1983: 139–40.

———. "Travel—and Escape from your Friends." *The Essays, Articles and Reviews of Evelyn Waugh.* Ed. Donat Gallagher. London: Methuen, 1983: 133–34.

———. *Vile Bodies.* 1930. Boston: Little, Brown, 1977.

———. *When the Going Was Good.* London: Reprint Society, 1946.

Williams, Julia McElhattan. "'Fiction with the Texture of History': Elizabeth Bowen's *The Last September.*" *Modern Fiction Studies* 41.2 (1995): 219–42.

Chapter 4

Contemporary German Journeys to Italy

Cecilia Novero

My Italian dream—this would be a good title. A German title. Dream and Italy, the old bond, indivisible, since Redbeard.... —Christine Wolter

How do German writers and intellectuals today travel to Italy? How do they travel in and to the country that has filled the imagination and inspired the work of writers and archeologists since the Modern Age? The journey to Italy continues in the present. It suffices to look at the number of publications about Italy now available in the bookstores. My article addresses the tendency of contemporary German texts to "erase" Italy, the country and its people, from the postmodern European world.

Most of the texts considered, which have been written by writers and journalists in the past ten years, reproduce some of the recurrent pitfalls of "travel literature" as we know it from the colonial age, that is, the age of discovery, the age of fieldwork and ethnography. Thus, the texts do not question the notion of travel and its meaning in and for modernity, let alone postmodernity. Furthermore, some texts indulge in naturalizing and objectifying the country the authors have chosen to "love." My article asks why contemporary travel literature seldom engages in a critique or, at least, an investigation of notions such as national identity and national culture, given that it indirectly contributes to their "meaning." In other words, why do German contemporary travel texts avoid "metalevels" of reflection and thus often essentialize or naturalize Italy, its beauty as well as its crises?

Typically, some authors compare Italy to the Earth, which is to say, for them Italy embodies "paganism" and sensuality, both associated with sexuality and primordial, instinctive "true life." For these writers, the Italian journey is tantamount to experiencing life; in a way, they travel to Italy and write about their journeys—or stays—to recuperate forgotten origins: the origins of western civilization and culture. At the same time, this Italian journey represents the occasion for the German traveler to witness the decline of western civilization. The notion of decline as both "naturally" Italian while dangerously familiar to German history is paradoxical and stereotypical. The writers conceive of decline as already implicit, natural, as it were, within the context of Italian history since the Roman Empire, which these texts reconstruct as static, in a state of constant crisis. Thus Italian history itself is "naturalized" here. The affinity between German and Italian history, or the possibility that Germany be involved in the same state of crisis, is at once apprehended and disavowed in the stereotypical representations of Italy as both the same and the Other of Germany.

With the exception of a few "writerly" (Barthes 4) texts—less about the country than about writing about Italy as textual site—travel is generally linked to the notions of return and *oikos* (home) in the majority of the commercial travel texts. As Georges Van Den Abbeele illustrates, these two notions informed the concept of travel and its experience at the peak of the modern age (xx–xxii). He refers to the definitions of travel in the Encyclopédie article of 1765 "Voyage," in which the author touched upon three epistemological categories: grammar, commerce, and education. The grammatical definition involves an anthropological perspective: the transport of a person from one place to another; in this transport, the agent is unclear, thus pointing to the "necessity" of travel. This in turn implies the transition from the realm of life to that of death, from the necessity of taking the Grand Tour to acquire knowledge to the figurative meaning of voyage as death. The semantic shift to the inevitability of death involves anxiety. One is anxious about not being prepared for the final voyage, which means not having accumulated enough "gain" (knowledge or provisions), thus not having moved enough. The preoccupation is of an economic nature, just like the second definition of the term in the same article. Travel is defined commercially as the moving back and forth of furniture and other things (furniture in French means something movable) by a mercenary or else a person who makes a revenue (returns). The third definition posits the educational value of travel. Van Den Abbeele writes: "As the anthropological agent of the voyage is thus secured by the revenue (in profits, in knowledge) of a return, do does the space of that trajectory become available to be read as the grammar of a topography....If travel posits the risk and anxiety of death, it also signals the way to health, wealth and wisdom" (xvi). Hence he shows how a certain kind of "utilitarian" reason informed the traveling experience, and—consequently—its narration.

Within the *topoi* of travel literature since the sixteenth century, the moral impulse constitutes one of its motivations; in other words, travel and travel writing happen as a lesson for life. The lesson indicates a "return," both economically and physically. The traveler profits in knowledge by risking a potential loss, which the "return," however, already denies at the outset. Travel requires a home, *oikos,* a domestic return, and as such travel domesticates—or brings home (*domo*) the experience of displacement. Writing itself—in the form of the letter or the journal—becomes yet another attempt to fix memory, to freeze experience into a monument, a souvenir, a fetish.

In contrast, other written or cinematic genres have participated in dismantling and dissolving the ethnographic images associated with travel memoirs, and indirectly, with the sites first visited and then captured in words or images. National boundaries dissolve, and these writerly or cinematic texts are about both *identity* crises and identities in *crisis.* They often help discard organic notions of national culture and national belonging. For instance, Italian intellectuals writing and filming Italy go abroad, to the eastern European countries, in order to reconceive of their own subjectivity and culture. It suffices to mention the films by Gianni Amelio, Pupi Avati, and Mazzacurati; Germans use the media to deconstruct the notion of territoriality, as for instance in the films by Wim Wenders, and the texts by Peter Handke; Turkish-German authors write about their experience of 1968 in Germany as this is mediated through Turkey (a case in point is writer Emine Sergi Ozdamar) and Afro-Italians give rise to new languages and cultures that belong in Italy today.

Even so, the German "journey to Italy" is mostly singular: It romanticizes and aestheticizes Italy without taking into account its fragmentary, fractured, and refracted aspects, both in its cultural products and in its societal multiplicity. Italy embodies the paradox of the ultimate experience of the Other that is familiar and the familiar that is Other. However, the Other is constructed as the absolute signifier. Thus, the representation of Italy does not avoid essentializing "Difference" itself. Difference*s* within Italy are erased and naturalized into the ahistorical Italian crisis of civilization, into the truism of "Italian chaos" implicit in the necessary self-identical, never-changing, natural history of Italy itself.

What determines the difference between "critical," "writerly" texts and "a-critical," "readerly," and "affirmative" ones? The term affirmative is borrowed from Herbert Marcuse, who used it to describe bourgeois culture as the site where the dominant ideology is reconfirmed. Is it legitimate to speak of a divide between commercial and "writerly" texts in order to pinpoint this difference? Considering the texts selected, the distinction lies less in the category or genre of the texts than in their status or provenance—their cultural matrix.

I am grouping the texts in two main categories: In the first group are Barbara Bronnen's autobiographical narrative on her stay in Tuscany, and the collection of articles by the correspondent for the *Süddeutsche Zeitung,* Klaus Brill. Although belonging to two different genres, they both dehistoricize and typify Italy. The former essentializes Italy into the Other elective country that provides the occasion for Bronnen's authorial experience to coincide with her intellectual and emotional landscape. In this text, the traveler becomes an "author" and thus finds her authorial "identity" when describing Italy in writing. Her authorial voice needs to construct Italy as both an object of narration and an occasion for experience. Bronnen uses Italy "ethnographically," as an ethnographic experience, but she does not reflect on her "subject position" as ethnographer and writer.

With the aim to provide information on contemporary Italy, Brill's collection of essays is so caught up in the anxiety about details and contemporaneity that it reduces history to an everyday and immediate consumption. Bronnen's account places Italy's essence before its own history and the European context, while Brill's work conflates history with information, the "then" with the "now," and thus explains Italian phenomena also within the static framework of a given Italianness.

My second category includes Thomas Valentin's *Schnee vom Ätna,* Christine Wolter's *Italien muss schön sein,* and Alice Vollenweider's *Italia!* These texts construe Italy as anti-site, a forcefield that extends beyond the organic nature of a naturalized crisis. They question Italianness and Germanness in tandem: Valentin and Wolter come from the former German Democratic Republic (GDR), and Vollenweider is a freelance writer from Switzerland, who is a "tourist" by chance. Because of their somewhat marginal and other location within the Germanic world, or, in other words, their status as "minor literature," these texts are intertextual, and deconstruct Italy and the experience of the journey. "Travel," and more specifically the "Italian journey," become for these authors metaphors for a mobile view of national and individual subjectivity that is represented as multiple and complex. Hence, only those self-reflexive texts authored by minor German writers come to terms with the internal displacements and confusions between the subject traveler and the traveled space with its people, with the plurality of the various and varied specific*s*, difference*s* and transnational characters. The texts by the GDR and Swiss authors bear some of the subversive features that Gilles Deleuze and Felix Guattari ascribe to minor literatures. Their difference within the linguistically "one" German panorama is either evidently invoked or only evoked, however it intersects with the construction of Italy. These few texts present Italy less as site of travel than as traveling site.

The traveled site becomes a net of subjects that reinvent and reconstruct the national temporal and spatial interconnections. The "minority" status of the literature of departure is first projected and reflected upon in the journey to contemporary Italy, which embodies the place in Europe, whose "national" and modern history well reflects the condition of minor. The "minor" country, with a long and—ironically—important and "major" history, mirrors the "minor subject's" marginalization, from which position, however, the minor author enjoys a privileged, because both marginal and central, cultural perspective on Europe. It is the perspective of the minor as always already a traveler between center and periphery.

In this regard, the "minor" German texts bear affinities with "postcolonial" literatures. At the same time their role within the German context is closer to the role played by minor literatures within the majoritarian, identical dominant cultural and linguistic empire of the German-speaking states. The minor authors's dilemma and strength lie as well in their being internal to the dominant paradigm, and yet totally alien, thus able to produce a de-familiarizing effect. Minor literatures exist both within and outside of the "cultural empires," practically clinging to the frontier, occupying the threshold, and dispersed in the interstices between classical and shared literary and cultural traditions or canons. To put it in a less abstract way, the German texts by "minor" authors considered here are dialogic: "Their" Italians are cross-cultural subjects, expressions of traveling cultures that are not easily fixed and that, just like the minor texts themselves, have to be renegotiated constantly in relation to the dominant gaze, a gaze that tends to incorporate and unify.

One text escapes both classifications, and yet falls short of its ironic and self-reflexive impulse. Robert Gernhardt's *Die Toscana-Therapie* (The Tuscany Therapy) attempts to use irony and sarcasm to critique the narcissistic and self-absorbed manners of the German "intellectual" travelers to Italy. However, this satirical radio play shows that irony does not suffice to "displace" the "textual place" that Italy occupies in contemporary travel literature. Here, the German infatuation with Italy springs from a narcissistic love that is blind to external reality and lives off an ideal image, in this case, the romanticized rural and idyllic Tuscan landscape. In effect, the contemporary German travelers—or the protagonists of the radio play—instrumentalize the idyll and the notion of travel as valuable experience because they explicitly, and yet unconsciously, transform their stay inside the Italian landscape into the conventional and most popular form of contemporary life-experience and journey: "therapy."

Notwithstanding the author's exposure of the contemporary German manipulation of the ancient and everlasting Italian myth (by which the German imagination is imprisoned), the playwright's irony, which revolves around the metaphor of therapy, loses its critical potential in the final scenes. A reconciliatory ending shows how the journey to Italy has failed because of the impossible recuperation of the idyll, the failure being due to the German neuroses that affect most intellectuals today. Furthermore, they are incapable of recapturing the idyllic Tuscan landscape because of the intruding presence in this landscape of "modern artifacts," industrial "finds" that produce "noise," both physically and metaphorically. And yet the ironic element that might subvert the concept of return and thus resist objectification of the Italian landscape flips into its opposite and provides the reader with a return after all: The catastrophic results of the main characters' "stay in utopia" are therapeutic, thus cathartic, and cohere in a happy end.

The failure of a life in utopia generates closure, the acknowledgment of one's own "mistaken" identity and lost desires that need not be projected outwards. Thus, despite the critique of the German stereotypical representation of Italy, as well as its instrumentalization on the part of the German traveler, the radio play actually makes Italy into an *occasion* to criticize the German character, but also to praise failure with the prize of "understanding." The happy end thus reinscribes and resolves the intellectuals' anxiety about absolute loss in an almost Hollywood fashion.

My article shows that contemporary German works about Italy tend to invent Italy as an organic text that functions as a medium to reaffirm identity and self-identity. This Italy is a colony of the authors's imagination, a space from which they univocally reaffirm their authorial voice, their self-identity. Italy is a point of departure as well as arrival; the text involves a return to the origins, and this return often reconciles the traditional counterpoised categories of German spirit and Italian earthy sensuality in an idealistic fashion, and yet from an economic perspective too. Finally, the Italian journey reveals itself to be a true Hegelian "phenomenology of the Spirit" in which the educational and moral return is guaranteed in a newly found home that sublates plurality.

Common Places and Self-Identity: The Italianness of Italians

Tuscany becomes the author's "own"—as the possessive adjective in Bronnen's title indicates, *Meine Toskana*—and she defines her text as a *Liebeserklärung,* a love declaration:

> Peace became my friend, the birds are my companions, and the wind, the smells, the soul of this land allow my absence of mind to vanish—all these are things, which I store before I return to the city.
>
> And as I have become free here, I have also felt a solid ground, grounding, just like Florian who took his first steps here. (8)

> Esimio, the farmer, he himself is an olive: gnarled, shriveled, brownish, pointed in his spirit and intricate too. Just like the olive tree, he wants to be courted, only then he offers us the bitter fruit of his Tuscan wit, insolent and to the point like a Berliner. (13)

The stress is laid on the author's subjective perspective, on an "intimate" relationship, while at the same time pointing to the public aspect of this love: The fact that it is a *declaration* immediately grants agency to the author of the letter; it involves an object, which, however, in the case of Tuscany, differs from the recipient. The latter is an audience of witnesses to this love. The distinction between the object-object and the audience-recipient testifies to the final and absolute objectification and alienation of the object itself, Italy. Tuscany is constructed as pure object.

In addition, the publisher's introduction of the book identifies the lover's discourse as that of a woman and classifies her love as "maternal" and "natural." Her words are like birds's songs (nature), and they capture the Italian lifestyle with Behutsamkeit, care, and consideration (mother). Bronnen's rhetoric is comparable to the publisher's, and the effects of the book are analogous to those analyzed above in the title. Her style captivates the subject, the object, and the addressee in an emotional landscape, inexplicable because it is the fruit of a natural motherly love. Empathy takes over analysis, and the Italian landscape becomes static, like nature that a naturally everlasting love preserves in its unquestioned and unquestionable way.

Although depicted in their individuality and with proper names, the Italians represented merge with the landscape. Thus they become a function of the *Kantian sublime*. They reconfirm the author's moral position, which they help her recognize: Italians are like Kant's starry sky; they induce the moral law within the contemplating subject.

Naturalization

In the chapter "Passeggiata" (69–70), Bronnen describes the stroll as "high and low tide," a typical ekphrasis that naturalizes a social phenomenon:

> Inevitable just like the tides, the dance of the "passeggiata" begins on the Piazza, every afternoon, at five o'clock. It is a device of the Mediterranean that generates movement, a chat, a cup of coffee or ice-cream….This urge to get together, at least for an hour a day, this desiring to touch or be touched, of conversations and contact! This longing to see and be seen, this impulse to engage in exchange, to reassure one another, to be persuaded by one another. A performance of multiple meanings and a ritual against isolation. (69)

Despite the author's attempt to look at this "activity" as social, the subtext redefines the stroll as an intrinsically Italian custom. Italian means mostly "naturelike." As with the possessive adjective *mein* in the title, the author first has to distance herself from this natural landscape and then can envy it for its difference. Difference is thus kept at a distance. She establishes a connection, and yet it is one that underscores both "nonidentity" with the landscape and possession. Similarly, the possessive *mein* of the title both indicates possession and distance: The desire to belong in "nature" is disavowed in its fetishization as "described object" that can be possessed, objectified, and fixed in the text.

The topos of the sea returns in another passage (54–56). Bronnen does not ignore the fact that the sea is a cultural construct, and in effect underscores the multiple perspectives that go into the myriad meanings ascribed to the sea in and outside Italy. However, after having offered a vast array of views including farmers, city dwellers, young men, and couples, the author homogenizes into *one* plurality their various, individual perspectives. For example, one sentence starts with the words: "The sea shows its teeth to the ones, and it is motherly mild to the others"; then it changes to: "The sea *is* (my italics) heavy and sweet, and light," and the paragraph finally ends with a totalizing "we": "[W]e come to look for life and we ban death" (55). Such a sentence forgets the farmer's "angst" that Bronnen has just mentioned a few lines above. In contrast, she naturalizes the sea, which here is made into a metaphor of "life" as one. The sea and life are like synonyms: both in the singular, they are absolute and circumscribed existential concepts encompassing every one of *us*, against difference*s*.

Even when mentioning the "modern" aspects of the sea, i.e., its pollution, Bronnen erases the potential disturbing and disrupting "meaning" pollution could entail. Indeed, the polluted sea is immediately domesticated within the poetic, nostalgic framework. The sea will always live as *one* legend, as poetry, or rather as the landscape of poetry itself, suspended halfway between truth and the imagination. Here the author does not question the more complex relation between experiences of the sea and their cultural, textual mediations. She textualizes without reflecting on the construction behind her own text. Her depiction of Italian life as tantamount to the sea does not consider or incorporate any other, actual text in which the metaphor has been reproduced, discussed, or deconstructed. Her story is a prisoner of tautology: Italians symbolize because they are like nature and they represent nature because they are a clear manifestation of "life."

Luigi Malerba's representation of the sea in "Everyone at the Seaside" may serve as a counterpoint (Vollenweider, *Italienische Reise* 64). Malerba does not "universalize" or dehistoricize the relation between the sea and the Italian people. Rather, his text is borne out of the contradictions between his objections to the notion of enjoyment as leisure, distraction, mass tourism, and consumerism, on the one hand, and his unwillingness to resist these compulsions, and hence to distinguish himself from the rest of the Italian crowd. The relation between the author, the crowd, and the sea is Malerba's way to historicize the Italian "landscape," which is not "abstracted" from its social context. Malerba thus describes nature as a way to question the meaning of "enjoyment" in contemporary Italian society. Both Malerba's and Bronnen's texts use Italian *chiasso* as their main character. In contrast to Bronnen, however, Malerba reads his own experience as already inscribed by the culture that surrounds him and to which he necessarily contributes, willingly or not. He questions the forms of his "belonging" to Italian culture as well as the meaning of belonging, and Italian culture, too. Hence, his text is ironic, political, and does not explain any existential position or aesthetic judgment with the ready-made concept of Italianness. Malerba takes the symbol of the sea and explodes it, while Bronnen takes the sea and its multiple meanings and turns them into an icon of an always already existing and fixed Italianness that is never questioned. In the same way she does not question the meaning of nature.

Essentialism

Naturalization becomes "essentialism" in Bronnen's story "Bread." She equates Italy once again with nature, which she then keeps distinct from culture, or rather from civilization and technology:

Doctors say that we should not eat too much of it [bread] if we don't want to burden our stomach, they suggest that we nourish ourselves with fluids and light foods, which keep us slim.

Elsa is someone who appreciates bread. Unrelenting, she deepens her teeth in it and clarifies between two bites: "My entrails do not understand these theories. I don't give up my love for bread and sometimes I think that I eat the rest only as bread condiment....Bread has also to do with us women, and I am disturbed by a world that has nothing feminine any longer. Should we really give up all our forms and all those things to which our soul depends? Because bread is a part of me, it is warm and soft and it smells like soul." (96–97)

Italy is tantamount to tradition, and what is most disturbing is that this conflation occurs on the basis of the equation women = traditional food = warmth and softness. The passage sets up the Italian culinary tradition of bread making and consumption against the modern world of nutritional science. Furthermore, because bread is "warm and soft and smells of soul"—as Elsa puts it—bread becomes a synonym for Italian women, who then are themselves set up against modernity. Elsa's comments become even more problematic than they already sound because Bronnen frames her character's narrative about being "nourishing, simple, essential, earthy and sensual" within the questionable dichotomy between progress and tradition.

Elsa's love for bread is the expression of one of the two poles. It does not dialogue with science or the modern diet in Bronnen's text. Elsa's agency is annihilated because she is that traditional world, the repository of an essential truth, fully organic, and self-sufficient. Elsa's identity with bread and with herself is holistic and pure, not affected by external modern impulses, diets, and foreign worlds. Bronnen uses the dichotomy between progress and tradition so that writer and reader may travel from one world to the other, establish their differences and gain a point of view. Elsa figures in this narrative as the ethnographer's constructed primitive society—static and impermeable to the "outside" modern world. Bronnen never suggests that Elsa could be a metaphorical traveler herself within Italian and other cultures, or, in other words, that Elsa's act of eating bread could have also been represented as her way of questioning her own identity—after all she *is* bread, she *eats* bread, and she also *makes* bread.

Bronnen's narrative, as well as Klaus Brill's articles about modern Italy and its idiosyncrasies, experience a block of the imagination when it comes to Italy, which in their texts still functions like a colony of the German imagination since the eighteenth century. Bronnen's main flaw lies in blurring the particular, on which she and Brill focus, with the universal. The universal exists as a goal and as the return that *makes travel happen* in the first place. In effect, in both texts, the universal is the Italian character and then, metonymically, Life as a whole.

Thus, Klaus Brill's selection of Italian "topics" results in truisms and tautological expressions of Italians' Italianness. For instance, when he analyzes the national passion for cellular phones, his explanation is essentialist: Italians are the manifestation of life, life is exchange, Italians understand communication as the best expression of life—in other words, it signifies their identity—hence Italians cannot do without the *telefonino.*[1] Brill analyzes the use of cellular phones less from a social or cultural-anthropological point of view than as a naturalized extension of the Italian way of life. Italian lifestyles are not examined. Cell phones become modern incarnations of that same Italian Spirit that Bronnen wanted to capture by rediscovering the origins of a traditional world.

Traveling Inhabitants and Inhabiting Travelers: Thomas Valentin's *Schnee vom Ätna* and Alice Vollenweider's *Italia!*

Valentin and Vollenweider take a different approach. Their stories start and end with the "particular." The particular remains particular, the peculiar adds to the peculiar, and the result is a collage of contrastive, multifaceted, and elusive moments. As opposed to the experiential knowledge set forth in Bronnen's and Brill's texts, both Vollenweider and Valentin—although differently—exhibit their experience, and journey, as textually mediated, and their texts are dialogical, both with respect to other texts and to the people, the encounters with Italians and Italian landscapes.

Valentin's characters are oxymoronic and quite the opposite of stereotypical figures. For instance, they are Germans disguised or mistaken for Italians by Germans, or blind witnesses, or, finally, racist Neapolitans living in the North and contemptuous of the South. Valentin's Sicilian landscapes are complex micro-realities whose actors are unstable figures always "outside of themselves."

These characters question identity in all its forms: individual, regional, and national. In effect, Valentin's choice of Sicily as destination for his travel and topic of his text is already different in and of itself. Sicily has been a destination for centuries, a site typically visited for its archeological ruins, its ancient past as Greek "colony" ("Magna Graecia"). Even so, Sicily has also been a difficult place to visit and describe, because of its particular plurality of geographical, but especially human and cultural, landscapes, at once representative of historical occupations and thus differences, and of an intense, "protective," "insular" isolation from the rest of Italy. Sicily, as Gesualdo Bufalino puts it in the collection of articles on Sicily he edited in 1993, challenges the stereotype, and stands for the paradox. It is constantly ambivalent, it is "an island in the plural," as Bufalino titles his preface: an island, a colony, a continent, at once part of Italy, and separate from it, one of its regions and a nation of itself, multicultural and multiethnic (Bufalino and Zago v–viii). As the subtitle of the collection states, the articles selected can only be "testimonies *toward* a portrait" (emphasis added). Thus, the editors underscore that Sicily cannot be possessed (unlike Bronnen's Tuscany), not even reached. Rather it is a "travel*ing*" space, a voyage in itself, a journey that moves in the direction of a "portrait" that hence will always remain incomplete.

Valentin's journey to Sicily mirrors the fragmentation and paradoxes of this land and its people, like the "intellectual" itineraries, or "approaches," proposed by Bufalino and Zago. Valentin's text also engages with contemporary Sicily from a transversal point of view: Sicily is not any longer a center, not in Italy and not in the western world. It rather has embodied a question mark since at least Antonio Gramsci's *La Questione Meridionale*. Valentin's representation of Sicily makes into a central question the issue of the marginality of the South of Italy, of its "Mediterranean" roots. In so doing, the author first turns upside down the relation between "center" and "periphery," and then uses the new "twisted" relation to rethink—indirectly—both the German-Italian connection, as well as the Federal Republic of Germany-German Democratic Republic one. Interestingly enough, the first story in Valentin's collection is entitled "A Wall," where the indefinite article preceding the word "wall" is a clear reference to "the wall" that divided Berlin and that is evoked by a Neapolitan taxi driver in Milan who thinks it would be the best solution to separate the South from the North of Italy.

Despite the evident projection of Valentin's own historical and national "identity" onto what appears to be a preconceived image of Italy—or of Sicily in Italy—the text's true stake lies in the exposure of its own cultural and textual devices, of its own mechanisms of construction and deconstruction of national identities. In this respect, Valentin's stories demonstrate how textual journeys maintain a "truthful" basis only when their textuality (inter- and intratextuality too) becomes a constitutive part of the journey described, thus of the "place" visited.

Vollenweider's travel book is intertextual and textual as well: It mixes historical sources with excerpts of famous memoirs or stories about Italian authors or film directors. In addition, she chooses her written itineraries according to verbal connections: She follows the stream of erudite literary or etymological associations and thus prevents the reader from identifying experience with its narration.

One example is, for instance, Vollenweider's description of Parma (68–72). Her visit is immediately textualized—thus her experience is mediated—because both she and the text follow a series of verbal associations with Parma as both a word and a place. Vollenweider's point of departure is the cheese "Parmigiano" (Parmesan); her point of arrival is both the same and another: Contrary to the reader/traveler's knowledge, Parmigiano also denotes a dessert, one which is typical, as the proper name indicates, and atypical, unexpected, since the cheese's fame has erased the dessert. She goes one step further and qualifies Parmigiano as the common name of the citizen from Parma, one that is both singular and plural, and "Parmigianino" as the signature of *the* painter from Parma. Each of them is typical and exceptional—they are names and words defined by the place in which they are used, but they also describe it through their multiple, historical, and anthropological meanings. Finally, the text travels from "physical taste" to "aesthetic taste," from cheese to art. By using both "references," that of sign and that of place, she opens up new ways of entry into the semiotic and semantic space of the city. Every word used to describe the

semiotic and semantic space of the city. Every word used to describe the specificity of Parma becomes relevant with respect to the word's own cultural-historical
itinerary, an itinerary that is rooted in the history of Parma and whose meanings
have traveled via multiple texts, in language and through language.

Historical information and "other" texts become "active" interventions that
interfere not only with her own Italian text—Vollenweider's Italy is explicitly a
text—but also with the construction of the idea of Italian culture itself. Italy's
organicity dissolves into a complex "hypertext," in which, like for Valentin, the
text's complexity helps subvert the stereotypical notions of North and South,
center and periphery. Politics and aesthetics are thus intimately and clearly related in these travel stories: Verbal connections gradually displace both the word,
its origin, and the "place," thus effecting yet another kind of travel, the journey
of thoughts that accompanies Vollenweider's wordy places and displacements.

Just to mention a few examples: Vollenweider subverts the canon and shows
Milano, the industrial Northern city, to have the greatest fruit and vegetable
market in Europe. Rather than the "traditional" Southern open-air markets,
Milano's market (*mercati generali*) sell, and distribute, the freshest produce (31–
37). Vollenweider refers indirectly to the open-air market tradition only to show
that industrial mass consumption and production have in fact changed the tradition for the better, in this instance. Organization and money as essential functions of the market complicate the stereotypical imagination about markets in
Italy and the relation between the idyllic countryside and self-subsistence, on the
one hand, and industrialization and technologization of the Italian economy, on
the other.

Furthermore, when describing Italian fare in Rome, Vollenweider underscores the cross-cultural and transnational roots of a fictive national cuisine
(105–9). She thus undermines the topic "Italy" as nationally bound and defined.
She gives a brief history of the clerical origins of Italian cooking, points to the
moment when the clerical pleasure of the table reached the French courts
through the Italian courts. Finally, she recommends that the reader go to a Roman restaurant intended for the French missionaries in Rome and frequented by
the clergy of the Vatican. Here the visitor has a "taste" of the Italian experience
in sitting with the clergy while eating French food that is being served by Viet-
namese nuns. That which appears to be "non-Italian" becomes uniquely Italian,
in fact, specifically Roman.

Valentin and Vollenweider offer complex images of Italy that show its multiple dimensions and whose contrasts and contradictions only demonstrate the
interconnectedness of different national icons, constantly played against and
atop one another. The traveler is a reader of Italy, and Italy is a collection of
open texts. Thus, like the act of reading, the journey is a quest. Both reading and
traveling are identifiable with the desire to continue reading, constructing, and
reconstructing texts that always escape their own definitions. The inhabitant is
the traveler *of* and *in* this text. Similarly, the traveler inhabits the text while she

or he reads and "receives" it. The foreigner's and the insider's gazes are insepa-
rable and in effect coexist. In these two books, the authors do not reduce experience or the text, writing, to *Difference* and *Identity* as absolute signifiers. The
writers deconstruct identity as "national identity." What matters here are the
differences of the particular*s*.[2]

Whereas in Bronnen's and Brill's texts the reader finally travels home with
one or another picture of Italy, as "experience gained"; Vollenweider's and
Valentin's readers partake of the developing narratives and narrative voices. For
instance, the "foreign observer" is as foreign as the native to the situations described. Hence, the reader's exotic eye loses its exotic object or the native reader
perceives his/her own non-belonging in Italy and takes on the foreign gaze.
These texts do not commodify and fetishize experiences or ideas into myths or
souvenirs. They dissect them and question them so that a quest may begin—one
where return and *oikos* are exhibited as utopias, impossible sites of desire, beyond the text.

Conclusions: Italy, Another Stereotypical Other

What is theoretically innovative, and politically crucial, is the need to think beyond narratives of originary and initial subjectivities and to focus on those moments or processes that are produced in the articulation of cultural differences.
These "in-between spaces" provide the terrain for elaborating strategies of self-
hood—singular or communal—that initiate new signs of identity, and innovative
sites of collaboration, and contestation, in the act of defining the idea of society itself (Bhabha 1–2).

To conclude, I mention one more text, Christine Wolter's *Italien muss schön
sein* (Italy Must Be Beautiful) published in 1994. Wolter, who is from the former
GDR, has lived in Italy for many years, also prior to 1989. In contrast to *Schnee
vom Ätna* (Snow from Etna), written in the 1980s and published in the GDR,
Wolter's book came out after the fall of the Wall. *Italien muss schön sein* is not
only a text about Italy, but also a reflection about the meaning of travel, now
and then, when in the GDR traveling meant either a privilege or exile. Travel
literature thus played a very particular and different role in this country than, for
instance, in the Federal Republic. The title of Wolter's reflections underscores
the fantasy concealed behind the notion of travel as well as the foreign country.
This fantasy—known to be and remain a fantasy for the general readership—
had to resist and constantly renegotiate its "meaning" in relation to the "material
reality" of the experience of the traveler who could "physically" visit a foreign
country. In contrast, the foreign space could only exist as a narration for the
GDR readers who could travel only while reading the texts. As texts of others
and by others, travel literature was not expected to just fulfill an informative role;
rather, the audience would expect the text to exceed information, and even experience. Thus, in Wolter's words, "Italy *must* be beautiful" because it is beauti-

ful—and rare—to travel to Italy. Similarly, it is beautiful also to travel and be "the only" witness to another "world," or to be in the position of a storyteller who can marvel at his or her own experience.

From the traveler's perspective, Wolter—like most East German travelers and writers—was caught in multiple contradictions and anxieties: One would never know whether the travel could ever be repeated. The possibility of repetition would exist through writing and reading, both one's own memories and other texts that would "preserve experience." Thus, the essential paradox of travel literature reached its climax in GDR texts. The experience of travel had to be always textually constructed, as ready to be "read" and "reread."

Even so, these texts clearly demonstrated the impossibility to share experience, to communicate the journey, other than in a mediated form. The traveler—a privileged citizen—had to overcome the hostility of the underprivileged, their foreignness to the travel experience, the fact that travel abroad existed as an individual "narrative" in a vacuum, based on an individual experience not to be shared other than necessarily through a text. Travel literature elicited the fantasy or the dream of the author as revived storyteller. In fact, the best travel texts exhibited the authors's anxieties about the failed mission of the modern GDR storytellers.

Paradoxically, traveling and travel texts are always already mediated texts to be passed on, to be shared, to be remembered, and yet impossible to be communicated as "real." GDR travel stories (those written by writers who were not involved in "propaganda") had to deal more or less explicitly with the complex relation between travel and narration, and therefore they show a hidden awareness about processes of construction of texts about "the Other."

Unlike Valentin's text, Wolter's book pivots around the issue of textual complexity. She positions herself in the present and looks to a distant time. She remembers and tries to understand her first travels to Italy, her returns to the GDR, her loneliness, her fears, her split existence in Italy, a world literally outside her compatriots' experience and thus purely textual, practically "lived" to be read and written over and over again. Her Italian journey in the present occasions a literary journey/journal of other journeys, her own, and others. These multiple journeys question the "reality" and "singularity" of a space and of the spatial-temporal relation as we know it, a linear, historically and nationally defined relation.

Wolter shatters continuity when she includes images of refugees and migrants among the Italian snapshots, figures she does not distinguish from those of Italians. The people of Brindisi gradually become Albanians, or in effect discover that they fundamentally are Albanians when the Albanians disembark in their harbor. What they discover is a symmetry between the two countries: Brindisi is Albania in Italy because of the poverty and the marginality of Puglia (73–78).

A better and more metaphorical example is Wolter's choice to look at Italy from one of its own frontiers: Trieste and central Europe (79–85). The chapter is seminal because Trieste becomes both the traveler's body and the space he or she travels through. Thus, the text leaves behind the one-way movement from subject to object, from one site (that of the traveler's identity) to another (that of the city as identical to its origin and self). The author textualizes Trieste in a threefold way: First, Trieste is Wolter's text; second, it is a site crossed by frontiers; third, it is populated by foreign translators, who both represent the city and are represented by its frontiers. Italy is literally translated into multiple frontier texts that exist all at the same time, and coexist in the same space. Wolter's Italian journey shows that travel and traveled spaces merge as acts of constant cultural translations.

Two questions are still pending: What does Italy stand for in Bronnen's and Brill's texts and why? Why is it that East German and Swiss writers, the exponents of so-called "minor" literatures, are more inclined than *German*-German authors to view the Italian nation as a complex society and their texts as "complicit narratives of national constructions"? The following answers are pure speculations based on the texts themselves as considered within the German context and analyzed through the lenses of Bhabha's theories of the "Stereotype" (66–84). According to Bhabha, stereotypes are the fetish of colonialist discourse.

The first point is to see whether one can define Bronnen's and Brill's texts as colonial narratives and as such determine whether they are grounded in a system of truth that functions according to the ambivalent power of the stereotype. In Bhabha's opinion, this ambivalence follows the same rules of the game of recognition and disavowal of difference one finds in Freud's theory of the fetish. The stereotype is the fetish of colonial discourse, one in which the Other is both constructed and disavowed as Other, made into a mockery of the same, the same being the colonizer. The reassurance deriving from the fetish character of the stereotype is one of suture between two contradictory narratives: one of origins, in which identity is always affirmed and guaranteed, and one in which identity is shattered, threatened, and even nonexistent. The stereotype's repetition keeps alive the fetishistic belief of control over the threat that an originary identity may be a misperception after all.

In the travel accounts about Italy, stereotypes are seldom negative, in contrast to most colonial texts. However, the representations of Italy are stereotypical for their fetishistic nature. They bear the typical traits of the stereotype: the force of its ambivalence and its universalizing technique of "binding of a range of differences" (Bhabha 67), among other instances. Like otherness that is both object of desire and derision in the colonial stereotypical discourse, idealization too may function as a form of reification—paradoxically—within a space that is colonial. Idealization subjects its object to the same processes and functions of the stereotype in the way the object is imagined and constructed.

In these narratives, Italy is forced to take one position in the dichotomy between same and Other, present and past, tradition and progress, origins and modernity. Italy occupies the site of origins, the past. It both preserves the truth of western identity and the infantile aspects of the childhood of modernity. The stereotypes of Italy as archaic origin, failed or imperfect modernity, show the dangers of modernity while they displace them onto a different time-space framework (i.e., Italy and not Germany). However, this stereotypical representation also erases Italy as space in which the past-present connection could be reinvented according to multiple perspectives and multilateral, cross-cultural connections. It provides instead the way for Bronnen and Brill to find again the archeological site for a lost national and cultural origin (identity). The threat of identity loss is displaced onto the bipolar truth-system of the stereotype, so that contradictions or ruptures are here reduced to oppositions that can be laid out according to the two-dimensional, dialectical processes of the various national histories, antagonisms, and dynamics.

Then, how do these German travel texts about Italy reappropriate the German past and the Germans's nostalgia for tradition? They transform Italy into the fetish that disavows the absence of these topics and emotional states from German texts. I speculate that Italy as fetish helps to manage the German anxiety about the impossible reappropriation of the rural, idyllic Germanic character within German history after the Nazi past. Nature and Romanticism are displaced onto the Italian human and cultural landscape from which the German authors may believe in the continuity of a history devoid of catastrophes. As the synonym of life, Italy allows the recuperation of a past emptied of death, devoid of the memory of death. In this sense, Italy is nature and its time is empty. The archaic images of Italy as well as its failed modernity erase the memory of the link between technology and mass destruction. This failure and the repression of modern death produce fantasies about the welcome failure of absolute control. They represent the chance to reinvent the past as freed of the death provoked by the totalitarian Nazi regime.

The commodity-fetish Italy is both desirable and pleasurable on the one hand, and a threat on the other: It facilitates the repression of the historical trauma (by repressing Italian modern history as well); it prevents mourning; and yet it guarantees suture between past and present. Italy's threat is the possibility that its fascist past might resurface from behind the idyllic landscape. However, even then Italy may be the object of desire, despite the reprehensible and frightening context—in effect, though, Italy is depicted as having been able to mourn.

By the same token, minor travel literatures from the GDR are less imbricated in the colonial imaginary occupation of Italy as the one other German spatial-temporal dimension. First, the status of "minor" within the German literary panorama (and this is valid also for the Swiss author) develops a different connection to Italy as South of the European world. Second, the image of Italy played a political role for its present, postwar, modern history: as an example of humane European communism, a potential alternative to both the Federal Republic of Germany and the Soviet Union. Third, the modern history of the

GDR state revolved around narratives of resistance, liberation, and anti-Nazism much more similar to the Italian postwar cultural discourses than to those in the FRG. Fourth, the reconfiguration of a national and state history from within the history of the Eastern Block, the Slavic countries and the countries formerly belonging to the Hapsburg Empire involved the conscious reconsideration of the meaning of "national culture." In contrast to the FRG, the only official beholder of the German national-cultural legacy, GDR culture renegotiated its position also from within the newly rediscovered connections with Czechoslovakia, Russia, Poland, Yugoslavia, as well as the socialist countries of Africa, America (Cuba), and Asia. In addition to the specific and peculiar cultural meanings ascribed to "travel" in the GDR, as Wolter shows, these reasons are the grounds on which the German modern tradition of the "journey to Italy" is renegotiated, deconstructed, and reconceived in GDR texts.

"Italy's beauty" is a must, however, that discloses its *truth* only if and when it is acknowledged as a textual fiction ready to be translated into other new texts, new translations. These texts already start from "borderline," transfixed subject positions, as multiple fields of interceptions and diverse connections. Although hardly postcolonial, these texts are "effects" of minor cultures and as such constitute "minor" literary events that redefine western culture and civilization as beyond self-identity.[3]

Notes

1   Brill writes: "Italians and their *telefonino*—it is a "Passion" that leaves way behind the practical uses of this mobile machine. This is not to say that the cellular phone is an object of prestige in Italy only, but a sign that it is such is that its owner is a significant representative of the present with significant duties and connections. However, in Italy as well as in other Mediterranean countries the natural act of showing off one's own outstanding "features" is more common than in Northern or Central Europe. Denunciation is not shameful; modesty is a little ornament; one lives on the wide 'piazza,' and is to be seen. In any event, nothing is taken too seriously anyway. Furthermore, Italians are more loquacious than the people from Mecklenburg. For the former, chatting expresses love of life; it does not have to be "profound." It is fundamental that one calls *mamma* every day (very important!). In other words: The Italian ability to communicate is extraordinarily developed. Could it be any different in such a land than unswervingly ringing telephones and *telefonini?*" (46–47)

2   Homi Bhabha identifies the problem of the construction of "difference" and "otherness" as a form of "theoretical narcissism." He writes: "The difference of other cultures is other than the excess of signification or the trajectory of desire. These are theoretical strategies that are necessary to combat 'ethnocentrism' but they cannot, of themselves, unreconstructed, represent that otherness. There can be no inevitable sliding from the semiotic activity to the unproblematic reading of other cultural and discursive systems. There is in such readings a will to power and knowledge that, in

failing to specify the limits of their own field of enunciation and effectivity, proceeds to *individualize otherness as the discovery of their own assumptions*" (70, emphasis added).

3   See Bhabha: "Postcolonial critique bears witness to those countries and communities—in the North and the South, urban and rural—constituted, if I may coin a phrase, 'otherwise than modernity.' Such cultures of a postcolonial *contra-modernity* may be contingent to modernity, discontinuous or in contention with it, resistant to its oppressive, assimilationist technologies, but they also deploy the cultural hybridity of their borderline conditions to 'translate,' and therefore reinscribe, the social imaginary of both metropolis and modernity" (6, emphasis added).

Works Cited

Barthes, Roland. *S/Z. An Essay.* New York: Hill and Wang, 1974.

Bhabha, Homi. *The Location of Culture.* London: Routledge, 1994.

Brill, Klaus. *Die Köchin, die Pornodiva und der Papst. Römische Begegnungen.* Wien: Picus Verlag, 1998.

Bronnen, Barbara. *Meine Toskana: Eine Liebeserklärung.* München: Wilhelm Heyne Verlag, 1998.

Bufalino, Gesualdo, and Nunzio Zago, eds. *Cento Sicilie.* Firenze: La Nuova Italia, 1993.

Deleuze, Gilles, and Felix Guattari. *Kafka: Toward a Minor Literature.* Trans. Dana Polan. Minneapolis: U of Minnesota P, 1986.

Gernhardt, Robert. *Die Toscana-Therapie: Schauspiel in 19 Bildern.* Zürich: Haffmans Verlag, 1986; München: Wilhelm-Heyne Verlag, 1996.

Gramsci, Antonio. *La Questione Meridionale.* Roma: Editori Riuniti, 1966.

Malerba, Luigi. "Alle am Meer." *Italienische Reise. Ein Literarischer Führer Durch das Heutige Italien.* Ed. Alice Vollenweider. Berlin: Klaus Wagenbach, 1985.

Marcuse, Herbert. "The Affirmative Character of Culture." *Negations: Essays in Critical Theory.* London: Free Association, 1988.

Valentin, Thomas. *Schnee vom Ätna.* Berlin: Ullstein, 1985.

Van Den Abbeele, Georges. *Travel as Metaphor: From Montaigne to Rousseau.* Minneapolis: U of Minnesota P, 1992.

Vollenweider, Alice, ed. *Italia! Unterwegs zu den Verborgenen Schönheiten Italiens.* Frankfurt am Main: Schöffling & Co., 1997.

———. *Italienische Reise. Ein Literarischer Führer durch das heutige Italien.* Berlin: Klaus Wagenbach, 1985.

Wolter, Christine. *Italien muss schön sein.* Berlin: Das Arsenal, 1993.

Chapter 5

Constance Fredericka Gordon Cumming's "Picturesque" Vision: A Christian, Westernized Hawai'i

Andrea Feeser

If it could be said that there is an observer specific to the nineteenth century, it is only as an effect of a heterogeneous network of discursive, social, technological, and institutional relations. There is no observer prior to this continually shifting field; the notion of an observer has meaning only in terms of the multiple conditions under which he or she is possible.

—Jonathan Crary, "Modernizing Vision"

In the past several years, the study of travel writing has exploded into a full-fledged discipline. Scholars are investigating an extraordinary range of material and are developing a variety of perspectives through which to view travel accounts. Women travel writers have become the subject of numerous articles and books, many of which stress the differences between travel narratives authored by men and those authored by women. Some scholars who write about nineteenth-century women travel writers have argued that because nineteenth-century masculinist rhetoric produced binaries such as man/woman and civilized/savage—which link and devalue the female and the nonwestern—nineteenth-century women travel writers were in a position to recognize and critique social injustices perpetrated by western men at home and abroad.[1] As Inderpal Grewal observes in *Home and Harem,* for some such scholars of nineteenth-century female travel narratives, critiques of patriarchy collapse directly into critiques of imperialism.

Seeing feminist discourse not in its multifaceted resonance, or through its negotiations with discourses of state, nation, empire, and modernity that provide conditions of possibility, some analyses of western women's travel literature suggest that English women who traveled, for instance, were subversive both to English patriarchy and to a masculine imperialism, and that, in fact, to be oppositional to the patriarchy in England was to be in opposition to imperialism (Grewal 10).

Like Grewal, I contend that nineteenth-century British women's challenges to male authority were often partial versus systematic. The subject of my study—the Victorian travel writer and artist Constance Fredericka Gordon Cumming—while determined to experience the world as actively as any man, adhered to a great many gender, race, and class stereotypes typical of her times. Gordon Cumming set herself up as a female pioneer in foreign travel, but she neither consciously nor unconsciously assumed an anti-patriarchal position, nor one opposed to colonization. Indeed, she was wholly invested in Victorian imperial logic, namely that western beliefs and practices girded by Protestant faith were the most benevolent and constructive on earth, and should therefore spread far and wide.

When the fervently Protestant Gordon Cumming landed in Honolulu in 1879, she was forty-two, widely traveled, and established as a travel writer and artist. She had already journeyed to India, Fiji, Tahiti, California, China, and Japan, and published many articles along with the book *From the Hebrides to the Himalayas,* which featured her own illustrations. Traveling, as well as writing and drawing her experiences traveling, had become a way of life for her, and she therefore came to Hawai'i with the goal of representing it to others. In 1883, her two-volume travelogue *Fire Fountains: The Kingdom of Hawai'i, Its Volcanoes, and the History of its Missions* was published in her native Scotland.[2] The book purports to record Hawai'i's history and current circumstances, and contains several drawings by Gordon Cumming of Hawai'i's terrain.

Gordon Cumming's images are largely picturesque, a term that in its broadest sense refers to aesthetically pleasing representations that balance irregular (or uncommon) and regular (or common) elements. "Picturesque" is a word that appears repeatedly throughout Gordon Cumming's writing: She classifies virtually everything that she encounters as picturesque or nonpicturesque, and catalogues with irritation all that is not exotic and yet in some sense familiar. Her complaints about Hawai'i center largely on the land itself, which Gordon Cumming compares unfavorably to southern Polynesia. After having spent time in Tahiti, she finds the Hawaiian islands too arid, except for their lush rain forests and luxuriant, man-made gardens.

Given Gordon Cumming's passion for green growth, it is surprising that her desire for the both exotic and familiar is ultimately satisfied by the active lava flow on the island of Hawai'i. Hawai'i's volcanoes enthrall Gordon Cumming, although she is not so spellbound by them that she cannot give shape to her experience through writing and drawing. Indeed, Gordon Cumming draws on her strict Protestant faith to turn her overpowering encounter with the "fire fountains" into didactic description: She converts her stunned fascination with the power and beauty of Hawai'i's volcanoes into pedagogical discourse. In *Fire Fountains,* Gordon Cumming ties together her visual and textual representations of volcanoes to proselytize her twinned faith in Protestantism and capitalism as civilizing forces in Hawai'i.

Western Control of Hawai'i's Lands

Gordon Cumming visited Hawai'i when it was still a sovereign nation, but a kingdom experiencing the erosion of its autonomy through the capitalist system of private land ownership, which was largely facilitated in Hawai'i by American missionaries who counseled Hawaiian rulers in foreign ways. Lilikalā Kame'eleihiwa explains the cultural and historical significance of Christian power in Hawai'i thus:

> In reflecting upon Hawaiian history, it is obvious that foreign disease and the re-sulting depopulation have made Hawaiians prey to foreign interests. In traditional terms, the massive depopulation experienced by Hawaiians, beginning in 1778, indicated a lack of *pono* (harmony), the maintenance of which was the responsib-ility of the *Ali'i Nui* (high chiefs and chiefesses). In their search for a new *pono* that could stem the death of their people, the *Ali'i Nui* abandoned the *'Aikapu* (sacred eating) religion and the traditional *Akua* (gods and goddesses) because they no longer seemed to sustain life. The rejection of *'Aikapu*, however, left a re-ligious void—an absence of any *Akua* whatsoever. When the Calvinists arrived (in 1820) six months after the breaking of the *'Aikapu*, representing themselves as the source of foreign *mana* (divine power), and offering a religious respite from the foreign diseases, they effectively forestalled the emergence of a new form of Ha-waiian religion more appropriate to the governing of Hawaiian society....The Calvinist definition of *pono*...included Hawaiian acquiescence to foreign meth-ods of governance and to Western laws of which Hawaiians had little under-standing. Those Western laws included the establishment of a capitalist economic model and the private ownership of *'Āina* (land). (316)[3]

Just as foreign missionaries made it their business to convert Hawaiians to Christianity (the missions were predominantly Protestant, and twelve missionar-ies were sent to Hawai'i from America between 1820 and 1848), foreign businessmen and their supporters made it their mission to convert Hawaiians' shared stewardship of their homeland into plots that could be bought and sold. These supporters of private land ownership were themselves often missionaries, especially from the later 1830s on when the missions lost funds from their New England board, and worked to become self-supporting through capitalist in-vestments, especially in sugar mills (*Rise and Fall of the Hawaiian Kingdom* 40).

William Richards and Gerrit P. Judd, two American missionaries who coun-seled Hawai'i's *Mō ī* (paramount chief, or king) and *Ali'i Nui,* facilitated legisla-tion informed by their Christian and capitalist values that contributed to the loss of Hawaiian sovereignty. Richards was hired in 1838 by *Mō ī* Kauikeauouli and his *Ali'i Nui* to "be their chaplain and interpreter, and teacher of political econ-omy, law, and the science of government" (Kame'eleihiwa 174). Richards worked hard to teach the *Mō ī* and *Ali'i Nui* about capitalism, and in 1841, Richards drew up a secret contract between the *Mō ī*, one of his principal advisors, and the sugar growers Ladd and Company—which Richards deemed an upstanding Christian company—to lease all of Hawai'i's unoccupied lands (179). Through this measure, Richards tried to engineer colonization and development by Christian Americans who, he felt, could be trusted to enlighten and enrich Hawai'i. In fact, Ladd and Company's representative tried to sell the company's lease rights to the highest bidders irrespective of their religions' values, and in 1842, Richards left Hawai'i on a diplomatic mission to protect his plan.

In his absence, Gerrit P. Judd, a missionary physician and personal doctor to the *Mō ī* and many *Ali'i Nui,* became the court's primary foreign advisor. As secretary for foreign relations, Judd worked with the American lawyer John Ricord to Westernize Hawai'i's government, which was largely accomplished with the passing of the 1845 Organic Acts. The second of these acts established the Land Commission, headed by William Richards. This body oversaw the division of land known as the *Māhele,* which set aside vast tracts for private ownership. A controversial piece of legislation, the *Māhele* was resisted by Hawaiian *ali'i* (chiefs, both male and female) and *maka'āinana* (all Hawaiians other than *ali'i*) before and after it was passed. Petitions to the king from *maka'āinana* of the Big Island of Hawai'i, Māui, and Lāna'i argued strongly against foreign influence and presence in Hawai'i because both were eroding Hawai'i's sovereignty (Kame'eleihiwa 188–198, appendix: documents 2–5). However, through the *Māhele* and by 1850, non-Hawaiians were able to buy land, much of which came to support more foreign-owned sugar plantations.

Gordon Cumming's Vantage Point

Gordon Cumming admired what she viewed to be the sugar plantations' productive use of Hawai'i's soil. In her description of Māui in *Fire Fountains,* she lauds western agriculture, deems indigenous land barren, and implies that Hawaiian husbandry is negligent:

> As seen from the sea, Maui is a pile of red, scorched-looking, bare volcanic hills...and the only representatives of vegetation are the mournful *pandanus*, with...blue-green drooping leaves, or that most unlovable of all tropical plants, the weird, grey prickly-pear....Yet dreary as it appears from the sea, I am told that there are wonderfully fertile tracts all around the isle, wherever water can be obtained. There are great sugar-estates and cattle-ranches and sheep-runs, while thousands of cattle roam at large through the forest-belt which clothes the lower slopes of the mountains. (1: 70–71)

Gordon Cumming privileges western-controlled agricultural enterprises that produce or rely on lush, green expanses. She laments uncultivated land and suggests that common plants in Hawai'i are impoverished; she makes no note of the fact that the *pandanus,* which Hawaiians call *pū hala,* provide ample materials for Hawaiian goods, notably long, tough leaves used to make house thatch, mats, baskets, sandals, fans, and pillows. Although Gordon Cumming discusses western farming in Hawai'i at length, she does not detail Hawaiian wetland agricultural systems—*loko* (fishponds) and *lo'i* (fields)—tended by Hawaiians for centuries to harvest fish and taro, key staples in the Hawaiian diet. Largely in the company of fellow westerners devoted to "cultivating" Hawai'i's land and people through western practices, Gordon Cumming may well not have seen *loko* and *lo'i.* If she did, however, she may not have recognized and/or validated them as productive agricultural practices. *Loko* and *lo'i* do not dramatically alter their natural surroundings as large fields of sugar cane and cattle pastures do: Because sugar and cattle farming often take place in areas that must be irrigated, the green fields of plantations and ranches often contrast markedly with drier neighboring areas. *Loko* and *lo'i* are embedded within and work in conjunction with their natural aqueous and semi-aqueous environments. If Gordon Cumming encountered *loko* and *lo'i,* she might not have recognized them as consciously cultivated areas, and to her western eyes, they might not have appeared to be worked upon.

The cultural conditioning that affected what Gordon Cumming saw and did not see and the ethnocentricism evident in Gordon Cumming's construction of positive and negative land use extends to her descriptions of Hawai'i's people as well as their relationship to soil. A Scottish noblewoman[4] with ties to English aristocracy, Gordon Cumming admired Hawai'i's *Mō'ī* and *Ali'i Nui,* chiefly, however, when she viewed their comportment as westernized. For example, in her descriptions of Hawai'i's monarchy, she often notes those instances in which Hawaiian kings and queens resembled or cultivated relationships with Britain's monarchy. Gordon Cumming had no respect for Hawaiians of any rank whom she considered heathen—those who were not Christian or westernized in her terms. This form of judgment is evident in Gordon Cumming's description of the *Ali'i Nui* Ka'ahumanu (c. 1768–1832) who was *Kuhina Nui* (a principal advisor) to the *Mō'ī* Kamehameha I, Kamehameha II, and Kamehameha III. Gordon Cumming states that prior to Ka'ahumanu's embrace of Christianity she was "a cruel, haughty, and imperious woman"; after her conversion, Gordon Cumming maintains that Ka'ahumanu's character "was marked by extreme gentleness and kindness" (*Fire Fountains* 2: 116–17). This investment in portraying Christianity as an enlightening influence—and ultimately as the vehicle to spread other western institutions that Gordon Cumming deemed righteous— marks Gordon Cumming a product and promoter of nineteenth-century British imperialism framed as civilizing mission.

As Mary Louise Pratt maintains of the devout imperialist Queen Victoria, she "ascended the throne of England ready to codify what would be the European woman's Imperial Question *par excellence*: the Civilizing Mission" (Pratt 171). Although British male explorers, missionaries, soldiers, colonial officials, and businessmen were the primary architects of Victorian imperialism, British women contributed too. Although most Victorian women did not experience the freedom of movement and occupation that their male counterparts enjoyed, it was by no means unheard of for British women with financial means and strong wills to travel abroad for work or pleasure. Those women who published accounts of their experiences helped shape perceptions of foreign lands and of Britain's role abroad.

Indeed, as Grewal argues, the "production of the imperialist subject" in Britain was in large part the work of "travel books, exhibitions, newspaper accounts of politics and imperial ventures, children's books, didactic and 'improvement' literature" (87), and Gordon Cumming's work folds "improvement" narratives into travel accounts. In her memoirs, Gordon Cumming maintains that she was the first lady to go to India who was not a "wife or sister of some official" (*Memories* 195), a claim that suggests a competitive interest in positioning herself as a female pioneer in travel abroad. However, as Pratt argues, "by 1828 there were enough European women travel writers in print to form a category for men to complain about" (170). Therefore, although Gordon Cumming was not a typical Victorian lady, she was not unique, but part of a small group of women who had the resources and wherewithal to visit foreign places and to represent them to others.[5]

Gordon Cumming's resources and wherewithal were the products of her family circumstances. Gordon Cumming was likely inspired to travel abroad by her brother Roualeyn Cumming—the "Lion Hunter of South Africa"—renowned as the author of the 1850 *Five Years of a Hunter's Life in the Far Interior of South Africa*. An avid sportsman who first pursued riding and shooting abroad in the East India Company Madras Cavalry and the Cape Mounted Rifles in Africa, Roualeyn Gordon Cumming took up big game hunting as a full-time pursuit in South Africa between 1844 and 1848. He exhibited his vast number of trophies (the skins, bones, and stuffed remains of animals), as well as an African guide who helped him hunt, at London's 1851 Universal Exposition. The success of his book and exhibition made Roualeyn Gordon Cumming a well-known figure, and he launched a popular and financially successful lecture tour across the United Kingdom. In 1858, he established a museum with his hunting trophies near the Caledonian Canal in Scotland, a museum that became a great tourist attraction.[6]

Roualeyn and Constance Fredericka Gordon Cumming's journeys in distant lands, as well as their records of adventures abroad (his trophies and writing, and her artwork and writing), reflect the privilege and mindset of their class and of their family. British aristocrats of the nineteenth century traveled for pleasure, education, and work: In terms of the latter, they often filled posts in colonial governments and military commissions. The large Gordon Cumming family had influential relations and friends scattered throughout Britain's empire, and they used their powerful network of associates to facilitate their own ambitions. Indeed, Constance Fredericka Gordon Cumming's career as a travel writer began when she decided to accompany her half-sister and her half-sister's husband—who had just inherited his family fortune—on a yearlong visit to India. Because Gordon Cumming was unmarried and had no relations to look after, she was free to explore new worlds through family money and overseas contacts. Throughout her trips in India and beyond, she was hosted by prominent kinsmen, friends, and acquaintances who lived abroad as politicians, missionaries, and globetrotters. Although Roualeyn and Constance Fredericka Gordon Cumming used their class and family privilege to travel toward different ends—he to bag game and she to "bag" reportage in text and drawings—they were both invested in gathering exotic cultural capital to promote themselves as skilled and knowledgeable adventurers.

Roualeyn Gordon Cumming dictated his book on hunting in South Africa to his sisters, who produced the manuscript for him. Although this suggests that women in the Gordon Cumming family were conditioned to subordinate their accomplishments to the achievements of their male relations, Constance Fredericka Gordon Cumming and her sisters were in fact encouraged to examine and learn about the world around them on their own terms. Gordon Cumming's mother Eliza Mary modeled a version of independent womanhood for her daughters. She was a skilled sportswoman, painter, and amateur geologist who sponsored and went on geological expeditions. Lady Gordon Cumming saw to it that her daughters were well educated and trained in drawing and painting.

Education and art came together for the Gordon Cumming women in Lady Gordon Cumming's fascination with geology. Because the family estate was near quarries with red sandstone fossils, the Gordon Cumming home became a gathering place for noted scientists such as Louis Agassiz, Hugh Miller, and Sir Roderick Murchison. Lady Gordon Cumming involved her elder daughters in geology and art by encouraging them to produce watercolors of the fossils discovered on expeditions to the nearby quarries. This linkage between art and geology had broader currency in Britain as well. For example, in his 1851 *Modern Painters,* the art critic John Ruskin espoused "the new sciences of geology, meteorology and biology…claiming that artists must study the landscape scientifically" (Howard 80). In addition, beginning in 1863, the popular art magazine the *Art Journal* published geologist Professor Ansted's articles on science and art (Howard 80; 228, n. 4).

The Gordon Cumming children were exposed to a range of art in addition to the small-scale illustration practiced by the family daughters. Sir Edwin Landseer, a famous painter and sculptor of animals much admired by Queen Victoria, visited the Gordon Cumming home, and a family relation, Anne Seymour Conway, was a noted sculptor of busts and figures. The family therefore had a history of associating with professional artists and of validating female artists in the family. Although much of Constance Fredericka Gordon Cumming's work was relatively small scale—inviting associations with the genteel tradition of amateur painting for ladies—she also created large-scale landscapes that record her treks through the Scottish highlands and abroad. By creating larger format works and including her drawings as illustrations to her travel writing, Gordon Cumming established a professional profile for herself. Indeed, in her memoirs she writes with pride that her work was placed on view in venues such as the British Indian and Colonial Exhibition, and forestry and missionary exhibitions.[7]

Although Gordon Cumming occasionally notes in her writing that her adventures as a travel writer and artist are not typical for most people of her era—especially women—she generally discusses her presence abroad as a natural phenomenon. Like many travel writers in the Victorian period and in our own times, Gordon Cumming does not question her intervention in a foreign place: Her freedom to record another land and its people is an assumed right. In Gordon Cumming's mind, Westerners like herself who possess financial means and cultivation (for her, educated Christians), are entitled to leave their mark on foreign places. In *Fire Fountains*, Gordon Cumming sets herself up as an enlightened member of an Anglo-American community that deserves to be present in Hawai'i to enjoy what is thrilling and to domesticate what is "savage" about the island kingdom. This dynamic is particularly stark in Gordon Cumming's account of Hawai'i's volcanoes. In *Fire Fountains*, Gordon Cumming "tames" Hawai'i's volcanoes through western representational practices in visual and textual allegories that promote Hawai'i's betterment through Christian and capitalist ideals. Hawai'i's volcanoes become the focus of her enterprise because through them she is able to combine her expertise in landscape art, geology, and travel writing on foreign lands: the primary vehicles through which she cultivated her own cultural authority.

Gordon Cumming Draws (on) the Picturesque

Gordon Cumming utilizes a number of literary and pictorial conventions in *Fire Fountains* to excite her audience and to tame the landscape. This dynamic unfolds over time while reading her text, but is immediately evident in her eight illustrations for the book, which are interspersed at random throughout her travelogue. Seven of Gordon Cumming's pictures represent Hawai'i's volcanoes. In her drawing *Halemaumau: "The House of Everlasting Burning," Temporary Crags* (Figure 5.1.), her characteristic energetic, precise pen strokes describe craggy lava fields with molten rivers and smoke-belching volcanic chimneys. Two very small onlookers in western attire comfortably inhabit the foreground of the tumultuous terrain; one is a female figure who represents Gordon Cumming at work sketching. In *Halemaumau: "The House of Everlasting Burning,"* literally explosive landscape is arranged into a dramatic, pleasing, and information-filled composition through lively yet ordered marks. Like much of Gordon Cumming's voluminous text, this drawing expresses the exotic and potentially harmful world the traveler encounters through several

Figure 5.1: *Halemaumau: "The House of Everlasting Burning," "Temporary Crags,* from Constance Fredericka Gordon Cumming, *Fire Fountains: The Kingdom of Hawaii, its Volcanoes, and the History of its Missions,* vol. 1 (Edinburgh, 1883) opposite 167. Hawaiian Collection, Hamilton Library, University of Hawai'i at Manoa.

western framing devices: factual description, the sublime, and most notably, the picturesque.

For those who have seen volcanic activity on the Big Island of Hawai'i, or for those who have viewed it on films or through photographs, much of Gordon Cumming's drawing appears accurate: The fingers of sulfuric vapor gliding over the hardened, jagged lava and molten, liquid lava that she renders capture the genuine extremes of volcanic elements. However, this factual information is organized into a composition that heightens the volcano's awesome qualities. By creating a panoramic image rather than staging a close-up view, Gordon Cumming courts a sublime effect instead of inviting a more disinterested response characteristic of topographical renderings. She relies on pictorial conventions in nineteenth-century Romantic landscape painting to register the sublime, which artists and writers of her era understood to be overwhelming experiences (often of natural phenomena) that elicit extremes of often contradictory emotions. Gordon Cumming exaggerates the innate power of volcanoes to amaze by focusing the viewer's attention on her depicted figures's smallness in relation to the vastness of the exploding crater. Her tiny figures are placed in the middle foreground of the picture and are made clearly visible through the contrast of their darkness with the roiling lava's brightness. Gordon Cumming conveys a sense of human beings's fragility in the face of nature's power; however, because her figures are highly visible and stationed at the center of her image, she implies that they have a certain and sure position in their tumultuous environment. Gordon Cumming even conveys a subtle sense of human control over the elements, for the sketching figure who reads as a surrogate for Gordon Cumming herself is shown calmly working on a drawing that will capture the explosive landscape in a self-contained picture.

Although Gordon Cumming fuses factual pictorial description with visual elements that signify the sublime—awesome subject matter combined with stark contrasts in size and value—her drawing predominantly features picturesque characteristics. The term *picturesque* was deployed in the late eighteenth century and early nineteenth century as "a third aesthetic category to set against [Edmund] Burke's 'Sublime' and 'Beautiful'" (Copley and Garside 1). However, from the earliest theoretical usage of "picturesque," through the term's broader applications in the nineteenth century, the word *picturesque*'s meanings were not stable. As Copley and Garside maintain

> the widespread adoption of picturesque terminology in conversational use in the later eighteenth century, in relation to a broad range of cultural practices, confirms the problematic nature of the aesthetic: Even in this period, it can seem so ill-defined as to be virtually meaningless. This lack of precise definition is not an indication of its cultural and ideological insignificance, however. On the contrary, it can be argued that the cultural importance of the picturesque stands in direct proportion to the theoretical imprecision of its vocabulary. (1)

Although there was and is no consensus about what meanings *picturesque* captures, broadly speaking, picturesque images are understood to focus on irregular and mutable forms arranged into compositions that reference what is found to be pleasing in already sanctioned artistic conventions. This general aesthetic is spelled out in countless nineteenth-century manuals on drawing, and developed from late eighteenth-century discourse on art and travel, notably the English Reverend William Gilpin's 1792 *Three Essays: On Picturesque Beauty, On Picturesque Travel, and On Sketching*. In this illustrated text, travelers are instructed to appraise and analyze the scenic qualities of geographical areas according to pictorial modes of landscape painting that include the serene and the violent, two poles of Italian painting represented by the seventeenth-century work of Claude Lorrain and Salvator Rosa (Lukacher 116). Art historian Brian Lukacher notes that this aesthetic encouraged "The tourist well versed in the playful formalism and classifying criteria of the picturesque...[to] take visual possession of a prospect and thereby entertain an illusory domination over nature" (116).

Pratt has analyzed this dynamic—which she literally embodies in the phrase "the monarch of all I survey"—in the context of nineteenth-century travel writing. Pratt's following observation demonstrates how verbal and visual representation work together in Victorian travel narratives to convey a metaphoric sense of proprietorship: "Victorians opted for a brand of verbal painting whose highest calling was to produce for the home audience the peak moments at which geographical 'discoveries' were 'won' for England" (201). This representational logic is evident in Gordon Cumming's preference for high-level vantage points that provide her with a sense of all-encompassing vision. Not long after she arrives in Honolulu on O'ahu, she seeks out a vista that enables her to embrace her surroundings visually. In a letter from the Honolulu Hotel she writes: "After breakfast I began a sketch from the glass observatory at the top of this hotel, which commands a very fine panoramic view of the place, looking up the valley and over the embowered town (only revealing an occasional glimpse of a roof) to the wide, calm, blue ocean" (*Fire Fountains* 1: 27).

In the nineteenth century, such an outlook—an interest in visual domination implicit in the picturesque aesthetic—informed many artists's approaches to representing landscape. This perspective often included an investment in erasing or veiling markers of ruinous land development and human privation. Such concealment insured that artists and viewers had calming or exciting looking experiences that enabled them to idealize and/or romanticize relations among people and nature. Key examples of this dynamic appear in the work of the nineteenth-century British landscape painter John Constable, and the nineteenth-century American artist Joseph D. Strong, the latter of whom worked in Hawai'i.

Constable produced images of rural England that avoid references to "economic depression and civil unrest on the part of the agrarian working class" (Lukacher 122). As Ann Bermingham notes, agricultural laborers in England suffered great hardships during Constable's career. Heavy taxes after the Napoleonic wars, combined with a fall in agricultural prices and self-interest among a new class of landowners (who rejected "the genteel paternalism of their predecessors"), contributed to dire conditions that fed riots in 1816, 1822, and from 1829 to 1830 (88–89). However, when Constable included representations of agricultural workers in his paintings—human figures do not loom large in his oeuvre—he mostly portrayed them as peaceful folk at one with nature. This is evident in his most famous painting, the 1821 *Haywain,* which shows a mill and two peasants fording a stream. Labor is beautified in the work: The mill and peasants are pretty, integrated components of a lush, sparkling portrayal of the countryside. Constable infuses the painting with a sense of ease and comfort: The men appear embraced by the water, air, and land that cradle them visually. Constable's laborers, as Grewal notes of the poor in much nineteenth-century British art, become "aesthetic objects to be looked at and judged by their suitability as objects in a view" (101).

Strong's 1885 *Japanese Laborers on Spreckelsville Plantation* aestheticizes the labor of Asian immigrants, many of whom entered Hawai'i under the 1850 Masters and Servants Act, a piece of legislation that provided field-workers for the hard labor of tending and harvesting sugarcane. Because the Hawaiian population was radically reduced through the spread of foreign disease, and because a number of Hawaiians refused to labor as plantation workers, Chinese and later Japanese immigrants were brought to the Hawaiian islands to toil on the sugar estates that dominated Hawai'i's economy by the later nineteenth century. Strong's painting, in the tradition of the nineteenth-century French Barbizon School, renders working figures heroic by making them monumental and strong, and ideal by representing them as attractive and clean. Strong implies that the plantation laborers' activities are nurturing—for them and for the land itself—by depicting among the workers a drinking child sitting directly underneath a woman with bared breasts. Although immigrant labor did indeed feed Hawai'i's extremely successful sugar economy—260 million pounds were exported from Hawai'i by 1890 (Wilcox 20)—laborers' work was backbreaking, and the physical hardship they experienced is not indexed by Strong's painting. Moreover, the picture, like Constable's work, in no way references unrest in agricultural communities. In Hawai'i, some oppressed plantation workers attacked their overseers or deserted their positions, and others organized strikes to improve their conditions (Takaki 127–52). In addition, the diversion of water in Hawai'i to irrigate sugar regularly took water from indigenous agricultural systems and small-scale farms, which bred hostility toward plantations. The Spreckel plantation in Strong's painting was irrigated by one of the largest water diversion mechanisms in Hawai'i (Wilcox 61–62).

This will to romanticize land and people in artwork by obfuscating difficult economic and political realities is evident in Gordon Cumming's drawings, although in a less straightforward manner, for unlike Constable and Strong, she was not interested in showing agrarian labor. All her pictures but one depict Hawai'i's volcanoes. The exception shows a verdant Hilo homestead with tiny figures of a mother and children, the typical equation of nurturing nature and motherhood also evident in Strong's painting. Gordon Cumming's focus on drawing volcanic terrain versus rural imagery makes evident that she chose to illustrate the exotic (by western standards) elements of Hawai'i instead of its diverse topography increasingly compromised by foreign intervention. Although she wrote about Hawai'i's varied terrain, she clearly did not deem much of it picture worthy, and her written complaints about the appearance of much of Hawai'i's land not cultivated by westerners make this evident. Gordon Cumming's illustrations reduce Hawai'i to an exotic natural phenomenon that functions as a mere spectacle for onlookers (both herself and her readers) who do not inhabit the complex realities of the island nation.

Gordon Cumming's Allegorical Treatment of Hawai'i's Volcanoes

Gordon Cumming's family interest in geology, as well as the combination of art and geology in critical and practical art texts of the period, certainly influenced her interest in picturing Hawai'i's volcanoes. Additionally, when Gordon Cumming arrived in Hawai'i in 1879, the country's volcanoes on the Big Island were already renowned and a growing tourist destination. The Volcano House Hotel (a grass hut in its earliest incarnation), had "perched on the edge of Kilauea Caldera since the mid-1800s" (*On the Rim of Kilauea* 6), and began recording visitors' experiences of the volcano in 1865. That year, a visitor named O.H. Gulick donated a register to the hotel, which contains several entries from travel writers who preceded Gordon Cumming to the volcano, notably Mark Twain (his entry is dated 1866), and Gordon Cumming's compatriot Isabella Bird Bishop (her entry is dated 1873).[8] Shortly after Gordon Cumming's trip to Hawai'i, at the time of the 1880–1881 volcanic eruptions, shipping companies promoted further tourism to the volcano. The Oceanic Steamship Company sent "a number of striking red-and-black volcano scenes" to California to generate interest in visiting the Big Island; and the Wilder Steamship Company created Hawai'i package tours that included inter-island transportation and a stay at the Volcano House Hotel, which Wilder owned at the time (Forbes 174).

In her written representation of Hawai'i's volcanoes, Gordon Cumming builds upon her verbal binary oppositions that contrast growth (aligned with Christian westernization) with sterility (associated with the indigenous). Her writing about the Big Island sets up parallels between the natural environment and people: Dry, sparsely planted soil is equated with "lazy," "heathen" natives, whereas verdant land is equated with "civilizing" missionaries, "productive" plantation owners, and converted Hawaiians. These linked associations are evident in Gordon Cumming's descriptions of the Big Island's Christian settlement at Hilo, pictured as a peaceful, orderly place in her one drawing not dedicated to volcanoes. In her writing, Gordon Cumming notes her disappointment at her first glimpse of the island of Hawai'i from the deck of the boat that ferries her from O'ahu: She finds the arid, volcanic coastline hideous and uninviting. Her description of the island from the ocean parallels her account of sighting Maui from shipboard. However, as the town of Hilo comes into view, Gordon Cumming's spirits lift, and she writes: "I see that here the country is all green—very green (indeed the color beyond the town is so brilliant that it must certainly mean sugar)—and only the church spires and tower reveal the existence of a town or village embowered in foliage" (*Fire Fountains* 1: 73).

In the text that follows, Gordon Cumming provides positive, data-filled reports on the sugar, cattle, and sheep farming developing on the Big Island, as well as sentimental accounts of the lush, landscaped properties of hardworking Hilo missionaries. Both narratives delight in the productive, attractive land that these settlers have created for themselves and their communities. Gordon Cumming is particularly impressed with the Protestant missionaries' efforts to combine proselytizing with western education and the development of a capitalist work ethic. She admires the missionary schools for boys and girls that teach Christian values and western, gender-specific tasks (such as farming for boys and sewing for girls). Speaking of a missionary school for Hawaiian girls begun on the Big Island by Mrs. Coan, the wife of Reverend Titus Coan, Gordon Cumming effuses: "Mrs. Coan was assisted in her labor of love by two carefully trained native women; and soon the school became the ideal home of a company of contented, bright-faced little maidens, docile, industrious, and affectionate" (*Fire Fountains* 2: 139). Nowhere in the midst of this account does Gordon Cumming discuss the fact that indigenous culture continued to thrive in the face of missionary-induced westernization.

Noenoe Silva recounts the many ways that Hawaiian people (she focuses on Hawaiian women in particular), resisted western assimilation promoted by western churches, schools, and newspapers. Silva notes that Hawaiian newspapers published genealogies, legends, chants, and songs from Hawaiian oral tradition, texts that celebrated strong indigenous heroes (6). Silva observes that

> Native literary and oral traditions in the mother tongue which represented women as strong, independent, intelligent, resourceful, and unruly, were at the very least an inspiration and a relief from the tensions and demands associated with trying to live an alien and restrictive lifestyle. They provided a way for *Kanaka Maoli* [Hawaiian] women to reaffirm their alternative (Native) identity. (13)

Gordon Cumming's ignorance about, or repression of, these vital Hawaiian forms of resistance to Westernization—like her inability to see Hawaiian husbandry—reveals her monocular cultural perspective. A brief, written meditation on land that has not been cultivated by westerners makes evident Gordon

Cumming's readiness to claim that Hawai'i's indigenous plants and people are destined to disappear due to a supposed lack of strength and initiative. Gordon Cumming maintains:

> Although imported trees and shrubs seem to take so kindly to this soil, I cannot say that I am happily impressed by the indigenous vegetation. It almost seems as if the natural products of the soil were doomed, like the people, to fade away....All the trees I have seen are suffering from a blight like smut in wheat....In some of the isles it is said that this can be cured by planting the great forest lily closer to the roots of the diseased tree. Whether true or not, no one here takes the trouble to try such the simple experiment. (*Fire Fountains* 1: 97)

More direct associations between the sterile, nonproductive, and native occur in Gordon Cumming's description of Mauna Loa on the Big Island, and her ascent up this mountain to active volcanic craters. She writes:

> Mauna Loa is unquestionably a very ugly mountain...if it were not so careless and wasteful, it might very soon far transcend...[Mt. Fuji in Japan], for the amount of good building material which it is ceaselessly manufacturing would, if properly applied, soon reach up to heaven. Apparently the fire-spirits are like idle boys, and find it more amusing to throw stones in every direction than to build up their own houses. So year after year they waste as much good solid lava as would build the grandest cone in creation; and expend all their energy in annoying their neighbors, instead of providing them with an object of beauty for perpetual delight.... (*Fire Fountains* 1: 121–23)

Despite her disenchantment with the nonproductive, nonpicturesque mountain—which she associates with "idle boys" (read lazy heathens)—Gordon Cumming is determined to witness its volcanic activity, although she defers her ascent until she finds a white escort for this adventure. When he is secured—and happily for her he proves to be a minister—she commences a journey that is both irksome and satisfying.

Gordon Cumming's accounts of her exposure to Hawaiians on her trek contrast markedly with her rapturous tales of missionary life. She is repelled by a "wretched grass hut" rest station run by Hawaiians. Gordon Cumming is irritated that her hosts supposedly do not tend their flowers or plant fruit trees "for a future generation," and she finds their food and home dirty, and their dress poor and uncouth. Key passages of her description of the service provided by her hosts betray how close-minded and culturally biased Gordon Cumming's assessment of her surroundings is. She passes negative judgments on conditions that her own words detail as pleasant, for she states: "My hostess invited me to rest on a large four post bed, with mattress of soft *pulu* fern stuffing, and a gay quilt. It was tempting to weary limbs, as the *pulu* is deliciously soft silky stuff; but

I thought it safer to spread my own waterproof over a tolerably clean mat...."
(*Fire Fountains* 1: 137).

Gordon Cumming's frustration with the rest station and its inhabitants—which she finds unpleasant in spite of her own accounts of comforts extended to her—carries over into her experience of the lava fields. At first, she sees no "sportive fire fountains," but vast expanses of black lava hardened into ropy coils, jagged crusts, and brittle mounds. She hungers for the dramatic color and exotic activity that other western visitors to Hawai'i have described, and she therefore wanders tirelessly throughout craters to locate eruptions. With the help of a guide, she is ultimately successful, and eagerly seeks sweeping perspectives for a commanding view from which she can draw. In her narrative, she luxuriates in her productive capacity to render the violent volcano picture worthy:

> I had little time for sleep. So often as I lay down, the fascination of the scene recalled me, and I watched fresh fountains and rivers of fire continually bursting forth, till their glow paled in the light of the risen sun, and only the points of most intense heat continued to show red, the general color of the new lake and its rivers becoming wondrously silvery and glistening in the white light of day. (*Fire Fountains* 1: 190)

Gordon Cumming's account of the volcano and of herself represents in-between states. The fiery terrain she views is neither the supposedly nonproductive, barren land Gordon Cumming associates with "undeveloped" Hawaiians, nor is it the fecund, verdant land she links to hardworking Christians. The restless Gordon Cumming she describes herself to be is momentarily neither the judge of supposed indigenous sterility nor assumed western productivity. In a fleeting passage of her writing, she suspends her judgment and becomes absorbed and compelled by what she sees. However, Gordon Cumming hastens to present both the land and herself as finally contained: The lava stills and her agitation passes.

Her subsequent writing on Hawai'i's volcanoes demonstrates that Gordon Cumming's awesome experience does not jolt her enough to in any way reorient her thinking. Instead, Gordon Cumming's post-volcano writing suggests that she sought to contain her destabilizing experience through a reassuring Old Testament allegory about God-fearing righteousness. Gordon Cumming's need to frame her encounter with Hawai'i's volcanoes in terms of her overarching belief system is evident in the following passage:

> I think my chief feeling tonight is thankful wonder that we should have returned from such an expedition as safely as from a ramble in English meadows, without so much as a boot singed or a garment damaged. In truth, as we toiled up the steep ascent to the house, I could not but compare myself and my two comrades to the three Hebrew children [Book of Daniel heroes saved by God after they were thrown into a furnace for refusing to worship Nebuchadnezzar's golden

image], emerging unscathed from the midst of the fires in the burning fiery fur-
nace. (*Fire Fountains* 1: 196)

Most of Gordon Cumming's subsequent written descriptions of volcanoes serve
as vehicles for her to proselytize her vision for religious and moral development
in Hawai'i. Gordon Cumming's verbal imagery becomes increasingly symbolic,
with green growth representing the spread of Christian righteousness. She
writes: "As the *menenia* grass creeps silently and invisibly along the surface of
the dry volcanic soil, only revealing its presence when the refreshing dews or rain
showers call it into fullness of life...so the good influence extended insensibly
among the people; while in every isle some were found to whom the message of
the Gospel proved a life-giving reality" (*Fire Fountains* 2: 115). This metaphor
opens onto narratives that ascribe real power to the Christian God. In her account of Chiefess Kapi'olani's 1825 repudiation of the Volcano Goddess Pele in
favor of God, Gordon Cumming maintains that when Kapi'olani stood at the
edge of Halema'uma'u crater, God shielded the chiefess from the destructive
forces of the volcano. To further emphasize God's ability to protect Hawai'i's
people from volcanoes, Gordon Cumming contends at the conclusion of her
travelogue that Hilo was spared from the formidable 1881 lava flow because the
town's inhabitants prayed to God for safety. The final sentences of her book
revel in the freedom and succor that Christian faith supposedly brings to the
people of Hilo, and by extension to all of Hawai'i: "So day by day do they walk
in the midst of the flows, fearing no evil, as those who believe that the Fire-floods
will not be suffered to overwhelm them, because One, Who is the true Lord of
the Fire, is ever present to shield them from its power" (*Fire Fountains* 2: 279).

For Gordon Cumming, Christianity is at the root of the many western systems that she privileges, from the aesthetics that shape her illustrated travelogue,
to the economic practices that shape the work of foreign sugar growers she admires. She consistently foregrounds what she believes to be the benevolent, constructive properties of westernization in Hawai'i, although she very occasionally
alludes to what this perspective in action destroys. Tiny snippets of Gordon
Cumming's writing detail the painful specifics of the natural, social, and political
landscape that her pictures and most of her text excise. She notes that many
Hawaiian beliefs, practices, and creations were repressed or dismantled by westerners. She laments these losses if they were in her mind picturesque—such as
colorful modes of attire—but she celebrates the loss of them if they were "savage"—such as indigenous religious rituals. Gordon Cumming's recognition of
loss, therefore, is uncritical, for she never considers how Hawaiians experience
these losses. This is especially evident in her ruminations on the destruction of
Hawaiian carvings. She writes:

With all possible reverence for the great work so nobly accomplished by the early
missionaries, it is certainly a matter much to be regretted that, in the wholesale

sweeping away of idolatry, so many subjects deeply interesting to the ethnologist and the antiquarian should have been hopelessly swamped, and everything bearing on the old system treated as being either so puerile as to be beneath contempt, or so evil as to be best forgotten with all speed. (*Fire Fountains* 1: 55)

Although Gordon Cumming suggests that her foreign predecessors infantilized and/or demonized Hawaiians, thereby justifying the ruin of Hawaiian creations, her text treats Hawaiians in much the same manner. Furthermore, she laments the disappearance of what she terms idolatry on behalf of western science and art instead of Hawaiian community and culture. For Gordon Cumming, collectors of native "curios" lose, not Hawaiians.

Writing Travel in Hawai'i Today

Fire Fountains lays bare a key ideological conceit many travelers to Hawai'i had and continue to have: namely that Hawai'i conform to the fantasy of an exotic paradise that both excites and seduces, but which is "tamed" and "saved" by imported western institutions. This representation of Hawai'i—a native place "bettered" by western intervention—is characteristic of much historical and contemporary travel writing in general. As Grewal has demonstrated with regard to nineteenth-century British travel narratives, such texts helped shape the project of imperialism by suggesting that "indolent" natives in foreign places were incapable of cultivating their lands. Instead, only hardworking Britons could make the soil productive (44–45), and the British therefore deserved to settle in other countries that they could "improve." This logic, embraced by other western nations, describes the impetus for the agricultural imperialism that guided a great deal of nineteenth-century European and American colonization of foreign lands such as Hawai'i. In many former or current colonies today, agricultural imperialism has given way to tourism, a business venture that also moves outsiders into foreign territory supposedly to better all participants and the place in question.

In 1959, when Hawai'i became the fiftieth American state,[9] as the large sugar plantations that dominated business in the islands continued to fail economically, state-sponsored tourism steadily increased to shore up the economy. Today, Hawai'i's tourists and residents alike are encouraged through state-sanctioned tourist literature to believe that tourism is wholly productive: Such texts maintain that tourists are enriched by their experiences in Hawai'i and that tourist dollars enrich Hawai'i' itself. This dynamic is evident in the following text written for the October 1997–January 1998 *Maui Drive Guide* by publisher Winona Higashi (her photograph next to her statement establishes that she is Caucasian):

Aloha and welcome to the Valley Isle. Maui residents have a saying: *Maui no ka oi*—Maui is the best. We hope your time on Maui brings you to the same conclusion. Maui offers something for everyone. The *MAUI DRIVE GUIDE* is designed specifically for visitors who want to get the most out of their vacation. With a consistent No. 1 rating for "usefulness in getting around," the *MAUI DRIVE GUIDE* is supported by dozens of businesses islandwide. We appreciate it when our readers tell these businesses that they learned about them in the magazine.

This text establishes that present-day tourism occurs through consumption of goods and services advertised by businesses. The use of Hawaiian words to welcome and excite the reader about his or her vacation on the "best" Hawaiian island, lends an exotic mood to an otherwise mundane sales pitch. The use of Hawaiian with English in the publisher's statement also suggests that American and Native Hawaiian culture have mutually embraced one another. However, like *Fire Fountains,* the *Maui Drive Guide* copy does not communicate a Native Hawaiian perspective on western presence in Hawai'i.

Native Hawaiian scholar and activist Haunani-Kay Trask has responded to this erasure of Hawaiian voices in state-endorsed tourist literature. In "Lovely Hula Hands: Corporate Tourism and the Prostitution of Hawaiian Culture," she demonstrates that this literature obscures the fact that tourism in the islands is the "major cause of environmental degradation, low wages, land dispossession" of Native Hawaiians, and the exploitative marketing of "Native values and practices" (190). Trask writes:

> In Hawai'i, the destruction of our land and the prostitution of our culture is planned and executed by multi-national corporations (both foreign-based and Hawai'i-based), by huge landowners (like the missionary-descended Castle and Cook—of Dole Pineapple fame—and others) and by collaborationist state and county governments. The ideological gloss that claims tourism to be our savior and the "natural" result of Hawaiian culture is manufactured by ad agencies (like the state-supported Hawai'i Visitors Bureau) and tour companies (many of which are owned by the airlines), and spewed out to the public through complicitous cultural engines like film, television and radio, and the daily newspapers. (180–81)

Grewal's and Trask's analyses of travel writing suggest that Victorian and contemporary travel narratives share an interest in encouraging readers to see themselves as individuals entitled to consume land (through labor or leisure) in foreign places. Kame'eleihiwa's, Silva's, and Trask's demonstrations that native voices challenge and resist this assumption in Hawai'i's past and present ensure that what western representations of Hawai'i fail to show, Native Hawaiian representations will reveal.

Notes

1   See Bohls 107 for a nuanced version of this perspective.

2   Gordon Cumming's text and others that I cite do not make use of the *'okina* and *kahako,* which are diacritical marks in Hawaiian language words. I have not added these marks to texts that do not employ them.

3   Translations of Hawaiian words into English are based on Kame'eleihiwa's glossary.

4   She was a direct descendant of John Comyn, a claimant to the Scottish throne murdered by his rival Robert the Bruce in 1306.

5   In the 1880s, Gordon Cumming met two such female travelers: the botanical artist Marianne North who spent time in North and South America, the Far East, South Asia, Borneo, and Australasia; and the travel writer Isabella Bird Bishop who visited North America, Hawai'i, Australasia, South Asia, and the Near and Far East. Although the three women must have recognized that they shared the unusual distinction of having recorded what many women and men would never see, their meeting ended rather abruptly. Bird Bishop, the hostess for the meeting, greeted her guests in a colorful outfit comprised of "gold-embroidered slippers, a silver and gold petticoat from Japan...and a favor presented to her by the King of the Sandwich Islands [Hawai'i]" (Russell 27). Bird Bishop's cultural cross-dressing must have suggested to her guests either a lack of learned seriousness about her travels or an impulse to "go native" (certainly superficial and naïve), for Gordon Cumming and North rather quickly departed from the gathering.

6   For biographical information about Roualeyn Gordon Cumming, see Constance Fredericka Gordon Cumming's *Memories* and "Roualeyn Gordon Cumming," *Dictionary of National Biography,* 1885 ed.

7   For biographical information about Constance Fredericka Gordon Cumming and her immediate and extended family, see her *Memories.*

8   See *On the Rim of Kilauea,* a facsimile of the register, for Twain's, Bird Bishop's, and numerous other nineteenth-century travelers' accounts of Hawai'i's volcanoes.

9   Hawai'i's economic and strategic value to America resulted in its 1959 inclusion in the federal union. The qualified voters for statehood were U.S. military personnel and all those with U.S. citizenship who had lived in Hawai'i for at least one year. Those who declared themselves Hawaiian citizens could not vote.

Works Cited

Bermingham, Ann. *Landscape and Ideology: The English Rustic Tradition, 1740–1860.* Berkeley: U of California P, 1986.

Bohls, Elizabeth A. *Women Travel Writers and the Language of Aesthetics, 1716–1818.* Cambridge: Cambridge UP, 1995.

Copley, Stephen and Peter Garside, eds. *The Politics of the Picturesque: Literature, Landscape and Aesthetics since 1770.* Cambridge: Cambridge UP, 1994.

Crary, Jonathan. "Modernizing Vision." *Vision and Visuality (Discussions in Contemporary Culture, No. 2).* Ed. Hal Foster. New York: New Press, 1988,

Dictionary of National Biography. Eds. Leslie Stephen and Sidney Lee. 63 vols. London: Smith, Elder & Co., 1885.

Forbes, David W. *Encounters with Paradise: Views of Hawaii and Its People, 1778–1941*. Honolulu: Honolulu Academy of Arts, 1992.

Gilpin, William. *Three Essays: On Picturesque Beauty; On Picturesque Travel; and On Sketching Landscape*. 2d ed. London:R. Blamire, 1794.

Gordon Cumming, Constance Fredericka. *Fire Fountains: The Kingdom of Hawaii, Its Volcanoes, and the History of Its Missions*. 2 vols. Edinburgh: William Blackwood and Sons, 1883.

———. *From the Hebrides to the Himalayas*. London: Sampson Low, 1876.

———. *Memories*. Edinburgh: William Blackwood and Sons, 1904.

Gordon Cumming, Roualeyn. *Five Years of a Hunter's Life in the Far Interior of South Africa*. New York: Harper & Brothers, 1850.

Grewal, Inderpal. *Home and Harem: Nation, Gender, Empire, and the Cultures of Travel*. Durham: Duke UP, 1996.

Howard, Peter. *Landscape: The Artist's Vision*. London: Routledge, 1991.

Kame'eleihiwa, Lilikalā. *Native Land and Foreign Desires. Peheā La E Pono Ai?* Honolulu: Bishop Museum Press, 1992.

Lukacher, Brian. "Nature Historicized: Constable, Turner, and Romantic Landscape Painting." *Nineteenth Century Art: A Critical History*. Ed. Stephen F. Eisenman. London: Thames and Hudson, 1994. 115–43.

On the Rim of Kilauea: Excerpts from the Volcano House Register, 1865–1955. Hawai'i National Park: Hawai'i Natural History Association, 1992.

Pratt, Mary Louise. *Imperial Eyes: Travel Writing and Transculturation*. London: Routledge, 1992.

The Rise and Fall of the Hawaiian Kingdom: A Pictorial History. Honolulu: Pacific Basin Enterprises, 1979.

Russell, Mary. *The Blessings of a Good Thick Skirt: Women Travelers and Their World*. London: Collins, 1986.

Silva, Noenoe K. "Kū'ē! Hawaiian Women's Resistance to the Annexation." *Social Process in Hawai'i* 38 (1997): 4–15.

Takaki, Ronald. *Pau Hana: Plantation Life and Labor in Hawaii, 1835–1920*. Honolulu: U of Hawaii P, 1983.

Trask, Haunani-Kay. *From a Native Daughter: Colonialism and Sovereignty in Hawai'i*. Monroe, Maine: Common Courage Press, 1993.

Wilcox, Carol. *Sugar Water: Hawaii's Plantation Ditches*. Honolulu: U of Hawaii, 1996.

Part Two

Spectacle:

Mapping Cultural and

Spiritual Landscapes

✥ Chapter 6

Travel as Spectacle: The Illusion of Knowledge and Sight

Kristi Siegel and Toni B. Wulff

When I was training as an art historian, we were instructed in staring at pictures. The assumption was that the harder we looked, the more would be revealed to us; that a rigorous, precise and historically informed looking would reveal a wealth of hidden meanings.

— Irit Rogoff, "Studying Visual Culture"

"Seeing" as a Form of Knowledge

A college professor remarked, expressing a common sentiment, that "You cannot be a serious literature student without seeing Europe." It was the type of comment that could go unquestioned, or even unnoticed. However, a great number of assumptions were embedded within his remark, i.e., that seeing equals knowledge, that cultured "intellectual" people have traveled to the right places, that classic literature comes from Europe exclusively, and that viewing the site or object of literary creation directly correlates to one's understanding. In the medley of assumptions listed above, the notion that "seeing equals knowledge" piqued our curiosity (and skepticism) the most.

The importance of vision—as opposed to our other senses—dominates modern culture. Not speaking may be viewed as wisdom, while not seeing—blindness—surfaces instead as a metaphor for not understanding or even lacking in intelligence. To indicate "understanding" one says, "I see," or, conversely, asks, "Don't you *see*? Don't you get the *picture*? Are you *blind*?" However, the process of vision, merely seeing an image, does not equal knowledge. We assume that sight is our most important sense and often fail to realize that what we see is not universally equivalent or even necessarily shared within a culture. As travelers, then, we "read" visited cultures not in their own terms, but rather in our old, familiar ones. Vision, though, is always culturally mediated. We learn, literally, how and what to see. In a case study ("To See and Not See"), Dr. Oliver Sacks tells of a man [referred to as Virgil], happy, content, and blind since early childhood who, at the age of fifty, has his sight restored. Sight, rather than being a glorious revelation, brings confusion. When the "moment of truth" arrives and Virgil's bandages are removed, he does not—as so many movies would have us believe—instantly see: "No cry ["I can see!"] burst from Virgil's lips. He seemed to be staring blankly, bewildered, without focusing, at the surgeon, who stood before him, still holding the bandages" (Sacks 114). For Virgil, the world of sight is meaningless; without a sighted person's vast store of "visual memories" and without a lifetime spent "*learning* to see" (114), Virgil simply cannot interpret the images and objects in front of him. Instead, Virgil must learn to see, little by little, in a long, exhausting process that, ultimately, is not very successful. Similarly, the process of "seeing" another culture is no less challenging. While a culture's "reality" appears seductively accessible via vision, the traveler's view is always partial and biased. The vast number of unconsciously learned and assimilated beliefs, values, and norms that make up cultural patterns, the "mental programming" of any culture, remain veiled. The phrase "seeing a culture" has an accomplished and comprehensive ring to it, implying that we have in some sense acquired it. Learning a culture's language, preferably through some sort of immersion experience, may provide partial entry into a cultural "system" and allow a traveler—at least sporadically—to participate in its reality. Like vision, however, language is also complex, culturally mediated, and resistant to easy interpretation.

Until the early twentieth century, western thought tended to consider language as a neutral medium with little influence on an individual's experience of life. It was seen as a vehicle for conveying ideas rather than a major factor in a closed system, a force shaping perception and values. Edward Sapir and Benjamin Whorf (the Sapir-Whorf hypothesis) argue that the language and thought of a given culture are integrally related, forming and perpetuating a sort of internal code of communication and perception for the speakers of a language within a culture. For example, American English contains words and concepts having no denotative equivalent in certain other languages—like "homecoming" and "yard"—and definable only by circumlocution. The same is true of other languages, like Inuktitut (Eskimo) with its dozens of words for (literal variations of) snow, and Mandarin Chinese with its many words for rice. More complexly, the syntax of many languages (all Romance languages and Japanese, among others) has historically reflected and perpetuated the subordinate position of women in those cultures. Perhaps even more profound in its implications is a language like that of the Alaskan Native American Athabaskan-speaking nation visited by anthropologist Michael Dorris. The Athabaskan language both reveals and reinforces the fundamentally collectivistic nature of the people who speak it by offering no linguistic option for the expression of individual preference or will. Dorris explains:

> Much of my time was spent in the study of the local language, linguistically relat-ed to Navajo and Apache but distinctly adapted to the subarctic environment. One of its most difficult features for an outsider to grasp was the practice of al-most always speaking and thinking in a collective plural voice. The word for peo-ple, "dene," was used as a kind of "we"—the subject for virtually every predicate requiring a personal pronoun—and therefore any act became, at least in concep-tion, a group experience. (2)

Dorris's study of Athabaskan allowed him to access Alaskan Native American culture, enabling him to penetrate what to non-Athabaskan speakers would nec-essarily remain a closed system. Linguistic knowledge is a critical key to "unlock-ing" cultures, and yet linguistic skill alone will not give the visitor the visceral sense of the culture that defines the insider. The process involved is similar to the one we experience when grappling with the meaning of a culture's/language's idioms: First we learn the literal words (which often remain relatively meaning-less) and then, through time, we intuit their real meaning within a culturally spe-cific context. "Time" then surfaces as a critical necessity in even beginning to learn a culture. Accordingly, Dorris's insights into the Alaskan Native American culture via language provide entry but not mastery. Language may provide more knowledge, but like sight, eludes an outsider's complete understanding. As Virgil's experiences demonstrate, *time*—perhaps—surfaces as the largest barrier to comprehension. Jamie Zeppa, who describes her three years in Tibet in the book, *Beyond the Sky and Earth: A Journey into Bhutan,* comments on the need for time to even start assimilating a culture. Zeppa remarks that, in contrast to rapid traveling and arriving, "Entering [a culture] takes longer. You cross over slowly, in bits and pieces" and—after a great deal of time—"You are just *begin-ning* to know where you are" (emphasis added, 101). Similarly, Virgil could not open up his eyes and immediately see what sighted people have spent a lifetime learning; a traveler, visiting a new culture, faces parallel impediments. Further, Virgil had created a culture of his own, and for Virgil, like Molly Sweeney in the play Brian Friel loosely bases on Sacks's account, more is lost than gained by being able to see. Just like Virgil, Molly Sweeney ultimately receives vision as an assault, disrupting the gentler, less intrusive world of touch she has created.

Sacks's study proves suggestive to travel theory in a couple of ways: Simply seeing something, e.g., collecting images, does not provide knowledge in itself, and our ability to interpret what we see in other cultures may not be much better than Virgil's ability to interpret his new world. Virgil, for example, had a great deal of difficulty distinguishing between his cat and dog. He could not—by look-ing at a cat—assimilate what he saw until he had painstakingly touched each part of the cat, over and over, in an attempt to link the pieces to the "whole." In a like manner, travelers to a new country—whether they come armed with informational guides or not—are often seeing merely "fragments" that they will not be able to assimilate into meaningful wholes without actively "working" at the connections. Knowledge, therefore, does not emerge naturally from the sight itself.

Virgil's experiences also demonstrate that "seeing" itself is not an involuntary impulse. As Virgil becomes more depressed (and more overwhelmed), he often chooses not to see. Interestingly, Virgil does not need to close his eyes in order to stop seeing; he can simply choose not to "look." Sacks provides an explanation on the role of "motivation" and seeing: "It is insufficient to see; one must look as well. Though we have spoken, with Virgil, of a perceptual incapacity, or agnosia, there was, equally, a lack of capacity or impulse to look, to act seeing—a lack of visual behavior" (117–18, n.1). The voluntary nature of seeing also proves suggestive for travel studies. To simplify, how many sights do travelers miss, not because they did not see but, rather, because they did not look? Virgil's experiences, while proving fertile for travel study, also call into question the entire notion that vision and knowledge are inextricably linked, and intimate instead that a life might be quite complete without vision: "that the blind may...construct a complete and sufficient world, have a complete 'blind identity' and no sense of disability or inadequacy, and that the 'problem' of their blindness and the desire to cure this, therefore, is ours, not theirs" (Sacks paraphrasing Diderot 139).

Though the cultural dominance of vision has been termed "modern," it is modern only in a relative sense. For example, Paul Houlgate quotes John Dewey who asserts that western philosophy since Plato and Aristotle has been "dominated" by a "spectator theory of knowledge" where "the theory of knowing is modeled after what was supposed to take place in the act of vision" (87). Later advances in science, e.g., the microscope, the telescope, x-ray machines, and so forth, suggested that soon we would be able to "see it all," and in seeing it all, know it all. The notion of seeing equaling knowledge persists and has long been a tradition in travel literature. As Mary Louise Pratt articulates, travelers have tended to view other cultures through all-seeing, all-knowing "imperial eyes" and take a "monarch-of-all-I-survey" stance (201). Today's travelers, generally equipped with guidebooks or some knowledge of the important "sights," have an even greater premeditated/mediated vision. To seek what you already intend to find (e.g., I'm in Paris so I must see the Eiffel Tower) betrays a structuralist impulse that spatializes landscape. The process of sightseeing, in essence, makes an implicit statement, "Here's what is important," and the journey is thus reduced to a trek from valued spot to valued spot. Though sightseeing and "tourism" highlight the process of giving some sites/sights prominence while literally not seeing others—a checkered mode of cognition—all insight, as Paul de Man has explained in such works as *Blindness and Insight*, relies on blindness. To simplify (and perhaps oversimplify), when everything is foregrounded, nothing is foregrounded. In a sense, therefore, we are all always sightseers by necessity, articulating landscapes in order to see at all. By this criterion, however, the dichotomy between tourist and traveler, sightseer and connoisseur begins to break down.

The "Hierarchy" of Sight: Travelers versus Tourists

In Michel Foucault's sense of the word "gaze," knowledge is paramount. The gazer—all-seeing, all-knowing—quickly penetrates depths and layers to perceive a subject's essence (135–37). In the last paragraph of his book, James Urry refers to Foucault's gaze and its relation to travel and tourism:

> But what now is happening, as tourism develops into the largest industry world-wide...[is that] almost all spaces, history and social activities can be materially and symbolically remade for the endlessly devouring gaze....To return to Foucault, contemporary societies are developing less on the basis of surveillance and the normalization of individuals, and more on the basis of the democratization of the tourist gaze and the spectacle-isation of place. (156)

Although John Urry refers to Foucault briefly in both the beginning and ending of his book, *The Tourist Gaze,* Urry is not using the term *gaze* in precisely the same sense as Foucault. As Urry explains, the tourist's gaze, though ostensibly quite different from the medical gaze Foucault describes, is just "as socially organized and systematised as is the gaze of the medic" (1). Nevertheless, a major difference exists between the knowledgeable, totalizing gaze of a physician Foucault describes and the variety of gazes a tourist deploys. In terms of reception, the physician's gaze is respected; by implication the tourist's gaze is that of an amateur. In devoting an entire book to analyzing the tourist's fairly shallow gaze, Urry creates an implicit dichotomy. If the tourist's gaze is marked by superficiality, kitsch, and inauthenticity then surely there must exist "something else," a gaze that would somehow be different from that of a tourist. Commonly, distinctions are drawn between a tourist (the gauche novice) and the traveler (the knowing connoisseur). In many ways, the tourist is the modern-day version of Mary Louise Pratt's colonialist travelers who presume to "acquire" the countries they visit via their "imperial eyes." In one ironic passage Pratt explains the motivation of a particular set of imperialist travelers who epitomized condescending discourse: "No one was better at the monarch-of-all-I-survey scene than the string of British explorers who spent the 1860s looking for the source of the Nile...[these] Victorians opted for a brand of verbal painting whose highest calling was to produce for the home audience the peak moments which geographical 'discoveries' were 'won' for England" (202). These Victorian travelers who wrote about exotic landscapes and adventures for the armchair travelers' consumption prefigure the "pilgrims" Mark Twain lampoons in *Innocents Abroad,* the "ugly American" that figured in the mid–twentieth century literature and film, and the weary tourists satirized in such movies as *If It's Tuesday, This Must Be Belgium.*

Urry dates the advent of mass tourism to the beginning of the twentieth century when—for the first time—people other than just the upper classes of modern society were able to travel. Though Urry does comment that with the breakdown of boundaries characteristic of postmodernism "people are much of the time 'tourists' whether they like it or not" (83), the distinction (and the stigma) nevertheless persists. The tourist has become an object of study, and the scholar (or literary travel writer), who catalogues their identifying features, looks "down" on tourists with the much same "imperial eyes" that surveyed colonized nations. In *Sunrise with Seamonsters: Travels and Discoveries,* Paul Theroux distinguishes between real travelers and mock travelers. Michael Kowalewski (*Temperamental Journeys: Essays on the Modern Literature of Travel)*—paraphrasing Theroux—describes the distinction as follows: "Real travelers are the enterprising loners who put up with often hazardous, comfortless conditions"...[versus] mock-travelers "who aspire, like Anne Tyler's 'accidental tourist,' to make a journey without ever seeming to have left home" (5). Kowalewski adds, for he appears to agree with this dichotomy, that mock-travelers, who "are deeply opposed to exertion and dislocation...are afflicted by what I [Kowalewski] would call the Winnebago Syndrome. Like so many self-contained turtles or snails, these travelers take their homes with them, not just in cavernous RV's on America's backroads but abroad as well" (5). For Theroux and Kowalewski, the difference between a traveler and mock-traveler[1] seems to rest on one's comfort level. In short, the mock-traveler (or tourist) tries to replicate the comforts of home while the (true) traveler is willing to endure hardships and dislocation.

Although Paul Fussell remarks (famously) in *Abroad* that "we are all tourists now, and there is no escape" (46), it is clear from his book that the quip is ironic and does not refer to the way he views *himself.* In fact, Fussell creates three categories of voyagers: the traveler, the tourist, and the anti-tourist. Like Theroux, Fussell similarly sees the traveler as one willing to undergo discomfort but also someone, as in Caren Kaplan's trenchant summary of Fussell, who "can be characterized as a Western individual, usually male, 'white,' of independent means, an introspective observer, literate, acquainted with ideas of the arts and culture, and, above all, a humanist" (Kaplan 50). Additionally, Fussell creates another category. Not content with the term "tourist," Fussell also develops the term, "anti-tourist." While the tourist is obvious and always "moves toward the security of pure cliché" (Fussell 46) the anti-tourist is savvier. In what Mary Louise Pratt might term a "crescendo of arrogance" (a phrase she does use to describe Fussell's writing in another context, 211), Fussell describes the anti-tourist as a traveler-"wannabe":

> Perhaps the most popular way for the anti-tourist to demarcate himself from the tourists, because he can have a drink while doing it, is for him to lounge—cameraless—at a café table and with palpable contempt scrutinize the passing sheep through half-closed lids, making all movements very slowly....Any conversation gambits favored by lonely tourists, like "Where are you from?" can be de-

flected by vagueness. Instead of answering Des Moines or Queens, you say, "I spend a lot of time abroad" or "That's really hard to say." If hard-pressed, you simply mutter, "Je ne parle pas Anglais," look at your watch, and leave. (49)

Of particular interest here is Fussell's point of view. While satirizing the "anti-tourists" for snubbing and dissociating themselves from the bourgeois tourists, Fussell looks down on both categories and distinguishes them from the more cultured, knowledgeable class of "travelers" that would, of course, include Fussell—however much he might assert that "we are all tourists now." Tourist studies have become so sophisticated that one college tourism center identifies at least eight different types of tourists (or travelers) including such dichotomies as "allocentrics" who are "adventurous, self-confident, curious…[i.e., travelers]" versus "psychocentrics" who are "anxious, somewhat inhibited, non-adventuresome, inner-focused [i.e., tourists]"; or the hierarchy implied in this four-tiered analysis of travelers and tourists:

1. The "Independent Travellers" are travelers [*not* tourists] who "make their plans independently, allowing individual choice, freedom of itinerary" and who generally "stay away from specially developed tourist resorts."
2. The "Non-Institutionalised Tourists" are tourists who need little help from tourist agencies and often serve as "pathfinders for the mass tourism industry."
3. The "Mass Tourists" are tourists who do use "the travel industry to plan, package, and organise their holiday in specially developed tourist resorts."
4. The "Institutionalised Tourists" [obviously the neediest, most lowly of tourists] require their "tourism experience…planned, controlled and provided by the mass tourism industry" (McIntosh 8–10).

Among the many issues evident in the various analyses of tourists and travelers presented above is the question of *power*. At heart, the tourist is led while the traveler leads, the tourist is timid while the traveler is adventurous, the tourist cannot properly "see" the journey while the traveler is erudite and knowledgeable. For Inderpal Grewal the underlying, and not often acknowledged, difference between a traveler and tourist resides in social "class," which, of course, the traveler has and the tourist does not. In reality, Grewal asserts that the travelers' observations are "no more 'authentic'" than are the "tourist's 'sights'" (95).

James Clifford, in *Routes,* also remarks on the elitist distinction often made between traveler and tourist, but prefers to define travel as a "more inclusive term embracing a range of more or less volunteerist practices of leaving 'home' to go to some 'other' place" (66). In a chapter about his own travels, Clifford does use the word "tourist" but uses it ironically and often targets himself in the process. In one instance Clifford acknowledges that tourists are "everyone's 'Other,' [and] never given any social or individual complexity" (225). In a later passage, when Clifford wants to be alone with a Mayan ruin, his tone is bemused: "Alone with the stones, with nature. This much is required if ancient sites are to transmit wisdom and sublimity to romantic individualists. 'Alone' meaning with special people like oneself. Not with *tourists*...." (emphasis added 233).

Motive surfaces as an implicit concern in the various distinctions between travelers and tourists. What do travelers want? Travelers' motives may range from the trivial (diversion, recreation, good food, a good tan) to the more profound: nostalgia (a desire to find an untarnished Eden), insight (some knowledge or sense of other cultures), or, possibly, escape (the sense that one might become someone "else" away from home). Inherent in Fussell's assertion that we have all (inescapably) become tourists is that what we now see has become corrupted by travel and the tourist industry. What we see now, as many theorists posit, is spectacle—the hyperreal.

Guy Debord, in *The Society of the Spectacle,* argues that we have become a society of passive spectators who spend vacations capturing

> moments portrayed, like all spectacular commodities, *at a distance*, and as desirable by definition. This particular commodity [e.g., sight-seeing] is explicitly presented as a moment of authentic life whose cyclical return we are supposed to look forward to. Yet even in such special moments, ostensibly moments of *life*, the only thing being generated, is the spectacle—albeit at a higher-than-usual level of intensity. And what has been passed off as authentic life turns out to be merely a life more *authentically spectacular.* (112)

Like Debord, Jean Baudrillard and Umberto Eco similarly zero in on the depthless spectacle of modern society, a type of spectacle they refer to as the "hyperreal," which might be defined as the representation of representation or, in other words, the fabrication of the "absolute fake" (Eco 8). For both Baudrillard and Eco, Disneyland surfaces as the epitome of glorified simulation (and by extension, just the type of spectacle a "tourist" might desire). Disneyland, for Baudrillard, exists as a sort of "nostalgia-fix" that makes us feel that what is outside of Disneyland is *real.* Though we may desire the "real," Baudrillard argues that the real no longer exists: "Disneyland is presented as imaginary in order to make us believe that the rest is real, whereas all of Los Angeles and the America that surrounds it are no longer real, but belong to the hyperreal order and to the order of simulation" (12). Though Eco would certainly concur with Baudrillard's description of Disneyland, he explains the tourist's desire and motivation to see the hyperreal differently. After explaining the care taken in Disneyland to use "real" objects whenever possible, Eco remarks that when a "fake" is used, it is deliberate *and* desirable:

> When there is a fake—hippopotamus, dinosaur, sea serpent—it is not so much because it wouldn't be possible to have the real equivalent but because the public is meant to admire the perfection of the fake and its obedience to the program. In

this sense Disneyland not only produces illusion, but—in confessing it—stimulates the desire for it: A real crocodile can be found in the zoo…but Disneyland tells us that faked nature corresponds much more to our daydream demands. (44)

Disneyland may fulfill the "daydream demands" of tourists, apparently, but not those of Eco, as he goes on to prove in the next sentence where his parenthetical aside distinguishes him as a scholar/observer rather than a tourist: "When, in the space of twenty-four hours, you (*as I did deliberately*) travel from the fake New Orleans of Disneyland to the real one…" (emphasis added, 44). While Eco's tourist appears to make little distinction between the authentic (whatever that might be) and the inauthentic, Maxine Fiefer, in *Going Places,* gives the postmodern tourist a bit more credit. "Post-tourists," to use Fiefer's term, do not worry about whether they look at the wrong thing or whether they look like tourists because they are self-aware; post-tourists know that they are tourists and "that tourism is a game" (Urry paraphrasing Fiefer 100).

The Contemporary Mode of Perception

If, as Walter Benjamin has posited, each age has its own "mode of human sense perception" that "changes with humanity's entire mode of existence" (*Illuminations* 222) our present perceptual mode may be characterized more accurately as a "scan," rather than a "gaze," and its origins might be located in the rapid growth of mass media and technology. Urry's notion of the gaze, particularly in reference to Foucault, presupposes a form of perception that lingers long enough on a discrete object to determine its essence or value. Popular sights/sites are often so saturated by consumer apparatus (shops, advertisements, accommodations, amusement parks that have become "linked" to the original landmark) that the landscape itself has become de-articulated and what once was the "spectacle" may not be readily apparent. Conversely, for cultures whose perception has been shaped by landscapes of speed, saturation, and spectacle, topographies less "cluttered" may appear blank or desolate.

Our present mode of perception—transformed by the type of rapid scanning necessary to navigate shopping malls, to find one's destination on high speed freeways or crowded highways, to skim ever-burgeoning amounts of text, to surf television channels, or to browse the Internet, to name but a few—may differ radically from the way we perceived reality just a few decades ago. Further, if vision has long been associated with knowledge, our present culture ups the ante by its pronounced emphasis on the speed with which we may access images (and thus knowledge). The Internet, tellingly dubbed the "information highway," serves as the present touchstone for acquiring knowledge. In this "information age," the ability to access images and data has become synonymous with obtaining knowledge: "Whereas in the past information used to be a prerequisite for knowledge…nowadays information equals knowledge. Seeing the invasion in Somalia live means knowing about it (not understanding it): The possibility of handling millions of databases (not using them usefully) equals knowledge. Hence, knowledge is no longer a cultural product" (Burgelman 6).

Similarly, a lengthy report by the United States Commerce NTIA (National Telecommunications and Information Administration) expresses concern for the growing "digital divide" and by implication asserts that those not connected to the Internet (referred to as the "have-nots") are disconnected from knowledge itself:

> Overall, we have found that the number of Americans connected to the nation's information infrastructure is soaring. Nevertheless, this year's report finds that a digital divide still exists, and, in many cases, is actually widening over time. Minorities, low-income persons, the less educated, and children of single-parent households, particularly when they reside in rural areas or central cities, are among the groups that lack access to information resources. (Irving 1)

In addition to those not connected to the Internet at all, a new "digital divide" has occurred between those connected by modems (indicating slower access to information) and those connected by DSL or cable (indicating high-speed access to information). In accord with the current logic of technology, those not connected to the Internet cannot travel the "nation's information infrastructure" at all, and those with slow connections cannot access as much information (knowledge). Although few activities involve less motion than sitting in front of a computer screen, using the Internet has—since its inception—been associated with metaphors of travel, speed, and space (e.g., hypertext, hyperlink, information highway, search engines, surfing, connection speed, cyber-space, the new frontier, the world wide web, web *sites,* and so forth). What is often neglected in discussions about cyber "travel" is the acknowledgment that the Internet is merely one way to get (some) valuable information and does not necessarily (any more than watching television) provide knowledge in itself. Of more interest, however, may be the effect technology and the sheer volume of images we receive daily have had on our mode of perception. If our visual practice has become more hurried, more impatient, and more inclined to skim surfaces, how does that change the way we see a journey or later recollect our journey?

Further, voluntary travel—to use James Clifford's distinction—whether done by members of a "shopping-mall society" or not, may be marked by scanning as its *initial* perceptual mode. When Jamie Zeppa travels to Bhutan to teach in a remote village, she first receives a thorough orientation on Bhutanese history, culture, customs, and language. Even when armed with quite a bit more knowledge than most travelers would possess, initially Zeppa really cannot "see" or interpret Bhutan. Thimphu, the capital of Bhutan, seems small, cluttered, and old to Zeppa, and she scoffs when she is told "Thimphu will look like New York to you when you come back after a year in the east" (15). Zeppa grows impatient at a bank where people push and shove rather than forming lines, while the bank clerk, chatting idly with a guard, blithely ignores them all. Silently, Zeppa fumes, "Do these people have all the time in the world *or what?* (23). The food and water terrify her, and when traveling to her village, Zeppa thinks the landscape looks blank: "The country seems almost empty to me" (30). Finally, she loses her bearings entirely: "Somewhere south is Pema Getshel. Somewhere west is Thimphu. And beyond Thimphu—but no, I am too tired to retrace the journey mentally. I want to just click my heels three times and be home" (38).

Prejudiced by her own cultural baggage, initially Zeppa sees Thimphu as unimpressive, disorganized, and inefficient. The surrounding landscape seems vacant and desolate. After spending five months in Bhutan, Zeppa re-"sees" her surroundings: "The rains have turned Pema Gatshel a thousand shades of green: lime, olive, pea, apple, grass, pine, moss, malachite, emerald. The trees are full of singing insects, flowers, birds, hard green oranges, children" and then remarks: "It's hard to believe now that I once thought this a landscape of lack" (137). Like Virgil, Zeppa could only see the landscape after she learned *what* to see.

Provocatively, Zeppa's culture shock occurs both arriving and returning. When Zeppa travels back home to visit, after having spent two years in Bhutan, she finds Toronto enervating. She views her surroundings as "glossy and polished and unreal," and is "overwhelmed by the number of *things*" (262). Television is "incomprehensible," the "images fly out of the screen too fast....Ten minutes of television exhausts" her for hours, she's "shaken by the traffic, the rush, the speed at which people walk," and she finds the "number of stores...overwhelming" (263). Zeppa's reactions demonstrate that her inability to interpret her home now parallel her earlier inability to make sense of Bhutan. Significantly, Zeppa's confusion, her sense of being too slow in the midst of so much "rush and blur," emphasizes the steady scrim of images typifying industrialized culture (267). In short, Zeppa has lost (at least temporarily) the ability to "scan"—the mode of perception that may be necessary to decipher the "society of spectacle."

Remembering the Journey

From a negative standpoint, scanning may mark our present perceptual mode and suggests a type of seeing characterized by superficiality. In a more positive light and in the terms of travel, scanning may be inevitable. When Jamie Zeppa arrives in Bhutan, she can do no more than skim its surface and her vision, her ability to interpret her landscape is similarly compromised when she arrives in Toronto after being away for two years.

Zeppa's and any other traveler's ability to remember the journey may fare no better. Just as the initial perception of travel is partial at best, the journey's recollection, i.e., the "stuff" of travel literature, becomes distorted by the degree our cultural lens blinds us to the journey initially, the amount of time we can spend within a culture, our imperfect memory of the journey itself, and the changes that will occur once our memories have been exposed to the shaping forces of narrative. For Benjamin, the narratives (of one's life or one's travels) necessarily become a collection of fragments, an allegory of disjuncture and discontinuity, no matter how seamlessly these fragments are presented. Nevertheless, Benjamin finds as "one of the strongest impulses in allegory"—and by extension, in travel writing—the "appreciation of the transience of things, and the concern to rescue them for eternity" (*German Tragic Drama* 223). Yet, Benjamin's scattered reminiscences may be both "fleeting or eternal" (*Reflections* 28) just as the ruined landscape of allegory stands at the crossroads between "transitoriness and eternity" (*German Tragic Drama* 224). It is the devalued status of these reminiscences and allegorical ruins that effects their redemption. The honesty and humility of allegorical fragments, like the carefully unearthed fragments of "genuine reminiscences," ultimately redeem them from the very realm of "profane things" they appear to depict (*German Tragic Drama* 175). By not elevating these memories to symbols, to succumb to the immediate temptation of totality and eternity, Benjamin's reminiscences and fragments enact the theme of *contemptus mundi;* by falling, they might rise. Benjamin locates memory's value, the value that would also hold true for travel literature, in its ability to collect images from the past (or one's memory), severed from any connections that would threaten to totalize these images and thus elevate them to the status of symbols, so that they may then be contemplated by the present. The travel writer, like a collector, takes images/objects that are "out of circulation and confronts cultural history with them" (Abbas 14). For Benjamin, as becomes particularly evident in his later works, the importance of collecting images, reminiscences, shifts in emphasis from "remembering" to "not forgetting." Travel writings—as fragments of history and culture—achieve redemption by their ability to affect the present. Benjamin, writing under the shadow of the Third Reich, does not take the collection of memories lightly, seeing the tendency to forget the past threatening the return of the same: "For every image of the past that is not recognized by the present as one of its own concerns threatens to disappear irretrievably" ("Theses on the Philosophy of History" 581). Travel writing—a kind of history, autobiography, and cultural narrative in motion—leaves traces. For Benjamin, the motive and the worth of travel writing would be to make sure these traces are not forgotten.

Jamie Zeppa, similarly, understands that she will always remain an outsider in Bhutan but wishes—nonetheless—to present her fragments as honestly and completely as possible. Though Zeppa often finds Bhutan a kind of Shangri-la, she presents its political complexity unflinchingly, and never pretends to understand or agree with it. Like Virgil, Zeppa recognizes that sight itself does not bring knowledge. What she learns most of all—a lesson with which Benjamin would certainly concur—is that "Travel should make us more humble, not more proud. We are all tourists, I think. Whether we stay for two weeks or two years, we are still outsiders, passing through" (204–5). At best, Zeppa might feel she reaches an enlightened confusion, and perhaps this *is* the most that any traveler can attain.

Note

1   While Paul Theroux and Michael Kowalewski do not use the word "tourist," with the exception of businessmen whom Theroux also categorizes as tourists, this is certainly the word they imply.

Works Cited

Abbas, Ackbar. "Walter Benjamin's Collector: The Fate of Modern Experience." Working Paper No. 3. Milwaukee: Center for Twentieth Century Studies, 1986.

Baudrillard, Jean. *Simulacra and Simulation.* Trans. Sheila Faria Glaser. Ann Arbor: U of Michigan P, 1994.

Benjamin, Walter. *The Origin of German Tragic Drama.* Trans. John Osborne. London: NLB, 1977.

———. *Reflections.* Trans. Edmund Jephcott. New York: Schocken, 1986.

———. "Theses on the Philosophy of History." *Critical Theory Since 1965.* Ed. Adams, Hazard and Leroy Searle. Tallahassee: Florida State UP, 1986.

———. "The Work of Art in the Age of Mechanical Reproduction." *Illuminations: Essays and Reflections.* Ed. Hannah Arendt. Trans. Harry Zohn. New York: Schocken Books, 1969. 217–51.

Burgelman, Jean-Claude. "Traveling with Communication Technologies in Space, Time, and Everyday Life: An Exploration of Their Impact." *First Monday.* 5.3 (March 2000). URL: http://firstmonday.org/issues/issue5_3/
bur burgelman/1, p. 9.

Clifford, James. *Routes: Travel and Translation in the Late Twentieth Century.* Cambridge: Harvard UP, 1997.

Debord, Guy. *The Society of the Spectacle.* Trans. Donald Nicholson-Smith. New York: Zone Books, 1995.

de Man, Paul. *Blindness and Insight: Essays in the Rhetoric of Contemporary Criticism.* 2nd ed. Minneapolis: U of Minnesota P, 1983.

Dorris, Michael. *Paper Trail: Essays.* New York: Harper, 1995.

Eco, Umberto. *Travels in Hyperreality.* Trans. William Weaver. San Diego: Harcourt, 1986.

Foucault, Michel. *The Birth of the Clinic: An Archaeology of Medical Perception.* Trans. A.M. Sheridan Smith. New York: Vintage Books, 1973.

Fussell, Paul. *Abroad: British Literary Traveling between the Wars.* Oxford: Oxford UP, 1980.

Grewal, Inderpal. *Home and Harem: National, Gender, Empire, and the Cultures of Travel.* Durham and London: Duke UP, 1996.

Houlgate, Paul. "Vision, Reflection, and Openness: The 'Hegemony of Vision' from a Hegelian Point of View." *Modernity and the Hegemony of Vision.* Ed. David Michael Levin. Berkeley: U of California P, 1993, 87–123.

If It's Tuesday, This Must Be Belgium. Dir. Mel Stuart. Perf. Suzanne Pleshette, Ian McShane, Mildred Natwick. Stan Margulies. 1969.

Irving, Larry. "Falling Through the Net: Defining the Digital Divide." National Telecommunications and Information Administration (NTIA) U.S. Department of Commerce. http://www.ntia.doc.gov/ntiahome/

Kaplan, Caren. *Questions of Travel: Postmodern Discourses of Displacement.* Durham and London: Duke UP, 1996.

Kowalewski, Michael, ed. *Temperamental Journeys: Essays on the Modern Literature of Travel.* Athens and London: U of Georgia P, 1992.

MacCannell, Dean. *The Tourist: A New Theory of the Leisure Class.* Berkeley: U of California P, 1999.

McIntosh, Alison. "Toux 711: Tourist Behaviour." New Zealand: U of Otago. http://www.commerce.otago.ac.nz/tourism/

Pratt, Mary Louise. *Imperial Eyes: Travel Writing and Transculturation.* Routledge: London and New York, 1992.

Rogoff, Irit. "Studying Visual Culture." *Visual Culture Reader.* Ed. Nicholas Mirzoeff. Routledge: London and New York, 1998.

Sacks, Oliver. "To See and Not See." *An Anthropologist on Mars: Seven Paradoxical Tales.* New York: Alfred A. Knopf, 1995. 108–52.

Theroux, Paul. *Sunrise with Seamonsters: Travels and Discoveries, 1964–1984.* Boston: Houghton Mifflin, 1985, 126–35.

Twain, Mark. *Innocents Abroad.* 1872. Introd. Mordecai Richler. New York: Oxford UP, 1996.

Urry, James. *The Tourist Gaze: Leisure and Travel in Contemporary Societies.* London: Sage Publications, 1990.

Whorf, Benjamin Lee. *Language, Thought, and Reality; Selected Writings.* Ed. John B. Carroll. Cambridge: Technology Press of Massachusetts Institute of Technology, 1956.

Zeppa, Jamie. *Beyond the Sky and the Earth: A Journey into Bhutan.* New York: Riverland Books, 1999.

Chapter 7

Baudrillard's Explorations of Tocqueville's America: Wandering in Hyperdemocracy

Marco Diani

Jean Baudrillard, to say the least, is not an accessible traveling companion. It is difficult to imagine him walking, eating, talking, or engaging in any routine interaction without him remarking on it as a symbolic representation of the simple banality and emptiness at the heart of an entire nation. Nothing escapes his eerily hollow sense of the profound: breakdancers recall "the ironic, indolent pose of the dead"; the "smiling eyes" of squirrels betray "a cold, ferocious beast fearfully stalking us"; a must-exit sign is "a sign of destiny"; jogging, "like so many other things," is "a form of voluntary servitude" (19, 48, 53, 38). These digressions are, we discover, equally important and ominous pieces of the "giant hologram" America, where "information concerning the whole is contained in each of its elements" (29). Baudrillard's relentless seriousness is, at bottom, an outgrowth of worry: He identifies America as the obvious model of the modern society, and proceeds to examine it with concern for the future of Europe, the next in line to receive what in America has become a fatally barren, self-perpetuating future.

The same worry possessed and guided Tocqueville throughout his travels in America: He explored the country "so as at least to know what we have to fear or hope therefrom" (*Democracy* 19). One of his more prominent fears was democracy's tendency to "favor the taste for physical pleasures," which in excess "disposes men to believe that nothing but matter exists," which in turn leads to a pursuance of material goods with blind, "mad impetuosity" (544). The similarity of their ends nearly dissolves, however, in consideration of their wildly divergent means. Baudrillard declares early on, "I went in search of *astral* America, not social and cultural America, but the America of the empty, absolute freedom of the freeways, not the deep America of mores and mentalities, but the America of desert speed, of motels and mineral surfaces" (5). His real goal "is not the discovery of local customs…but discovering the immorality of the space you have to travel through." This approach, he rightly judges, "is on a quite different plane" (9) from traditional methods. Such a layered, otherworldly approach seems to be a direct affront to Tocqueville, who championed his discovery of the revolution of mores, and who took as only a small conceit seeing "more in America than America" (*Democracy* 19). Tocqueville's focus is so conscious, so concentrated, that if the reader does not "feel the importance attached to the practical experience of Americans, to their habits, opinions, and, in a word, their mores, in maintaining their laws," then, says Tocqueville, "I will have failed in the main object of my work" (308).

Baudrillard selects an approach and a tone well removed from Tocqueville's: "I sought the finished form of the future catastrophe in geology, in that upturning of depth that can be seen in the striated spaces" (5). Pared down, Baudrillard is not searching for America per se, nor for American democracy: He is seeking the image that best expresses America, the symbol that was once not a symbol, but with the birth of the symbol-oriented modern society, became one. That image, that symbol, is the desert, whose history has been forgotten, leveled, made an object of preservation, and whose meaning has vanished in its own heat. Baudrillard's giddy overlapping of the metaphoric and the real, of nature and the unnatural, is often overwhelming, and his concerns must punch through thick webs of prose and theory before they can be recognized. Finding air, they appear dark and unencouraging: To search for depth in America is to search for a meaningless, desert space that is America's past, present, and future, filled only with hollow desire for material wealth. So while Tocqueville found a country full of clearly expressed trends and tendencies, Baudrillard found an illusion, a transparent landscape where Tocqueville's most overt concerns disappear—they become part of the landscape that Baudrillard uses to express the literal and figurative character of America.

This is precisely the effect that Baudrillard intends. For him, the most appropriate way to experience and report on America is to do so as an American, or, since America is not a populace but a desert, as an accelerated element in the "nuclear form" (5) of the country. He accomplishes this by driving, the most convenient way to attain speed, "the rite that initiates us into emptiness" (7). America's lifeless atomization is not just a concern but a frank presupposition. Baudrillard admits that he "knew all about this future catastrophe when I was still in Paris, of course," going on to explain that "to understand it, you have to take to the road, to that traveling which achieves what Virilio calls the aesthetics of disappearance" (5). This is a difficult assignment: to literally lose oneself in a search for a form that you know to be meaningless; to disappear into the history-less, culture-less desert—indistinguishable from the deserted American city—while retaining a sense of identity and foundation enough to record it with some sense of distanced coherence. Baudrillard tentatively suggests, "no one is capable of analyzing [American society], least of all the American intellectuals shut away on their campuses" (23), but he later admits, "It may well be that the truth of America can only be seen by a European, since he alone will discover here the perfect simulacrum" (28). Since Americans exist as a model—they were born a model, rather than having developed into one—they cannot "possess the language in which to describe" (29) the nature of what they represent. Finally, he reasons, "I know the deserts, their deserts, better than they do, since they turn their backs on their own space" (63). Tocqueville concedes as much, finding that while Europeans "think a lot about the wild, open spaces of America," the "wonders of inanimate nature leave the Americans cold." They do not see the forests "until they begin to fall beneath the ax" (*Democracy* 485). Baudrillard, in any case, commits himself to the dilemma of speaking the country's subconscious language without rendering his prose as meaningless as the language itself. If his writing can be considered an abstraction, it is because of the nature of the journey, and further, the nature of the country.

So when he writes, "This country is naive, so you have to be naive" (63), he seems admirable for his intentions, and vulnerable for his naïveté. What better cue for critics to display a laundry list of what Richard Poirier terms "patent absurdities" (6) as proof of Baudrillard's immanent shallowness. Poirier hardly has to labor to find embarrassing bits of authoritatively delivered verbiage that is crushed by the weight of its own self-importance. Drop-dead lines like "There are no cops in New York" and "Americans have no identity but they have wonderful teeth" provide Poirier with ample ammunition to accuse Baudrillard of living up to the hollowness of his own subject. The examples are almost less harmful taken out of context than when liberally mixed with Baudrillard's verbose theory. Poirier's final thrust is delivered in Baudrillard's own words: *America* falls victim to the author's—not the country's—"surface intensity and deeper meaninglessness" (Poirier, qting Baudrillard , 62). Baudrillard cannot plunge into emptiness and emerge full of meaning.

Poirier's criticism of Baudrillard's "efforts of language by which he hopes to register his momentary transformations from European savant to new American mutant" (6) is well grounded but misplaced, especially as a support of Poirier's more far-reaching accusation, that Baudrillard "knows nothing whatever of American history or American literature" (3). This is a weak point of attack in light of Poirier's astonishing refusal to acknowledge Tocqueville as an obvious and authoritative presence in *America*. Poirier mentions Tocqueville only as a complement to D. H. Lawrence, using both to highlight Baudrillard's pompous ineptitude. Lawrence, however, is a suspicious counterpoint, and Tocqueville is a conspicuous absence. Poirier's assertion about Baudrillard's lack of historical foundation is meant to disprove Baudrillard's claim that America possesses neither history nor culture. Lawrence, though, is guilty of Baudrillard's crime as well: "Americans don't know what they want to be, but they know what they're not" (10). What they are not, according to Lawrence, is European. "They came to get away from everything they are and have been" (9). "Democracy in America," he continues, "is just a tool with which the old master of Europe, the European spirit, is undermined" (14). American democracy was a "false dawn" (14), a wrongheaded illusion that society could be filled with masterless individuals. Baudrillard does not simply accept this illusory quality—he pushes it to its extreme.

Tocqueville, though, is Baudrillard's true reference point. Aside from committing the occasional out-of-context embarrassment—Poirier might find Tocqueville's observation that there are "no peasants in America" (*Democracy* 342), and "no poets" (485), equally as damning as Baudrillard's "no cops" reference—de Tocqueville might be subject to Poirier's deeper suspicions that he finds an absence of history in order to substantiate his own visions about the hollowness of the future. Tocqueville finds "no tradition, no common beliefs" (473) in America; whereas immigrants came to America "with the germ of a complete democracy" (331), they were, in a sense, reborn as Americans through their experience in settling a "new," open land, empty and wild, in forming a revolutionary society without a typical revolution, but a revolution of mores. American history vanishes in the whirl of a new society, a society born in motion, each individual exercising his equality in a constant state of displacement, a search for space of his own. "In the United States," writes Tocqueville, "society had no infancy, being born adult" (303). Baudrillard senses the same kind of radical, spontaneous birth—Americans are "born modern, they do not become so" (73)—and finds its effects have left Americans addicted to simulation, caught in the vacuum of their own lack of history, forced to create a history and culture out of the material objects that are the source of their desires. Tocqueville, too, finds that Americans have "only come into the world to gain affluence and the comforts of life" (*Journey* 366).

Later in the same journey through the wilderness, Tocqueville spends an abnormal amount of verbiage on "an almost lyrical meditation on the appearance of the virgin forest" (Shiner 194)—a digression that Poirier would find as distasteful as Baudrillard's "lyrical descriptions of the deserts," which to Poirier seem offensive in their symbolic existence as "evidence that the country as a whole consists in its very landscape only of space waiting to be filled by Baudrillard's thought" (3). Tocqueville's "meditations," as well as his more grounded writing, consistently evoke comparisons—both symbolic and literal—that place Poirier in the awkward position of reconsidering the value of metaphors as indicators of a society's nature. Tocqueville doesn't make Poirier's burden any lighter with the subjects of his comparisons: the forest and the desert; the wilderness and the "natural, quiet growth of civilization" (*Journey* 32); the supernatural and the material; the death of nature and the death of civilization. "Comparison and antithesis," writes Shiner, "are the dominant rhetorical devices" (196) in Tocqueville's prose.

America is a conscious attempt to exploit and expand the same devices, the same images that Tocqueville left floating. For Poirier to remain unaware of such a large contribution to Baudrillard's work seems a grave, if deft, oversight. Tocqueville is relieved of such scrutiny perhaps because he did not presume to bear the same methodological burden as Baudrillard. Though both pursued a vision of the future in America, Tocqueville went to America to examine a new social form, and Baudrillard went to experience a predetermined social theory. In a very literal sense, Baudrillard is traveling through a country that is his own creation. As he "disappears" into the desert, he senses the "mental desert form" expanding "before your very eyes"; this is the "purified form of social desertification" (5). The journey into the desert of America is as much a mental process as a physical one, perhaps more so. Baudrillard cannot shake the immensity, the indifference of the deserts and of the cities; the deserts do not simply influence their surroundings, but—in his mind—they take on the form of civilization, they "form the mental frontier where the projects of civilization run into the ground" (63).

America is perhaps best defined not as a portrait of the country, but as a portrait of the man trying to portray the country, struggling to communicate an urgent, fearful message. The same can be said of Tocqueville, though his prose and method seem comparatively structured and methodical. His descriptions show flashes of instinctual images and sensations that betray an undercurrent of a more lyrical, symbolic sense of concern. It is a sense that Baudrillard takes as his own and—in his words—mutates, rather than changes, as the country has mutated. It is a particular image of conflict and paradox, of the real and the implied America that ripples beneath Tocqueville's prose, an image developed unconsciously by Tocqueville. It is an image that Baudrillard willingly gives full expression to, reintroducing Tocqueville to the outer limits of his own instincts.

"One's soul," Tocqueville wrote during his "Fortnight in the Wilds," "is shaken by contradictory thoughts and feelings" (*Journey* 372). It is difficult to read his description without sensing the constant rendering of instincts that he struggles to define: Even the title can be translated with equal accuracy as "A Fortnight in the Desert." Though "desert" and "wilderness" seem to be disparate images, Tocqueville uses the two interchangeably, both being subsumed under nature. In his earlier "Journey to Lake Oneida," he finds the forest filled with "a solemn silence," and remarks, "man is missing, but this is no desert." Minutes later, he encounters a "dwelling cleared like an oasis in the desert" (*Journey* 322) and the reader wonders which image Tocqueville wants taken seriously. What appears to be reckless symbolism, however, is meant to stress what Shiner calls the polarities within Tocqueville's "metaphysical context" (197). Tocqueville seems to have spent parts of the fortnight traveling through Baudrillard's "mental frontier." The forest's "sombre savage majesty strikes a religious terror" (*Journey* 321) in his soul; he admires the "sublime horror of the scene," where "so deep a silence, so complete a calm, prevailed in these forests," so that "all the forces of nature were paralyzed" (352). Engulfed by the forest's dark, moody "solemn silence" he envisions a grand battle between the "majestic order" of the "dome of vegetation" above him, and the strange, chaotic death surrounding him (322, 356, 321).

The forest floor's static violence holds a particular fascination for Tocqueville. At one point, struck by the aforementioned "religious terror," he "sees nothing but a field of violence and destruction...everything testifies that the elements are here at war." Then, in a sudden about face, "the struggle is interrupted. One would say that at the behest of a supernatural power, movement is suddenly halted" (*Journey* 357). His own sense of the impending revolution, of the onset of civilization, turns nature into a symbolic predecessor to the new form of life sweeping its way through the wilderness. The silence of the forest prods Tocqueville's instincts—he senses a wild, chaotic life within nature, a supernatural force, but one that will inevitably suffer a unique death at the hands of civilization. He sees "many generations of the dead lying side by side"; he witnesses "life and death meeting face to face"; he shouts and his echo is "the silence of the dead" (356, 353). The power of nature, of the forest and the "wildest open spaces," is in its overwhelming silence, its simultaneous indifference and "creative force" (328).

The violence, the battle, the death, are as much a product of Tocqueville's imaginative senses as of his surroundings. He does not simply journey through the wilderness, just as Baudrillard does not simply travel through the desert: He uses the natural as a counterpoint, a symbol, and a model for the unnatural and for civilization. The wilderness is a separate world, filled with laws and procedures of its own. "In the solitudes of America nature in all her strength is the only instrument of ruin and also the only creative force." These he distinguishes from "forests subject to man's control," but in both, "death strikes continually" (356). The death in man's forests, however, is more disturbing, as it involves more than a figurative conflict, but a real, immediate one, that of the "triumphant march" of civilization encountering "forceful, wild nature," and experiencing a mutual destruction that leaves both forces changed. The forest does not die a literal death—it vanishes symbolically and reappears in Tocqueville's descriptions of civilization.

Tocqueville, however, does not want to predict, and does not claim to observe, at least not overtly, what Baudrillard would later term America's "social desertification." His imagery is beyond his control, beyond his understanding. He makes remarkable allusions to the forest resembling both the desert and the ocean, often simultaneously. An emigrant's dwelling, to him, "forms a little world of its own. It is an ark of civilization lost in the middle of an ocean of leaves, it is a sort of oasis in the desert" (356). Baudrillard writes, "The secret of this whole stretch of country is perhaps that it was once an underwater relief and has retained the surrealist qualities of an ocean bed in open air" (3). Tocqueville struggles to communicate his instincts, searching for appropriate images, and then finding himself unsure of their implications. Toward the end of the fortnight he makes a last attempt at communicating the immense, otherworldly power of nature:

> The universe seems before your eyes to have reached a perfect equilibrium; there the soul half asleep hovers between the present and the future, between the real and the possible, while with natural beauty all around, and the air tranquil and mild, at peace with himself in the midst of a universal peace, man listens to the even beating of his arteries that seems to him to mark the passage of time flowing drop by drop through eternity." (*Journey* 371)

Then, turning sober and needing to account for such an unusually long digression into the cosmic, he warns, "Many men will not understand" his experience. It is not an overstatement to say that Baudrillard did understand it; Tocqueville's out-of-character passage only hints at the tone that Baudrillard sustains throughout *America*.

Tocqueville's character is just as prone to sweeping generalizations of civilization's alignment with Providence, of man's "natural greatness," and of the inevitability of the democratic revolution of mores (which, in any case, "assumes the existence of a civilized, knowledgeable society") (*Democracy* 208). "The whole world here," he wrote to Ernest de Chabrol, "seems like a malleable material that man turns and fashions to his liking" (*Letters* 392). He prefaces his description of the forest's "universal peace" with a more ambiguous tribute to the wilderness' "flowering solitude, delightful and scented; a magnificent dwelling, a living palace built for man, but to which its master has not yet reached" (*Journey* 371). Tocqueville does not exploit the master-servant image—"Fortnight," in fact, becomes a sad farewell to proud, wild nature. He stands aside to let the "march of civilization" pass and feels at once "proud to be a man," and regretful "at the power that God has granted us over nature" (372). The meeting of two forms guided by forces (the supernatural, Providence) beyond their control seems to result in one replacing the other.

The transformation, however, is not so one-sided, despite Tocqueville's occasional black-and-white references. "The forest was felled; solitude turned to life," (328) he states bluntly at the beginning of "Fortnight," as if with the introduction of the civilized world the natural world is extinguished, the noisy life of civilization having replaced the silence of the dead. He still senses the power of nature, though with *Democracy,* he filters out the infrequent flashes of nature-inspired lyricism and concentrates on the social and political form of democracy. He sounds more like a journalist than a melancholy observer when he reports, "Immutable Nature herself seems on the move, so greatly is she daily transformed by man" (328). In both *Journey* and *Democracy,* his sense of nature's place in the civilized world must be found in his descriptions of the civilized man, the modern society. During the fortnight, he comes upon the village of Saginaw, "a sort of observation post" of civilization, and calls the society "a scarcely formed embryo, a growing seed entrusted to the wilds, which the wilds must fertilize" (*Journey* 365).

Frederick Jackson Turner used this theme sixty years later as the core of his proof that Americans are, quite literally, products of the frontier. He detailed the transformation: "The environment is at first too strong for the man. He must accept the conditions which it furnishes, or perish, and so he fits himself into the Indian clearings and follows the Indian trails. Little by little he transforms the wilderness" (201), and finally becomes not a deformed European but a strong, individualistic American. Turner's example is not mentioned to accuse Tocqueville of employing the same process, but to suggest that Tocqueville's most subtle imagery—not the polar "nature dies, civilization lives" process—stays with him throughout. Turner's description lends nature a more tangible power that Tocquequeville expressed more unconsciously. Tocqueville watches "the most civilized of Europeans" become "a worshipper of savage life," though "still remaining a Frenchman" (*Journey* 365). Significantly, Tocqueville uses passive sentence structures to describe the process: he "has been snatched away," "has been transplanted," "has been inflamed by new sights." This is a curious way to describe what would seem to be an active transformation—it is as if Tocqueville wants to show the subtle, silent power of nature, the static action he observed in the forest. Still, this man is to be distinguished from the "emigrant from the United States" who, instead of giving himself up to nature, engages in "continual contest" (*Journey* 366) against it. This is not a quick, decisive battle—it is "man struggling with nature hand to hand" (325). So while Tocqueville predicts "the noise of civilization will break the Saginaw," civilization's echo, like the echo of Tocqueville's own shouts, "will be silent," the silence of the dead, the continuation of the struggle (372).

Civilization, despite its ties to Providence, and despite its natural, irrepressible greatness, clearly is not flawless for Tocqueville. The civilization he observes in "Fortnight" is "a nation of conquerors that submits to living the life of a savage without ever letting itself be carried away by its charms, that only cherishes those parts of civilization and enlightenment which are useful for well-being." "Like all great peoples," he continues, they "press forward to the acquisition of riches, with a scorn of life" (*Journey* 340). The Indian, then, is not "great," but is as savage as the wilderness, since the wilderness transfers its primitive state onto those not strong enough to resist it. Once, traveling through the wilderness, "where everything is ready to receive man," Tocqueville suffers a break in his will as well: He feels "a vague distaste for civilized life; a sort of primitive instinct that makes one think with sadness that soon this delightful solitude will have changed its looks" (348).

Baudrillard, 150 years later, calls America "the last primitive society"; accuses it of possessing a transparent, empty history; complains that it is inhabited by cold, indifferent, object-obsessed individuals; and sees its character in the "irony of geology." Tocqueville's journey is both frozen in time and accelerated:

Baudrillard heightens every conscious effect of equality, every unconscious effect of nature, that Tocqueville observed and places it on the flat, empty, perpetual-motion surface of the desert. Americans are still banal, possess unremarkable intelligence, see only what is useful to themselves, and are filled with a sameness that renders their identities meaningless. Baudrillard looks to the desert to express this, rather than to the country's moral and political state. He wonders briefly what happened to Tocqueville's revolution of mores, but admits that that is not his concern, that he simply does not know what happened, that, indeed, the state of the country's mores is meaningless in its depth. Tocqueville finds that, with democracy, "the darting speed of a quick, superficial mind is at a premium, while slow, deep thought is excessively undervalued" (*Democracy* 461). In this state, mores become irrelevant, as all action takes place on the superficial level and, Baudrillard would add, anything deeper becomes more meaningless through the country's pervading irony.

Baudrillard recalls Tocqueville's paradox of equality producing equally forceful tendencies toward "insignificance" and "originality"; he only feels responsible for noting that the dilemma has been "multiplied by geographical extension." He then restates it in his own (italicized) terms: "*This is a world that has shown genius in its irrepressible development of equality, banality, and indifference*" (89). The italics seem somewhat out of place: It is more of an anticlimax than a revelation to observe that America has grown over the past century and a half, and that the tendencies exhibited at its birth have become as bloated and disfigured as its size. This is exactly Baudrillard's point: Nothing, he says, has changed: "To land in America is, even today, to land in that 'religion' of the way of life which Tocqueville described. The material utopia of the way of life, where success and action are seen as profound illustrations of the moral law, was crystallized by exile and emigration and these have, in a sense, transformed it into a primal scene" (75). America, born modern, has remained the same since: ironically primitive, single-mindedly pursuing the hollow goals of wealth, ignoring the existence of nature, culture, history, or society.

America begins and ends with "space and the spirit of fiction" (181), the sense of the unreal, the faith in the unnatural. This spirit is a product of its own obsession, its own power of creation, and its own dramatic displacement: its wish to get away from what it once was. Knowing nothing and admiring nothing but its own creations, it willingly creates itself over and over again, pretending the repetition is the creation of "something more real." "Democratic peoples may amuse themselves momentarily by looking at nature," wrote Tocqueville, "but it is about themselves that they are really excited" (*Democracy* 484). They live, he said, "in a state of perpetual self-adoration." Ironically—thus appropriately, since everything that makes up America revolves around its self-created meaninglessness, its illusory character as a social desert—this unnatural state is now best understood through geology, the crowning example of the most natural and primitive of elements made into an object, an empty symbol. The reliefs of the desert, writes Baudrillard, "because they are no longer natural, give the best idea of what a culture is" (3).

American civilization is not a product of nature in the direct sense—Americans did not experience Turner's step-by-step transformation, nor did they come to master nature. Their mastery, their power, is illusory, since it is another one of their creations—it bears no relation to reality, to the real state of nature or society. America is a trip through a timeless, infinite illusion, one that affects everything within its reach. The mountains, the desert, are real outside America—Baudrillard sees them with European eyes and knows they exist—but within America they become part of the fiction, the most extreme fiction, since they were once the most extreme reality. The competitive, individualistic Americans saw nature, and their first instinct was not to destroy it but to match it, to reproduce it in their own form, to master it by recreating it. The vision of "subduing nature...of diverting rivers, drying up marshes, plays a real part in the actions of every man" (*Democracy* 485), writes Tocqueville. "A human race," says Baudrillard, "has to invent sacrifices equal to the natural cataclysmic order that surrounds it" (3). Nature cannot be nature on its own—it has to be nature as created and defined by humans.

This, of course, is a paradox: Nature becomes unnatural while America—its cities, its civilization, its society—is unnatural but exhibits all the characteristics of nature, of Tocqueville's cold, indifferent, supernaturally immense and silent wilderness. In Tocqueville's wilderness, "nothing awakens thoughts of the past or of the future" (*Journey* 364); in his civilization, "it is the interest of the moment that prevails" (*Democracy* 264). In Baudrillard's America, civilization and nature absorb each other to create an image and a reality of the "perpetual present, perpetual simulation." The two worlds—natural and unnatural—meet and, instead of repelling, perform what Baudrillard calls "a stunning fusion of a radical lack of culture and natural beauty...this mixture of extreme irreferentiality and deconnection overall, but embedded on most primeval and great-featured natural scenery of deserts and ocean and sun" (128).

"In America," writes Tocqueville, "there is one society only....One goes without transition from the wilds into the street of a city, from the most savage scenes to the most smiling aspects of a civilization" (*Journey* 333). Society has been "levelled out" by equality, both in terms of mores, laws, and political and legal structures, and in a vision of absolute barrenness, an erasing of culture and history and meaning. For Baudrillard, "culture has to be a desert so that everything can be equal and shine out in the same supernatural form" (126). There is no difference between a desert and a city, the peak of civilization. The "sight of such universal uniformity chills me," (*Democracy* 704) Tocqueville writes of civilized America. He worries too that, with equality, individuals lose their power, and if they do not learn to gain it through forming associations they will "soon fall back into barbarism" (514); Baudrillard claims this prophecy was fulfilled at their birth. They never progressed from the state of nature they encountered in the wilderness, in the desert—their only motion was the hurried pursuit of their own empty desires.

As ominous as the desertification of civilization is—with Tocqueville it is only an unconscious warning—with Baudrillard it is, simply, the state of the model modern society. "This country has no hope," he writes; the cycle that America runs on, creates, and cannot see, is sufficiently tied in to the cosmic abstraction of geology that it cannot be altered by human intervention (37). Americans "have lost the formula for stopping" (39). One cannot hope to change America—one can only hope to contain it. Most frightening about Baudrillard's vision is its similarity in nature to that of Tocqueville's democratic revolution. Americans "attained democracy without the sufferings of a democratic revolution, and they were born equal instead of becoming so" (509). The real revolution—the revolution of mores—occurred within the people before its expression in the American Revolution.

The democratic revolution was subversive, occurring without the knowledge of the participants, but unable to proceed without them. It was a slow, creeping revolution, the seeds of which came, in part, from Europe, but which ultimately took form in America, in the search for space, the agitated desire to be masterless, to find an equality defined only by the self. More than this, it was inevitable, irresistible, irrefutable.

Baudrillard calls his journey "the irreversible advance into the desert of time" (11); from its origins, as from the country's, *America* is touched with the sense of a process that is infinitely finite. The signs, to Baudrillard, are everywhere: The smiles of Americans are "the equivalent of the primal scream of the man alone in the world," "the smile the dead man will wear in his funeral home"; the sight of a "man preparing his meal in public" provokes the thought that "he who eats alone is dead"; the villas of Santa Barbara are "like funeral homes" (33, 34, 15, 30). He comes across a "dwelling" in the city, and it fills him with a sadness so deep and so empty that he writes, "everything here testifies to death having found its ideal home" (31).

These are not random, flashing signs, but fixed parts of the cycle in which "everything is destined to reappear as simulation" (32). They are the whirling atoms within the desert's nuclear form, but their motion is stagnant, meaningless, and hollow. The signs—people—are unaware of their nature, too obsessed with their own fictions. That which they create is swallowed up by its own emptiness. "The paradox of this society," writes Baudrillard, "is that you cannot die in it any more since you are already dead" (42). As Americans create the uncreatable—nature—it vanishes from their reality; so too do Americans disappear into the desert of their unique creation, *democratic civilization*.

Works Cited

Baudrillard, Jean. *America*. London: Verso, 1988.

Lawrence, David Herbert. "The Spirit of Place." *Studies in Classical Literature*. Harmondsworth: Penguin, 1977. 7–14

Poirier, Richard. "America Deserta." *London Review of Books*. 16 February 1989. 3–6.

Shiner, Louis. *The Secret Mirror*. Ithaca, NY: Cornell UP, 1988.

Tocqueville, Alexis de. *Democracy in America*. 1835. Ed. J. P. Mayer. New York: Harper & Row, 1969.

———. "A Fortnight in the Wilds." *Journey to America*. 1836. Ed. J. P. Mayer. London: Faber and Faber, 1959.

———. *Selected Letters on Politics and Society*. 1859. Ed. Roger Boesche. Berkeley: U of California P, 1985.

Turner, Frederick Jackson. *The Significance of the Frontier in American History*. Ed. Harold P. Simonson. New York: Ungar, 1963.

Willis, Sharon. "Spectacular Topographies: *Amérique's* Post Modern Spaces." Eds. Marco Diani and Catherine Ingraham. *Restructuring Architectural Theory*. Evanston: Northwestern UP, 1989. 60–69.

✥ Chapter 8

Simone de Beauvoir's America Day by Day: *Reel to Real*

Gary Totten

On January 25, 1947, Simone de Beauvoir arrived in New York at the start of a four-month speaking tour of the United States. Upon returning to France, she published the record of her American trip, *America Day by Day,* in 1952, after it first appeared in the French periodical, *Les Temps Modernes.* Similar to other French intellectuals traveling in America, such as Alexis de Tocqueville, Jean Baudrillard, or Michel Butor, Beauvoir uses her narrative to cast a critical gaze on American culture and recount how America discloses itself to her consciousness (xvii). Amidst candid commentary on New York's Bowery district and Chicago's seedy underside, the apathy of Ivy League students, the mass frigidity of American women, the South's tangible atmosphere of racism, and the American curse of superabundance, Beauvoir weaves an adventure tale of her search for an American essence. She wanders through San Francisco, New Orleans, and Santa Fe into the early morning hours searching for key experiences (usually in ethnic neighborhoods, nightclubs, or slums) that will unlock each city's secrets. Beauvoir accumulates these impressions, which become clearer as her trip progresses (xvii), in order to decode America and test her assumptions about American culture, making her journey a version of what Kris Lackey terms "deep-travel": the penetration of "pastoral surfaces and the superficies of ethnic and regional stereotype to examine latent economic and cultural tectonics" (30). In her version of deep travel, Beauvoir does not comment on the sources of economic and cultural production, however; indeed, she admits in her preface that she manages to spend four months in America without experiencing its factories, and without meeting its working class population or its political and economic elite (xvii). Similar to what Lackey suggests Theodore Dreiser accomplishes in *A Hoosier Holiday* (1916), Beauvoir reverses the notion of deep travel, rendering visual details and sensations with astonishing acuity, relying on her impressions of intellectual and social trends, material objects, and cinematic images to comprehend American culture. In her 1952 review of the text, Mary McCarthy notes that to Beauvoir America was literally "movieland" (44), and Beauvoir's narrative ultimately reveals that her assumptions about American cultural reality are largely filtered through the lens of American cinema, a perspective which both facilitates and complicates her access to authentic American experience.

Disembarking at the Paris airport, Beauvoir indicates that she sees her journey to the United States as both physical and ontological. While she views most of her travels as attempts to attach a "new object" to her experience, she senses, as she departs for the United States, that she is leaving her old self completely behind. The flight itself portends this effect. In the air, she feels as if she has "escaped" herself: The earth seems to retreat to the "bottom of an alien ether," which she characterizes as both "nowhere" and "elsewhere" (3). Beauvoir's observations parallel Frances Bartkowski's suggestion that travelers and travel texts use language to negotiate issues of selfhood and identity in relation to movement and cultural dislocation to an "elsewhere." "Travel, or mobility between here, there, and elsewhere, seems to seduce new selves into being," contends Bartkowski (86). Beauvoir clearly assumes that her trip to America will initiate a complete remaking of her self. Her sense of estrangement leaves her feeling disembodied, and is most pronounced when she first arrives in New York. During the plane's descent into New York City, Beauvoir is reminded of her physicality: Her temples throb; her eardrums hurt. At first, she is merely "a gaze, an expectation," but her physical discomfort reveals that she possesses a body of "separate and ill-fitting parts" (4). While these physical discomforts remind her of her body, when she looks out at the city below, she is once again only a gaze, and describes what she sees as a glittering array of gemstones, "ruby fruits, topaz flowers, and diamond rivers" (4). Beauvoir's response reflects the "voluptuous pleasure" of "looking down" and "seeing the whole," which Michel de Certeau ascribes to the voyeur's experience atop New York City's World Trade Center. According to Certeau, elevation and distance "transfigure" the spectator into a voyeur: "It transforms the bewitching world by which one was 'possessed' into a text that lies before one's eyes. It allows one to read it, to be a solar Eye, looking down like a god. The exaltation of a scopic and gnostic drive: the fiction of knowledge is related to this lust to be a viewpoint and nothing more" (92). During her descent, Beauvoir exults in her role as the all-seeing eye.

Beauvoir's totalizing gaze also generates a sense of nostalgia, for her aerial view of New York at night allows her to recall childhood memories and desires: the treasures of *The Thousand and One Nights,* merry-go-rounds, fair booths, stage sets and chandeliers at the Chatelet Theater, and jeweled clusters of glossy candy on Palm Sunday (4–5). Roland Barthes suggests that "to read" a country is first of all to perceive it in terms of the body and of memory, in terms of the body's memory....That is why childhood is the royal road by which we know a country best. Ultimately, there is no Country but childhood's" (8–9). Beauvoir's initial reading of New York through her vivid childhood memories, wearing, as

McCarthy suggests, "metaphorical goggles" (45), confirms Barthes's observations. As the narrative progresses, Beauvoir's reading of America depends on comparisons she makes between her previous experience with America's images, particularly images she recalls from American film, and the physical experience of her American trip. Ultimately, the pleasure she receives from these images, and from the act of looking itself, the "lust to be a viewpoint and nothing more," jeopardizes her ability to move from voyeur to participant.

On Beauvoir's first night in New York, the magical spectacle she observes from the air continues as she glides, as wide-eyed and full of wonder as a child, through the city's streets, whose supernatural light and feeling of order and serenity (created by the regular sequence of the traffic lights) renders the city ghostly, silent, and unreal, similar to a silent film (6). "Tomorrow New York will be a city," Beauvoir observes, but her first night is "magical" (6). Beauvoir mirrors the unreal nature of the city; she describes herself as "invisible...traveling incognito, like a phantom," wondering if she will ever be able to "reincarnate" herself in America (7). In the daylight, the city's mirage-like images fade, and the city's geometric shapes, space, and steel establish its material density (8), but it takes longer for Beauvoir herself to achieve a sense of corporeality. She fades in and out of existence like a ghost, gradually acquiring tangibility in an American reality that emerges from the dim lights and illusion of the movie house—film, she claims, helps to "anchor" her in America (74). Indeed, Beauvoir notes that movies have long represented America for her (22). She knew America first through its film images, and she still considers these black-and-white movie images as America's "real substance" (74). Thus, film is the comforting and familiar medium through which Beauvoir survives her first disorienting days in New York. However, now that she is in America, these cinematic images do not satisfy her, and she takes to the streets to experience the physicality of New York with her hands, her eyes, and her mouth. Waiting in line for movies on Broadway beginning in the morning, killing time at animated films or newsreels during the day, or mingling amongst moviegoers on crowded Forty-second Street at night allows Beauvoir to believe that she is becoming part of New York life (74). She observes that if she wants to understand New York, she must meet its citizens (10), and she claims that she becomes "embodied" by seeing and (more importantly) being seen, jostling people and making them notice her (21). The physical contact allows her to materialize: As a hairdresser massages her scalp, she loses her ghostliness: "there's a meeting between me and these hands—it's really me turning into flesh and blood" (11–12).

In addition to physical contact, Beauvoir also requires movement to achieve corporeality. She organizes the city around herself during walking tours, and acquires a geographical knowledge that allows her to believe that she is becoming psychologically and physically situated. Even so, her walking actually reveals her dislocation. Certeau notes that "To walk is to lack a place. It is the indefinite process of being absent and in search of a proper [place]" (103). Beauvoir has difficulty moving beyond this absence; as she establishes a route and revisits favorite bars, restaurants, and movie houses, she struggles to recapture the sense of the city as a whole that she experienced in the air. Certeau observes that, although walking can be "transformed into [visible] points" on a map, such mapping "has the effect of making invisible the operation that made it possible....The trace left behind is substituted for the practice." The geographical system may "transform action into legibility," notes Certeau, "but in doing so it causes a way of being in the world to be forgotten" (97). Through her wandering, Beauvoir achieves an appearance of locatedness, but the city's true "presence" continues to elude her.

Beauvoir tacitly acknowledges the "absence" inherent in wandering the city, and she seems to transform her sense of this phenomenon into a belief that she must efface her former self and identity to truly find her bearings within America's vastness. America's enormity eclipses her. The skyscrapers of Brooklyn and Manhattan exist, but she no longer exists. The city's massive scale allows her to sense what she describes as the "plenitude" of childhood, "when we're utterly absorbed by something outside ourselves" (13). Beauvoir further heightens her dislocation by differentiating her American trip from all other travel experiences, noting that she did not experience such plenitude in previous travels to Greece, Italy, Spain, or Africa, where she was able to believe that Paris was still the center of the world (13). America exists, however, as a world (not just a country) apart from Paris, a world "too dazzlingly clear" for her to comprehend (13). She attributes part of America's complexity to its conglomerate character. Beauvoir reflects that if she thinks about New York or Chicago while in Los Angeles, she has the sensation of being completely "elsewhere," but still part of the same country (113). She assumes, however, that this strange mixture of regionalism and uniformity will somehow become clearer to her. As she begins her trip, she believes that the revelation which will unlock America will occur beyond the scope of her physical existence; she is a "charmed consciousness through which the sovereign Object will reveal itself" (13–14). She insists that she will need to fashion an "American self" in order to comprehend America. When Beauvoir is with French people in America, she experiences the sensation similar to her childhood impression that nothing is "completely real"; indeed, as a child, she remembers feeling as if a glass wall existed between her and the outside world (15). She believes that her French sensibilities and perspective impede her ability to break through the glass wall now that she is traveling in America, and she attempts to create an American self by seeking out and pursuing what American films have suggested to her are authentic American experiences. Thus, for example, we find her dutifully drinking scotch until three o'clock in the morning because she considers scotch to be a key to America's reality (15).

Beauvoir senses the need to surrender to America while somehow maintaining a critical perspective on her experience. Her adventures in American movie houses reveal this tension. She attends the movies during her American trip to feed her addiction, claiming that she needs movie images "like a drug" (22), but she finds that now she is in America, narrative cinema often distracts her rather than satisfying her need to grasp American reality. She notes that while watching movies, she forgets New York (21). At one point she tries a newsreel so that a cinematic narrative will not distract her from comprehending America; yet, she only achieves the reflective engagement she desires with a film that does not completely absorb her, one insipid enough for her to remember that "This is New York, and I'm in a New York movie house" (22). Her need to experience and interpret the physical objects of American culture persists throughout the text, and she relies on the physical presence of the mailboxes, doorbells, deserts, and cowboys she has seen in American films to "flesh out" her experience of America. These images constitute the most significant traces of presence on Beauvoir's American "map," and as such, substitute for actual practice and constitute the "procedures" through which she "forgets" (Certeau 97) or misapprehends American culture.

Beauvoir's method of approaching America through its cinematic representations seems to position her as a passive spectator, contradicting existentialism's experiential stance. In her May 25, 1947, article for the *New York Times Magazine,* "An Existentialist Looks at America," Beauvoir distills the new philosophy for her American readers, emphasizing existentialism's focus on meaningful human action and humankind's need to exert itself in remaking existence and enacting a "will to live." According to Beauvoir, existentialists believe that the reality of humankind is not "hidden in the agreeable mists" of men's and women's own fancy, but exists in the physical world, and can only be discovered there (13). Beauvoir applies this philosophy to American civilization, asking whether America vindicates its citizens' existence and provides them with satisfactory reasons for living. She answers with a qualified "yes," for she finds much in American culture to facilitate an existentialist "will to live." She suggests that the "American dynamism" allows men and women to assert themselves "against the inertia of the given" (13). She notes, apparently from personal observation, that the European newly arrived in America is initially struck by the nation's "spiritedness and generosity": skyscrapers, factories, drugstores, bridges, and roads all carry on the "victorious movement of the first pioneers" (13). She discovers poetry in the drugstores and the ten-cent stores, whose grand displays of products indicate the ability to transform raw materials into clever devices designed to further human aspirations (13). However, Beauvoir believes that Americans are restricted by their inability to deal with the "enormous reality of their country"; she predicts that America will only achieve its potential when its citizens recognize themselves as "concrete individuals" and thus introduce a "real content" into American civilization (54). Beauvoir sees America in the state of innocence, described by Hegel, in which the object and the subject are not yet "divided by the pang of the unhappy consciousness" (54). The American individual needs to relinquish his "voluntary blindness," discover himself, and take the risk of living authentically "in the jeopardy and glory of his lonely freedom"; only then can America realize its potential (54). In her own attempts to grasp American reality, Beauvoir emphasizes this need for human action. Indeed, on her last night in New York City, before setting off to tour the rest of the country, she observes that the philosophical task of fashioning an American self requires that she thrust herself into the physical American world in order to attain the plenitude she imagines. She believes that "something real" must happen to her, "and the rest will follow in abundance" (72).

By documenting her personal struggles to experience the real America, Beauvoir designs her narrative as a sort of philosophical guidebook to model for Americans how they might deal with their country's enormous reality. However, while she claims in her introduction that her journey reveals America to her consciousness, at the end of the text she admits to being no more enlightened than when she began. She makes it clear that her American existence is tenuous and even illusory, briefly definable only in those moments when she is actively pursuing authentic experience. Indeed, some aspects of American culture, such as racial tension, seem ultimately inaccessible through her experience. For example, she is only able to describe the American South by referring to reading she has done on racism, specifically, *An American Dilemma,* an "authoritative" account of American blacks by the Swedish economist, Gunnar Myrdal (236–48). Beauvoir is much more successful dealing with American culture through familiar cinematic images. Thus, although she spends a great deal of time, especially early on, in American theaters passively watching movies, the cinematic images literally propel her physical and mental movement through the country, provoking fascinating comparisons between America's physical reality and its cinematic image. Her dependence on these images complicates her purpose and her journey, however. She asserts herself "against the inertia of the given" which these images represent (i.e., the screen's prepackaged and safe version of American culture) by authenticating real American experience against its screen version, suggesting that human reality is not "hidden in the agreeable mists" of fancy or cinematic illusion, but is located and revealed in the actual world. At other times, however, she privileges movie images over actual experience, making her journey more fantastic than realistic.

Often, Beauvoir's actual experiences do not measure up to their cinematic representations. For example, her disappointing meeting with Charlie Chaplin at a New York cocktail party reveals that she is more impressed with his screen persona than his physical presence. She describes the offscreen Chaplin as he defends his latest film, *Monsieur Verdoux.* At various points in his tirade against American society, Chaplin abandons his rant, using his facial expressions and entire body to act out his story. Beauvoir notes that this delightful "first-class number" is short-lived, however, and he reverts back to speech. Beauvoir watches him leave with regret, convinced that she has not "really seen" Charlie Chaplin (296–97). Beauvoir's reaction suggests that for her, the real Chaplin is the screen Chaplin, and she considers his physical presence authentic only when it approximates the silent clowning figure she has seen in film; as a mime, "he's Charlie again" (296).

Beauvoir expresses a similar preference for film images over reality when she describes screening three films in Los Angeles: *The Best Years of Our Lives, Lost Weekend,* and a special RKO studio showing of *The Ox-Bow Incident.* Beauvoir says that these three films allow her to "rediscover" on the screen New York's elevated trains and shops, the garages, drugstores, and parking lots of all the cities she has visited, the airplane repair facilities she passed outside Las Vegas, and the Nevada desert—"*and this rediscovery is an even greater pleasure than that of seeing the images themselves*" (168, emphasis added). Beauvoir's reaction to these film images illustrates how she privileges cinematic representation over reality; indeed, at one point she notes that she regards the screen as a "platonic heaven" that allows her to comprehend the pure Idea of America, a concept only approximated in its physical objects (74). While these images initially promise her access to a pure American essence, she later concedes that American film cannot adequately represent American social reality. America is unable to express itself, Beauvoir complains, while considering how film censorship, the star system, a fear of the truth, and, perhaps above all, capitalism, prevents most American screenplays from living up to their potential (172). She observes that the actual lives of Americans never appear in film. Movies construct a "papier-mâché America" in which only the physical landscapes and material objects seem real. Although Beauvoir believes that literature has not yet been affected in this way, she considers the cinema, which she assumes has more direct ties to capitalism, effectually silenced (173). After screening a documentary about the pursuit of happiness in America, Beauvoir notes that the film confirms her suspicion that only in consumer product posters and advertisements do Americans actually have the "round cheeks, radiant smiles, calm gazes, and faces glowing with good conscience" (63). Beauvoir concludes that Americans would be much better off if they did accept that there is unhappiness in the world, and that such unhappiness is not necessarily bad (64). She seems to believe that film could facilitate such a vision, but in its present state, fettered by American capitalism, it is unable to do so.

Beauvoir's critical attitude toward American film gradually develops during her stay, and after being in America for three months, her respect for American cinema begins to fade. She discovers the pleasure in watching a film that is not American, observing how Anna Magnani's sensual performance in *Rome, Open City* contrasts with the frigidity of American women and the "hygienic" attitude fostered in America toward sexual relations and functions as an antidote for the ineffectual Hollywood heroines whom American women idealize (334). Beauvoir's reaction to this film, and the English film, *Odd Man Out,* again leads her to criticize the inability of American film to accurately represent America. At this point in her travels, when she comes out of an American film to walk in New

York's streets, she sees with a more experienced eye, indignant that the street's picturesque poetry is not expressed in film. She claims that foreign directors would have expressed American social reality: Marcel Carné would have captured the "blond brides smiling in the mists of the Bowery"; Grémillon would have shown us the East River's ships, ferryboats, and fish crates at dusk. We would have seen the silent tramps along Chicago's nighttime streets, and the bars of the city's underside would have been more startling than the Western saloons we usually encounter in American film (334). Beauvoir refers to scenes she has personally encountered during her American travels, further confirming that the text functions as a philosophical tour book for Americans, with Beauvoir as the tour director who seems to ask, "Why haven't you been able to see as I've seen?" Apparently, American movies, like American citizens, do not possess the ability to interpret or express America's overwhelming cultural reality, but Beauvoir sees no reason why this must remain so. New York, Chicago, and New Orleans could be given as much cinematic presence as London, Paris, or Rome and American movies made into "great art" (335). Beauvoir's desire for social realism in contemporary American film is perhaps a little unreasonable, considering the climate of fear and suspicion generated by the McCarthy hearings at that time, one of which Beauvoir attends while in New York.

She believes film's inability to reflect American social problems and conditions is further revealed in San Antonio, where Disney's *Song of the South* is playing. For Beauvoir, the film attempts to disguise real social problems under a thin veneer of visual spectacle. The film's animated images hardly counteract "the irritation and disgust provoked by this insipid story in Technicolor: the greens and russets of the idyllic countryside hardly conceal the hatred, injustice, and fear in which they are rooted" (208). Although the screen's anemic representation of America's cultural drama disappoints Beauvoir, she values the accurate depiction of landscapes and material details in American film. These images fascinate her and stir her memory; indeed they mesmerize her much like her initial childlike reaction to New York City's visual delights. Film's realistic portrayal of physical objects allows Beauvoir to recognize those objects when she encounters them in the actual world, and provides her with a useful anchoring device: The details function as visual moorings from which she can launch cultural commentary and interpretation. Her experience with these American objects also provides her with a sense of cultural expertise; her contact with such objects allows her to believe that she is turning native, becoming "a little American" (334).

For example, Beauvoir claims that since being in America, the exoticism of American drugstores, streets, elevators, and doorbells has disappeared and she views these items now as simply realistic details; however, she considers this realism "more poetic than any invention." The screen transfigures ordinary objects, and reestablishes the distance between herself and American culture that allows her to reflect (74). Even so, she is unable to actually comprehend the cultural significance of a drugstore until she visits one. The physical experience produces real cultural insight: Drugstores represent a simultaneous primitivism and modernity, descending from the general stores of the Old West where pioneers procured all the "necessities of life" (18). Ultimately, the drugstore represents the height of American poetry for Beauvoir; its products establish the nation's cheerful, though perhaps naive, cultural norm which, she concludes, has existed for centuries.

Thus, throughout the narrative, film works in tandem with physical reality to conjure Beauvoir's America. The physical presence of filmed objects moves her perspective of American material culture from exoticism to realism, but it becomes clear that American reality actually renders itself more "poetic," and unrealistic, through the comparison. Not long after she arrives in New York, she notes how disconcerting it is to find that the movie sets that she had "never really believed in" are now real (12). Mere place-names conjure up film images to compare to the actual scene. Wondering how she can experience Chicago in a short thirty-six hours, she thinks of the fascination of its name, and her memories of gangster stories fill her with expectation. She enters California on a train in a damp gray fog, reflecting how the name "California" is "almost as magical as 'New York.'" Since the fog blurs her vision, she considers the California of her imagination, a state that, through the movies, has become a legendary place where pioneers and cowboys walk streets paved in gold (107). On an excursion with the director, George Stevens, to Lone Pine, California, where Stevens shot *Gunga Din,* Beauvoir is surprised at the simultaneous magnificence of Mount Whitney (used to represent the Alps, the Himalayas, and the Caucasus in film) and the diminutive dimensions of a large plain on which an army marched in *Gunga Din* (a cinematic vastness achieved through camera angles, according to Stevens). Only steps away are African sand dunes and the Australian bush. Beauvoir is astonished that this "false Tibet" and "illusory Switzerland" exist as real landscapes (154). Later, in Death Valley, where von Stronheim made the final scenes of *Greed,* Beauvoir suggests that the old epics have never seemed so unreal to her than here where they actually occurred. She notes that cowboys, sheriffs, buffalo herds, horses, mountain passes, and desert towns enchant her because she recognizes them from film. However, the desert's actual boundlessness shocks her; the valley's depth frightens her. No landscape has seemed so overwhelming as these vast desert vistas, and the physical effect of the landscape inspirits the film itself. By physically "touching" the movie images and witnessing the "startling truth of the setting," Beauvoir says, "the drama itself becomes real: I believe in the agony of von Stronheim's heroes" (157). The realness of the physical experience heightens cinematic reality, making it difficult for Beauvoir to determine which representation is the most real.

The narrative is riddled with further examples revealing how the distinction between film and reality becomes increasingly blurred for Beauvoir. Traveling with her friend, Nathalie Sorokine Moffatt, from Sacramento to Reno, Beauvoir passes through Placerville and various ghost towns, and is delighted to see land-scapes that she had only imagined through movies and books. She reports that the discovery of these places moves her as much as if she had turned a bend in the road and come upon Sleeping Beauty's castle. She notes that this is where the figures that peopled her childhood dreams actually lived, where, for exam-ple, Chaplin filmed *The Gold Rush* (145). Once in Reno, Beauvoir is fascinated by the clubs, which she enters through swinging doors like the ones she has seen in Westerns. The gritty and authentic clientele interest her the most, a group so visually captivating that they remind her of "movie extras." Apparently, though, this is too much raw realism, even for the movies, and Beauvoir notes that the most skilled director could not have conjured this much reality; the scene is too "authentic" (147).

When they resume their road trip and, just after crossing Devil's Gate pass in California, are pulled over by a sheriff, complete with a big hat and badge, Beauvoir notes that "the most famous character in all Westerns" has stepped off the screen to accost them (151–52). In Las Vegas, Beauvoir walks into a lavish and gaudy club and immediately notes that it evokes gangster hangouts she has seen in the movies. She imagines Edward G. Robinson drinking whiskey in the smoky room, sporting sideburns, and lounging in an armchair (159–60). Travel-ing toward Albuquerque, the bus comes within a few miles of the Petrified For-est, where Beauvoir's ability to distinguish between film images and the physical landscape is again compromised. She wishes she could have seen the forest be-cause of the film by the same name that she liked so much, and which intro-duced her to this landscape. She suggests that the film's "magic" is no longer instilled in just a word or place, but has been internalized into her being; al-though the visual idea of the Forest infatuates her, the physical presence of the fossils themselves interests her very little (181). Later, at a Santa Fe party, she has the sensation that she is in a movie comedy routine, noting that the arrival of guests into the early morning hours reminds her of a scene from the Marx Brothers's *Night at the Opera,* where people crowd into a small cabin (196–97). She finds herself on a movie set again when she steps off the Greyhound in Pe-cos, Texas, and suggests that the bus is a time machine that has transported her to a village from an old Western movie. In a Pecos lunchroom, she finds tanned cowboys in big hats, leather pants, and boots, all "young, manly, and handsome, like Tom Mix." "Once again," says Beauvoir, "we think we're in the movies" (201). Beauvoir has internalized these images into her consciousness; the visual impact of such images, not the actual fossils, casinos, or cowboys themselves, seduce her into believing that she is experiencing the real America.

Because Beauvoir recreates the movies in her American journey, the trip re-mains in the realm of fantasy. Indeed, fantasy becomes difficult to distinguish from physical reality as cowboys walk off the screen to eat with her in Nevada or scold her for speeding in the California desert. Beauvoir is in search of the real America, but she relies on film images to validate the realness of what she sees and experiences, problematizing the authenticity of her trip. "America is nowhere" (126), she realizes at one point, but she believes that she occasionally touches that reality. For example, while Beauvoir listens to her friend's record collection of cowboy and pioneer songs in California, the music seems to escape the limits of time and space, and she imagines that at least for a brief moment that night, the music captures something ephemeral out of the air and gives it to her (126). She also believes that she has gained access to authentic American experience at the Savoy in New York City where, with Richard and Ellen Wright, she experiences jazz at the one place in the world where it can "fully express its truth." Listening to jazz or watching blacks dance in Paris seemed to promise her a "more complete reality," which seems fulfilled in New York. At the Savoy, she feels as if she has "come out of the cave," to experience the "fullness" that "allows the surrendered soul to contemplate a pure Idea" (39). Similarly, she also feels that she has really experienced Houston when a professor takes her to a "typically American" wrestling match (215). After the fight and a visit to a Houston bar decorated with giant bull horns, photos of prize bulls and cows, and a covered wagon, Beauvoir goes to sleep assured that, through her experience, Houston's secrets have been revealed to her (216).

Cinema has taken Beauvoir to America before, and these preconceptions remind us of the texts upon which she relies to read America. McCarthy is correct when she observes that Beauvoir "does not [really] wish to know America but only to ascertain that it is there, just as she had imagined it" (46). Bartkowski suggests that the travel writer's reference to the texts which have allowed him or her to name and preconceive of a place demonstrates the ways in which travelers differ from explorers (21). Beauvoir's passionate search for authentic American experience reveals her desire to function as an explorer, hoping to recreate that pioneer spirit which the skyscrapers and drugstores represent. As much as Beauvoir tries to lose herself in American culture, however, she is perpetually distanced by her reliance on cinema. Like a promise unfulfilled, Beauvoir's cinematically produced preconceptions about America draw her into pseudo-realistic encounters with American life, ultimately barring her access to authentic experience. She wishes to represent herself as the explorer, but she is ultimately too much the tourist, consuming America through its film image and natural spectacle with the same detachment that she finds distasteful in other tourists. For example, she is disgusted by the way that natural wonders such as the Grand Canyon and Niagara Falls are turned into consumer products. Through reflective panes of glass which "absorb the overly intense light" in a Grand Canyon visitor's center, Beauvoir finds that a mediated and softened vision replaces a clear view, which would be "raw and violent" (178). Similar to Americans' affinity for canned, homogenized, and artificial consumer products, this mediated view of the landscape offers the tourist an unnatural method to subdue nature's unrestrained spectacle. Americans love nature, Beauvoir observes, but only if it has been "inspected and corrected" first by human beings (179). Even so, traveling through the desert between Las Vegas and Los Angeles, the road's visual spectacle, generated by the same mechanisms of tourism evident at Niagara and the Grand Canyon, is suddenly acceptable and delightful. She is infatuated with the gas stations and inns along the road, and she is charmed by the fact that this all exists solely for her and her fellow tourists. Beauvoir notes tourism's privileged status in America: "[I]t doesn't cut you off from the country it's revealing to you; on the contrary, it's a way of entering it...the average American [unlike the European] devotes a great part of his leisure time to driving along the highways. The gas stations, roads, hotels, and solitary inns exist only for the tourist and because of the tourist, and...are profoundly part of America" (164–65). Beauvoir believes that she experiences a sense of intimacy with America on the road. She characterizes America as a nation of travelers, defined by movement, and she feels a certain communion among American tourists functioning as tourists in America. "By traveling in America, I'm not distanced from it," she observes (165). If there is authenticity in her American journey, she seems to attain it while enjoying American tourism with "native tourists." Capitalism, tourism, and America's overexposure in the cinema may have scripted her trip, but it is also apparent that it is a script that cannot be duplicated elsewhere. Similar to her need to walk around New York City when she first arrives in the country, her physical movement through the desert gives her a sense of geographical and psychological locatedness, but never a complete access to American experience. Like her fellow American travelers, Beauvoir cannot penetrate past the forces of tourism, the film image, and capitalism. Ultimately, Beauvoir fails to comprehend America because her prescripted notions of American culture establish a glass wall between her self and her experience as surely as the Grand Canyon visitor's center mediates the tourist's view of the landscape. The traces of these visual texts, through which she maps America, deny her the presence she desires.

Indeed, Beauvoir really seems no more successful grasping America than her French counterparts whom she accuses of viewing the country through a glass wall. Her desire for authentic and real contact is thwarted by the insertion of these visual screens between herself and her experiences that form a protected voyeurism through which she objectifies America. Beauvoir attempts to pursue a less mediated perception of America through forms of practice, but she is continually seduced by film. Whenever she attempts to travel into the alien territory of America, filmed images appear as distracting memories, blocking her ability to truly see, and exposing her as an outsider. Back in New York near the end of her journey, she receives a vivid sense of her outsider status. She observes a native New Yorker watching, as she is, the setting sun, and realizes that, although she wants to believe that she is as much a part of the city as he, such impressions are only illusions. She remains on the outside, a spectator. Her perspective undergoes a dramatic change when compared with her first impressions: New York becomes an overwhelming, opaque, and resistant reality rather than a "mirage" for her to "convert into a city of flesh and blood." She recognizes that in order to know such reality she will have to "give" herself to it, finally a transformation more radical than she is willing to make: "To be a visitor, a traveler—that is my fate here" (351–52).

Beauvoir may not become as "American" as she would like, but her experiences do reconfigure her self to an extent, and she finds that she has to rediscover how to live in France once she returns. Unlike the native inhabitant, Beauvoir is a traveler, who, as Bartkowski notes, has "chosen her place, her routes, her questions...[thus] the traveler...will share the desire to make the writing of [her]...displacement lead [her]...to a reshaped sense of self. Writing will lead [her]...back to a new home" (101). Beauvoir's travel narrative betrays this desire to make sense of cultural displacement through a refashioning of the self, and when she returns to Paris, she finds that she has to remake France as her home. Toward the end of the narrative, ostensibly in Chicago, she reflects how, over the course of the journey, her "phantom" self slowly took on tangibility: "I saw the blood flow in its veins, and I was happy when its heart was beating like a real human heart" (381). However, whatever semblance of an American self she has achieved, it cannot be exported, for as her travels in America end, Beauvoir notes that her phantom becomes quickly "disembodied" (381). Beauvoir manipulates her chronology here, for the details she includes about Chicago near the end of the text are actually from her second trip to visit her lover, Nelson Algren, in September of 1947 (Keefe 52). Beauvoir returned to North America again in May 1948 to travel through New Orleans, the Yucatan, Guatemala, and Mexico with Algren. The false chronology is instructive, however, for since the entire narrative is written after her return to France, the text becomes a reflective post-travel treatise on America. Deirdre Bair suggests that she began writing the text soon after she returned to France in May 1947 as a method to work through her obsession with Algren, whom she missed intensely (347). Conceivably, then, part of her purpose in writing the narrative may be, as Bartkowski suggests, to reconstruct, through writing about her American experiences, a new sense of self, home, and, in this case, her relationship with Algren.

These final pages of Beauvoir's narrative are also replete with critique and reflection about the promised reality America offers but never allows her. She notes that each day she has been both exhilarated and troubled by American culture (382). During her last days in New York City, she observes that the skyscrapers and drugstores are just as magical as the first day she arrived; they create the illusion of an existence characterized by a tremendous force of forward movement (382), revealing, as in her road trip through the west, that American culture depends on movement for its energy and uniqueness. The skyscrapers suggest the triumph of "imagination over matter" and reveal that human beings are not stagnant, but filled with "energy, expansion, conquest" (382). Indeed, Americans are "fully alive" because of their dissatisfaction with inertia and their obsession with action; in America, "to be you must do." The great bridges, skyscrapers, airports, train terminals, city streets, and interstate highways affirm this particularly American faith (383).

However, Beauvoir concludes that American's love of movement and action is ultimately unproductive. She maintains that Americans live in the abstract, unwilling to look inside themselves to question and to reflect, but regard things, not themselves, as the "source of values and truth" (384). Americans' focus on things leads to a negation of the subject and the triumph of abstraction: "The object, erected as an idol, loses its human truth and becomes an abstraction be- cause concrete reality envelops both object and subject. This is the paradox of all the positivisms, of all the pseudo-realisms that turn away from man to affirm the thing—they miss the thing itself and attain only concepts" (384–85). Ironically, Beauvoir describes precisely what she has experienced while traveling in Amer- ica. Her American experience remains tangled in her emphasis on objects, al- lowing her to contemplate abstract concepts, but miss the real America. Perhaps Beauvoir's frustration with the ineffectiveness of her trip is largely due to her inability to experience America except as Americans do. She can imagine an existential engagement with America, but she cannot actually enact it—America denies her the kind of access she desires. She achieves a sense of American real- ity by physically moving through the country with other Americans on the road, but the meaning in the movement remains concealed behind a glass wall, or in this case, a movie screen. American culture is as difficult to permeate as that screen—an illusion of depth on an opaque surface, reflective but impenetrable.

In her review of the text, McCarthy suggests that Beauvoir's impressions re- tain "the flavor of an eyewitness account, of confirmation of rumor," the purpose being not so much to "assay America as to testify to its reality" (45). America's reality seems to depend on a world that is not real, "but only a half-frightening fantasy daydreamed by the Americans" (45). When Beauvoir returns to Paris, however, she realizes that she must step back into her "own skin" to refamiliarize herself with France, whose gray, dreary appearance provides a sharp contrast to America's glamour. In Paris, Beauvoir finds that the streets are dark and the people are petty, while she continues to think of America as a "sparkling" conti- nent across the ocean (390). Although Beauvoir believes that she has not assimi- lated American reality into her consciousness to the extent and in the manner she anticipated, traveling and writing have produced a version of the self that leads her "back to a new home" (Bartkowski 101). Similar to the Americans whom she criticizes for reifying objects, Beauvoir has allowed abstraction to overwhelm her subjectivity: Concrete reality (in this case, the visual representa- tion and physical embodiment of cinematic objects) cloaks both object and sub- ject, negating the subject and creating a space for abstraction. When Beauvoir has to put on her old skin back in France, she enacts the American paradox of the pseudo-real that she identifies at the end of her narrative; she believes that her fate in America is to be a visitor and traveler, but upon her return to France, she also finds herself a visitor and traveler, transformed by the cultural displace- ment of travel. Ultimately, her travels through the actual and cinematic landscapes of American culture position Beauvoir as a tourist in her own culture, longing for a new home that does not exist outside the borders of illusion and fantasy.

Works Cited

Bair, Deirdre. *Simone de Beauvoir: A Biography.* New York: Summit Books, 1990.

Barthes, Roland. "The Light of the Sud-Ouest." *Incidents.* Trans. Richard Howard. Berkeley: U of California P, 1992. 3–9.

Bartkowski, Frances. *Travelers, Immigrants, Inmates: Essays in Estrangement.* Minneapolis: U of Minnesota P, 1995.

Beauvoir, Simone de. *America Day by Day.* 1952. Trans. Carol Cosman. Berkeley: U of California P, 1999.

———. "An Existentialist Looks at America." *The New York Times Magazine.* May 25, 1947: 13, 51, 53–54.

The Best Years of Our Lives. Dir. William Wyler. Perf. Fredric March, Myrna Loy, and Teresa Wright. Samuel Goldwyn, 1946.

Certeau, Michel de. *The Practice of Everyday Life.* 1974. Trans. Steven Rendall. Berkeley: U of California P, 1984.

The Gold Rush. Dir. Charles Chaplin. Perf. Charles Chaplin, Georgia Hale, Mack Swain, and Tom Murray. Charles Chaplin, 1925.

Greed. Dir. Eric von Stroheim. Perf. Gibson Gowland, ZaSu Pitts, and Jean Hersholt. MGM, 1924.

Gunga Din. Dir. George Stevens. Perf. Cary Grant, Victor McLaglen, and Douglas Fairbanks, Jr. RKO, 1939.

Keefe, Terry. *Simone de Beauvoir: A Study of Her Writings.* Totowa, NJ: Barnes & Noble Books, 1983.

Lackey, Kris. *RoadFrames: The American Highway Narrative.* Lincoln: U of Nebraska P, 1997.

Lost Weekend. Dir. Billy Wilder. Perf. Ray Milland, Jane Wyman, and Philip Terry. Paramount, 1945.

McCarthy, Mary. "Mlle. Gulliver en Amérique." *Critical Essays on Simone de Beauvoir.* Ed. Elaine Marks. Boston: G. K. Hall & Co., 1987. 44–59.

Monsieur Verdoux. Dir. Charles Chaplin. Perf. Charles Chaplin, Martha Raye, and Isobel Elsom. Charles Chaplin, 1947.

A Night at the Opera. Dir. Sam Wood. Perf. Groucho Marx, Chico Marx, Harpo Marx, Margaret Dumont, and Kitty Carlisle. MGM, 1935.

Odd Man Out. Dir. Carol Reed. Perf. James Mason, Robert Newton, and Kathleen Ryan. Universal, 1946.

The Ox-Bow Incident. Dir. William Wellman. Perf. Henry Fonda, Henry Morgan, Jane Darwell, and Anthony Quinn. Twentieth Century Fox, 1943.

Rome, Open City. Dir. Robert Rossellini. Perf. Anna Magnani, Aldo Fabrizi, and Maria Michi. Excelsa Films, 1945.

Song of the South. Dir. Harve Foster. Perf. Ruth Warrick, Bobby Driscoll, and James Baskett. Walt Disney, 1946.

Chapter 9

St. Lawrence and the Pagans in The Marvels of Rome

Cynthia Ho

Sigmund Freud in *Civilization and Its Discontents* compares the jumble of monuments in the city of Rome to the complex memories in a human brain in order to illustrate "preservation in the sphere of the mind." Freud argues that "If we want to represent historical sequence in spatial terms, we can only do it by juxtaposition in space—the same space cannot have two contents" (70–71). The conglomeration of Roman landmarks which speak so clearly to Freud about the crowded and competing landscape of meaning is also the subject of the much read, copied, and revised *Mirabilia urbis Romae* (*MUR*). The twelfth century *MUR* has typically been read as a pilgrimage manual for medieval travelers to Rome, but it is also a multifaceted work that seeks to describe and decode the typography of Rome. In doing so, *MUR* argues for an acknowledgment and absorption of Rome's significant "other," the pagan past, into the aesthetics of Christianity.

The Marvels of Rome is the conventional English title for *Mirabilia urbis Romae,* a manuscript written in Rome about 1143 by a canon (probably named Benedict) describing the sites of medieval Rome. The many versions and revisions in the manuscript's history demonstrate it was often used as a pilgrim guide to Christian sites throughout Rome, despite its concerns with ruined Roman glories as well as Christian monuments. Although the work has been categorized as a tour guide, it is much more a treatise about knowing Rome in the fullest sense. Mary Campbell has demonstrated that one aspect of the pilgrim experience was the desire to confront strange sites, new people, and the exotic (3). *MUR*'s view of Rome as "other"—the powerful pagan past conquered by the great Christian martyrs—tempts pilgrims to read Benedict's version of the Christian triumph or to make a journey across Europe themselves. Descriptions of the great monuments and the narratives attached to them are keys to the meaning of the work. Most particularly, the tale of the martyred Saint Lawrence shows

Rome as another world, visited and conquered, simultaneously known and unknown.

Rome as Christianity's Significant Other

MUR represents a classical and Christian synthesis dating from the very expansion of Christianity into the Roman Empire. The persecutions of the third century that pitted paganism against Christianity had paradoxically left Rome rich in martyrs completely intertwined in the history of imperial Rome. The *Depositio martyrum* compiled in 354 names 32 such Christian martyr saints. Physical witnesses to this important fund of sanctity were preserved very early on by many church officials including Damasus Pope from 366, who preserved bodies of the martyrs in catacombs, and Leo IV, who in 846 extended the Roman walls around the Vatican Hill (Llewellyn 218). The development of the cult of martyrs, connected so intimately with the physical city of Rome and the memories of its pagan past, made it an early and important pilgrimage site. Fourth-century Rome was particularly venerated (Markus 72). Symbolically, then, in that important transitional moment between pagan and Christian, Rome represents Christianity as its finest hour. However, for most medieval Christians, Christianity's sacred territory was displaced, "emphatically Elsewhere" (Campbell 18). Originally Jerusalem, subsequently Rome, the longed-for locality of Christian worship was somewhere different from the common world and thus in need of interpreting and absorbing. Hildebert of Lavardin's poems make the point that Rome was a "regio dissimilitudinis," or region of difference (Witke 403). Paradoxically, Rome was also the Eternal City, the root of Christian culture, the place from which all were displaced and to which they yearned to return.

The imperial, or pagan, heritage of medieval Rome made itself felt two ways. First were the physical remains that served as the backdrop for Christian ceremony and enthralled visitors. Second was the very language of the church: the Latin, which in its grammar, rhetorical models, and literary illusions formed the bulk of Christian texts. Although appreciation of the Roman past was always present, official reactions within the Christian establishment to these monuments of the pagan past varied. On the one hand, St. Gregory the Great feared their appeal. He urged destruction of all the antiquities, because the believers who came to Rome spent so much time admiring them (Labarge 87 and Kinney 208). Specific sites were seen as particularly pagan locations of the anti-miracle. For example, *Legenda Aurea,* a collection of exempla roughly contemporary with *MUR,* describes the construction of the Pantheon as an example of the pride of the pagans, since the ground plan was laid out with such dimensions that the dome could be finished only with the help of the devil (*Golden Legend* 642). In contrast, St. Augustine praised Rome's secular achievement and virtues reflected in her monuments (Thompson 154–56). Much later, John of Salisbury's *Policraticus* of 1159 continues the consistent tradition of appreciation of ancient monuments. Contemporaneous with *MUR,* both pagan and Christian monuments were carefully preserved by the restored republic which in 1143 threatened those persons who defaced or damaged the columns of Trajan (Sumption 223). Although destruction of pagan monuments did take place, it is not clear if they were destroyed solely because of their pagan associations (Buddensieg 260). Richard Krautheimer suggests the possibility that animosity against Roman remnants was a fearful reaction of the less educated, while Saradi-Mendelovici has argued that hostility of Christians toward pagan monuments sprang from the agendas of local institutions. Altogether, evidence seems to indicate that on the whole classical monuments never ceased to be appreciated for their artistic value (Krautheimer 60 and Saradi-Mendelovici 47–61). Christian appreciation and use of pagan literature reflects this same sensibility: Despite disclaimers from some quarters, many authors from the Roman period were brought into accord with Christian theology. Virgil's alleged conversion and prophetic pronouncement in the *Fourth Eclogus* and Cicero's supposed understanding of the messianic promise are two of the most famous examples. It is not surprising, then, that the best-known medieval legend of a virtuous pagan involves Trajan, Roman emperor from 98–117 (Vitto 37–39).

Pilgrimage to Rome

MUR is a state-of-the-art answer to pilgrim interest in the twelfth century. In a sense, the Rome of the ancients had been colonized by Christians, forcing a shift from what had been paganism. The ancient ruins, and what they represented, displayed a strange, frightening, and titillating world to the weary pilgrims. Early pilgrims to Rome concentrated their veneration on the churches and monuments in the cemeteries on the radial roads outside the city which held the bodies and shrines of early martyrs. These tombs were soon expanded with the addition of their own churches. These provided visitors with increased access to the saint's relics and satisfied what Robert Finucane calls "the pilgrim desire for conflation of relic and altar" which were fueled by expectations of posthumous miracles at these holy places (39). Early pilgrim guides suggest that in the sixth and seventh centuries, pilgrim trails began at St. Peter's and went around the perimeter of Rome (Llewellyn 3). By the close of the eighth century the focus of the city changed as the Lateran and the Vatican became the power centers of the church. Consequently the centers of pilgrim veneration expanded to include churches located within the city walls as well. Moving to sites within the old Rome intensified pilgrims's realization of the cohabitation of pagan and Christian spaces, and increased the number of possible holy locations. Surviving pilgrim texts of travels to Rome show, by their selection (and rejection) of sites, their deliberate devotional choices. When Archbishop Sigeric of Canterbury pilgrimaged to Rome in 900, for example, he visited 23 churches out of the existing 117 (Ortenberg 197). In the same way, Nikolas of Munkathvers in 1150 was overwhelmed with the pilgrimage sites available to him: "[N]o one is so wise as to know all the churches in the city of Rome" (Birch 107). By the twelfth century, the churches of Peter and Paul were premier sites followed by the city's three other patriarchal basilicas: Saint Lawrence Outside-the-Walls, Saint Maria Maggiore, and Saint John in the Lateran (Birch 107–10). The popularity of pilgrimages in twelfth-century Europe brought many devout to Rome's sacred sites and created a demand for travel literature and guidebooks that *MUR* answered.

The Marvels of Rome

The *MUR* has traditionally been categorized as a pilgrim guide (Bloch 632). However, the author himself never identifies it as a handbook for travelers. Rather, Benedict states that his purpose has been "to bring back to the human memory how great was their beauty in gold, silver, brass, ivory and precious stones" (46).[1] Many take him at his word that it is simply a paean to the past, the old city still visible, in as "a sort of palimpsest with one civilization written over the other" (Brentano 80). It has also been seen as a political document, connected with the revival of pride in the renovation of the Senate in 1143–44 and the desires of Pope Innocent II.[2] A number of factors make it an improbable pilgrim handbook. Both the expensiveness of the manuscript and the sophistication of the Latin indicate another audience (Birch 117). In addition, the content itself is not conducive to perambulating the city. As J. K. Hyde puts it, "The instant and lasting popularity of the *Mirabilia* may be ascribed to its being written for one body of readers but appealing to another" (322).

If not primarily a tour guide, what is the genre of the *MUR*? Hyde has argued for its importance as one of the medieval descriptions of cities which were "a manifestation of the growth of cities and the rising culture and self confidence of the citizens" (320). Structural peculiarities such as the opening description of the city wall and the lists of notable features by category are consistent with earlier examples of the genre. Benedict's first work, *Liber politicus,* a handbook that detailed the routes of papal processions, positioned him to write an independent treatise on the topography of ancient Rome (Bloch 632). Benedict's desire to describe the city in words suggests a prose map—a work of literature that, in its inception, attempts to create in words the physical reality of Rome along with its attendant meanings. This medieval prose map seeks to recognize Rome as a rich code of cultural signification: not a fixed scheme, but a rapidly changing source of historical meanings. Seeing *MUR* as a geography of memory, as a recollection of history, makes possible our understanding of how the text's verbal representations of spatial Rome manipulate seemingly superfluous details and suppress supposedly important, even essential, details in the pursuit of meaning. Although the Roman Empire had been proficient in spatially representative map making, medieval Europe had lost the skill. Medieval maps, then, at best were diagrams, "an open framework where all kinds of information might be placed in relevant spatial position, not unlike a chronicle or narrative in which information would be arranged chronologically" (Harvey 19). The earliest travelers' maps are clearly more narrative and symbolic than topographical. [3]

While scholars have long identified the credibility problems of medieval maps, they have only now begun to discuss the essential unreliability of all maps, exposing our reliance on the truth-value of the map over other forms of expression. In fact, though, the process of making a readable map requires cartographers to limit the stories they tell and "so allows them to manipulate their audience with the information they choose to include. This combination of power and subjectivity has repeatedly put maps at the center of controversy" (Monmonier 1). Modern studies of cartography have increasingly come to realize how the map itself is an argument, a visual corollary to a rhetorical text. As Denis Wood has convincingly demonstrated, "Maps serve interests. Every map shows this and not that. Not only is this inescapable but it is precisely because of this interested selectivity—this choice of word or sign or aspect of the world to make a point—that the map is enabled to work" (1). Maps, then, are the siblings of literary texts, for they provide an accessible example of the ways in which reading and writing involve representation and misrepresentation. Maps invite speculation about what has been removed, revised, renamed, or replaced (McQuillan 4). As Robert Scholes argues in *Textual Power,* structuralist and poststructuralist theories apply not only to verbal systems but also to "maps, diagrams, painting, sculpture, film, ideograph, hieroglyph, and all other motivated ways of signifying" (102). The *MUR,* then, blends the ideas of spatial description with the compatible genre of narrative to produce a version of Rome. As a verbal map it exaggerates all of the potentials of a map for the construction of meaning. Although not intended as a traveler's map and guidebook, its spatial orientation made it an obvious text to be appropriated by pilgrims whose agendas were perhaps different from those of the author. Benedict's prose map is a rigidly controlled presentation of the sites and relationships he considers important.

Reading Structure

As a text and as a map *MUR* invites readers to read its structure. What is and what is not included, the location within the text of different pieces of information, and the approach to the stories themselves signal meaning. The overall work is a frame to present stories about Rome, but these framed tales vary tremendously in length and purpose, from one-line tags to the extended exemplum of Saint Lawrence. Gardner's printed edition and translation of *The Marvels of Rome* reflects several editorial intrusions that differ from the medieval manuscript tradition: Some parts are deleted, selections from later manuscripts are inserted, and the body of the work is divided into three named "Parts." Nevertheless, this modern redaction offers an accessible vehicle to understand the way the text is constructed. The first "Part" begins with an urban genealogy that both introduces the entire work and this particular section on sites. The beginnings of the other sections echo the themes of harmony and consolidation advanced here. An amazing opening names Noah (the founder of Janiculum), Saturn (founder of a city on the Capitoline), Aborigines, and finally, Romulus, descendant of Priam, King of Troy, as the founding patriarchs of Rome. In according all of them the same level of reality, it establishes the equal truth-value of all the narratives that follow whether they are of pagan or Christian origin. Next, the pagan ruins of Rome (listed in categories of architectural types such as Walls, Gates, Arches, and so forth) are linked to very brief, important facts in Roman and Christian history. These short narrative snippets are "tags"—references to prior existing, larger stories outside the text, residing in the reader's memory. Tags are mini-examples, core fragments, which gesture to an understood body of commonly held information. These tags remark on what happened on the site, or what is there now, or what was there once, or where the name came from. However, these references are not pious additions; the leap we might expect to moralization is absent, for the inherent value of the identification lies in itself, in demonstrating to the reader how both pagan and Christian heritage lie in the same geography of our remembrance. Mary Campbell notes that "like an archaeologist, the Christian pilgrim is looking for the past, but it is a past made up of singular events and personalities" (19). The important past here is the assumed shared cultural knowledge of the author and audience. This opening clearly establishes that this is a retrospective text, bent on seeing only the past. Here are no current events, no occupants of contemporary Rome. Interestingly, there doesn't even seem to be a narrator's voice. All "today" is obliterated in the pursuit of a commonly remembered past, and the architectural signposts function to "know" old Rome.

The second part also begins with a synthetic prologue in which the pagan emperor Octavian envisions and accepts the revelation of the Blessed Virgin. Thus Roman foresight and good sense are linked to Christian truth. Here, longer narratives about Roman history are each connected to a specific place. The Pantheon, for example is discussed as a site that demonstrates how Rome turned from Cybele, the mother of the gods, to the "Blessed Mary, ever-virgin, who is the mother of all the saints" (22). In the same way, S. Pietro in Vincoli evokes the story of Eudoxia and the chains of St. Peter (26–27). Between these two paradigmatic examples, the Pantheon and Saint Peter's, appears the remarkable and atypical story of St. Lawrence and the early martyrs. The third, concluding part of *MUR* is often labeled a "Perambulation" of the city, although it is really an idiosyncratic list of places and relative locations without the narrative tags or exempla of the earlier parts of the work. Because this verbal chart offers an itinerary that is not really walkable, it presents a mapping of potentialities. As it talks us across the topography of the city, the fusion of pagan and

Christian becomes so insistent that the pagan implications of the sites control the text.

Saint Lawrence

Within the center of the structure of *MUR* lies the important story of Saint Lawrence. With the exception of Peter, Bishop of Rome, Lawrence is the most often mentioned martyr in *MUR*. His appearance accurately reflects his importance in the early church. He is continually remembered in the liturgy where he is mentioned in the Communicantes list in the Eucharistic prayer; the tale of his suffering sometimes appears in the Recession as well (Jungmann 173 and 461). Four great basilicas, numerous chapels, and many smaller churches were dedicated to Lawrence in Rome, and all four of Lawrence's famous churches are mentioned in *MUR*. The first and in a unique category is S. Lorenzo fuori le mura, or St. Lawrence Outside-the-Walls on the spot where Lawrence's relics were originally buried in a catacomb on the Via Tiburtina (*MUR* 1.11). According to the *Liber Pontificalis,* in the fourth century Constantine built a funerary hall next door with flights of stairs leading up and down from the grave. Thus, veneration of Lawrence was intertwined with the emerging sensibilities of the new Christian Rome (Birch 30 and Brown 87–88). In the sixth century, Pelagius II increased pilgrim access to Lawrence's actual vault by laying out a new basilica in which the tomb was on the ground level in the center of the church. In both renovations, considerable wealth in silver decoration was expended. His second church is San Lorenzo in Lucina (*MUR* 1.4 and 1.7). Although the exact founding date of the church is unknown, it was surely in existence by 365. Pilgrims flocked there to see Lawrence's most famous relic, the craticula, or gridiron, upon which he was broiled. The church was important enough to undergo a number of expensive renovations in the Middle Ages, and among the many fine donations was a "silver statue of the martyr St Lawrence, weighing 200 lb" (*Liber Pontificalis* 36). Lawrence's two other churches are San Lorenzo in Panisperna (1.4 and 3.9) and San Lorenzo in Miranda built on the Temple of Antoninus and Faustinus in the Roman Forum (3.10). In addition, the Chapel of St. Lawrence in the Lateran was famous for its collection of relics including the foreskin and umbilical cord of Christ and a piece of the true cross (Sumption 222 and Birch 111). Another site of veneration for Lawrence was created when his body was later moved to an altar in the monastic church Saint Stephen with an inscription by Pope Leo, "Preserved in this altar are the relics of the holy martyrs and deacons Stephen and Lawrence" (Wilson 19). These monuments provided pilgrims with access to the real presence of the saint. The devotees who flocked out of Rome to the shrine to ask for his favor hoped to meet him there, *ad dominum Laurentium* (Brown 87–88). That his very body was endowed with power was often demonstrated. Stories abound about Lawrence's willingness to perform miracles for supplicants, and to punish the sinful and unwary as well. *Legenda Aurea,* for example, lists twelve such exempla, including the often told story from Gregory the Great of unfortunate workers who died from accidentally touching Lawrence's body (*Golden Legend* 443 and Llewellyn 174).

Although Lawrence is a conventional and understandable choice for Benedict's longest tale, the telling of his story is strikingly unconventional for a work used by pious pilgrims. Lawrence's story is not, like all the other exempla, linked to a certain location, it is remarkably lacking in the miraculous, and it focuses more attention on a host of other participants than on the saint. Lawrence's passion is strangely represented because it is much less about Lawrence himself than the synthesis he represents. The section begins, "One approach for preaching the passions of S. Abdon and S. Sennen, or Saint Sixtus, Saint Lawrence and the rest would, as the legend relates, examine why the emperor put them to death and would begin thus: 'After a tempest arose under Decius, many Christians were slain, while Galba ruled in the city of Rome'" (2.5). In this approach, the preacher would move immediately to these saints's tales of martyrdom, focus on their acts of heroism, and celebrate Christian triumph. This version, however, is tacitly rejected by the swift move to the second, lengthier, alternative. Benedict continues with another option: "The other approach, as the Roman legend relates, would begin like this and preach: 'There was a certain emperor, Gordian by name, whose standard-bearer in the legions was Philip.'" As the story unfolds, Philip the Christian slays the Emperor Gordian and takes the empire for himself and his son, also named Philip. One of Emperor Philip's heathen knights, Decius, gains the favor of the emperor, the soldiers, and the Senate because of his good reputation, wit, and prudence. After becoming chief captain, pagan Decius is tempted to murder the elder Philip in his tent. The soldiers rally around Decius out of fear rather than love or loyalty, and the younger Philip flees to the sanctuary of Sixtus and implores the pope to take the elder Philip's treasure and keep it hidden. After Decius has murdered Philip the Younger, he begins his search for the imperial treasure. Decius himself is not able to attend to searching for the treasure, however, because the bell of the Persian image is ringing (which a previous chapter has already explained means that the Persians are in revolt). Galba, now temporarily in charge of Rome, dies. (It is at this point in the narrative that the first option would begin). Decius returns and slays (in the Colosseum) the two Persian Christian noble hostages Abdon and Sennen he has been carrying around with him all this time. Sixtus is beheaded for the treasure and now the famous Lawrence finally appears and pleads, "Holy Father, do not leave me behind, for I have spent the treasures that you put into my hands" (25). Lawrence is now seized and the text concludes "the rest that follows."

By offering these two versions, Benedict asks us to consider the importance of origins in telling a historical exemplum. Promoting the importance of beginning with the past, he aims to present Rome to his new age, accommodating the many tensions of within and without to absorb the Roman "other" in twelfth-century culture. Lawrence's passion in its longer version is about something else, and that something else, the gap, is a key to meaning of the text. Not only the four early martyrs, but also Philip and Decius, are the stars of the tale. Philip, emperor of Rome from 244–249 was, it seems, guilty of the death of Decius. Although historians now doubt that Philip was indeed Christian, Benedict here follows the medieval conviction, apparently derived from a statement by St. Jerome, that Philip was the first Christian Emperor of Rome. Eusebius tells the story that Philip tried to join the Christians' prayers at Easter, but the bishop told him to stand in the ranks of the penitent and Philip had obeyed. Bishop Dionysius described Philip's reign as "more kindly to us Christians" (Fox 453). The emperor Decius (249–251), best known as the instigator of the first sustained persecutions of the Christians, was a traditionalist, a politician who felt he could reverse the downward spiral of Roman life by revitalizing worship of the Roman gods. Nevertheless, historically it seems that it was under the persecutions of Valerius, the emperor who followed Decius, that Lawrence was martyred in the year 258 (Fox 454). Another source, *Legenda Aurea,* pointedly questions the chronological accuracy of this traditional story (*Golden Legend* 442). Since narrative is often subordinated to argument in this kind of ideological framework, the author uses Decius for his own purpose (Lyons 43).

All that is known for certain about the life and death of the historical Lawrence is that he died four days after the death of Pope St. Sixtus in 258. The legendary details are chiefly supplied by St. Ambrose and the poet Prudentius. The conventional story is as follows: Saint Lawrence was one of seven deacons who were in charge of giving help to the poor and the needy. When a persecution broke out, Pope St. Sixtus was condemned to death. As he was led to execution, Lawrence followed him in tears and the pope promised Lawrence he would also suffer in three days. Joyfully, Lawrence gave all of the church's treasure to the poor. The greedy pagan Prefect of Rome ordered Lawrence to bring the Church's treasure to him. The Saint said he would, in three days. Then he went through the city and gathered together all the poor and sick people supported by the Church. When he showed them to the prefect, he said: "This is the Church's treasure!" In great anger, the prefect condemned Lawrence to a slow, cruel death. The saint was tied on top of an iron grill over a slow fire that roasted his flesh. In his bravery, he called out, "Turn me over, I'm done on this side!" And just before he died, he said, "It's cooked enough now." Then he prayed that the city of Rome might be converted to Jesus and that the Catholic faith might spread all over the world.

Three topoi consistently appear in the tellings of Lawrence's tale. First is Sixtus's prophecy, second is Lawrence's connection with the "treasure" and third, of course, is Lawrence's famous grilling in which he calls himself well done. Medieval readers would know that St. Lawrence's story is particularly notable for its contrast of earthly and heavenly treasures and for his explicit claim to have merited divine reward: by his sufferings during his martyrdom, by the conversions he made through his preaching after being arrested by Decius, and most notably, by his distribution of the material goods of the church to the poor. When Ambrose (340–397) praises Lawrence in "Duties of the Clergy" it is for his monetary priorities, his martyrdom, and his affection for the pope (*Nicene* 65). Important nuances about the relationship between the priest and the deacon concerning the chalice at mass also come from the story of Lawrence's relationship with Sixtus (Jungmann 59). Lawrence's ministry thus illustrates the right use of earthly treasures and paradoxically legitimizes the Church's rights to property given to her (Tavormina 245). His connections with the biblical verses Ps. 111:9/2 Cor 9:9 (which both stress charity) can be found as early as a late sixth-century mosaic at St. Lawrence-Outside-the-Walls in Rome and in sixth- to eighth-century manuscripts of the sermons of Maximus of Turin.

Most surprising, then, is the one sentence attributed to Lawrence in Benedict's version: "I have spent the treasure" (2.5), which seems to undervalue Lawrence's character and sufferings. Benedict demonstrates elsewhere that he knows the details of Lawrence's martyrdom. In Part I the Baths of Olympias are identified as the place "where Saint Lawrence was broiled" (1.12), and again in Part III he relates that these Baths of Olympias, where Saint Lawrence was broiled, were once the Temple of Apollo (3.14). The text contains many references to Lawrence's monuments as well. What can we make of the fact that the story of Lawrence and the other martyrs does not say much about them? Medieval literature of all genres overflows with semantic "gaps" or "blanks," holes that require the reader's participation by supplying what is missing from the text. As Wolfgang Iser puts it: "The reader will only begin to search for the meaning if he does not know it, and so it is the unknown factors in the text that set him off on his own quest" (9). Moreover, these medieval works are not merely conceptually incomplete; they insist upon their own incompleteness, upon "the gaps that make interpretation not only possible but necessary, and necessarily indeterminate" (Sturges 2). Medieval theorists were themselves interested in identifying and then reading the "gap." When John Scottus Eriugena reflects on language in the ninth century, he focuses precisely on the hidden nature of the sign, its abstract conjecturality, rather than on its status as a phenomenal manifestation. Stephen Nichols argues that Eriugena's metaphor of the fountain is consistent with poststructuralist theories that hold that the nature of the sign is to be found in the wound or opening—that constitutes it and annuls it—at the same time. The sign exists as absence, as potential (55–56). The noticeable absence of Lawrence and of the saints's suffering points to unstated agendas: Benedict's emphasis is on reading the unfamiliar "other" of the past rather than the familiar.

The tale of St. Lawrence illustrates the importance of acknowledging and appreciating the alterity of the Roman past which is still ever present and beckoning to pilgrim tourists. While the story of Lawrence was used to address certain issues within the church, his is also a tale of origins and the larger world. He maps the intersection of the two meanings of the name "Rome": Christian universal church and pagan empire. Martydoms link these two periods. G. W. Bowersock argues that the Christian martyrs reflect the "mores and structure of the Roman Empire, not to the indigenous character of the Semitic Near East where Christianity was born. Martyrdom had nothing to do with Judaism or with Palestine. It had everything to do with the Graeco-Roman world, its traditions, its language, and its cultural tastes" (Bowersock 28). The gaps in the story of Lawrence point to the moment at the end of the pagan past and the beginning of Christianity. This conflation of two worlds was evident in anyone's perambulation of the city.

Beyond a singular, personal example, Lawrence provides the opportunity for Benedict to produce a "public exemplum" that focuses on secular persona and "insists on the inherent disorder of the historical world it addresses" (Scanlon 81). Philip and Decius do in fact have important parts to play here. The pagan emperors of the narrative become evil examples, men whose violations of noble truths demonstrate their ultimate efficacy. Philip, who, despite being Roman Emperor, was not particularly Roman (his father was an Arab sheik) is the secular counterpart of our Roman saint who is from Spain, not Rome. Medieval historical writing becomes an important concern in the twelfth century in an effort, in Lee Patterson's words, to "reestablish the historical world as itself a locus of value" (158). More precisely, here Rome is reclaimed as an essential topography in the creation of Christianity. The Spanish poet Prudentius, who himself visited Rome during the late fourth century, became a devotee of the cult of the martyrs. His hymn to St. Lawrence is his longest, 584 lines, and it offers a remarkable source for the tale of *MUR*. In Prudentius' version, Lawrence dies after he has just finished a speech prophesying Rome's conversion. Michael Roberts argues that in several rhetorical moves throughout the poem, Prudentius sets up a Roman versus non-Roman opposition in which Rome is converted to Christianity under the leadership of the martyrs (Roberts 130). The city becomes the homeland of not just Roman Italians, but the entire universal community of Christians in a new kind of Roman Empire. Prudentius proposes a new founding legend of Christian Rome, "one that has its origins in the past but continues in the present to be part of the experience of individual Christians as they celebrate the saints's feast days and move about the city" (Roberts 185–86). This important moment conjoining Rome and other-Rome is also reflected in the *Legenda Aurea*; it comments that Philip "reigned in the thousandth year of the foundation of Rome, God having disposed that this anniversary should be dedicated to Christ" (438).

Almost four hundred years later the problem of Rome's past and present relationships were still vexed. Machiavelli argues in *Discourses* that Christianity attempted to wipe out the city's memory of its glorious past (Lyons 43). Benedict's text, in contrast, anticipates and refutes this argument by demonstrating that Christianity and an appreciation of the pagan past are compatible and can cohabit the same geography of memory. "Two Approaches to Teaching the Passions" demonstrates the superiority of beginning with origins in truly knowing Rome. For those viewing the crowded landscape of Rome (whether they be pilgrims or armchair readers), Benedict selectively maps the highlights of Rome's treasures, both familiar and other.

Notes

The author expresses special thanks to Dale Kinney, Birgitta Wohl, and the National Endowment for the Humanities for their help and support in this project.

1   All quotations are from *The Marvels of Rome. Mirabilia Urbis Romae*, ed. and trans. Francis Morgan Nichols. 2nd ed. Eileen Gardiner (New York: Italica Press, 1986).

2   For differing views on the genre of *MUR* see Panofsky 73, Davis 14, Krautheimer 198, and Kitzinger 648.

3   For maps that accompany Roman tour guides and their accuracy see Birgitta Wohl, "Mental Images and Late Medieval Maps of Rome," in *Paradigms in Medieval Thought Applications in Medieval Disciplines: A Symposium*, ed. Nancy van Deusen and Alvin E. Ford (Lewiston: Edwin Mellen 1990).

Works Cited

Birch, Debra. *Pilgrimage to Rome in the Middle Ages.* Woodbridge: Boydell Press, 1998.

Bloch, Howard. "The New Fascination with Ancient Rome." *Renaissance and Renewal in the Twelfth Century.* Eds. Benson, Robert, and Giles Constable. Toronto: U of Toronto P, 1991: 630–55.

Bowersock, G. W. *Martyrdom and Rome.* Cambridge: Cambridge UP, 1995.

Brentano, Robert. *Rome Before Avignon. A Social History of Thirteenth-Century Rome.* New York: Basic Books, 1974.

Brown, Peter. *The Cult of Saints.* Chicago: U of Chicago Press, 1989.

Buddensieg, T. "Criticism and Praise of the Pantheon in the Middle Ages and the Renaissance." *Classical Influences on European Culture A.D. 500–1500.* Ed. R. R. Bolgar. Cambridge: Cambridge UP, 1971. 259–67.

Campbell, Mary B. *The Witness and the Other World.* Ithaca: Cornell UP, 1988.

Davis, Raymond, ed. *The Lives of the Eighth-Century Popes (Liber Pontificalis).* Liverpool: Liverpool UP, 1992.

Finucane, Robert C. *Miracles and Pilgrims. Popular Beliefs in Medieval England.* London: Macmillan, 1995.

Fox, Robin Lane. *Pagans and Christians.* New York: Alfred Knopf, 1987.

Freud, Sigmund. *The Future of an Illusion. Civilization and Its Discontents and Other Works.* London: Hogarth Press, 1964.

The Golden Legend of Jacobus de Voragine. Trans. Granger Ryan and Helmut Ripper-
ger. New York: Longman, 1969.

Harvey, P. D. A. *Mappa Mundi: The Hereford World Map.* Toronto: University of Toronto Press, 1996

Hyde, J. K. "Medieval Descriptions of Cities." *Bulletin of the John Rylands Library* 48
(1966): 308–40.

Iser, Wolfgang. *Prospecting: From Reader Response to Literary Anthropology.* Baltimore: Johns Hopkins UP, 1989.

Jungmann, Joseph. *The Mass of the Roman Rite.* New York: Benziger, 1949.

Kinney, Dale. "'Mirabilia Urbis Romae.'" *The Classics in the Middle Ages.* Eds. Aldo S.
Bernardo and Saul Levin. Binghamton: Medieval & Renaissance Texts and Studies,
1990. 207–22.

Kitzinger, Ernst. "The Arts as Aspects of a Renaissance." *Renaissance and Renewal in
the Twelfth Century.* Eds. Robert L. Benson and Giles Constable. Cambridge: Harvard UP, 1982.

Krautheimer, Richard. Rome. *Profile of a City, 312–1308.* Princeton: Princeton UP,
1980.

Labarge, Margaret. *Medieval Travelers.* New York: Norton, 1982.

Liber Pontificalis (Book of Pontiffs). Trans. Raymond Davis. Liverpool: Liverpool UP,
1989.

Llewellyn, Peter. *Rome in the Dark Ages.* New York: Praeger, 1971.

Lyons, John. *Exemplum.* Princeton: Princeton UP, 1989

Markus, Robert. *The End of Ancient Christianity.* New York: Cambridge UP, 1990.

Marvels of Rome, the. Mirabilia Urbis Romae. Ed. and Trans. Francis Morgan Nichols.
2nd ed. New York: Italica Press, 1986.

McQuillan, Gene. "YOU ARE HERE (?) Cartography, Unreliability, Erasure, Vigi-
lance." *CEA Critic* 9 (1993): 4–8.

Monmonier, Mark. *Drawing the Line: Tales of Maps and Cartocontroversy.* New York:
Holt, 1995.

Nicene and Post-Nicene Fathers. Vol. X. Ed. Philip Schaff and Henry Wace. Grand
Rapids, MI: Wm. B. Eerdmans Publishing Co., 1989.

Nichols, Stephen. "Remodeling Models: Modernism and the Middle Ages." *Modernite
au Moyen Age: le defi du passe.* Eds. Brigette Cazelles and Charles Mela. Geneva:
Droz. 1990.

Ortenberg, Veronica. "Archbishop Sigeric's Journey to Rome in 990." *Anglo-Saxon
England* 19 (1990): 197–246.

Panofsky, Erwin. *Renaissance and Renascences in Western Art.* New York: Harper &
Row, 1969.

Patterson, Lee. *Negotiating the Past: The Historical Understanding of Medieval Literature.* Madison: U of Wisconsin P, 1987.

Roberts, Michael. *Poetry and the Cult of the Martyrs. The Liber Peristephanon Prudentius.* Ann Arbor: U of Michigan P, 1993.

Saradi-Mendelovici, "Christian Attitudes toward Pagan Monuments in Late Antiquity
and Their Legacy in Later Byzantine Centuries." *Dumbarton Oaks Papers* 44 (1990):
47–61

Scanlon, Larry. *Narrative, Authority and Power.* Cambridge: Cambridge UP, 1994.

Scholes, Robert E. *Textual Power: Literary Theory and the Teaching of English.* New Haven: Yale University Press, 1985.

Sturges, Robert. *Medieval Interpretation. Models of Reading in Literary Narrative, 1100-1500.* Carbondale: Southern Illinois UP, 1991.

Sumption, Jonathan. *Pilgrimage, An Image of Mediaeval Religion.* Totowa: Rowman and Littlefield, 1975.

Tavormina, M. Teresa. "*Piers Plowman* and the Liturgy of St. Lawrence: Composition and Revision in Langland's Poetry." *Studies in Philology* 84 (1987): 245–71.

Thompson, David. "Dante's Virtuous Romans." *Dante Studies with the Annual Report of the Dante Society* 96 (1978): 154–6.

Vitto, Cindy. *The Virtyous Pagan in Middle English Literature.* Philadelphia: The American Philosophical Society, 1989

Wilson, Stephen. *Saints and Their Cults. Studies in Religious Sociology, Folklore and History.* Cambridge: Cambridge UP, 1983.

Witke, Charles. "Rome as 'Region of Difference' in the Poetry of Hildebert of Lavardin." *The Classics in the Middle Ages: Papers of the Twentieth Annual Conference for the Center for Medieval and Early Renaissance Studies.* Eds. Aldo S. Bernardo and Saul Levin. Binghamton: Center for Medieval & Early Renaissance Studies, 1990. 403–15.

Wohl, Birgitta. "Mental Images and Late Medieval Maps of Rome." *Paradigms in Medieval Thought Applications in Medieval Disciplines: A Symposium.* Eds. Nancy van Deusen and Alvin E. Ford. Lewiston: Edwin Mellen Press, 1990. 173–91.

Wood, Denis. *The Power of Maps.* New York: Guilford Press, 1992.

✾ Chapter 10

John McPhee's Spiritual Journeys: The Authenticating Eye

Theodore C. Humphrey

Yet once a little while and I will shake the heavens, and the earth, the sea, and the dry land; and I will shake all nations... —G. F. Handel, *The Messiah*

John McPhee explores our world, seeing it through the authenticating lens of "deep time" provided by contemporary geological theory; the result is an account both wonderfully scientific and unexpectedly spiritual. His explanations of plate tectonics, glaciation, volcanism; his understanding of the forces of fire, water, and tectonics in creating and shaping the face of the globe; his ecological journeys into Alaska and Maine—all contribute to the conclusion that John McPhee is a writer whose artistically crafted reports of his journeys of experience lead to an overwhelming sense of the complexity and wonder of the earth as our physical home. His travel writings, profiles, and essays on tools, toolmakers, and tool users celebrate the inquiring minds of our species, lamenting at times their limitations, but always, I think, moving us inexorably toward a Blakean acknowledgment of the goal of our own spiritual journeys—"To see a World in a Grain of sand/And a Heaven in a Wild Flower/Hold Infinity in the palm of your hand/And Eternity in an hour" ("Auguries of Innocence," ca. 1803). His work enacts a profoundly spiritual interpretation of this planet, the results of his lifelong quests and his authenticating eye.

Mankind has always sought to make sense of this earth, our origins, our location in the cosmos. Creation myths are found in nearly every culture. McPhee's journeys and his subsequent reports of his findings are those of one who seeks to know the grounds of his experience, or, as Thoreau put it in *Walden*, "drive life into a corner...[and] if it were sublime, to know it by experience, and be able to give a true account of it in my next excursion." It is work informed, I think, always by the sort of purpose perhaps best expressed in *Annals of the Former*

World (winner of the 1999 Pulitzer Prize for General Non-Fiction) where McPhee seeks to present the science of geology and its practitioners "in a form and manner...meant to arrest the attention of other people while achieving acceptability in the geologic community" (*Annals* 9).

To do so he makes a pilgrimage from the eastern root of Interstate 80 westward to its terminus near San Francisco. His journey enacts a quest that is as much spiritual as it is scientific; indeed, its enactment blurs the distinctions one might be inclined to make between these two domains of human inquiry: science and spirituality. Its goal is to understand the very foundations and roots of these geophysical entities called continents that float upon great tectonic plates along the surface of our earth's molten core. The enormous forces that drive the motions of these plates and the reaches of time in which they take place stretch the limits of the human imagination. To articulate and create an understanding of these titanic forces at work over the eons requires language and vision that might well approach the vatic and the visionary, but McPhee chooses instead the language and the vision of modern geological science. Does work in this linguistic register render the vision articulated somehow nonspiritual? Or does it rather close the gap (as does contemporary astrophysics) between the "spiritual" and the "physical?" I claim that it does and that McPhee's travels over the physical road of Interstate 80 from New York to San Francisco, approximately the 40th parallel, across the United States in the company of different geologists, each an expert in his or her own portion of this fundamental discipline, yield a profound understanding of our small place in the great scheme of creation. Clarifying the mind-bending contrast between the eyeblink-time of our species's existence and its efforts to "control" nature, on the one hand, and the great and nearly incomprehensible travels of tectonic plates, the rise and fall of mountain ranges, and the opening and closing and reopening of oceans and seas, on the other, McPhee's pilgrimages testify to that divine light in the human mind which seeks always to illuminate the facts of our existence.

This essay explores some of the contexts in which McPhee's spiritual journeys take place, and focuses on the elements of his writing that create the special persona of the spiritually motivated scientific voyager, whether in *Annals* or in any number of his other works. His portraits of the experts whom he has interviewed at length, often over periods of years, observing and communing with them about topics such as the place of the bear in the wilderness; the origins and composition and ages of rock; the relationships between cattle ranching, rustling, and branding; the short-term conflicts between mining and wilderness interests; and the tensions between stewardship, exploitation, science, and ecology—all contribute powerfully to the sense of wonder and discovery that informs McPhee's writing. As he writes in "The Encircled River" Section of *Coming into the Country,* the antlers of a caribou, like the grizzly bear, imply the country; when he sees the bear there, in color, on the side of the hill, it represents a vision of a whole land, a metonym. In *Coming into the Country,* McPhee provides a number of spectacular examples of his methods for creating a sense of place—of different places actually—that are as successful and compelling as any in literature. In the first volume his encounter with a grizzly bear is a moment that defines not only the general nature of human-bear encounters as ecological and environmental issues but also figures the grizzly bear as totem for the state and especially for the specific area of the Brooks Range he is exploring on the Salmon River. And the power of this identification is so powerful, so compelling that "To be there was to be incorporated...into its substance—his country, and if you wanted to visit it you had better knock" (70–72), a perception of reverence and respect.

***

If the aim of travel writing, as one analyst of travel literature puts it, is "to chart the world afresh" (Gray 49), then in McPhee's *Annals of the Former World,* we see an extraordinarily successful charting of the "world afresh" in writing that opens the geological structures of our country, various explanatory theories and arguments, and the investigative tools and techniques of geologists to our view and our understanding. If the essential quality of travel writing as a genre, its central impulse, is to discover "the territory" by traveling over it, to it, through it, or in it; exploring it fully, whether "it" is a known or an unknown area; experiencing its different cultures; learning its different languages and customs, then such work is clearly purposive, cognitive, at times emotional, always responsive, and always working to transmit the resulting visions of the world to the reader. In McPhee's "geological" essays his purpose is to transmit a vision of the "old" world that will deeply transform our existing vision of surface topography into a four-dimensional understanding of its deep structure, not only to reveal the world's fundamental properties but also to model a way of seeing, a way of understanding, a way of knowing this land upon which we live and travel through time in all its incredible dynamics. In each of John McPhee's essays in "the literature of fact," this cognitive, epistemological impulse fully informs his work. McPhee's compulsion to see and experience, to know and understand every aspect of this world, and to teach is perhaps nowhere clearer than in his luminous *Annals of the Former World.*

In 1978 McPhee began a long-term project to research and write about the science of geology and its practitioners, journeying repeatedly across the United States in the company of various experts. However, he discovered that he had bitten off a much larger project than he wanted to attempt all at one time. Subsequently, he published over the next twenty years four book-length essays, including *Basin and Range, Assembling California, In Suspect Terrain,* and *Rising from the Plains. Annals* reprints these earlier essays and adds two new pieces: a short *Narrative Table of Contents* that serves as an overall guide to the volume by giving a clear statement of his method and purpose, and *Crossing the Craton,* which develops the narrative for the relatively stable section of the country from Chicago to Cheyenne where for more than a thousand million years, not much happened to its deep structure, its geology (*Annals* 6). *Annals,* then, is the completed result of those travels, a unique and masterful travel book.

As with all of McPhee's books and essays, his structural principles and patterns for *Annals of the Former World* emerged as he analyzed his materials, especially the voluminous notes resulting from his extensive, detailed, and repeated interviews and experiences with the geologists who are his principal scholarly resources. His challenge was to find a structure and a style that would explain clearly and accurately and without condescension the arcane theories employed by the geological sciences that show us the country itself as mobile, as terrane in motion over vast, barely imaginable reaches of time, creating for his readers a special kind of vision, a four-dimensional vision that enables us to see below the surface topography and behind the face of time. His subject is challenging to us humanoids whose time as a species on earth is not yet even the pencil mark at the end of the yardstick. Although the basic plan of his "travels" that comprise the book's narrative thread is the journey from New York to San Francisco, the narrative itself is not linear; it jumps around the country and detours to various other points. This "jumpiness" is driven by the need to understand and explain older tectonic activity in the eastern United States by visiting examples of tectonics working in the same way today, in Nevada, for example, as they were in New Jersey two hundred million years ago. In addition, he added a new section, *Crossing the Craton,* because his initial overall device of traveling over the country to reveal its geology had left a significant "epic caesura," a blank in his analysis of the middle of the country, from "Chicago to Cheyenne." However, the geophysical insights of recent years and recent advances in a number of fields allowed him to travel down in the "basement" of the mid-continent, as it were, in the company of W. R. Van Schmus of the University of Kansas, to see how it had been constructed in the Precambrian eons, covering about 4,000 million years.

In another new section written for *Annals,* "A Narrative Table of Contents," McPhee instructs us how to read the book, written entirely in the form of journeys, as "an unfolding piece of writing and not as a catalogue of geologic topics" (7), a document of discovery rather than a document of results. Thus, using the devices of an accomplished travel writer, McPhee engages his readers, taking us into the country to visit the "hot spots." He helps us, as tourists and students, see the country deeply in all its dimensions including deep time, attracting a popular audience while winning the approval of the scientific community. In set pieces, sketches, flashbacks, and "histories of the human and lithic kind," he establishes and explains clearly plate tectonics as the theoretical basis of his exploration. He develops compelling narratives of discovery. He profiles the experts with whom he travels in significant and satisfying complexity. The characters and contexts of the six geologists with whom he travels on different segments of his trips across the United States (with a number of relevant side trips) give geology the human face of its researchers and balance his "set pieces," essays *in situ,* on such necessary matters as geologic time, plate tectonics, and glaciation. In the process, he constructs his readers as fellow travelers, intelligent, resourceful, and above all curious about the ground beneath their feet, and of whom he requires a capacity for wonder, an imagination great enough to embrace the fantastic vistas afforded by thousands of millions of years. Furthermore, he instructs these readers by crafting a particularly credible and attractive narrative persona, an insatiably curious person in love with both the science of geology and its language who is also informed by a subtle spiritual vision. He is enthralled with the language of geology, a discipline, he writes, that dispensed "language of the sort that would have attracted Gilbert and Sullivan" (32), its words "floating down the [class]room like paper airplanes" (31). McPhee loves the vigor, the muscularity, the enormous reach and range of contemporary English, and manipulates it like a modern-day Shakespeare to create the landscapes of then and now with equal persuasion and clarity.

While he does not use such terms as "spiritual" or "vision" in these essays, I read his work as fundamentally spiritual, a consequence of the strong tension between the facts of our geological and evolutionary existence and the minds that imagine, theorize, and discover those facts, that seek the means to explain and understand satisfyingly the relationship between the knower and the known, between enormous time scales out of which we have arisen and our own impossibly brief encounter with them. It is not the traditional spirituality of most "organized" religion; perhaps one should simply call it a spirituality induced by contemplation of the perfection of mathematics, physics, and molecular biology. However one may address the qualities of joy and wonder in the discovery of the facts of our physical world that come through McPhee's prose, it is in the geological terms and narratives of plate tectonics, of glaciation, of "continental drift," of enormous and incomprehensible stretches of time seen and seeable in the rock and "explained" by geological theories that the presence of an almost classical spirituality emerges. I think that *Annals* is filled with epiphanic moments in which McPhee brings the reader up before very hard, very physical facts, and illuminates them with the powerful light of contemporary science that overwhelms us with a twin sense of our own short-term lease and an exalted sense of the complexity and dynamism of this earth. Titans shake the floors of our existence.

McPhee's exposition of the exhumation of the Rockies after they were buried in the Miocene, for instance, is breathtaking, his prose crackling as he presents the burial of the mountains of early Miocene Wyoming followed by the mysterious elevation of a significant chunk of the earth's crust about a mile—"the complete interred family of underthrust, upthrust, overthrust mountains" (*Annals* 314). As the land mass rose, water and wind excavated the Wyoming ranges transferring about fifty thousand cubic miles down rapidly straightening rivers that cut through the ancestral mountain ranges like sharp saws through soft wood to deposit that material ultimately in the Mississippi Delta, creating Louisiana. The fierce and unrelenting wind of the region probably carried at least half of the total volume removed from the Rockies, moving it as far away as the Atlantic Ocean and Hudson Bay, according to David Love, McPhee's geological expert for this section. McPhee's recitation of the facts and their expert interpretation stuns the reader into ever larger understandings of the power of geological and meteorological forces over the eons. He relies on understatement, cataloging, the testimony of experts, and always the careful, concrete description of the places, the actions, and the forces, bringing the awesome forces into human scale with the occasional voice of others who live or have lived in the areas.

Because McPhee conceives his audience as curious but not necessarily well informed about the geology of our country or the theories with which geologists are making sense of the rock, he employs the standard strategies and devices of the travel writer to make known the arcane and technical words, theories, and discoveries of geologists, paleobotanists, and paleogeomorphologists, among others. However, he is not one of these experts. He is one of us—curious, well-read, with a variety of interests, who, while perhaps not robustly heroic, is capable of extraordinary physical explorations of this earth. His narrative persona is that of one who, even as an English major designate while in prep school at Deerfield Academy in Massachusetts, developed a generalist's background in geology with the aid and inspiration of a talented teacher. As a professional writer, mostly for the *New Yorker* (*Annals* is his twenty-seventh published volume, all published by Farrar, Straus and Giroux), McPhee has earned a solid reputation as an extraordinary stylist, a writer of clear, detailed expository prose in a genre that he has termed the "literature of fact." He earns our trust as the quintessential, well-informed charter of the territory—whether that territory is a profession, a person, a scientific theory, or a road cut. By his powers as a writer, McPhee makes us see and understand not only his travels but through them the travels of enormous land forms themselves, the continents and crustal plates and island arcs and "exotic terranes," over thousands of miles and hundreds of millions of years and persuades us of the veracity of his vision, his understanding, his reporting.

How does he do this? One of his essential techniques is the pilgrimage—to the road cuts, to the tops of mountains, to the front porches of geologists. We travel with him. In Book 2 of *Annals,* for example, *In Suspect Terrain,* he takes us into road cuts along I-80 just east of the Delaware River with Anita Harris, a geologist for the U.S. Geological Survey, who, although skeptical of plate tectonics, reads rock very well. We learn in the field with McPhee and Ms. Harris that the Delaware River is a hundred and fifty million years old. However, the Tac-onic mountains are fifty million years older. The river 150, and the first ancestral mountains another 250 million years, rising 450 million years before the present. McPhee acknowledges the difficulty of our comprehending the meaning, let alone the significance of these dates, unless we can draw an analogy between "a hundred million years of geology and one human century, with its upward-fining sequences, its laminations of events, its slow deteriorations and instant catastrophes" (209). He invites us here and elsewhere to imagine the mountains themselves coming up like waves, the rivers running first one way then another, the mountains cresting and breaking before there is a period of geologic calm after which the rivers run the other way again. McPhee's landscape seen through the lens of current geological theory is very much in motion, unlike that of the painter, George Innes, who painted "The Delaware Water Gap" in 1859. If we have seen and understood the story that the rock itself tells us, we can see the whole story in the Innes landscape. "The composition is almost infinitely less than the sum of its parts, the flickers and glimpses of a thousand million years" (*Annals* 209).

On every page McPhee is a poet who makes us see that rock. In seeing the rock, we see and learn and know the country in its four dimensions, the landscape never more to be a static picture of "the everlasting hills," but instead a dynamic, ever-changing event, a process that McPhee makes us see despite our inability to experience directly the lands and the waters of this country in their balletic display.

***

In the early years of her career, Anita Harris (then Epstein) and her husband Jack were doing geology in the Madison and Gallatin Ranges of southwestern Montana. They were present for the 1959 earthquake that brought down half a mountain, created Earthquake Lake, and killed scores of campers, an event that made Anita Epstein a catastrophist, one who subscribes to a view of geological formation that takes into account the function of those geological catastrophes like huge earthquakes or volcanic eruptions that punctuate the gradual shaping of the surface of the earth. As if to explain Epstein's strong reaction, McPhee again creates dynamic prose to figure a compelling contrast of human time with geologic time and our typical human responses to such events as the Mount Saint Helens volcano, a tsunami, or a catastrophic landslide. Such events are so rare in the lives of individual humans that only in the last two hundred years or so have humans,

> begun to sense the patterns the events represent....[But] if geologic time could somehow be seen in the perspective of human time...sea levels would be rising and falling hundreds of feet, ice would come pouring over continents and as quickly go away. Yucátans and Floridas would be under the sun one moment and underwater the next, oceans would swing open like doors, mountains would grow like clouds and come down like melting sherbet, continents would crawl like amoebae, rivers would arrive and disappear like rainstreaks down an umbrella, lakes would go away like puddles after rain, and volcanoes would light the earth as if it were a garden full of fireflies. (*Annals* 170–71)

Human time is too thin to attract attention; thus, man arrives on the scene and is astonished. It is in such passages, I think, that we may appreciate McPhee's methods and his skills as a very special kind of travel writer, one who can manage all sorts of perspectives, chronological as well as spatial. His poetic devices, if you will, are the devices of good writing generally—metaphors and similes ready at hand and cached in shoals of parallel structures to enable discovery, convey movement, and illuminate perspective; historical and artistic allusions to bring the awesome geologic facts within the scope of human understanding via human creativity; instruments of travel including the interstate, various vehicles, and his feet and those of his knowledgeable guides. McPhee profiles the geologists, their *Indiana Jones* adventures, and their tools of discovery to bring geology to vivid life through the perceptions and reports of these very human beings. McPhee invites his reader certainly to share in the scenery, but I think he also invites us to ponder the significance of what we see in terms that remind us—as does much sacred literature—of the puny and insubstantial nature, vision, and understanding of mankind. He clearly scorns the suggestion of a *New York Times* letter writer that Mount Saint Helens be bombed to shut down the volcano.

In another context, we stand with Ms. Harris and McPhee on a cool April morning, looking at the consequence of a relatively slow geologic event, a river's crossing a mountain range, "eighteen miles west across a gulf of air to the forested wall of Kittatinny Mountain, filling the skyline of two states, its apparently endless flat ridgeline broken only by one deep notch, which centered and arrested the view and was as sharply defined as a notch in a gunsight: the Delaware Water Gap, where the big river comes obliquely through the mountain, like a thief through a gap in a fence" (*Annals* 182). In this geology lesson, we learn more about the dimensions of time, for in no way could human perception literally see the forces that constructed the big river's attack on the mountain. Nevertheless, through the lens of theory and an altered perception of time, we can see it all in the rock.

Thus, McPhee's passion for the authentic experience as a passport to deeper understanding leads him to stand with Ms. Harris in an I-80 road cut, the roar of traffic in their ears, the backwash from hundreds of huge trucks sweeping over them. He takes us with him to share with Ms. Harris the work of geology with hammer, glass, seismological data, topo maps, hydrochloric acid, and drill bores. We put our noses on the rock face, swing the sledge and the rock hammer to take samples, grow fascinated with and accustomed to the poetry inherent in the naming of rock types, time periods, and terms that identify the mechanisms by which plates move and mountains rise; rivers appear, flow, and are captured; the Delaware Water Gap appears so that Mr. Innes may paint it; and exotic terranes accrete, form up, and move across thousands of miles and millions of years to form a California here, a Cyprus there. We learn to see with fourth-dimension eyes, a special kind of vision, so that the sheer eastern face of the Sierras rises up before us as its western side descends into the Great Central Basin of California;

we learn just how the Mother Lode was imported into the "country" as an exotic terrane, one of several island arcs that "docked" against what we now know as the North American continental plate. We see the "hot spots" of great magmatic upwellings over which continental and crustal plates move, the plumes puncturing those plates to create island chains and volcanic chains in numerous parts of the U.S. and elsewhere in the world, and, according to one theory, lift the entire Colorado Plateau, the Great Plains, and the Rocky Mountain platform (*Annals* 402).

Another important part of McPhee's method as a travel writer in the fourth dimension is that he always presents the testimony and questions of experts at just the right moment to test the depth of our understanding and the solidity of the theory, pacing our explorations like a skilled novelist. To help us appreciate the difficulty of explaining the Raton and Yellowstone plumes, for instance, those enormous upwellings of magma that created massive uplifts of different parts of the great Rocky Mountain range, he brings forward his traveling companion for that part of the journey and renders him with all the detail, color, background, and action of a fictional hero. David Love is a remarkable geologist from Wyoming, a true westerner, whose geologic expertise is rendered credible as much by his questions and reservations as by his methodology and conclusions. His intense query about the nature of "plumes" is an example: "'How do you reactivate a plume? We need answers,'" he says, 'to this sort of thing, and we don't have them. If the plume theory is correct, you've got to answer those questions'" (403). David Love is also a prospector as well as a pure scientist; an exploiter as well as an environmentalist who can see—and with McPhee's help makes us see—"not only what Jim Bridger saw but also—through dimming tracts of time—what no one saw" (404), a perspective that, perhaps, makes more acceptable (even in these times of ecological consciousness) Love's Old Testament view that the resources of nature were put here for the uses of mankind.

Because McPhee profiles each of the "knowing ones" in terms both heroic and human, we get to know and care about David Love's mother, Miss Ethel Waxham, a Phi Beta Kappa graduate in classical studies from Wellesley College. An expert horsewoman, she had never encountered such a remote region as Rawlins, Wyoming, until arriving there in 1905 to teach two little girls at the even remoter Red Bluff Ranch. According to David Love, Rawlins is a place where at one glance one may view twenty-six hundred million years in the rock—from the Archean Eon up to the Miocene Epoch (*Annals* 295). His mother's journals describe the country and her life in it, exuding good humor and resourcefulness in the face of the vast distances, challenging climate, and a sparse human society that included outlaws, sheepmen, and Native Americans. Her future husband, John Love, a "mirthful" Scott and nephew of environmentalist John Muir, having been expelled from the University of Nebraska for unauthorized posting of a sign in a dean's flowerbed, became a cowboy and decided to go to Wyoming. When his team died from poisoned water, he walked

200 miles into central Wyoming where he established a successful sheep and cattle ranch. Learning of Miss Waxham's arrival in the country, he lost no time in visiting her, riding eleven hours each way from his ranch to her residence, sometimes through daunting blizzards and snowdrifts, sometimes even pursuing her to Colorado and Wisconsin. Eventually they married on June 20, 1910. They moved to his ranch in the Wind River Basin where they flourished, raised three children who were basically educated by their mother and who became a petroleum chemist, a design engineer, and "the preeminent geologist of the Rocky Mountains" (*Annals* 308). McPhee's detailed portraiture of John and Ethel Love, his descriptions of the Love Ranch, and his narrative of their challenging life in the midst of such grand geography and weather help us understand David the geologist and, consequently, his insistence on answers to hard geological questions, his love of the country, and his various jobs, including that of mining engineer.

* * *

Another one of McPhee's geologic experts, Eldridge Moores of the University of California, Davis, argues that California has been literally formed by immigrants; not people, in this case, but exotic terranes, chunks of crustal plates in the form of island arcs like the Japanese or the Indonesian archipelagos of today that have traveled over hundreds of millions of years to attach to the plates of the North American continent. Traveling east to west across the Sierra Nevada, McPhee and Moores show us that what mountains are made of is not what made them, that great tectonic forces raise whatever crustal stuff is present up into the air as mountains. Crossing the Sierras, present-day travelers see a "congested lithic barn" containing "rock of such varied type, age, and provenance that time itself becomes nervous—Pliocene, Miocene, Eocene nonmarine, Jurassic here, Triassic there, Ypresian, Lutetian, Tithonian, Rhaetian, Messinian, Maastrichtian, Valanginian, Kimmeridgian, upper Paleozoic" (*Annals* 442). The rocks are from here and there around the Pacific world representing events and the vistas that are unknown to human observers.

This splendid exposition of how California, a marvelous collection of immigrant terranes from all around the South Pacific, came to be, illustrating, I think, a central aspect of McPhee's purpose and method: present the territory with the long view of geological time and processes and explain the processes by which geologists make sense of the jumble of rock thereby creating a coherent narrative of its creation, travels, and origins. This is "tourism," we might say, of a very special sort, and it seeks to explain among other things what the gold rush of the 1840s and 50s (454–72) and the Loma Prieta earthquake of 1989 (*Annals* 603–20) have in common. McPhee's narrative of the formation of the area we now know as California helps today's tourist and resident alike make sense of this edgy and shaky state. California literally has not existed for most of the history of the earth. Because, according to present geological theory, California is an assemblage of varied terranes and physiographic provinces, it is a "restless" place shaken by earthquakes along a host of faults—the great San Andreas, the Hayward, the Cucamonga, and hundreds of others. One result of this extensive faulting and shaking is that the San Gabriel Mountains of Southern California are at present the most rapidly growing range of mountains in the country. However, it is also a range that is coming down about as fast as it goes up, its incredibly incompetent and fractured rock, visible from every hiking trail, subject to the great and destroying processes of erosion. One is reminded of *Isaiah:* "For the mountains shall depart and the hills be removed..." (54:10).

In his capacity as interpreter *par excellence* of current geological theory, McPhee carries us to San Francisco's famed Mussel Rock, where we face north, place our right foot on the east side of the great crack in the earth's crust known as the San Andreas fault, our left foot on the west side, and almost feel our stride lengthening. Then he tells us that some granite under the sea off Mussel Rock that apparently originated from the southern Sierra Nevada, "has traveled three hundred miles along the San Andreas system, and continues to move northwest" (*Annals* 432). To comprehend the implications of that statement requires an act of imagination and faith strengthened by theory and knowledge.

McPhee summarizes the arguments that California has only recently come into existence, that for most of the history of the world, no landforms existed where California exists now. What we know as the North American continent and the continental shelf ended far to the east, just blue sea reaching down some miles to ocean-crustal rock, which was moving as it does into subduction zones to be consumed. Spreading centers like that presently expanding the Atlantic Ocean were creating vast areas of new ocean floor that were in turn being moved around the world and recycled in subduction zones and trenches before any particle of California appeared. Then, however, a piece at a time, chunks of crust banged into the continental plate and stuck, although, McPhee says, "Baja is about to detach....Some parts of California arrived head-on, and others came sliding in on transform faults, in the manner of that Sierra granite west of the San Andreas" (*Annals* 423).

The crustal block on the west side of the San Andreas, that, in its rising transform pressure has pushed up the San Gabriels and the San Bernardino mountains, gives the residents a bump every once in a while and reminds Angelenos of the frailty of their security and existence. The Great Valley of California is probably, according to Karen Kleinspehn, another of McPhee's geologists, "an example of a late-stage compressional basin—formed as plates came together" (*Annals* 25). McPhee's claims are breathtaking and take on the quality and character of contemporary origin myths (Turtle bringing up mud on a large scale, shall we say). They poetically explain and celebrate the origins of a state whose settlement and culture, politics, and sociology are, one might argue, uncanny reflections of its geology. Geology is destiny. In California, especially, where the edges of the North American plate collide with the edges of the oceanic crustal plates, plate tectonics announces its agenda clearly. The rocks which comprise California arrived here from elsewhere, their composition and contributions—consider the Mother Lode as just one example—are enormously significant to the state's economic and cultural history and mock its political boundaries. Plate edges collide, elide, slide over, transform, and are transformed in the process. Likewise cultural "edges."

The rhythms as well as the information presented at the beginning of *Book I: Basin and Range* reveal the motives and background of the author, a man determined to go upon a journey of discovery as mythic as any Odyssey, its "hero" as purposeful and changed as any Ulysses who sets out "to seek a newer world," to understand the recent revolution in the shift from the "old" geology to the "new" that had recently taken place. McPhee frames his quest in the metaphoric terms of his change from a lustful youth "staring up the skirts of eastern valleys" and learning the rudiments of Old Geology, to "middle-aged and fading" but filled with passion to learn something of the "New Geology," "to feel the difference between the Old and the New" (34). There is nothing neutral in his orientation, his commitment, his quest. In fact, one hears interesting echoes of Tennyson's "Ulysses": "I cannot rest from travel; I will drink/ Life to the lees...Come my friends, /'Tis not too late to seek a newer world. /Push off, and sitting well in order smite/The sounding furrows...." (6–7; 56–59). One also finds in McPhee's journeys a useful parallel with Joseph Campbell's formulation of *The Hero with a Thousand Faces*. McPhee sets off on his voyage of discovery from his "humble" village of Princeton, New Jersey. He encounters challenges, experiences conflicts, enjoys the passions of the search, and brings back the boon of his adventure: knowledge of the new geology. His narrative in all its plots and subplots argues the worth of his journey, the significance of his discoveries, the importance of his coming back to tell us all. McPhee is the hero of his mythic narrative, constructing new relationships of awe and understanding between us and geology, especially the geology of the United States, and bringing back the boon of knowledge that will be of benefit to the larger community. Because of McPhee's literary artistry in deftly handling the conventions of "literary nonfiction," we will never look at a road cut or a mountain range or either coast of our country in the same way again. Our lives are changed by McPhee's experiencing the country and telling the tale of it.

He, indeed, "charts the world afresh," not only with expert testimony but with homey metaphors, the lithic barns into which a wildly disparate collection of objects, the rocks of former worlds, has been assembled. Through the clarity of his convincing exposition of a revolutionary explanatory theory we see through the topography to visualize the rocks lying in four dimensions beneath the topography, to see the structure, and to understand that "structure on the move [through time] is tectonics" (*Annals* 446) and to see "landmasses converging to form superterranes and breaking apart to form new continents [to] become the outermost laminations of new landscapes" (449). Thus, Sonomia docked against western North America in early Triassic time, about 250 million years before present time, creating what has been called the Golconda Thrust. However, Sonomia was actually the second terrane to attach. The first arrived in Mississippian time, thrusting itself almost to Utah. A third terrane followed Sonomia in the Mesozoic, "smashing into it with crumpling, mountain-building effects that would propagate eastward through the whole of Sonomia, metamorphosing its sediments...and folding them at least twice" (450).

I think McPhee is successful in attaining his purpose because of his artful blend of expert testimony rendered credible by his careful characterization of experts and an unflinching deluge of technical vocabulary, analytical processes, summarized debates—and his own deep involvement in the learning process: reporter as the best observer. Not the expert, but, like you and me, passionately involved in discovering what the expert can show him and relating that information, those visions, to what he sees from the winding track of the mountain road or through his Hastings Triplet. He renders his experts credible by getting to know them often over periods as long as fifteen years or more. Kenneth Deffeyes (rhymes with "the maze") has a "tenured waistline," hair flying behind him like Beethoven's, his voice "syllabic, elocutionary, operatic," is a man devoted to "the entire narrative of geology in its four-dimensional recapitulations of space and time," a teacher whose goals "are ambitious to the point of irrationality" expecting at the very least that "a hundred mint geologists [will] emerge from his course" (35), a general education course at Princeton. We learn about their families, their living arrangements, their hobbies, their education and careers; we watch their beards grow white along with McPhee's—and, possibly, our own. In addition, he invites us to travel the same road cuts, stop at the same spots, and put our noses on the same outcrops. It is a journey, he says, "that above all else is physiographic, a journey that tends to mock the idea of a nation, of a political state, as an unnatural subdivision of the globe, as a metaphor of the human ego sketched on paper and framed in straight lines and in riparian boundaries between unalterable coasts" (26). McPhee's powers as a travel writer are informed, I believe, not only by scientific elements of geologic theory, but by spiritual wonder in the presence of our physical world. Although we have inhabited it for an incredibly short time in comparison with its own age, McPhee makes us aware that the human curiosity and passion to know, to investigate, to travel through time and space, make us able to see these tracts of time, these vistas of geological formation and movement and destruction as if they were indeed literally before our eyes rather than present only in the palimpsest of the rock.

What an absolute joy it is to be caught up in John McPhee's powerful and evocative prose, to gain a powerful sense of place, to feel and understand the edges of geological structures, theories, and terranes, to travel with him in the four dimensions of our physical world. As Gerard Manley Hopkins put it:

> And for all this, nature is never spent;
> There lives the dearest freshness deep down things
> And though the last lights off the black West went
> Oh, morning, at the brown brink eastward, springs—
> Because the Holy Ghost over the bent
> World broods with warm breast and with ah! bright wings.
> ("God's Grandeur," 9–14)

Geology *is* destiny.

Works Cited

Blake, William. "Auguries of Innocence." 1863. *The Complete Prose and Poetry of William Blake.* Ed. David Erdman. New York: Anchor, 1982.

Campbell, Joseph. *The Hero with a Thousand Faces.* Princeton: Princeton UP, 1990.

Gray, Rockwell. "Travel." *Temperamental Journeys: Essays on the Modern Literature of Travel.* Ed. Michael Kowalewski. Athens, GA: UP of Georgia, 1992. 33–50.

Handel, G. F. *The Messiah: An Oratorio for Four-Part Chorus of Mixed Voices, Soprano, Alto, Tenor, and Bass Soli and Piano.* Ed. T. Tertius Noble. Milwaukee, WI: G. Schirmer, Inc., 1938.

Hopkins, Gerard Manley. "God's Grandeur." 1877. *Poems of Gerard Manley Hopkins.* Ed. Norman H. MacKenzie. New York: Oxford UP, 1976.

McPhee, John. *Annals of the Former World.* New York: Farrar, Straus and Giroux, 1998.

———. *Coming Into the Country.* New York: Farrar, Straus and Giroux, 1977.

Tennyson, Alfred Lord. "Ulysses." 1842. *The Works of Alfred Lord Tennyson.* New York: NTC/Contemporary Publishing, 1998.

Thoreau, Henry. *Walden.* New York: W.W. Norton, 1966.

Chapter 11

Kurt Vonnegut's Search for Soul

Donna Foran

Oscar Wilde in "The Decay of Lying" suggests that the best of fiction is a lie (Adams 673–86). In short, he claims that art should not portray life as a realistic representation but instead should order it with a form actual life does not contain. In Kurt Vonnegut's works we see a similar benediction of art as lying in order to get at truth. Vonnegut says, "everything is a lie because our brains are two-bit computers, and we can't get very high-grade truth out of them...we do have the freedom to make up very comfortable lies. But we don't do enough of it" (Allen, *Conversations* 77). Most authors use the search for truth beyond factuality as their vehicle to produce this ordered "lie," which is the life of fiction, what John Steinbeck calls the "self-character." Vonnegut's characters and narrators journey to far-flung worlds Science can only hint at in a search for truth beyond factuality (Steinbeck 363–64). No matter where they travel in time or space, Vonnegut's characters and narrators come back to square one, searching for, wishing for, and hoping to find soul.

Vonnegut journeys inward in an attempt to get at truth itself. It is an American truth he looks for because it is American perspective he knows. It is the truth of his ancestry since his ancestors came to America from another country; it is the truth of the sum of his own familial and personal experiences. J. G. Keogh and Edward Kislaitis have suggested that a singular moment, the February 13, 1945, fire bombing of Dresden by American and British bombers which Vonnegut saw firsthand, forms the pivotal experience he writes about in all his novels to create "an intriguing polyphony" (38–40). The firebombing can certainly be seen as a catalyst for Vonnegut's *Slaughterhouse-five* and his desire to write. How, then, can one explain the journeys to Tralfamadore, Vonnegut's fictional planet, or to the center of Kurt Vonnegut himself? These journeys go beyond a single, physical, factual event, reaching into Vonnegut's genealogy and the philosophies by which America itself is driven. Explaining Vonnegut is explaining America, a complicated miasma of idealism and cynicism at once. The Great

Depression affected his own family profoundly, as it did America and its culture, even more than the world wars affected it. Vonnegut maintains that the immigrant-driven nature of Americans left it "without a culture" and that the Great Depression left it "embarrassed" and feeling useless because "The machines fired everybody" (Allen, *Conversations* 108).

In *The Sirens of Titan* (1959), that uselessness, a barren culture, and embarrassment is supported with Vonnegut's scientific education. Vonnegut had studied chemistry, biology, engineering, and archeology—not literature (Allen, *Conversations* xvii). Space travel is a given in *Sirens* (not so at the time of its writing); life on other planets is assumed. The point of the novel seems to be that life on Earth and especially in victorious, postwar America may be hollow, but because it is all we have got, it should be lived properly. The reader discovers that, for instance, the Great Wall of China and other of humankind's notable efforts were erected to serve as a signpost for a single space traveler who was looking for a part to fix his spaceship. We are told that even Stonehenge "is a Tralfamadorian word meaning 'Replacement part' being rushed with all possible speed" (*Sirens* 271). The traveler is Salo, a character from the planet Tralfamadore, who is a machine with somewhat human characteristics. He has been used by Earth's and his own planet's rulers. He was to carry a message but never to know it until the Earth-human Winston Niles Rumfoord—his friend—demands to know it. At this point Salo replies that he is being made to make war against his own nature as a machine. "His mind buzzes and pops" like a human being's "with thoughts of love, honor, dignity, rights, accomplishment, integrity, [and] independence" (300). Salo's journey, although physically comprising half a million years in Earth time and "over a distance of one hundred and fifty thousand light years in space," has taken him to the core of his being at which he finds he has been unnatural to himself. He cannot live, he says, because he is more human than machine-like. Thus, Salo kills himself by taking himself apart and throwing his parts in all directions, and all for a friend. Salo has become human, a role Vonnegut sees as perhaps the most difficult role there is. The original inhabitants of Tralfamadore, Salo's home, were human, but deliberately eliminated themselves on behalf of machines—who were much less trouble. Vonnegut explains that the Tralfamadorians felt so purposeless that they created machines who could be more useful. Those machines discovered that the humans were indeed useless. The Tralfamadorians then began killing each other—so efficiently that they turned that job over to the machines as well and, "the machines finished up the job in less time than it takes to say 'Tralfamadore'" (275). Nevertheless, Salo has become human; this machine entity has been unable to avoid taking on the characteristics of human beings. He has begun to search for soul.

Soul-searching, in fact, is a difficult task for any of Vonnegut's characters and occupies most of their time. The planet Earth that Vonnegut writes about here has a history he calls the Nightmare Ages, those occurring after World War II and before what he calls the "Third Great Depression." He describes this period of time as "a nightmare of meaninglessness without end" in which the souls of human beings have not yet been explored (*Sirens* 8). Vonnegut's omniscient narrator starts his story sometime after this "Nightmare Age," saying "Everyone now knows how to find the meaning of life within himself" (7). This ironic assumption is made so that the reader realizes he will be delving into a history of what has gone before the *Sirens* story, a history of our own times in America.

Vonnegut sees *The Sirens of Titan,* in fact, as being largely about Franklin Delano Roosevelt, the major political figure of his lifetime, and the notion of life being lived simultaneously rather than chronologically. One major character, Winston Niles Rumfoord, is described as being as aristocratic as Roosevelt was, from the use of a cigarette holder to his prep-school accent and the timbre of his voice. In *Conversations* Vonnegut said of Roosevelt, "He was elected to his first term when I was ten years old. And he spoke with this aristocratic Hudson Valley accent which nobody had ever heard before, and everybody was charmed. You know, here was an American. And we do love it so when we find a dignified American...." (159). The "chrono-synclastic infundibula" Rumfoord/ Roosevelt experiences, being able to appear in many different places in time, is an occurrence Vonnegut explains as natural to all human beings: "I honestly believe," he says, "that we are wrong to think that moments go away, never to be seen again. This moment and every moment lasts forever" (Allen, *Conversations* 63). Another character is Chronos, whose good-luck piece turns out to be the part of the spaceship that has triggered Salo's quest. In this manner, Vonnegut ties the events of his own time in America to a much broader picture. Salo has a quest—finding the part in order to deliver his message—and so does the story's main protagonist, Malachi Constant. Rumfoord is a catalyst allowing the quests to continue and also allowing them to stop at moments in time when characters must meet, disagree, and conflict with each other's lives.[1] The kinds of quests they are place Vonnegut's work squarely into American literature.

Leslie Fiedler has categorized Vonnegut's work as a popular rather than an elitist production as a result of Vonnegut's need to write for "slick" magazines—which paid well—and for a paperback rather than a hardcover market—which paid quickly—because he wrote to support himself and his family. However, Fiedler's praise is decidedly not faint when he says Vonnegut's critical approval was inevitable because his books are "thin and wide, rather than deep and narrow...which open out into fantasy and magic by means of linear narration rather than deep analysis; and so happen on wisdom" (Fiedler 196). Fiedler is seizing on American themes here to create a term for Vonnegut's work, "New Romanticism," such as "that tale of the male companions...in flight from women and in quest of the absolute wilderness," much like a Western saga or Fenimore Cooper's work (195–96). The difference in *Sirens*, however, is there is no "flight from women" here; Malachi's union with Beatrice produces not only Chronos but also a great deal of literature from Beatrice. Her own journey runs from Rumfoord to Malachi to Chronos to wisdom. Fiedler admits there are some vestiges of Modernism in Vonnegut's work, and indeed there are. A recurrent theme in the books is the quest for understanding by a man, and often by an artist. The most "romantic" aspect of this intricately composed and highly allusive and metaphoric text is that it is a story Vonnegut claimed easy to write, a kind of "lovechild" of a book. Vonnegut told an editor, Knox Burger, that he had an idea for this book when he had none at all. He says he began to tell the editor the story "of the Sirens of Titan. Every mother's favorite child is the one that's delivered by natural childbirth. *Sirens of Titan* was that kind of book" (Allen, *Conversations* 35, 159*)*.

The book may have come naturally but was, nevertheless, extremely complicated and multileveled. Lawrence R. Broer, has explained its copious allusions to *Alice in Wonderland* and *Through the Looking Glass,* for example, as leading him to decide that "it is not outer space but the 'uncharted terrain' of Malachi's own mind and soul where the main action of the novel takes place" (30). However, Broer's view of Vonnegut as producing schizophrenic characters gets in the way when he sees the Rumfoord door which Malachi Constant opens to enter a different life as "a psychical one suggesting that Malachi is the only verifiable character in the novel" (31). Why only Malachi? Why not Malachi as a self-character of Vonnegut's? It is one thing to think of an author's various characters as parts of an author's mind and another to distort a story by denying the existence of those who people it. As it is, *Sirens* contains a broad enough cast of characters, and at least one of them *is* split into variations upon a theme in the way Constant morphs into the different characters of Malachi Constant, Jonah K. Rowley, Unk, and the Space Wanderer. Only memory lapses, though, and differing circumstances define Malachi Constant's different names; all his actions fit into the characterization of Malachi Constant, a name meaning "Faithful Messenger" (*Sirens* 17).

Like old Salo, the Tralfamadorian space traveler, Malachi also wanders—and wonders. What is his message? Like Salo, he, too, is being used—to bring the necessary part to Salo's spaceship. Too late, we think at first, but not too late for his own use. Was Salo's journey ever important? Was Malachi's? Malachi's story is told chronologically; his and Beatrice's son, conceived on Mars and later to live on Titan, is named "Chronos." Chronos carries the spaceship part as his lucky piece, having accidentally picked it up on Mars where Unk has lost it after getting it from Rumfoord. When Malachi puts Salo back together again as a result of his loneliness after Beatrice's death, he tells Salo what he has learned from his wandering, that "a purpose of human life, no matter who is controlling it, is to love whoever is around to be loved" (*Sirens* 313). Rumfoord—not omnipresent but *often* present—disappears, annoyed to be used by the Tralfamadorians. Salo allows his reassembly, no longer minding being used. Beatrice, before her death, thanks Malachi for being used by him, saying, "The worst thing that could possibly happen to anybody would be to not be used for anything by anybody" (310).

Finally, Malachi asks Salo to take him to Indianapolis, Indiana (Vonnegut's hometown), because he remembers that it was the first city in the country which had actually hanged a Caucasian for the murder of a Native American (315). Malachi Constant is ready to die at this point, and when Salo's parting gift to him, a hypnotic vision of his former best friend, arrives to take him to Paradise, much to Malachi's surprise his friend says, "Somebody up there likes you" (319). Vonnegut ends on this note of irony. It is Salo, his fellow messenger, to which this vision refers, but Malachi's journeys do end happily. That they do does not mean that Vonnegut's vision of them is sentimentalized. Rather, Malachi's happiness rests on the science that Vonnegut sees behind Malachi's travels and their close connection with religion—at least Vonnegut's kind of religion, which is inextricably bound with his science.

Vonnegut's conceptions of time in *Sirens* rest on a partially Einsteinian universe in which his chrono-synclastic infundibulum "acts as a parody of the theological concept of eternity," as Joseph Sigman suggests (Mustazza, *Critical Response* 28). Vonnegut's character Rumfoord, while appearing to be omniscient, is not. He says, ".. the end is as much a mystery to me as to you" (*Sirens* 52). Because he is not omniscient, neither is he omnipotent. As Sigman points out, omniscience is a quality not only attributable to deities but also to narrators (Sigman 29). Vonnegut is an omniscient narrator in this novel, claiming on the first page that mankind has found the meaning of life in a religion different from earlier religions, a religion which "protects the innocent as a matter of Heavenly routine" (*Sirens* 6). In this story, a flashback to the "Nightmare Ages" he announces as the setting for the novel, Rumfoord's church is dedicated to "God the Utterly Indifferent" and Rumfoord's rocket fuel is "The Universal Will to Become." It is a universe built upon chance and yet depending upon purpose—which in turn provides meaning and self-knowledge. It is, again, a search for soul. A yet deeper look at the meaning of such voyaging can be seen in Vonnegut's most popular novel, *Slaughterhouse-five.*

Billy Pilgrim is *Slaughterhouse-five*'s main protagonist, but another important protagonist is Kurt Vonnegut himself. The author here is writing about the firebombing of Dresden, in which both he and Pilgrim share a specific time and place. The two "characters" should not be confused with each other. As Robert Merrill and Peter A. Scholl argue, *Slaughterhouse-five* "is not a novel simply about Dresden. It is a novel about a novelist who has been unable to erase the memory of his wartime experience and the Dresden fire-storms" (128). That author here warns us against Billy Pilgrim's "Tralfamadore," nearly an anagram for "or fatal dream" (Broer 87). Pilgrim cannot live with the horror of Dresden and escapes by becoming "stuck in time," traveling to and from that point to make sense of it, and finally succumbing to a Tralfamadorian understanding of time. This understanding allows Pilgrim, the optometrist, to "correct the whole erroneous Western view of time, and explain to everyone the meaninglessness of individual death" (Merrill and Scholl 128). That is, of course, if individual death ought to be considered meaningless at all.

It is important, therefore, that the reader understand both Vonnegut's (as narrator) and Pilgrim's points of view. Specifically, Vonnegut is angry about humankind's selfishness and cruelty. *Slaughterhouse-five* is not an anti-war book; it merely exposes the cruelty that too easily attaches itself to people who know they are fighting a righteous cause. In his address to the American Physical Society in New York in 1969, Vonnegut says,

> The Second World War was a war against pure evil. I mean that seriously. There was never any need to moralize. Nothing was too horrible to do to any enemy that vile. This moral certainty and the heartlessness it encouraged did not necessarily subside when the war was won. Virtuous scientists, however, stopped saying "Can do!" (*Wampeters* 99)

Perhaps, though, the virtuous scientists did not stop saying it soon enough. Neither war nor suffering is a plausible choice for Vonnegut. Discussing Hiroshima, Dresden, and the German extermination camps in his address to the graduating class at Bennington College in 1970, he explains his pessimism regarding the human race but asks the class to "...believe in the most ridiculous superstition of all: that humanity is at the center of the universe, the fulfiller or the frustrator of the grandest dreams of God Almighty" (*Wampeters* 163). If this were so, he says, there might be hope. Although Vonnegut has said he is an atheist, much of his work contradicts that statement, unless he considers imagination and creativity God-like. Later in his address to Bennington he says,

> The arts put man at the center of the universe, whether he belongs there or not. Military science, on the other hand, treats man as garbage—and his children, and his cities, too. Military science is probably right about the contemptibility of man in the vastness of the universe. Still—I deny that contemptibility, and I beg you to deny it, through the creation of appreciation of art. (*Wampeters* 165)

He lectures about less need for information or intelligence, concluding that people need to be less selfish and that America's free enterprise system "is much too hard on the old and the sick and the shy and the poor and the stupid, and on people nobody likes" (*Wampeters* 166–68).

Billy Pilgrim's views are substantially different because he is a student of Tralfamadorian philosophy. Pilgrim is an optometrist in Ilium, a city where the General Forge and Foundry Company requires its 68,000 employees to wear safety glasses and thus guarantees his success. However, he is deeply sad. He weeps from time to time without having any reason anyone—including himself—can understand. He is depressed because he is lonely. He has married for money and has a daughter who thinks he is senile at forty-six and who appears to rejoice whenever she is condescending to him or robs him of his dignity. In addition, he was at the firebombing of Dresden while a prisoner of war, as was Vonnegut.

Dresden was an open city, free of fear of bombing since it had no war indust-ries or troops quartered there. However, it was bombed anyway by America and England on Feb. 13, 1945. Both Billy and Vonnegut report on it. Billy describes the destruction to the lovely ex-porn star Montana Wildhack when he is her mate on Tralfamadore. He tells her, "It was like the moon" after the fire bomb-ing, describing "little logs lying around," which he does not at first recognize had been people before the firestorms (*Slaughterhouse* 179).

Then when he is asked by a Tralfamadorian what he has learned so far at the zoo where he is kept on that planet, he explains he has learned about peace. He had not seen it on earth but had instead seen "the bodies of schoolgirls who were boiled alive in a water tower by my own countrymen, who were proud of fighting pure evil at the time" (116). Vonnegut as narrator does not personally describe the scene but instead gives his words to Pilgrim. However, he does write elsewhere about the difficulty of describing the events of *Slaughterhouse-five,* admitting that he thought he could simply report it, whether from memory or from discussion with friends who served with him in the war, but that it had not been possible then or even later. In a *Playboy* interview, Vonnegut says, "There was a complete forgetting of what it was like...Dresden had no tactical value; it was a city of civilians. Yet the Allies bombed it until it burned and melted. And then they lied about it. All that was startling to us" (*Wampeters* 262–64). In *Slaughterhouse,* Vonnegut admits having been asked by Harrison Starr, a mov-iemaker, whether it is meant to be an anti-war book. He says "I guess," to which Starr asks, "Why don't you write an anti-*glacier* book instead?" Vonnegut re-sponds, "What he [Starr] meant, of course, was that there would always be wars, that they were as easy to stop as glaciers. I believe that, too" (3). The difficulty of enunciating horror and finding reasons to keep searching for meaning beyond that horror opens up differing critical perspectives.

Tony Tanner, for example, sees Vonnegut's comments reflecting a Tral-famadorian philosophy. He notes Billy Pilgrim's justification of the bombing of Dresden: "It was all right," said Billy. *"Everything* is all right, and everybody has to do exactly what he does. I learned that on Tralfamadore" (*Slaughterhouse* 198). Then, though, Tralfamadore may mean "or *fatal* vision" and should stand as a warning. Tanner questions whether this is a "culpable moral indifference," asking, "Can one afford to ignore the ugly moments in life by concentrating on the happy ones? On the other hand, can one afford *not* to?" He considers Pil-grim's time travels "fantasies...which serve to drug men to reality. When the reality is the Dresden fire-storm, then arguably some drugging is essential" (129). Such a view confuses the identities of the narrator and Billy Pilgrim, although understandably, since the Tralfamadorian "so it goes" is enunciated as much by the narrator as by Pilgrim.

Robert Merrill and Peter A. Scholl say, however, that such a view is Billy Pil-grim's wisdom alone and that Tralfamadorian wisdom must be questioned.

They cite Vonnegut's own words as proof:

> There are people, particularly dumb people, who are in terrible trouble and never get out of it, because they're not intelligent enough. And it strikes me as gruesome and comical that in our culture we have an expectation that a man can always solve his problems...that if you just have a little more energy, a little more fight, the problem can always be solved...This is so untrue that it makes me want to cry—or laugh. (*Wampeters* 258)

Merrill and Scholl point out that Pilgrim "is one of those people who are in terrible trouble and not intelligent enough to get out of it...unable to imagine a saving lie except one that denies personal moral responsibility" (148). The Tralfamadorians, who say "So it goes" after any mention of death—whether of person, place, thing, or action—are not only fatalists but do not believe in free will. They are concerned, however, with happiness; that is their first question to Billy on Tralfamadore, a question posed, significantly, from a speaker on a television set: "Are you happy here?" (*Slaughterhouse* 113).

The Tralfamadorians have told Billy they are responsible for the end of the universe when "a Tralfamadorian test pilot presses a starter button, and the whole Universe disappears." Pilgrim asks them if they can prevent the catastrophe and is assured they cannot. "He has *always* pressed it, and he always *will*. We *always* let him and we *always* will let him. The moment is structured that way" (117). Confused by the seemingly peaceful nature of the planet, Billy is told that not all moments there are peaceful and, since they cannot do anything about the bad times, they ignore them—and Earthlings ought to do the same thing. However, while this philosophy might suit the Tralfamadorians very well, it makes Billy Pilgrim cry and does not suit Vonnegut. Human beings are not machines; Tralfamadorians are. Humankind cannot ignore, among the deaths and atrocities determined by war, the "springtime" that comes with war's end, when "The trees were leafing out" and an abandoned wagon is "green and coffin-shaped" (215). Death and compassion and love form a trinity in *Slaughterhouse-five*. As Malachi Constant says in *The Sirens of Titan*, "a purpose of human life, no matter who is controlling it, is to love whoever is around to be loved" (313).

A facile answer? Vonnegut was allowed—critically—to get away with the only conclusion he could reach in *Slaughterhouse-five*, perhaps, but paid more heavily for his answers in *Breakfast of Champions,* maybe because they were supplied by his alter ego, Kilgore Trout, the writer of pulp science fiction. Trout shows up regularly in many of Vonnegut's books, sometimes as a character, sometimes simply as a writer whose ideas a character adopts. In *Slaughterhouse-five,* one of the books that Billy is given by his hospital-mate Eliot Rosewater is *The Gospel from Outer Space*. Rosewater describes Kilgore Trout as a terrible writer who has good ideas. He says he doubts if Trout has ever been out of America because all of Trout's characters sound like Americans while demographics argue that Americans are a distinct minority on Earth. Rosewater tells Billy he is the only one who has ever heard of Trout and that his letters to the writer always come back because Trout's many publishers all fail. Billy also meets Trout at a bookstore where he finds a copy of *The Big Board,* a novel he thinks he has not read. It is about "an Earthling man and woman who were kidnapped by extra-terrestrials...[and] put on display in a zoo on a planet called Zircon-212" (*Slaughterhouse* 201). Kilgore Trout, obviously, is incredibly important to Billy Pilgrim and to the interpretation of *Slaughterhouse-five.* Billy travels to Tralfamadore, all right, but does he travel mentally or physically? His ideas come from Trout. Rosewater's point about Trout always writing about Americans is also critical. From Vonnegut's first novel *Player Piano* (1952), based on his own work in public relations for General Electric, to his last at this writing, *Timequake* (1997), in which he proposes four new amendments to the Constitution, it is American themes and values he writes about—nowhere in a more blistering way than in *Breakfast of Champions.*

An early *Newsweek* review by Peter S. Prescott reduces its plot to a size "so small you could stuff it in an earthworm's ear," then describes it as full of "gratuitous digressions" and "eighth-grade obscenities." He concludes that it is "pretentious, hypocritical manure" denying man's complexity—a reaction which can easily be explained if a satirist is read literally (qtd. in Merrill, *Critical Essays* 39– 40). This review, however, was at least more enlightening than those of critics who simply ignored any references to sex made in the novel. The sex is impossible to ignore, as is the crassness. There is absolutely no subtlety whatsoever about Vonnegut's constant references to penis sizes and garish lifestyles; he is deliberately pointing out America's obsessions with sex and money. Kilgore Trout, for example, in accepting the Nobel Prize for Medicine in 1979, says in *Breakfast,*

> There were two monsters sharing this planet with us when I was a boy...the arbitrary lusts for gold, and, God help us, for a glimpse of a little girl's underpants. I thank those lusts for being so ridiculous...[Now] we can build an unselfish society by devoting to unselfishness the frenzy we once devoted to [them]. (25)

As William Rodney Allen has noted, "Vonnegut's purpose is not to titillate but to allow the reader to see through convention" (Allen, *Understanding* 107). He points out the ugliness of the American scene: "polluted, strip mined, and made horrifically ugly with advertisements...T-shirts with inane slogans...trucks [bearing] letters eight feet high" and even the title of the novel. Vonnegut explains,

> I learned politeness at my mother's knee...not to offend anyone by discussing excretion, reproduction, religion, or a person's sources of wealth...[but] if we are to discuss truthfully what America is and what it can become, our discussion must be in absolutely rotten taste, or we won't be discussing it at all. (*Wampeters* 216)

Truthfulness demands such an approach because the topics he mentions above *are* discussed freely now, and he believes that many "sinister taboos" interwove themselves among those his mother taught in the name of politeness. Kilgore Trout believes we must move beyond this kind of freedom to discuss "tasteless subjects" and devote our time instead to unselfishness. If Kilgore Trout's ideas are not taken seriously in the novel, it can have no value, will never move beyond the "tasteless."

Like *The Sirens of Titan* and *Slaughterhouse-five,* the novel follows the travels of a major character, this time Trout, and this time not to the edge of the universe or to a point in time—although the timing of Trout's trip is important in *Breakfast.* His odyssey is to the heart of America, "Midland City, Indiana,"[2] to celebrate an Arts Festival on a holiday weekend, November 11, Veterans Day. Philboyd Studge, the narrator of the preface to *Breakfast of Champions,* indicates that Veterans Day was once called something else:

> ...all the people of all the nations which had fought in the First World War were silent during the eleventh minute of the eleventh hour of Armistice Day, which was the eleventh day of the eleventh month...[when in 1918] millions stopped butchering one another...old men on battlefields during that minute [said]...that the sudden silence was the voice of God. (6)

The narrator explains that because Armistice Day was sacred and Veterans Day is not, he will forget about Veterans Day because of its lack of meaning but that he will commemorate Armistice Day because "I don't want to throw away any sacred things." His suggestion is that Americans do throw away important things and perhaps not always with their conscious assent. He is disturbed that "American experience has been an unhappy experience...living without a culture. When you came over here on a boat...you abandoned your culture" (Allen, *Conversations* 109). *Breakfast of Champions* takes place on this weekend in 1973, Vonnegut's fiftieth birthday, at a time when Studge/Vonnegut says he can no longer live without a culture (5).

In many ways, although Vonnegut's work is considered science fiction because it is so often placed in the future, he writes more about the past, but that is probably because he realizes the past cannot be changed. It is not unreasonable, when he sees past mistakes also being made in the present, for him to assume they will also be made in the future—thus, the crux in his works, a clash between determinism or hopelessness, and free will or hopefulness, which we see in all his writing. He assures his readers that *Breakfast of Champions* is about suicide and also that he is past suicide; things really are impossible—but it is possible to live with them. He is definitely concerned with the past—with the effect the Great Depression and wars have had on the country, and with the present—because American concerns seem to him to be absurd. So it is only the future with which he can deal to achieve any sort of optimism.

In *Breakfast of Champions* Kilgore Trout tries to prophesy the future while literally mired in the present. After hitchhiking to Midland City, he steps into Sugar Creek where his feet are covered with a plastic substance that dries in air instantly. He wants to leave footprints in the motel lobby but cannot because of the plastic. He wants to be able to say, "I am simply using man's first printing press," that is, putting one foot down after the other, making significant footprints indicating, "I am here" (*Breakfast* 226). Vonnegut explains that "life is now a polymer in which the Earth is wrapped so tightly" and that because the scientific diagram for plastics goes on and on, he tends to begin sentences with "and" and "so" and to end them with "and so on" or "ETC" (228).

As in the two novels previously discussed, there are two important protagonists. In the case of *Breakfast of Champions,* Kilgore Trout cannot carry the novel's message alone. Dwayne Hoover is also needed, with the narrator along for omniscience when necessary—and sometimes as a character. Dwayne is necessary for background, to depict the American scene against which the narrator rails, but he also shares in some of the narrator's own problems. Dwayne Hoover only travels mentally. Both Hoover and Trout suffer from the chemical menace, but while Trout sees it outside himself in the city and countryside—and only accidentally sheaths his feet in plastic—Hoover suffers internally from what Vonnegut calls the Yin and Yang of madness, bad chemicals and bad ideas. The chemicals are manufactured by his body; the ideas are supplied by Kilgore Trout. Trout had written a book convincing Dwayne that he was the only person in the world with free will and that everyone else was a robot. He had not meant it. The narrator says of Trout's book, "It was a *tour de force.* It was a *jeu d'esprit.* But it was mind poison to Dwayne" (15). This is reminiscent of the Prescott review above in which Vonnegut is chided for believing that human beings are machines: "If we pretend that we are only machines we cannot pretend to be interesting enough for a novel" (qtd. in Merrill, *Critical Essays* 40). There are also critics who insist that the novel has only one character: Dwayne Hoover. Satire is tricky, of course, but the narrator has clearly warned the reader to beware of Hoover's opinions. His body's chemicals and his brain's analysis of Trout's ideas have poisoned him and made him untrustworthy.

The Midland City Arts Festival never occurs but does provide a place for Hoover and Trout to meet. Trout is impressed by one of the works of art produced by Rabo Karabekian. The narrator says he is transformed by his own character, Rabo, at this point because he too has come to the festival "to be born again" (*Breakfast* 219). Rabo has painted "The Temptation of Saint Anthony," on a canvas twenty feet wide and sixteen feet high. It is avocado green and has on it a vertical stripe created by orange reflecting tape. He has been paid $50,000 for his work, and even the narrator thinks it is outrageous, a typically elitist fraud that takes money from the poor. He changes his mind, however, when he hears Karabekian describe it: "It is a picture of the awareness...the immaterial core of every animal—the 'I am' to which all messages are sent. It is all that is alive and maybe sacred in any of us. Everything else about us is dead machinery" (221).

From the suspicion that all men are machines without free will like Salo, from entertaining the notion that acting without free will and accepting death to avoid pain the way Billy Pilgrim does, from describing the inane preoccupations of American society and considering it machine-like, Karabekian's art has made the narrator—and Trout—value awareness and, further, value it as sacred.

From the corroding and pestilential world outside, the trip inward has produced joy through art—flawed joy, but joy. The novel itself, replete with simple drawings throughout its pages, shifts away from words entirely toward the end and becomes a series of basic sketches presented in silence. Richard Giannone suggests that this silence refers back to that sudden silence that World War I veterans described as the Voice of God on Armistice Day, reminding us that Vonnegut is playing God "in the oldest of artistic guises, the omniscient Creator" (111).

This core of awareness is where all messages are sent. We are reminded again of the meaning of Malachi Constant's name—faithful messenger—and that Vonnegut shares at least a part of all of the characters he creates. In *Breakfast of Champions,* seeing the bad effects Trout's words have had on Hoover, he talks about the words he himself creates. He says he will stop telling stories, letting other writers order the world they see. He says he wishes to do the opposite, to bring chaos to order, because if all writers did it perhaps their readers would finally understand that the world has no order. Robert L. Nadeau, beautifully connecting narrative theory with physics, explains that Vonnegut "is not simply stepping out from the blind of his fiction and revealing himself as narrator…but also affirming the possibility of freedom in a cosmos in which indeterminacy makes imaginative choice a possibility" (44). This nicely entrenches Vonnegut in the postmodern world where old cosmologies and old mind-habits simply do not apply.

Vonnegut bases his conclusions about chaos versus order on the belief that Americans try to live their lives like fictional characters with proper beginnings, middles, and ends. Further, he thinks that Americans are "treated by their government as disposable as paper facial tissues" because writers treat bit-part "players" in their fictions the same way (*Breakfast* 210).

Trying to break that mold, in this novel he introduces himself to his creation, Trout, and offers him an apple as a symbol. However, he says he must explain it because it is so simple, so "oriental in its simplicity," and Trout, like himself, is American. He explains that Americans like beautiful symbols and especially ones which "have not been poisoned by great sins our nation has committed, such as slavery and genocide and criminal neglect, or by tinhorn commercial greed and cunning" (293).

Of course, he does *not* explain it, but because of other references to Genesis in his works, it is self-explanatory.[3] Free will is a two-edged sword. When Kilgore

Trout offers three wishes to his parrot Bill, Bill is confused and hops back into his cage. Kilgore congratulates him: "You made sure you'd still have something worth wishing for—to get out of the cage" (*Breakfast* 35). When the character Trout is given his freedom, he pleads, "*Make me young, make me young, make me young!* " (295). However, the narrator merely sets him free with the final words "*Bon voyage*" (294). He will be on his own with no more help than any individual can expect in his or her own travels.

By setting his characters free and clearing his mind "of all the junk in there—the assholes, the flags, the underpants" the narrator says, he will be able to begin again. He can no longer perform as he has in the past because the ideas he had in the past were the ideas of others and did not fit into the reality he saw outside of himself (*Breakfast* 5). Vonnegut considers the old conventions of fiction as outmoded as Karabekian sees the cocktail waitress Bonnie's use of the phrase "Breakfast of Champions" every time she serves a customer a martini. Karabekian asks her if it does not get tiresome, and she responds that she only tries to cheer people up. She apologizes. She hopes she is not giving offense (5). Bonnie may apologize, but Vonnegut does not beg our pardon for his novel, and sometimes he does mean to give offense.

It is worth looking at one more book to explain the kinds of inward voyages in this search for soul that Vonnegut's characters and narrators take. Although *Mother Night* (1961) was published two years after his second book, *The Sirens of Titan* (1959), eight years before his most popular book, *Slaughterhouse-five* (1969), and twelve years before *Breakfast of Champions* (1973), its form and subject matter are completely different from any of the others. It is straightforward, or as straightforward as a postmodernist writer like Vonnegut can make a book after the technological influences of society have permeated his thoughts and actions. It cannot be called science fiction. William Rodney Allen calls it a spy novel but immediately notes that it is more than that, in fact, because it functions "by exploring the metaphysical implications of the network of conscious and unconscious fictions that make up human experience" (Allen, *Understanding* 46). However, Allen is even closer to the mark when crediting Vonnegut's scientific background for the real difference in his novels. Vonnegut in fact is in reality not particularly interested in or in favor of space travel. In *Conversations,* he relates in a 1973 interview with David Standish a conversation with a cab driver who, he said, expressed his own feelings: "...the money should be spent on space when we can *afford* it. He wanted better hospitals; he wanted better schools, he wanted a house for himself" (98–100). When Standish notes that Vonnegut is "closer to a scientifically minded writer like Thomas Pynchon than to Henry James, [it is because] Vonnegut creates *science* fiction—even when his work has nothing to do with outer space" (Allen, *Understanding* 9).

This view is particularly applicable to *Mother Night.* No omniscient narrator is present here, and Vonnegut does not appear as a character, although he does call himself an editor of Campbell's confessions. The first-person narrator is Howard W. Campbell, Jr., without even a split personality to guide the reader on this sometimes bumpy trip. This character has a German background, is involved—deeply—in World War II, and is an artist. As Hitler is gaining power, Campbell is writing rather romantic plays inspired by Helga Noth, the beautiful actress/wife whom he adores. He is idealistic and cares nothing at all for politics, having been transplanted from America to Germany as a child by his parents because his father's job—for General Electric—required the move. These details remind the reader of Vonnegut himself and are the way the author is able to work himself into the text. Campbell is writing his memoirs—or confessions— because he is about to go on trial for war crimes in Israel committed long after the war; in a nearby cell is Adolf Eichmann. The question is, is Campbell guilty? To determine whether he is the reader must travel Campbell's own path and think as he does, at least part of the time. Vonnegut announces the theme early in the introduction: "We are what we pretend to be, so we must be careful about what we pretend to be" (*Mother Night* v).

For the rest of the novel, the reader must think about this theme. Eventually, the reader must also question it. Is it possible for an artist, recruited as a spy by the United States, to ingratiate himself with the Nazis, to merely "pretend" and still be guilty of war crimes? Frank Wirtanen warns him that only Wirtanen and President Roosevelt will know he is a spy and that the United States will never admit it has recruited him. Thus, it makes sense for the Israelis to indict him for the brutal broadcasts he has made working for Goebbels, Hitler's Minister of Propaganda. However, it is the very moral which Vonnegut states so early, "We are what we pretend to be," which must eventually be called into question. Are we? Is Campbell? Is our use of free will "free"? Broer points out that the anagram for "Wirtanen" is "near twin"—and resembles "or fatal vision" for "Tralfamadore,"possibly a useful observation that also may further cloud the issue. Wirtanen and Campbell are both spies, but only Campbell is a double agent. In addition, Campbell seems to have a choice here.

Campbell's search for meaning begins and ends with love. He claims no political ties except to a "Nation of Two," the nation that is his wife and himself. In this special relationship filled with "uncritical love," Campbell explains, "Oh, how we clung, my Helga and I—how *mindlessly* we clung!...Away from the sovereign territory of our nation of two, we talked like the patriotic lunatics all around us. But it did not count (*Mother* 44)." Vonnegut emphasizes the word "mindlessly." It is an early warning of trouble ahead. Campbell is a romantic. He prefers writing plays with form, saying that he admires orderly art with a beginning, a middle, an end, and even a moral (136). He sees his own life as a play, in fact. While he has been creating highly effective propagandistic radio broadcasts for the Nazis, he has also been sending information to the Allies through a code of coughs and pauses he does not himself understand. Inadvertently, he has broadcast the news of his own wife's death. When Wirtanen sees him still alive years later, he explains that he thought Campbell would kill himself because of the news. Campbell says, "You would think that a man who's spent as much time in the theater as I have would know when the proper time came for the hero to die...I missed my cue for the great suicide scene" (136).

Indeed, at the novel's end, Vonnegut implies Campbell's suicide. However, the suicide does not come in time to prevent Campbell from a life of betrayal by others, just as he has betrayed all decency in supporting the basest of Nazi aims. Campbell is so torn by the results of those betrayals that long before the novel's end, he reaches a point when he literally cannot move: "I had absolutely no reason to move in any direction. What had made me move through so many dead and pointless years was curiosity" (167–68). Campbell no longer has a center, a belief, anything to prod him. He allows outside sources to move him, in this case, a policeman who asks him to move on. His paralysis is extreme and indicates the struggle with which he has dealt throughout his ordeal as a counterspy—or simply as a person who tried to live with too many different kinds of "truth" without ever really examining any of them.

Broer suggests that Campbell's (and Vonnegut's) struggle with guilt and pessimism "is that same spiritual journey made by Conrad and James, and by Hawthorne and Melville before them. It is a plea for the recognition of the Devil within and its power for distorting our humanity, and it is an act of expiation carrying with it a hope for renewal" (46).

Perhaps. But no real hope appears to exist for Campbell. He believes that he *is* the man he has pretended to be. Love—as he has understood it, in a highly romantic manner—is gone. He seems to see no real awareness in himself. Vonnegut might agree. In an interview with Robert Scholes in which Scholes says *Mother Night* "seems a little darker" than Vonnegut's other novels, Vonnegut responds, "It's more personally disturbing to me. It had meanings for me. Oh, because of the war and because of my German background" (Allen, *Conversations* 129). In an interview with Laurie Clancy in 1971, Vonnegut said his German background "made it very touchy to seem to be in any way an apologist for Nazi Germany. I had to be very careful about that" (Allen, *Conversations* 50). Allen points out that Vonnegut's title, coming as it does from Faust, "makes clear that the threat comes not only from the man-made folly of war, but from the nature of the universe itself" from the principle of entropy itself, that systems tend toward death. He believes, too, that Vonnegut's fiction reflects Schopenhauer's philosophy "that consciousness, the most complex of systems, itself may be a striking exception, an accidental and probably temporary anomaly in the vast unconscious process of the material universe" which indeed wants to return to nothingness (*Understanding* 49).

Mother Night's "Editor's Note" cites the quotation from Mephistopheles in Goethe's *Faust* which ends "I hope it won't be long till light and the world's stuff are destroyed together," indeed a cheerless conclusion. The editor says Campbell has chosen the title and the dedication ("To Mata Hari" because he, too, had whored in espionage), but the editor does say that now that he has read Campbell's confessions, he would prefer to dedicate the book to someone more contemporary. He then writes that he is dedicating the book to *himself* in the following words, "This book is dedicated to Howard W. Campbell, Jr., a man who served evil too openly and good too secretly, the crime of his times. —Kurt Vonnegut, Jr" (*Mother* xii).

Skipping this "Editor's Note," or indeed skipping Vonnegut's introduction preceding it, allows the reader to follow Campbell's memoirs easily and without confusion, with the exception of having to decide whether "you are what you pretend to be" is a valid statement. However, once these sections are read there is confusion. Mary Sue Schriber explains the confusion beautifully:

> The confessions are unavoidably filtered through the editor in spite of his efforts to the contrary. Moreover, the confusions of Campbell the confessant within the edited confessions themselves are multiple [because Campbell's false pro-Nazi stance was "true" to his German audience, and the reader] stands at a third rem-ove from all of this...to discover a merely subjective but nonetheless anticipated truth—that turns out to be unattainable. (176-77)

The fact that Vonnegut, as "editor" signs his own name but dedicates the book to "himself," as "Howard W. Campbell, Jr.," is quite enough to start the confus-ion. Deciding what is supposed to be real and what is actually fiction in the "confessions" seems to be a part of Vonnegut's game, part of the "lies" he advoc-ates for writers, establishing another kind of indeterminacy on the work. Schriber concludes that, "If the degree of truth in the written word is measured by its reflection of reality, whatever that is, then nothing in *Mother Night* is true except the problem of truth itself" (177). The problem of truth indeed appears to be at the heart of Vonnegut's search, and it is not a problem for scientific reas-oning. It is metaphysical, going to the essence of a human being. *Mother Night* is an early work ending on a note of despair even if its last line is "*Auf wiederse-hen?* " Allen, in *Understanding Kurt Vonnegut,* looks at the novel as leading to Vonnegut's next book, thus "ending not with Campbell's suicide, but with a question...Until we meet again?" (53). Of course, after *Breakfast of Champions,* in which Vonnegut dismissed his characters to set them free, he might not have written any other books either. However, he did, and his travels were extensive.

Kurt Vonnegut's works have traveled near and far, but especially inward, es-pecially toward a search for the sacred. The novels subsequent to the ones dis-cussed above have shared that search, including *Timequake*, published in 1997 when Vonnegut was seventy-five. The most welcome surprise in *Timequake* was the reappearance of Kilgore Trout, to whom he gives the last words of the book (although there is an epilogue). These are: "I have thought of a better word than *awareness*....Let us call it *soul* " (214).

Vonnegut often attracts readers because he can be humorous while dealing with serious topics. He is. Sometimes. Nevertheless, he is also dead serious, which is when he stops being funny. He makes us work, he asks us to consider, he begs us—please—to think. Vonnegut can be a migraine waiting to happen if we see that he is both simple and complicated. "All you need is love," said the Beatles, and Vonnegut seems to agree. Where does that "simple" love come from? For Vonnegut, it appears to come from a nonscientific, metaphysical concept. "Soul" is not a concept postmodern critics would agree on as a life force. However, it appears to have a serious place in Vonnegut.

Notes

1   For an extremely interesting view on how the books's characters come together in spiral formations, see David Ketterer.

2   Richard Giannone points out that Midland City recalls "Midland, Michigan, home of Dow Chemical, whose creativity has found unforeseen applications for plastic" like napalm and body bags (105).

3   See especially Leonard Mustazza's chapter on "Adam and Eve in the Golden Depths: Edenic Madness," in *Slaughterhouse-five:* pp. 102–35.

Works Cited

Adams, Hazard, ed. *Critical Theory Since Plato.* New York: Harcourt Brace Jovano-vitch, 1971.

Allen, William Rodney. *Understanding Kurt Vonnegut.* U of South Carolina P, 1990.

———. *Conversations with Kurt Vonnegut.* Jackson: UP of Mississippi, 1988.

Broer, Lawrence R. *Sanity Plea: Schizophrenia inn the Novels of Kurt Vonnegut.* Rev. ed. Tuscaloosa: U of Alabama P, 1989.

Fiedler, Leslie A. "The Divine Stupidity of Kurt Vonnegut." *Esquire* 74 (September 1970): 195–97, 199–200, 202–04.

Giannone, Richard. *Vonnegut: A Preface to His Novels.* Port Washington, NY: Kennikat Press, 1977.

Keogh, J. G., and Edward Kislaitis. "*Slaughterhouse Five* and the Future of Science Fiction." *Media and Methods* (January 1971): 38–40.

Ketterer, David. *New Worlds for Old: The Apocalyptic Imagination, Science Fiction, and American Literature.* New York: Anchor Press, 1974.

Merrill, Robert, ed. *Critical Essays on Kurt Vonnegut.* Boston: G. K. Hall, 1994.

Merrill, Robert, and Peter A. Scholl. "Vonnegut's *Slaughterhouse-five:* The Requirements of Chaos." Ed. Merrill *Critical Essays.* 142–51.

Mustazza, Leonard, ed. *The Critical Response to Kurt Vonnegut.* Westport, CT: Greenwood Press, 1994.

————. ed. *Forever Pursuing Genesis: The Myth of Eden in the Novels of Kurt Vonnegut.* London: Associated UP, 1990.

————. "Adam and Eve in the Golden Depths: Edenic Madness in *Slaughterhouse-five.*" Mustazza, *Forever Pursuing Genesis* 102–15.

Nadeau, Robert L. "Physics and Metaphysics in Vonnegut." *Mosaic XIII* (Winter 1980): 37–47.

Prescott, Peter S. "Nothing Sacred." *Newsweek.* May 14 1973. 114–18. Rpt. in Merrill. Ed. *Critical Essays.* 39–40.

Schriber, Mary Sue. "Bringing Chaos to Order: The Novel Tradition and Kurt Vonnegut, Jr." Ed. Mustazza. *The Critical Response.* 175–85.

Sigman, Joseph. "Science and Parody in Kurt Vonnegut's *The Sirens of Titan.*" Ed. Mustazza. *The Critical Response.* 25–41.

Steinbeck, John. *The Acts of King Arthur and His Noble Knights.* Ed. Chase Horton. New York: Ballantine Books, 1976.

Tanner, Tony. *City of Words.* New York: Harper and Row, 1971.

Vonnegut, Kurt. *Breakfast of Champions.* 1973. New York: Dell, 1991.

————. *Mother Night.* 1961. New York: Dell, 1991.

————. *Player Piano.* New York: Delacorte Press, 1952.

————. *Slaughterhouse-five.* 1969. New York: Dell, 1991.

————. *The Sirens of Titan.* 1959. New York: Dell, 1991.

————. *Timequake.* New York: G. P. Putnam's Sons, 1997.

————. *Wampeters, Foma & Grandfalloons (Opinions).* New York: Dell, 1974.

Chapter 12

Willa Cather's Nebraska Prairie: Remembering the Spirit of its Land and People

Heidi N. Sjostrom

As Jim Burden is leaving Black Hawk at *My Ántonia*'s end, he stumbles on a fragment of the old tracks that used to lead from town to his grandfather's farm. He describes the tracks as, "mere shadows in the grass" (418). Those symbolic indelible tracks in the landscape are what Cather leads readers along, back to the scenery and attitudes she learned to value when she traveled at age nine from Virginia to Nebraska in the late 1880s. The people and land of Nebraska so impressed Cather that, to her, what was "true" and "good" was embodied there. Cather catalogues weather and terrain, animals and plants, and many different prairie travelers in order to illuminate and enrich readers with the strong spirit she found when, in 1883, she first entered that country. Both Cather and her fictional alter ego, Jim Burden, left Nebraska for college and a life in New York City; therefore, Cather is clearly not requiring that people stay on or return to the prairie. However, she is celebrating the prairie values that enriched the rest of her life. Like Cather, the characters in *My Ántonia* (published in 1918) travel away from the Nebraska prairie, either permanently or for a time, and they come to value the prairie's spirit in a new way as they contrast it with the city.

Book I of *My Ántonia,* which contains two-fifths of the novel's total pages, fascinates readers with descriptions of the landscape and climate of 1880s Nebraska, a multicultural cast of characters with speech and stories from differing lands, and female characters strengthened by that land. However, Cather's aim in Books II through V is to show that her characters learned not only from their journey into the Nebraska prairie, but also from their journeys out of it. As Alfred Kazin has said of Cather, "She did not celebrate the Pioneer as such; she sought his image in all creative spirits—explorers and artists, lovers and saints, who seemed to live by a purity of aspiration, and integrity of passion or skill, that represented everything that had gone out of life or had to fight a losing battle for survival in it" (19). When immigrants and pioneers first traveled to Nebraska, they found a flat and unforgiving land that required all their integrity, passion, skill, and creativity. When their children left the prairie for the town, they found they most valued the virtues and stories of those prairie days. It is of that spirit and how the Nebraska landscape called it forth that Cather sought to remind *My Ántonia*'s readers.

Cather clearly endorsed a realm of the spirit, but she did not endorse a specific religion. She was interested in the spirit carried in the landscape and its people. Harold Bloom notes that, even *Death Comes for the Archbishop*, a novel about Catholic priests, is "easily misread as a growing religiosity by many critics.…Cather emulated a familiar pattern of being attracted by the aura and not the substance of Roman Catholicism. New Mexico, and not Rome, is her place of the spirit, a spirit of the archaic and not of the supernatural" (2). Cather's spirituality is illustrated by her insight as she looked at Dutch paintings. She wrote that in the detailed Dutch domestic scenes, there was often "a square window, open, through which one saw the masts of ships or a stretch of gray sea" (qtd. in Seaton 5). Cather thus began to see how she could use everyday events and landscapes to evoke the spirit of something greater. The prosaic events, words, and sights of 1880s Nebraska are in the foreground of Cather's painting, and the spirit that pioneers discovered in the landscape and climate to which they traveled shines through the window.

Like her characters who leave the prairie and live in towns, Cather herself lived many years in cities. However, her mind had been teased by the spiritedness of a Czech girl she had known in Nebraska, and she wrote,

> One of the people who interested me most as a child was the Bohemian hired girl [Annie Pavelka] of one of our neighbors [the Miners], who was so good to me. She was one of the truest artists I ever knew in the keenness and sensitiveness of her enjoyment, in her love of people and in her willingness to take pains...Annie fascinated me and I always had it in mind to write a story about her. (qtd. in Bennett 46–47)

Most of the events in *My Ántonia* did actually occur among Willa Cather's neighbors in Nebraska. For example, Annie Pavelka did follow a railroad man who deserted her, and Annie's father committed suicide and was buried at a crossroads (Bennett 48–51). Wick Cutter was modeled after Red Cloud's lascivious Mr. Bentley, who shot himself and his wife to prevent her from inheriting his money-lending fortune (84–85). The Harlings were directly modeled on the Miner family, to whose daughters Cather dedicated *My Ántonia*. Additionally, "a crayon enlargement of Annie Pavelka's...first daughter recalls the one that Jim Burden sees of Ántonia's baby Martha" (Rosowski and Mignon 3). Cather seems to have followed the method of writing that Jim Burden describes in the introduction of *My Ántonia* (xi). Cather wrote down her memories and then selected and arranged them to emphasize the importance of the prairie spirit.

When Cather herself traveled to Nebraska as a child, she found a landscape foreign to her previous experiences in Virginia. However, as critic Laura Winters has noted, Cather's books are often about characters traveling to "the place of exile that they make their own" (5). The young Jim Burden seems exiled but curious in passages like the one where her meets Otto Fuchs upon his arrival at the Nebraska train station. Otto asks Jim if he is afraid to have come so far west, and Jim looks at him with eyes wide with as much curiosity as if Otto were Jesse James (*My Ántonia* 6). Jim's excitement about being on the prairie is revealed in a passage where Jim thinks that the Swiss Family Robinson had no more exciting adventures than did early prairie settlers (74). The concomitant fear of the traveler who is first exposed to Nebraska is shown in passages like the one where, having just left the train station with Otto, Jim feels that this empty landscape cannot even be affected by the human heart. He says, "Between the earth and that sky I felt erased, blotted out. I did not say my prayers that night" (8). Jim felt his old spiritual ways rendered him a stranger on these blank and empty prairies. Cather's biographer postulates that, while Cather loved the open spaces of Nebraska, she retained an ambivalent fear of them because there was "no place to hide" (qtd. in O'Brien 69). For Cather and Jim Burden, this feeling of fear and emptiness in a wide, flat landscape forms an opening through which a new kind of neighbor- and land-centered spirituality, unlike what might have been found in a Virginia church building, can come in. When Jim moves to town three years after being transplanted to the prairie, he again realizes he must learn many new things. The contrast between the old and new landscapes opens him to find new spirit and energy.

In her books, Cather emphasized story and memory, rather than drama, because she felt they could bring important strengths and values into the present. Richard Millington quotes Fredric Jameson's remark in *Marxism and Form:* "[T]here is no reason why a nostalgia conscious of itself, a lucid and remorseless dissatisfaction with the present on the grounds of some remembered plenitude, cannot furnish as adequate a revolutionary stimulus as any other" (714). Cather's revolutionary critique was to point out that many city dwellers had lost the spirit available on the prairie. Unlike several people writing near the 1918 publication date of *My Ántonia,* Cather did not want immigrants to lose their native stories and memories. She hoped they would mix their past stories with those of the landscape to which they came. At the same time, Cather did not despair of a fulfilling life in the modern times developing around her. *My Ántonia* has "a characteristic Cather dual perspective: one eye lovingly, almost elegiacally, on the past, and the other—usually a hopeful eye—on the future" (Harvey 3). The plow silhouette is a strong reminder of the farming past, but it shrinks as the girls and Jim watch (*My Ántonia* 279). Like Jim, who goes away to college, then to the big city and an important career, Cather looked back to the spirit of early Nebraska to find sustenance: "[She found] in her present day some of the enduring values from earlier days...Cather seems to have remained hopeful that these values would continue to endure for future generations" (Harvey 5). In fact, Jim Burden's success as a New York railroad executive is attributed to strengths gained in his prairie days (*My Ántonia* x). Indeed, Burden and Ántonia function together to show how the blend of prairie strength and town polish is the ideal. Patrick Shaw writes, "by juxtaposing this idealized frontier female [Ántonia] with Jim, the successful capitalist who incidentally is articulate enough to write a book, Cather managed the...truly spiritual marriage, the integration of selves that was in fact impossible" (67). Impossible or not, writing *My Ántonia* was Cather's way of transmitting her feelings about Nebraska to future readers.

Instead of a driving plot, the substance of *My Ántonia* is Cather's memory of a new land and the stories that travelers to and from there made and told. The Bible is largely composed of stories and parables because of their powerful ability to affect faith, emotions, and values, and that is how *My Ántonia* passes on its truths, also. Walter Benjamin cites as characteristics of "the story" its usefulness and practical interests, its freedom from explanation of the story as it is being told, and its mingling of a religious view with worldly accuracy (86, 89, 96). The stories in *My Ántonia* use these characteristics effectively. It is when the people of Virginia, Austria, Bohemia, Russia, and other places tell stories from their home regions that the spirits of all those settling on the plains are enriched.

The mixing of languages is important to defining the culture of the prairie. For example, Jim Burden is interested to hear Ántonia's family speak at the railway station and says it was the first time he had heard people speaking a language other than English (*My Ántonia* 6). Soon he shows interest in his grandfather's use of an unknown word during devotional time: "Selah." Jim says, "[As] he uttered it, it became oracular, the most sacred of words" (14–15). Even the word "Selah" shows Cather's interest in mingling spiritual resources: "Cather shows how a commonplace devotion, a cornerstone of Protestant daily life, turns on a word [Selah] that is unknown. Domestic religious life is made strange and made sacred by the admission of the foreign" (Reynolds 82). Cather included much of the everyday, immigrant-enriched language people spoke in the Nebraska of her girlhood. She was a great observer and champion of this kind of talk:

> The language people speak to each other is the native tongue. No writer can invent it. It is made...in communities where language has been undisturbed long enough to take on colour and character from the nature and experiences of the people. The "sayings" of a community...imply its history, suggest its attitude toward the world, and its way of accepting life. (Cather *On Writing* 56)

The mix of foreign and domestic is what travelers to the town missed when they left the prairie. Jim comments on how amusing it is to hear Lena Lingard speaking in formal phrases, making commonplace remarks (*My Ántonia* 318). Jim is better pleased with Ántonia's broken, though honest, English when he returns to her at the book's end.

The strength of the prairies is personified in the character of Ántonia, who traveled to Nebraska from eastern Europe. A vital part of Ántonia's strength remains her Bohemian origins. Quite late in the book, when she is working for the Harlings, Ántonia tells Jim that she remembers even the forest paths of her own country (271). Ántonia's solidity helps Jim come to terms with the prairie in which they are both aliens: "Jim uses Ántonia to make the vast, threatening expanse of the prairie into a manageable, valuable, memory-laden place" (Winters 12). With Ántonia, Cather created a character who was marginalized by her immigrant status, female gender, and reduced economic class, but Ántonia's spirit is shown as unbowed: "[T]hroughout the novel, [Ántonia] 'tries on' various selves, and makes choices that extend her limits" (Harvey 52). Ántonia makes choices about her life rather than allowing her voice to be silenced and her spirit to be constrained. When the Harlings tell her to choose between being their hired girl and dancing at the tent in town, Ántonia chooses not to define herself as a lower-class, immigrant, female worker with no options. Instead, she quits so that she can enjoy the good times and the tent while they are present (*My Ántonia* 237). This spirited refusal to bow to convention foreshadows the courageous and forthright way Ántonia handled having a baby, although its father abandoned her. Ántonia is Jim's source of enlightenment because of her close connection to the earth's energy. Mrs. Harling says that, after Ántonia has worked for her in town a while, she will forget the hard days of farmwork (175). However, Ántonia herself says, when her railway fiancé wants her to live in Denver that she is not sure how well a country girl like herself can manage in a town without chickens and a cow (349). The town contrasts with the country, and Ántonia knows where her heart truly lies. Her repetition, near the novel's end, of her connection to the land reveals that her travels to town have sharpened her insight into her dependence on the earth's energy: "I'm never lonesome [on a farm] like I used to be in town" (387). Having weathered the difficult journey from prairie to town and back again, Ántonia finds she belongs on a Nebraska farm, where her strength and spirit are both required and fed.

Some readers feel that Ántonia's power as a symbol of earthy life force and spirit is weakened by her aging appearance when Jim travels back to revisit her. Most critics agree that "Cather's primary sexual attraction was to other females and...such attraction perplexed her throughout her life because homoeroticism clashed with her strong sense of social propriety" (Shaw 2). Whether or not Cather's disinterest in men meant that "lying at the heart of her design is the theme of submergence-emergence—an artistic manifestation of her personal conflicts and contradictions" (Shaw 58), Cather was perhaps more aware than some writers of alternative purposes for women's lives, beyond beauty and marriage. Ántonia's loss of teeth, gray hair, flat chest, and "battered" look in her mid-forties is not a particularly happy ending for the book, but Cather makes a point of contrasting how much better Ántonia looked than society women "whose inner glow had faded...as if the sap beneath [their skin] had been secretly drawn away" (*My Ántonia* 379). It was that sap, not sexual attraction, that Cather wanted to show as valuable. Certainly, Cather did not think writing about love relationships was the best route to the universal spiritual truths she was seeking. "She considered the vicissitudes of sexual passion a 'trite' and 'sordid' theme, which a writer as talented as Kate Chopin would do well to avoid in favor of 'a better cause'" (Seaton 1). Eudora Welty saw Cather's women refusing marital entrapment for the sake of Art. Welty insisted that "What [Cather's] characters are mostly meant for...is to rebel. For her heroines in particular, rebelling is much easier than not rebelling, and we may include love, too, in not rebelling...It is rebelling...for the sake of something a great deal bigger—for the sake of integrity, of truth, of art" (Welty 155). Integrity, truth, art—those universal truths interested Cather much more than sex and beauty. Ántonia is perfectly able to embody those truths and remind Jim of the land's lessons even when, or perhaps especially when, she is nearing the end of her life's journey.

Mr. Shimerda, Ántonia's father, also seems to have represented special spiritual truths to Cather. He is second only to Ántonia in emotional importance to Jim, and we realize that if Jim and the Shimerdas had not moved to a new homeland, they never would have met. Several times, Jim mentions how unforgettable Mr. Shimerda's appearance or words were. When Ántonia nestles a late summer katydid in her hair, Mr. Shimerda listens, and Jim says that he will never forget Mr. Shimerda's sad and pitying smile (*My Ántonia* 47). When Mr. Shimerda comes to visit the Burdens in their airy house that contrasted so sharply with his dark sod cave, Jim notices how Mr. Shimerda's spirit, so starved for culture and beauty, is fed (*My Ántonia* 98–99). Jim also remembers Mr. Shimerda when he writes his high school graduation speech. Jim tells Ántonia that he dedicated the speech to her father (*My Ántonia* 263). However, Mr. Shimerda is one traveler to whom the Nebraska prairies do not give strength. Instead, they exhaust him so that he finally shoots himself. Critic Patrick Shaw writes, "the motifs may be summarized thus: The mysterious prairie grows wheat, corn, wild flowers, and pragmatic people aplenty, but it cannot nurture artistic sensibility, sexual unorthodoxy, philosophical diversity, or idealists" (Shaw 22). Jim makes a similar interpretation. He feels that Mr. Shimerda's spirit was more suited to the refined culture of his native Bohemia than to the rough energies of the prairie. Jim admires Mr. Shimerda's cultured refinements and entertains the appealing fantasy that Mr. Shimerda's soul has returned, after his death, to Bohemia's woods and fields, where he was happy. The people of the prairie vote with Jim on whether Mr. Shimerda should suffer judgment for his unhappiness. Just as Jim's grandfather predicted, future prairie travelers never drive over the long red grass on Mr. Shimerda's grave. They drive around and leave a little island in the prairie. Jim says, "Never a tired driver passed the wooden cross, I am sure, without wishing well to the sleeper" (*My Ántonia* 136). The travelers who come after Mr. Shimerda seem to understand how the sometimes brutal landscape of Nebraska could exhaust one's hope, and they honor his spirit.

Cather sometimes evoked the spirit of Nebraska's pioneers by using traditional religious symbols. On the way to Peter's house the night Pavel dies, Jim and Ántonia look up at the night stars from the back of the wagon, and Jim reflects that, although he and Ántonia originally came from different continents, they both feel that the stars have a divine influence on their lives (59). In addition to stars seen by travelers all over the world, Cather uses Jim's grandparents' Christianity to illustrate the good of the people who came together in Nebraska. Grandmother visits the Shimerdas, and Jim notices that both she and Jake take so seriously their Christian responsibility to their fellows on life's journey that, on the way home, they discuss at length how easy it is for good Christians to forget that they are their brothers's keepers (84, 89). Grandmother even models inclusivity in her attitude toward the farm's badger, who occasionally kills a chicken. Grandmother will not let the farmhands hurt him, however, because "In a new country a body feels friendly to the animals" (19). In contrast to the Shimerdas, who condemn Mr. Shimerda to lie buried at a crossroads and are sure he will go to hell for committing suicide, Jim's grandfather shows compassion with his prayer at the graveside, saying that they were leaving Mr. Shimerda at "Thy judgment seat, which is also Thy mercy seat" (134). Traditional religion has a place on Cather's prairie.

Most often, however, Cather shows readers that travelers to Nebraska saw the earth itself as a spiritual presence. Religious imagery is present in this description of fall afternoons on the prairie: "The whole prairie was like the bush that burned with fire and was not consumed. That hour always had the exultation of victory....It was a sudden transfiguration, a lifting-up of day" (44–45). In addition to religious allusion, there is the vibrant life of Nebraska's earth itself. Critic Laura Winters says that "Cather's spaces...become transformed into sacred spaces when characters so identify with their resonance that the line between self and environment begins to dissolve" (8). The most famous passage in which this dissolving happens is when Jim Burden is lying in the sun with the pumpkins in the pumpkin patch one afternoon. He says, "[That] is happiness; to be dissolved into something complete and great" (*My Ántonia* 20). This quotation appears on Willa Cather's tombstone, a fitting tribute to her use of things such as pumpkins and sunshine to evoke spiritual truths. The earth seems to be a mothering spiritual presence several times in *My Ántonia*. The first is at Jim and Ántonia's initial meeting, when they nestle down in the grass, out of the wind, so that Jim can begin teaching English words to Ántonia (28–29). The spiritual energy and sustenance of the plains are in direct contrast with the deadness Jim perceives in the town of Black Hawk. There people try mainly to economize and prevent gossip (249–50). In town, even the daring of the marriageable young men has been depleted. The mothers worry their sons will marry the energetic immigrant girls who dance at the tent downtown, but Jim realizes that the sons are far too concerned about respectability to allow themselves to be carried away by desire (229). This lack of strength that results from not having grown up on the prairie lands themselves is a repeated theme in *My Ántonia*. Cather's view that pioneering travels created better people than days of relative ease is clear when Jim reflects that the younger brothers and sisters in immigrant families— the ones who did not have to struggle as hard—are not as interesting as their older siblings, who had come "at a tender age from an old country to a new" (225). The spirit and strength of having been pioneers in the land is clearly something Jim and Ántonia share. Still, drawn by the changing American economy, which was becoming more urban-centered, and Gaston Cleric, a teacher he respects, Jim leaves the plains and even Black Hawk to seek happiness and fulfillment as a lawyer married to a society lady, but it is not until he travels back to Ántonia and her family on their farm that he has the spirit to hope for good in the future. After visiting Ántonia's family, he can say, "I had escaped from the curious depression...and my mind was full of pleasant things" (417). The contrast between town and prairie has shown Jim how much he learned when he came to the Nebraska prairie. Having traveled to Nebraska's plains, to town, and then back to Ántonia's farm, Jim is stunned by a visible, not traditionally religious, expression of the strength Ántonia has drawn from the earth and made manifest in her life. After Ántonia's children show Jim their new fruit cellar, they all come running up from the cellar into the sunshine (382). Cather used no religious terms, but in her description she clearly shows the lifeforce of the children emerging from the earth where the family's preserved produce is stored. The Nebraska earth itself has spiritual and physical energy if the traveler is open to seeing it. Journeys to town create the contrast that makes this obvious.

In the following passage, Cather's Nebraska landscape is again shown to be a living presence, with its own spirit—symbolized by wine, the ocean, and spirited movement: "The red of the grass made all the great prairie the color of wine-stains; or of certain seaweeds...the whole country seemed, somehow, to be running" (*My Ántonia* 16). In a later passage, Jim notes about this new landscape, that here the earth and sky seethe with the energy of spring, but not with the signs of spring he knew in Virginia. Here, spring's energy is in "the swift clouds, in the pale sunshine, and in the warm, high wind" (137). Indeed the spirit of the land often seems stronger than that of the people in the first two-thirds of *My Ántonia*. Critic James Miller notes that "Almost every detail in 'The Shimerdas' [Book I] is calculated to shrink the significance of the human drama in contrast with the drama of the seasons, the drama of nature, the drama of land and sky" (53). Still, Books II–V show that most of the Nebraska settlers were not overwhelmed by nature; they benefited from the community it forced them to form and the strengths they had to develop to make the land productive.

The mothering earth is certainly not always sentimentally kind in *My Ánto-nia*. Jim notices, "The pale, cold light of the winter sunset did not beautify—it was like the light of truth itself" (197). The truth was hard for the Nebraska pioneers. The Shimerdas have already been overcharged for their land and implements by Krajiek when they arrive in Nebraska, and then Krajiek parasitically lives with them. When the hired girls are cutting elder blossoms and drowsing in the sun after playing tag, they list many of the hardships of prairie life: worn-out and ill-fitting clothes and shoes, no money for toys, missing the food of their homeland, too many babies, sick mothers, dark houses made of sod, sleeping with three in a bed, and no time for school when farmwork needed doing (272–75). Likewise, early on, Ántonia enlightens Jim about the difference between coming to Nebraska from Bohemia with little money, and coming from Virginia speaking English and carrying money (*MA* 159). But losing one's feeling for others and grasping for material success are never shown as the remedies for prairie life's difficulties. Wick Cutter is, of course, the most evil character in the book, with his plot to rape Ántonia, his fleecing of immigrants, and finally his shooting his wife and then himself. Mr. Harling, the autocratic grain and cattle merchant, is another unlikable, mercenary character. Interest in the details of people and landscape is the antidote to despair over Nebraska's hardships. If settlers can maintain their sense of community, they retain hope and build strength of spirit from their adversities. Grandfather perhaps illustrates it best when, during the feud between Jake and the Shimerdas, he goes to help his neighbors with a sick roan (151). Sick animals, bad weather, injuries—prairie settlers had to help each other with the harsh realities of settlement. That community is where Jim and Ántonia find strength.

Cather's work has been criticized at times for not dealing directly with the painful side of life, but tragedy is part of the experience for travelers to Nebraska. In *My Ántonia,* Jim's journey is, indeed, forced by the death of both of his parents, and part of his feeling of exile when he moves to live under the total blank of the Nebraska sky is his feeling that "I did not believe my dead father and mother were watching me" (8). Most striking is Mr. Shimerda's suicide, of course. Mr. Shimerda's loss of music, culture, and his beloved homeland are some of the most painful moments in the novel. When he comes to visit the Burdens, Jim thinks that Mr. Shimerda may have decided, after living in the dark, crowded sod hut with his quarrelsome wife and several children, "that peace and order had vanished from the earth" (98). Mr. Shimerda is as demoralized as Jim thinks the brown owls living in holes near the prairie dog town must be: "winged things that would live like that must be rather degraded creatures" (33). Jim realizes that Mr. Shimerda died of homesickness (115), but he is happy to think that the soul of the man he admired might be stopping off in his grandparents' kitchen on its way back to Bohemia. There is suffering on the prairie, but also much of the sacred.

The pluralistic community Cather advocates is also not without its tensions.

Otto says, "Bohemians has a natural distrust of Austrians" (23) and later is not surprised when the Shimerdas and Burdens have a brief feud. Jake says at one point during the feud, "These foreigners ain't the same. You can't trust 'em to be fair" (148). Grandmother voices her irritation at foreign settlers' mutual distrust when she says about the Norwegian church's refusal to bury Mr. Shimerda that they will have to create a "more liberal-minded" American graveyard if the different nationalities will not accept each other's dead (127–28). Even Jim is irritated that Ántonia can't speak English when a snake behind him terrifies her. He says, "What did you jabber Bohunk for?" (51). Later he adds to Ántonia, "People who don't like this country ought to stay at home" (101–02). Although Jim never truly wished that Ántonia or her family would go home and only made his cruel comment out of disappointment and anger, Cather is fair in presenting the tensions present in a journey like the one to Nebraska's prairie. However, it is in dealing with these tensions and showing compassion for those defeated by them that Cather's characters grow in spirit.

Other travelers besides those from Europe enrich the prairie's spirit in *My Ántonia*. Early Spanish explorers are mentioned as the ones who perhaps began the non-Native culture of the region. A farmer breaking sod finds a buried Spanish stirrup and a sword with a Spanish inscription on the blade (277). African Americans are present on the plains, too, and they contribute their spirit to its culture. A black piano player comes to town, and Jim notes about him that he has the happiest face he has seen since leaving Virginia, and that he played the piano terribly but with wonderful energy (209, 215). Non-European characters are essentialized in Cather's book, but their spirits add to the prairie in a way that cannot be ignored.

In her famous essay "The Novel Demeublé," Cather wrote about selecting details that evoke rather than catalogue emotions: "Whatever is felt on the page without being specifically named there—that, one might say, is created. It is the inexplicable presence of the thing not named" (*On Writing* 41–42). Cather selected everyday events and details of 1880s Nebraska to evoke the spirit or emotion she wanted the reader to experience, much as did French symbolist poets of her time: "Like them, she viewed art as a religion. Like them, she felt that literature should focus not on reality but on 'something else'—some ineffable emotional truth lying between the mind and the world" (Acocella 60). By finding the right physical image or shared story, Cather hoped to produce in her readers a sensation similar to that felt by *My Ántonia*'s Jim Burden as he left the theater after watching *Camille*. Although the actress was getting old and the play was from a different time and country, it still spoke deeply to him (*My Ántonia* 314). Similarly, Cather no doubt hoped that wherever *My Ántonia* was read, the universal truths she valued from her prairie days would live again. Literary theorists have problematized the term "universal," but Cather identified with dominant beliefs of her time and felt that "the themes of true poetry, of great poetry, will be the same until all the values of human life have changed and all the strongest emotional responses have become different—which can hardly occur until the physical body itself has fundamentally changed" (*On Writing* 28). Cather selected details to evoke these human responses.

Cather carefully noticed not only the spirit of the landscape but also its specifics so that "flora and fauna are described in detail sufficient to identify plant and animal species" (Rosowski and Mignon 4). Jim both notices details and responds with a traveler's emotion in this passage about how roads lined by sunflowers along cornfields always seemed to lead to freedom: "I used to love to drift along the pale yellow cornfields, looking for damp spots one sometimes found at their edges, where the smartweed soon turned a rich copper color and the narrow brown leaves hung curled like cocoons" (*My Ántonia* 32). Cather's feeling for individual specifics of this landscape resonates so clearly that readers see its spiritual meaning: freedom, coppery richness, life force. Trees, also, have deep meaning in *My Ántonia*. Jim tells readers that, on the prairie, trees were so rare that the settlers used to visit them as though they were people (32). Once Ántonia has her own farm and family, she too feels protective of her apple trees, to the point that she would worry about them at night and even get up to carry water to them (383). Cather's detailed depiction of trees and their care is not for the purpose of local color. She used details of nature to evoke the feelings of travelers interacting with a new landscape, caring for strengths and spirit they felt were vital.

Women, in *My Ántonia* and Cather's other novels, are uniquely connected to the earth and strengthened by it. Critic Beth Rundstrom suggests the reason may be biological: "Cather portrays harmonious relationships between women and the land. This connection is partially inherent, because women and the earth experience similar seasonal-menstrual rhythms and reach out to and are responsive to others..." (3). In any case, Ántonia, Grandmother Burden, the Widow Stevens, Mrs. Harling, and even Mrs. Shimerda are shown as hardworking, practical women who work the land and are part of it economically, spiritually, and finally physically. "Cather portrayed women as the solid, stable base for a growing nation...prairie women knew they were figuratively and would become literally, dust of the earth....Women would eventually be sustenance for the very earth from which they humbly sustained their households" (Rundstrom 6). The following admiring description of Ántonia and Mrs. Harling shows how much Cather valued their earthy spirit: "They loved children and animals and music, and rough play and digging in the earth. They liked to prepare rich, hearty food and see people eat it; to make up soft white beds....Deep down in each of them there was...a relish of life, not over-delicate, but very invigorating" (*My Ántonia* 205). Over-delicacy was not part of the spirit that Cather valued in memories of journeying to Nebraska. Similarly, Frances Harling is another not overly delicate, spirited woman of the prairies. She has such business talent that she and her husband eventually run her father's grain and cattle trading firm, but Frances also continues to care about the souls of the people with whom she deals (171). The Widow Stevens moves into Jim's grandparents' former white house and from there continues caring for Ántonia, helping her sew for her wedding and then helping with the baby's birth when Ántonia returns. She is earthy enough to see the good in Ántonia and is not bothered by the scruples that give Jim Burden pause when he hears how Ántonia fared with marriage. Jim Burden's grandmother is a more traditional prairie farmwife to whom Cather gives a voice, not without having undergone some inner struggle, according to Cather's biographer: "[Female] realms at first seemed limited and oppressive to Willa Cather....But by the time she created the portrait of Grandmother Burden in *My Ántonia* she regarded women's traditional tasks with respect" (O'Brien 24). Cather recognized that prairie women, despite being marginalized, were economically and socially central to travelers into the frontier landscape. Indeed, when prairie women's lives are in the foreground, the spirit of helping neighbors, finding a place in a strange land, and relishing children and food shines through the window like the aforementioned light in a Dutch painting.

The daughters who go to town have reserves of the same strength possessed by the women who remain on the prairie, but the hired girls seem to lose their prairie spirit as their separation from the land lengthens. Lena Lingard, for whom Book III is named, says emphatically that she is through with the work and troubles of the farm. She will be a dressmaker (*My Ántonia* 183). In fact, she becomes a very successful dressmaker, traveling from Black Hawk to Lincoln and on to San Francisco. But when Jim spends his first Lincoln evening with her, his happiest thoughts are not of the scholarly life he is planning with his teacher, Gaston Cleric, but of the people he and Lena knew on the prairie (297). Lena reminds Jim of images in his past, but she does not have the strengthening effect of Ántonia, who had told Jim when they lived in Black Hawk, not to waste his life in the little town but to go away to school and make a life for himself (255). Lena, the girl converted to town life, distracts Jim, and finally he must leave her and travel again to Harvard if he is to acquire the polish needed to be successful and not lose his own prairie strengths under Lena's tempting influence. In a similar vein, Ántonia rejected those "glittering and reckless" (313) ways, but is glad of having learned from her town years so that she raises her children knowing so much more about cooking, housekeeping, and "nice ways" (387). Tiny Soderball, another one of the hired girls, also contrasts with Ántonia, because Tiny learned from town but never found her way back. Tiny Soderball is a warning against unfeeling materialism and traveling too far from one's prairie strength. She made a fortune with an Alaskan gold mine, but Jim says, "She was like some one in whom the faculty of becoming interested is worn out" (341). Tiny Soderball never came back to experience that feeling of coming home to oneself that Jim had when he left Ántonia's farm at the novel's end (419).

Cather's work has been criticized for lacking plot. We can see the influence of regionalist writer Sarah Orne Jewett both in Cather's undramatic plotting and in her decision to write about the prairie. Cather said, "Miss Jewett wrote of the people who grew out of the soil and the life of the country near her heart, not about exceptional individuals at war with their environment" (*On Writing* 55). Jim, coming from Virginia, can explore this new place—Nebraska—and novelty can substitute for drama in piquing his curiosity and ours. As narrator, Jim can write down little scenes and occurrences that evoke the spirit of the prairie for him, and avoid sensationalism. Indeed, Cather wrote about not wanting to sensationalize her memories of Annie Pavelka, Ántonia's prototype, "There was material in that book for a lurid melodrama. But I decided that in writing it I would dwell very lightly on those things that a novelist would ordinarily emphasize, and make up my story of the little, every-day happenings and occurrences that form the greatest part of everyone's life and happiness" (qtd. in Bennett 47). Unlike most novels, *My Ántonia* does not end with all the plot lines neatly tied up in a marriage or a death. Instead, we hear many different stories from and about characters originally from many different regions, coming together on the blank slate of the Nebraska prairie.

Red Cloud, Nebraska, Cather's childhood home, was truly a pluralistic community. "In 1884...approximately 10 to 15 percent of [Red Cloud's] immigrant population was foreign born" (Rundstrom 2). Jim gets a glimpse of what the Old World was like when he sees how differently Mrs. Shimerda reacts to being relieved of her obligation to pay his grandfather for a cow. She kneels to kiss his hand (*My Ántonia* 154–55). However, Jim does not condemn Mrs. Shimerda's show of gratitude, perhaps because his grandparents have welcomed their immigrant neighbors. Indeed, Jim's grandfather is even able to accept Catholic, Bohemian religious traditions in a passage where Mr. Shimerda crosses himself and kneels in front of the Christmas tree. Jim is worried because his grandfather is a staunch Protestant, but "Grandfather merely put his fingertips to his brow and bowed his venerable head, thus Protestantizing the atmosphere" (99). Later, Grandfather tells Jim that "The prayers of all good people are good" (100). Jim's cooking ideas are even expanded when Russian Peter gives Ántonia a sack of cucumbers and a pail of milk in which to cook them. Ántonia assures Jim that cooked cucumbers taste very good (41). However, not all the American-born citizens of Nebraska are as accepting as the Burdens. At one point in *My Ántonia*, Jim repeats and counters arguments he has heard voiced in town: "All foreigners were ignorant people who couldn't speak English. [However] there was not a man in Black Hawk who had the intelligence or cultivation, much less the distinction of Ántonia's father. Yet people saw no difference...they were all Bohemians, all 'hired girls'" (228). In contrast, Jim admires what he learns from his immigrant neighbors, and Cather's readers learn to celebrate the spirit of those travelers as well.

If Cather's Nebraska novels have any political effect, it is in showing that a pluralistic society of travelers from different landscapes can succeed. In the Burdens's own household, Otto and Jake come from Austria and Virginia to combine resources and make the Christmas tree a sacred space using Otto's Austrian colored paper figures and Jake's pocket mirror for an ice-covered lake (94). Even in town, the dancing tent that so clearly shows the superior energies of the hired girls is brought by the Italian Vannis. *My Ántonia* is not the only place where Cather's pluralist sentiments can be seen.

> [Cather's] 1923 essay on Nebraska in *The Nation*, with its criticism of the "Americanization" of the richly cosmopolitan culture that immigration produced in the rural Middle West and its worries about the effects of a generational shift from makers to buyers suggests that for Cather..."progress" toward a triumphant, homogenous middle-class culture amounts to a kind of regression, a narrowing of experience against which *My Ántonia* registers an elegant protest...directing its celebration of the past toward the refreshment of a worn-out present. (Millington 692–93)

In that same 1923 essay for the *Nation,* Cather celebrated how the European immigrants "spread across our bronze prairies like the daubs of color on a painter's palette" (qtd. in O'Brien 71). *My Ántonia* is the manifesto of an author who felt that a mingling of spiritual resources was what gave the prairie settlers their strength.

Although Cather did not endorse rampant urban-style success as it began to be manifest in the early 1900s, she did not oppose all change on the Nebraska prairie, as is clear in these lines from Book IV of *My Ántonia:* "[A]ll the human effort that had gone into [new houses, wheat and cornfields, and big barns] was coming back in long, sweeping lines of fertility. The changes seemed beautiful and harmonious to me" (346). However, a character like Wick Cutter, so corrupted by his desire to amass his own fortune that he self-destructs, is a clear sign that Cather preferred another set of land-centered values. With Wick Cutter and other avaricious characters, Cather defines her prairie region of community against "the other" of heartless urban materialism. "In her fiction Cather seems to work toward a redefinition of success that sees a fulfilled self *grounded in* community" (Harvey 6). The region whose stories Cather tells in *My Ántonia* is definitely one to which the typically marginalized travel and where their spirits join together and are shown to be strong and valid, more valid in most cases than urban materialism.

Like Mr. Shimerda, the Widow Stevens, and Jim, who all say "My Ántonia" at some point, the reader is meant to say "My Ántonia" and gain strength from knowing her "look or gesture that somehow revealed the meaning in common things" (*My Ántonia* 398). The common things in Cather's life on the Nebraska prairie were the open sky and rushing grass, the snakes and prairie dogs, the blizzards and illnesses, and most importantly the people who she met on the plains. Though Cather and many of her characters left the prairie for a life of education and culture in cities, she clearly recalled the strength of spirit that was held in the land and sky and shared among the travelers who came to that land.

Works Cited

Acocella, Joan. "Cather and the Academy." *The New Yorker.* 27 November 1995: 56–71.

Benjamin, Walter. "The Storyteller: Reflections on the Works of Nikolai Leskov." *Illuminations.* Ed. Hannah Arendt. New York: Schocken, 1968. 83–109.

Bennett, Mildred. *The World of Willa Cather.* New York: Dodd, Mean, & Co., 1951.

Bloom, Harold. *Willa Cather.* New York: Chelsea House Press, 1985.

Cather, Willa. *My Ántonia.* New York: Quality Paperback Bookclub, 1995.

———. *On Writing.* New York: Knopf, 1949.

Hamilton, Kristie. (kgh2@csd.uwm.edu). "Re: a chinatown: a region?" E-mail to Theorizing Regionalism reflector (region@csd.uwm.com). 5 Dec. 1998.

Harvey, Sally Peltier. *Redefining the American Dream: The Novels of Willa Cather.* Cranbury, NJ: Associated UP, 1995.

Kazin, Alfred. "Elegy: Willa Cather." *Willa Cather.* Ed. Harold Bloom. New York: Chelsea House Press, 1985. 15–23.

Miller, James E., Jr. "*My Ántonia*: A Frontier Drama of Time." In Harold Bloom. Ed. *Willa Cather.* New York: Chelsea House P, 1985. 51–59.

Millington, Richard. "Willa Cather and 'The Storyteller': Hostility to the Novel in *My Ántonia.*" *American Literature* 66.4 (Dec. 1994): 689–715.

O'Brien, Sharon. *Willa Cather: The Emerging Voice.* New York: Oxford UP, 1987.

Reynolds, Guy. *Willa Cather in Context: Progress, Race, and Empire.* New York: St. Martin's, 1996.

Rosowski, Susan J., and Charles Mignon. "Editing Cather." *Studies in the Novel* 27.3 (Fall 1995): 387–401.

Rundstrom, Beth. "Harvesting Willa Cather's Literary Fields." *Geographical Review* 85.2 (April 1995): 217–39.

Seaton, James. "The Prosaic Willa Cather." *American Scholar* 67.1 (Winter 1998): 146–51.

Shaw, Patrick W. *Willa Cather and the Art of Conflict.* Troy, NY: Whitston Press, 1992.

Welty, Eudora. "The House of Willa Cather." *Willa Cather.* Ed. Harold Bloom. New York: Chelsea House, 1985.

Winters, Laura. *Willa Cather: Landscape and Exile.* Selinsgrove: Susquehanna University Press, 1993.

✠ Chapter 13

Dorothy Richardson's Pilgrimage as a Journey Down to the Center of Being

María Francisca Llantada Díaz

Early in 1913 Dorothy Richardson (1873–1957) completed *Pointed Roofs,* the first part in a thirteen-volume novel that was to be called *Pilgrimage* (1915–1967). The travel motif that is implied in the title of the novel runs parallel with the *Bildungsroman* educational journey through life. The protagonist, Miriam Henderson, is almost always in transit. She voyages through her formative years and moves from naïveté to experience, developing a sense of identity and searching for fulfillment. The goal of her journey is the discovery of truth, the creation of art in the form of writing.

When Richardson chose *Pilgrimage* as the title for her multivolume lifework, she was inscribing it in a complex network of mythical and religious references and allusions that endow it with a multiplicity of meanings and implications. The word *pilgrim* is derived from the Latin term *peregrinus* ("per" meaning "through" and "ager" meaning "land" or "field"). It refers to someone who journeys in alien lands, and it can also have the connotation of a search for some high goal, such as truth. This pursuit of some elevated ideal makes the notion of pilgrimage extraordinarily close to that of *Bildungsroman,* where the aim is the development of personality as the result of a life journey that takes its protagonist from innocence to maturity, so that the pilgrim finally achieves self-knowledge and understanding of the world. In Richardson's work the notion of pilgrimage is imbued with mystical ideas of a journey to the interior that parallels the protagonist's external life journey.

> Pilgrimage means embarking on an adventure, a quest, and this act of travel makes pilgrims have a liminal or transitional experience; that is, it situates them in a threshold. If mysticism is an interior pilgrimage, pilgrimage is exteriorized mysticism. Pilgrimage has its inwardness, while mysticism has its outwardness:

"Pilgrimage may be thought of as extroverted mysticism, just as mysticism is introverted pilgrimage. The pilgrim physically traverses a mystical way; the mystic sets forth on an interior spiritual pilgrimage." (Turner and Turner 33–34)

Pilgrimage, ideally, is charismatic, in the sense that the pilgrim's decision to make it is a response to a charism, a grace, while at the same time pilgrims receive grace as they make their devotions. In this sense Richard R. Niebuhr has defined pilgrims as "persons in motion—passing through territories not their own—seeking something we might call completion, or perhaps the word clarity will do as well, a goal to which only the spirit's compass points the way" (qtd. in Clift 1).

For Turner there is an initiatory quality in pilgrimage: "A pilgrim is an initiand, entering into a new, deeper level of existence than he has known in his accustomed milieu." In their way pilgrims will find trials, tribulations, and temptations. Pilgrimages offer liberation from profane social structures that are symbiotic with a specific religious system, but they do this only in order to intensify the pilgrims's attachment to their own religion. Pilgrimage has also been seen as a liminal phenomenon. "During the intervening liminal phase of the pilgrimage, the ritual subject (the 'passenger' or 'liminar')...passes through a realm or dimension that has few or none of the attributes of the past or coming state." When the passage is consummated the subject returns to classified secular or mundane social life (Turner and Turner 8–9).

In the paradigmatic Christian pilgrimage, the initiatory quality of the process is given priority, though it is initiation to, not through, a threshold. Initiation is conceived of as leading not to status elevation but to a deeper level of religious participation. Pilgrims are those who divest themselves of the mundane concomitants of religion to confront the basic elements and structures of their faith in their unshielded, virgin radiance.

The act of making the journey involved in a pilgrimage is a ritual, and, as such, a way of bringing symbolic meaning to everyday reality by speaking to the unconscious. Frequently, at the pilgrimage site, there are specific ritual actions which the pilgrim performs in order to be in touch with the reality of the place. Although rituals are sometimes viewed as superstition, they cannot be wholly obliterated. If traditional rituals were done away with, other rituals would arise in their place. Pilgrimage is simply one example of the human desire to make a connection with something beyond one's everyday experience. Like all archetypes, the archetype of pilgrimage is experienced as compelling. Sometimes the reasons to embark on a pilgrimage seem obvious to the pilgrim but do not seem adequate or compelling to the outsider. Pilgrimage is such a universal archetype that it arises universally, carrying the pilgrims to the possibility of some transformative energy for change when the need for change arises in their lives. Pilgrimage is a phenomenon that continues surviving despite the most determined attempts to stamp it out. In Clift's view "this determined human pattern of pilgrimage points to the human basic need to make a connection with something outside themselves, some holiness or value which helps ground the pilgrim in a new being, in a new lease on life, in something which gives meaning and direction" (152).

A pilgrimage is usually narrated in the first person, as the authentication of a real pilgrimage lies in the personal participation of the pilgrim. The pilgrimage motif provides Richardson's work with a dramatic and symbolic unity: the dramatic continuum of the frame of links, and the spiritual unity provided by the purpose and associations of pilgrimage. The idea of pilgrimage is, thus, a unifying thread, a device that brings together the whole novel. The notion of pilgrimage can be understood as "a key metaphor for life from the religious sphere. We are all pilgrims on the way to the heavenly city, and every journey, but especially a religious one, reflects the basic pattern of existence" (Bloomfield 186). This view of life as a pilgrimage to the shrine of heaven is developed by John Bunyan in his *Pilgrim's Progress* and deliberately suggested in *Pilgrimage*. For Jean Radford, the echo of Bunyan's *Pilgrim's Progress* signals an intentional and significant relationship between the two texts, so that she considers Richardson's novel-sequence a revisionary allegory of Bunyan's work. She holds that the form of *Pilgrimage* is framed or patterned around a series of extended metaphors of life as a journey with specific religious or spiritual reference that only the word "pilgrimage" could provide (25).

Miriam's journey begins, like Christian's in *Pilgrim's Progress,* with her as an adolescent leaving her family and setting out on "her lonely pilgrimage" (*Pointed Roofs* 27). By doing this she starts a new life only to come back to her center of being and discover herself. Miriam is different from Bunyan's pilgrim because her pilgrimage was to be modern and independent of any Heavenly City. She carries with her her own goal, the ever-unfolding self, so that by the end of the novel she begins to explore "the strange new light within her" (*Dawn's Left Hand* 153). Radford holds that although in Miriam's view *Pilgrim's Progress* was not "meant for modern minds" (*Backwater* 262), Richardson felt it had a reserve of power and enough cultural and religious resonance to provide a shape for her own construction. However, according to Radford, she did not keep her project till the end, where she not only provides a "Safe Arrival at the Desired Country," but also a destination that is a form of renewal and a starting point, this time with the pilgrim as a writer (Radford 34–35).

In his introduction to the 1968 Penguin edition of *The Pilgrim's Progress,* Roger Sharrock points out that there is a connection between Christian's life-long journey and the process of development portrayed in multivolume novels that are sometimes named *roman-fleuve:* "[T]he image of the purposeful journey through life still has great evocative power; it is reflected in all those long fictions of which the main theme is individual growth, from Proust to Anthony Powell and C. P. Snow" (25).

Both Bunyan's and Richardson's books are preceded by an apology where their authors explain the uncertainties they underwent when they were in the process of writing their books. Bunyan's reason for having written his book was to please himself, not the public: "I did it mine own self to gratify" (31). The ironic "heart-felt apology" Richardson offers her readers in her 1938 foreword to *Pilgrimage* is parallel to Bunyan's "The Author's Apology for His Book." She also wanted to please herself and to find a coherent frame for her literary innovations. She did not care about the difficulties her technique imposed on readers. Similarly, her concern for finding an adequate method parallels Bunyan's deliberations on style: "May I not write in such a style as this? / In such a method too and yet not to miss / Mine end, thy good? Why may it not be done?" (32)

Both *The Pilgrim's Progress* and *Pilgrimage* can be considered journeys toward the light. Horace Gregory sees Richardson's novel precisely in these terms: "The work is true to its title: it is a pilgrimage, a winding path toward the light, leading through stretches of beauty, bleakness and gloom and ending in the glow of a March moonlight" (108). In Bunyan's work the pilgrimage is characterized as a movement "from darkness to light, and from the power of Satan to God" (*The Pilgrim's Progress* 297). *The Pilgrim's Progress*, like the *Book of Common Prayer*, presents light as something external to human beings that has to be achieved with God's help. Darkness represents the dangers of the pilgrimage, and faith is necessary so that God will send light to show the way: "But let them that walk in darkness and have not light, trust in the name of the Lord, and stay upon their God...let us pray for light to him that can lighten our darkness...so they cried and prayed, and God sent light and deliverance...(*The Pilgrim's Progress* 295).

However, there is a difference between the idea of light in both *The Pilgrim's Progress* and the *Book of Common Prayer*, where it is presented as something external to human beings, and in Richardson's novel, where light is seen as something internal to its protagonist. This notion of the inner light is the central belief of Quakerism. Richardson's interest in this religion is present in the numerous references to it in her novel. In 1914 Richardson published an anthology on the founder of Quakerism entitled *Gleanings from the Works of George Fox,* and a book called *The Quakers: Past and Present.* In the latter she includes many expressions related to motifs such as the inner light and the journey to the center of being that would be essential in *Pilgrimage,* whose first installment appeared the following year. In *The Quakers: Past and Present* Richardson speaks of the Quakers as "pilgrims in the spiritual life" (15) and describes the activities of George Fox in terms of a journey towards the light, identified with truth: "He...wandered for four years up and down the Midland counties seeking for light, for truth,...for a common principle where men seemed to pull every way at once" (6). Fox propagates "the message of the inner light of immediate inspiration, of the existence in every man of some measure of the Spirit of God," and although Richardson thought that "this belief in the divine light within the individual soul was, of course, nothing new" (*The Quakers* 10), she incorporated many key elements of the Quaker doctrine into the writing of *Pilgrimage.*

What is characteristic of the Quakers is "a process of retirement into the innermost region of being, into 'the light'" (*The Quakers* 11), and that is the goal of the protagonist of *Pilgrimage*. Fox's concern was "to reveal to men their own wealth, to wean them to turn from words and ceremonials, from all merely outward things, to seek first the inner reality" (*The Quakers* 16). Richardson's explanation that "for Fox the relationship of the soul to the Light was a life-process; [where] the inner was not in contradiction to the outer" (*The Quakers* 22) reinforces the idea of the coexistence in her novel of an external journey or pilgrimage and an inward journey that could be called a spiritual or mystical pilgrimage.

Richardson considers silence "the first step taken by the mystic upon his pilgrimage," and this is also the first step taken by Miriam in her journey down to the center of being. Miriam considers the Quakers of the Dimple Hill farm easily capable of traveling down to their inner selves, even for such a simple activity as saying grace before meals. The tranquillity she achieves in their company is characterized as being much richer than that she attains in solitude. The experience of shared silence makes the Quakers cast a radiance that is also shared by her:

> As if here, too, as in every human activity there seemed to be, was a concrete spiritual rhythm; so many wing-beats of the out-turned consciousness on its journey towards stillness, a moment's immersion within its pulsating depths, and the return. To a serenity flooding her being and surrounding it, far richer than the same kind of serenity achieved in solitude....Every one had emerged from the silence luminous. Given back to themselves renewed, freshly available....(*Dimple Hill* 469–70)

For Dorothy Richardson everyone is a mystic, and thus we are all capable of experiencing reality in a way that would enable us to develop our potential as artists: "All have the light. We are all mystics. We all live our lives on our various levels, at first hand. But a full recognition of this fact need not blind us to the further fact that those who have mystical genius need not chart upon their journey, most of us need a plain way traced out for us through the desert" (*The Quakers* 47). In *The Quakers: Past and Present* Richardson maintains that the development of our potential as mystics and artists implies setting off on a journey. This is what she explores in *Pilgrimage*, where the journey enables Miriam to find her inner light and become a writer. Seret has pointed out that the modern artist's voyage involves a journey of the mind and soul, a movement away from the materialistic toward the abstract. The modern artist's final goal is creativity and the unlimited expression of his soul (2).

In *Pilgrimage,* Miriam shares many of the Quakers's concerns. Like them— and other mystics—she practices "the art of introversion and contemplation" (*The Quakers* 37) and is also a pioneer "for the world upon the upward way"

(49). In her process of becoming an artist, the inner light is very important for Miriam, as it is the mediator in her approach to reality and expression of it by means of writing. Richardson also considers that the inner light is the filter through which Quakers see reality: "From...[their] standpoint of obedience to the 'inner light' they [the Quakers] found within, they understood what they saw around them, and brought a fresh revelation to the world" (*The Quakers* 37).

Richardson's book on the Quakers has a chapter called "Quakerism and women" that opens with the following words: "Watching the pilgrims who pass one by one along the mystic way, we see both women and men" (*The Quakers* 71). She considers the fact that Quakers consider women on the same level as men extremely important: "Quakerism stands as the first form of Christian belief, which has...escaped regarding woman as primarily an appendage to be controlled, guided, and managed by man...It was a step that followed from a central belief in the universality of the inner light" (72–73).

Both *The Quakers: Past and Present* and *Pilgrimage* end with a question mark that highlights their respective key words: in the former, "light," the essence of the Quakers's doctrine, and, in the latter, "fulfilment," the fundamental goal in a *Bildungsroman*. Thus, both books end with a question that projects into the future the core of their subject matter:

> Will they [the Quakers] constitute themselves an order...a 'free' group of mystics ready to pay *the price,* ready to *travel* along the way trodden by all their predecessors, by all who have truly yearned for the uncreated Light? (*The Quakers* 93; emphasis added).

> If Jean's marriage with Joe Davenport brought her a child, should I feel, in holding it, that same sense of fulfilment? (*March Moonlight* 658)

The italicized words in the quotation from *The Quakers* are remarkably similar to a key passage from *March Moonlight* in which Miriam says: "To write is to forsake life. Every time I know this, in advance. Yet whenever something comes that sets the tips of my fingers tingling to record it, I forget *the price;* eagerly face the strange *journey* down and down to the center of being" (*March Moonlight* 609; emphasis added). In both texts, "to pay the price" means to face a journey, to travel, in a metaphorical way, to the interior in order to find "the center of being." The parallelism between both texts's aims is thus manifest. "Light" and "fulfilment" are sought as the result of a process of introspection and evolution, and they can be considered equivalent. The Quakers's aim is to achieve a communion with the inner light present in them and, ultimately, fulfillment. Thus, their search could be inscribed in the *Bildungsroman* frame, the same as George Fox's, who is presented in Jones's introduction to his *Journal* as "a genuine man engaged in a dramatic struggle for reality and for truth" (ix). Despite the fact that in the *Journal* darkness is identified with death and evil, Fox believes that even evil men have the inner light within them: "Then I warned him to repent, and to come to the light, which Christ had enlightened him with, that by it he might see all his evil words and actions, and return to Christ Jesus" (*Journal* 54). As in the *Book of Common Prayer*, George Fox identifies Christ with "the true Light" (*Journal* xix). The difference is that for him light is also in men: "We...directed him to the light of Christ...and manifested that it was divine and spiritual, proceeding from Christ, the spiritual and heavenly Man; and that which was called the life in Christ the Word, was called the light in us" (139).

The doctrine of the Inner Light, which is the cardinal principle of Quakerism, is Fox's real contribution to the progress of religious thought. However, he finds it as no new thing. For him it is the one great underlying thought of the entire Gospel as taught and exemplified in the life of Jesus (Knight 262–63). George Fox's mission was to make people discover God in themselves: "directing all to the Spirit of God in themselves, that they might be turned from darkness to light, and believe in it, that they might become the children of it" (*Journal* 63). In the *Book of Common Prayer* light is not naturally inside people, it is received from the outside: "Almighty God, give us grace that we may cast away the works of darkness, and put on the armour of light..." (47). Light is seen as something external to human beings, that is received from God—"O send out thy light and thy truth ..." (399)—and it will eventually come in the future, with Jesus Christ.

The idea of journey that is implied in *Pilgrimage* can be understood in a broad sense in the frame of the quest myth. Humanity's pattern of quest is marked by the search for knowledge and the changing focus from the outer to the inner world. Grace Stewart points out in *A New Mythos: The Novel of the Artist as Heroine* that "the journey or quest is an important element in myth, in fiction and in life." Stewart concentrates on how the female's journey to the interior and the mythic images used therein differ in some ways from the so-called universal pattern (7, 10).

For Gerald Jay Goldberg, the quest is also especially prominent in the *Künstlerroman*, where the journey involves a creative process in more ways than one. He claims that in the twentieth-century *Künstlerroman* "the theme of the quest for identity is intimately connected with the concept of the discovery of the self through the process of creation so that the actual creation of a work has become the subject of many contemporary artist-novels" (qtd. in Stewart 7). Roberta Seret points out that the *Künstlerroman* psychological voyage centers on the young artist's quest to develop a sense of identity and personal worth, so that self-realization and artistic expression are the dominant goals of this genre (143). Labovitz similarly declares that Miriam's *Bildung* and quest are motivated by self-discovery and self-realization: "Miriam's journey assumes the characteristics of the epic myth, her quest leading her into spaces not even experienced by the traditional *Bildungsroman* male protagonist" (18, 37).

The importance of the quest myth as both an inward and outward journey has been emphasized by many critics. Thus, for Paul Ricoeur, "the quest is absorbed into the movement by which the hero...becomes who he is." His voyage is a voyage toward the center, toward himself, the retardation in his arrival means growth (185–86). Some of Richardson's critics have been aware of the quest myth that joins *Pilgrimage* together. Among them, Staley has perceived the structure of the novel as derived from the archetypal journey, or the quest. Miriam's quest is for discovery and for understanding (38). The pilgrimage motif gives integrity and coherence to *Pilgrimage* as a novel. For Powys, "this pilgrimage of Miriam's is a sort of Quest of the Holy Grail" (22).

Richardson's novel is firmly rooted in such mainstream European genres as the *Bildungsroman* and the *roman-fleuve*. Richardson situates her novel in the tradition of the prototypical German *Bildungsroman, Wilhelm Meister,* and the French *roman-fleuve* as represented originally by Balzac and later by Proust. In her foreword to the 1938 collected edition of *Pilgrimage,* Richardson quotes a passage from *Wilhelm Meister* in order to explain her position in literary history. Her work is thus inscribed in the purest tradition of the *Bildungsroman* genre. Maurice Beebe argues that "Goethe deserves the major credit for initiating the vogue of the artist as hero, because a dominant theme of his work...is the conflict between art and life...[and] because he achieved a personal balance between the self and the world" (27). In *Pilgrimage* there is also an identification of the *Bildungsroman* with the *Künstlerroman* that has been pointed out by David Miles: "[T]he *Bildungsroman,* mirroring the autobiographical trend of nineteenth-century fiction...tends to become a Künstlerroman." He holds that "the viewpoint of the hero...shifts from the world without to the world within" by the transformation of the picaro into the confessor (980).

From the eighteenth century, the concept of *bilden* had been associated with "a religious, didactic process that was restricted to an individual sphere of activity and that had distinctly aesthetic connotations" (Cocalis 400). In fact, the hero of a *Bildungsroman* usually possesses a pronounced aesthetic sensibility that can easily develop into an artistic career. Thus, the strong aesthetic component of the *Bildungsroman* makes it evolve naturally into the *Künstlerroman,* where the protagonist's process of formation and aesthetic education culminates with his/her becoming an artist. Marc Redfield considers the *Bildungsroman* the genre of aesthetics. *Bildungsromane* are, thus, "the most pedagogically efficient of novels, since they thematize and enact the very motion of aesthetic education" (55).

Because the *Bildungsroman* has traditionally been defined in terms of content rather than form (Cocalis 399), its pedagogical subject matter could be easily associated with the multivolume shape of the *roman-fleuve*. For Lynette Felber it is the vastness of *Bildung* that makes it an appropriate subject for the *roman-fleuve* (12). This form has proved to be suitable for the *Bildungsroman* educational contents because it favors the progressive representation of the formation process of the protagonist in a detailed way. Dorothy Richardson's *Pilgrimage* and Proust's *Remembrance of Things Past* are examples of multivolume *Bil-*

dungsromane that result from the productive fusion of this genre with the *roman-fleuve*.

In *Pilgrimage,* the *Bildungsroman* genre is fused with the *roman-fleuve* in an intimate manner. This confluence of two genres makes *Pilgrimage* a complex text and is also responsible for the proliferation of meanings for which it is known. The *Bildungsroman* takes the form of the *roman-fleuve* and is expanded over a series of volumes where a sensitive young woman voyages from innocence to experience, struggling to become independent and mature and finally coming to an understanding of herself and the world. The internal rhythms of the *roman-fleuve* are responsible for its ultimate unity, rescuing it from the chaos associated with lack of external structure. Moreover, both the *Bildungsroman* and the *roman-fleuve* have in common a strong autobiographical tendency. Ausmus has pointed out that the majority of sequence novels are to a high degree autobiographical. They tell their authors's life history, although with varying degrees of fictional disguise (61). Jerome Buckley similarly holds that "most of the English *Bildungsromane* are highly autobiographical." This belief makes him study "the problem of the prevalence of the confessional impulse in Romantic and modern culture and...the general uses of subjectivity" (viii). T. Kelly situates *Pilgrimage* in this tendency to autobiography that characterizes modernist *Bildungsromane.* She maintains that the autobiographical nature of *Pilgrimage* and its account of an aesthetic quest place it along other modernist novels such as Proust's *Remembrance of Things Past* and Joyce's *A Portrait of the Artist as a Young Man* (153). Fleishman also reads *Pilgrimage* autobiographically as a journey entailing a spiritual quest: "*Pilgrimage* is distinguished among autobiographical writings not merely by its consistent figure of 'making a journey to the heart of reality' but by its repeated testimony to the central irony of religious experience, that the journey is always to where one already is, that the quest is for what is already possessed if not firmly grasped, that the discovery is always a rediscovery and the illumination a repetition" (433).

Pilgrimage traces Miriam's journey through life and her progress toward mental maturity and self-esteem, expanding progressively as she develops. Eric A. Blackall has also explained the structure of *Wilhelm Meister,* Richardson's prototype of *Bildungsroman,* as an expansion from themes that were present already in the first books of the novel: "The novel expands; it does not divide" (382).

Miriam Henderson's pilgrimage is simultaneously a life journey and a retreat into the center of her being. The inner and the outer are parallel during the life process, and this reinforces the idea of the coexistence of an external journey or pilgrimage and an inward journey that could be called a spiritual or mystical pilgrimage. The protagonist of *Pilgrimage* makes a journey to the heart of reality. For Shirley Rose, the important quest for the link between the subjective and objective reality, made apprehensible through a literary work, introduces the pilgrimage metaphor. Miriam becomes a complex unity of observer, mediator, interpreter, creator, and contemplator of her own creation ("Dorothy Richardson's Theory of Literature" 33). As Richardson says in *The Quakers: Past and Present,* all men are engaged in pilgrimage, but there is a difference between the quality and intensity of the light which illumines their way:

> The "artist" lives to a greater or less degree in a perpetual state of illumination, in perpetual communication with his larger self....The religious genius, as represented preeminently by the great mystics—those in whom the sense of an ultimate and essential goodness, beauty, and truth, is the dominant characteristic—have consciously bent all their energies to breaking through the veil of sense, to making a journey to the heart of reality, to winning the freedom of the very citadel of Life itself. (34–35)

The great mystics are the ones who make a journey to the heart of reality. Their pilgrimage is always toward what is already known. In Richardson's scheme, the artist is chief pilgrim, acting as informed and compassionate guide to the accompanying multitude. For the reader, the quest is a tour of the mind of the author, and for the writer, the quest is in finding her own form for expressing her own consciousness. Fouli holds that Miriam is a pilgrim in the sense of a traveler, as her pilgrimage is a metaphor for the metaphysical quest through experience for self-knowledge and vocation. In order to practice her vocation of writing about life, Miriam has to renounce life, just as the ideal believer has to renounce the world in order to give his/her life a meaning, and to achieve eternal life (25, 71).

Shirley Rose maintains that *Pilgrimage* has a philosophical cohesiveness that is the result of Richardson's imaginative rendering of the view that persists in all her writings: that the source and repository of life is the center of being, that here lies immutable reality, apprehended by the synthesizing capacity of the human consciousness ("The Unmoving Center" 381–82). Besides the inward journey that "traveling down to the center" implies, there are also many references to outward pilgrimages. The noun *pilgrimage* appears several times in the novel. Among these occurrences there is one that should be highlighted because of its literal connotations to a traditional pilgrimage. When Miriam accompanies her sister Harriett to meet their sister Eve, their walk is described as a pilgrimage that seems to be taking them to a goal, and the roadway is said to lead to paradise:

> The mile of gently rising roadway leading to the Heath was overarched by huge trees. Shadowy orchards, and the silent sunlit outlying meadows and park land of a large estate, streamed gently by them beyond the trees as they strode along through the cool leaf-scented air. They strode speechlessly ahead as if on a pilgrimage, keeping step....She [Harriett] walked along swiftly and erect, looking eagerly ahead as if, when they reached the top and the windmill, they would find something they were both looking for...the shaded road led on to paradise. (*Backwater* 299)

The description of the road as a *locus amoenus* brings to mind the ancient "pilgrim's way" mentioned in old pilgrimage narratives like Chaucer's *Canterbury Tales* and purposely sets Miriam's life pilgrimage in this context.

For Labovitz, Miriam's spiritual journey occurs through a series of mystical insight, revelation, and enlightenment. The process of self-discovery is heightened and linked with Miriam's writing career. Richardson reinforces self-development through Miriam's discovery of the ideal vocation to give meaning to her concept of human growth and understanding (60). Caesar Blake also studies *Pilgrimage* as a mystical novel and offers a reading in the framework of the "Mystic Way." These outlines of the view of personality provided by the novel are the rudiments of transcendental, mystical belief. Miriam is engaged in a particular kind of mystical experience, a quest for reality that promises the establishing of a conscious relation with the Absolute (61).

The idea of the spiritual journey pervades *Pilgrimage*. In *Dimple Hill*, there is a reference to a journey where the goal and the way are the same: "[O]ne had the feeling of being on a journey that was both pathway and destination" (485). This fusion of journey and destination could be applied to *Pilgrimage,* as the process of attaining the goal is as important as the goal itself. What makes the journey more important than the arrival is *Pilgrimage*'s inscription in the *Bildungsroman* genre, manifested in the heroine's personal and spiritual quest. Literary creation is the goal of Miriam's *Bildungsroman* journey. When she is writing, external reality disappears for her, as she puts life aside in order to recall the past and interpret it from the vantage point of the present. Thus, her center of being is the filter through which she sees reality and transforms it into art.

> While I write, everything vanishes but what I contemplate. The whole of what is called "the past" is with me, seen anew, vividly. No, Schiller, the past does not stand "being still." It moves, growing with one's growth. Contemplation is adventure into discovery; reality. What is called "creation," imaginative transformation, fantasy, invention, is only based upon reality. Poetic description a half-truth? Can anything produced by man be called "creation"?....Fully to recognize one must be alone. Away in the farthest reaches of one's being. (*March Moonlight* 657)

This idea of making a pilgrimage into herself is recurrent in the novel and it is developed in some important passages of *March Moonlight*. When Miriam finds herself prepared to write, she is aware that to write is to renounce life. In order to set herself to record past events, she has to leave the external world aside and descend to the inner center of her being: "Travel, while I write, down to that center where everything is seen in perspective; serenely" (619). Miriam's "strange journey down and down to the center of being" (609) in order to write becomes thus the goal of her pilgrimage and her lifelong quest.

Works Cited

Ausmus, Martin Russey. "Some Forms of the Sequence Novel in British Fiction." Diss. U of Oklahoma, 1969.

Beebe, Maurice. *Ivory Towers and Sacred Founts. The Artist as Hero in Fiction from Goethe to Joyce.* New York: New York UP, 1964.

Blackall, Eric A. Afterword. *Wilhelm Meister's Apprenticeship.* By Johann Wolfgang von Goethe. Trans. Eric A. Blackall and Victor Lange. Princeton: Princeton UP, 1989. 381–87.

Blake, Caesar R. *Dorothy Richardson.* Ann Arbor: U of Michigan P, 1960.

Bloomfield, Morton W. "Chaucerian Realism." *The Cambridge Chaucer Companion.* 1986. Eds. Piero Boitani and Jill Mann. Cambridge: Cambridge UP, 1987. 179–93.

The Book of Common Prayer and Administration of the Sacraments and other Rites and Ceremonies of the Church According to the Use of the Church of England. 1549. Cambridge: Cambridge UP, 1968.

Buckley, Jerome Hamilton. *Season of Youth. The Bildungsroman from Dickens to Golding.* Cambridge, MA: Harvard UP, 1974.

Bunyan, John. *The Pilgrim's Progress.* Hardmondsworth: Penguin, 1968.

Chaucer, Geoffrey. *The Canterbury Tales.* London: Edward Arnold, 1980.

Clift, Jean Dalby, and Wallace B. Clift. *The Archetype of Pilgrimage. Outer Action with Inner Meaning.* New York: Paulist Press, 1996.

Cocalis, Susan L. "The Transformation of *Bildung* from an Image to an Ideal." *Monatshefte.* 70 (Winter 1978): 399–414.

Felber, Lynette. *Gender and Genre in Novels Without End. The British Roman-Fleuve.* Gainesville: UP of Florida, 1995.

Fleishman, Avrom. *"Pilgrimage:* The Eternal Autobiographical Moment." *Figures of Autobiography: The Language of Self-Writing in Victorian and Modern England.* Berkeley: U of California P, 1983. 428–53.

Fouli, Janet. *Structure and Identity. The Creative Imagination in Dorothy Richardson's* Pilgrimage. Tunis: Publications de la Faculté des Lettres de la Manouba, 1995.

Fox, George. *The Journal of George Fox. With an Introduction by Rufus M. Jones.* Ed. Ernest Rhys. London: Dent, 1924.

Gregory, Horace. *Dorothy Richardson: An Adventure in Self-Discovery.* New York: Holt, Rinehart and Winston, 1967.

Jones, Rufus M. Introduction. 1923. *The Journal of George Fox. With an Introduction by Rufus M. Jones.* By George Fox. Ed. Ernest Rhys. London: Dent, 1924. ix–xiii.

Joyce, James. *A Portrait of the Artist as a Young Man.* 1916. Harmondsworth: Penguin, 1992.

Kelly, Theresa. "Pilgrimage and Modernism." Diss. The University of York, 1987.

Knight, Rachel. *The Founder of Quakerism. A Psychological Study of the Mysticism of George Fox.* London: Swarthmore, 1922.

Labovitz, Esther Kleinbord. *The Myth of the Heroine. The Female Bildungsroman in the Twentieth Century: Dorothy Richardson, Simone de Beauvoir, Doris Lessing, Christa Wolf.* 1986. New York: Peter Lang, 1988.

Miles, David H. "The Picaro's Journey to the Confessional: the Changing Image of the Hero in the German *Bildungsroman."* *PMLA* 89 (October 1974): 980–92.

Powys, John Cowper. *Dorothy M. Richardson.* 1931. London: Village Press, 1974.

Proust, Marcel. *Remembrance of Things Past.* Vol. I. *Swann's Way.* 1913. *Within a Budding Grove.* 1919. Trans. C.K. Scott Moncrieff and Terence Kilmartin. London: Chatto and Windus, 1981.

————. *Remembrance of Things Past.* Vol. II. *The Guermantes Way.* 1920. *Cities of the Plain.* 1925. Trans. C.K. Scott Moncrieff and Terence Kilmartin. London: Chatto and Windus, 1981.

————. *Remembrance of Things Past.* Vol. III. *The Captive.* 1923. *The Fugitive.* 1925. *Time Regained.* 1927. Trans. C.K. Scott Moncrieff and Terence Kilmartin. London: Chatto and Windus, 1981.

Radford, Jean. *Dorothy Richardson.* Bloomington: Indiana UP, 1991.

Redfield, Marc. *Phantom Formations. Aesthetic Ideology and the Bildungsroman.* Ithaca: Cornell UP, 1996.

Richardson, Dorothy. Foreword. *Pilgrimage* I. *Pointed Roofs, Backwater. Honeycomb.* 1938. London: Virago, 1995. 9–12.

————. ed. *Gleanings from the Works of George Fox.* London, Headley, no date available.

————. *Pilgrimage.* Vol. I. *Pointed Roofs.* 1915. *Backwater.* 1916. *Honeycomb.* 1917. London: Virago, 1995.

————. *Pilgrimage.* Vol. II. *The Tunnel.* Feb. 1919. *Interim.* Dec 1919. London: Virago, 1992.

————. *Pilgrimage.* Vol. III. *Deadlock.* 1921. *Revolving Lights,* 1923. *The Trap,* 1925. London: Dent, 1967.

————. *Pilgrimage.* Vol. IV. *Oberland.* 1927. *Dawn's Left Hand.* 1931. *Clear Horizon.* 1935. *Dimple Hill.* 1938. *March Moonlight.* 1967. London: Virago, 1979.

————. *The Quakers: Past and Present.* London: Constable, 1914.

Ricoeur, Paul. "Narrative Time." *Critical Inquiry.* 7 (Autumn 1980): 169–90.

Rose, Shirley. "Dorothy Richardson's Theory of Literature: The Writer as Pilgrim." *Criticism.* 12 (Winter 1970): 20–37.

————. "The Unmoving Center: Consciousness in Dorothy Richardson's *Pilgrimage.*" *Contemporary Literature* 10 (Summer 1969): 366–82.

Seret, Roberta. *Voyage into Creativity. The Modern Künstlerroman.* New York: Peter Lang, 1992.

Sharrock, Roger. Introduction. *The Pilgrim's Progress.* By John Bunyan. Harmondsworth: Penguin, 1968. 7–26.

Staley, Thomas F. *Dorothy Richardson.* Boston: Twayne, 1976.

Stewart, Grace. *A New Mythos. The Novel of the Artist as Heroine. 1877–1977.* Montreal: Eden Press. Women's Publications, 1981.

Turner, Victor, and Edith Turner. *Image and Pilgrimage in Christian Culture. Anthropological Perspectives.* New York: Columbia UP, 1978.

Part Three

Displacement:

Situating Identity, Home,

and Diaspora

Chapter 14

In the Ruins of Diaspora: A Southern Italian Perspective

Joseph Pugliese

The Affective Tropics of Diaspora

The dirt path leads to a view of the eighteenth-century bell tower. The path and the bell tower are framed by the branches of overarching trees. The scene is quintessentially pastoral and thus entirely removed from me, from the spatio-temporal coordinates that locate me somewhere else altogether. The fact that it was the final exposure in the roll of film has caused the edge of the photo, where the light reacted to the last of the emulsion, to be blurred and slightly hazy. The fact that the black and white negatives were printed on color paper has given the photo a sepia tone. Both these processes have enhanced the pastoralism of this photograph; they work, in that admixture of light and emulsion, to produce what Emmanuel Levinas terms "a time assemblable in a recollection of representable representation" (*Otherwise* 51). At the edge of the photo, along that liminal axis where the emulsion ends and the failure of representation begins, is located another strange admixture, one of memory and amnesia which insists on contaminating the image before me. This strange admixture produces a *parergonal* effect, in which "the parergon inscribes something which comes as an extra, *exterior* to the proper field...but whose transcendent exteriority comes to play, abut to, brush against, rub, press against the limit itself and intervene in the inside only to the extent that the inside is lacking" (*Truth in Painting* Derrida 56). The complex and contradictory emotions that mark my return "home," to Spilinga, Calabria, village of my birth, partly inscribe themselves in this photograph. Exterior to the proper field of representation, they nonetheless intervene in the inside to supplement the photo with what it lacks, with what remains unrepresentable within its empirical borders. At one level, this essay is a meditation on the historical specters that fail to register in this photo but that insist on inscribing themselves, silently, invisibly, on its surface.

Spilinga is already recollection, made available in such technologies of representation as photography, where past time secures its future through the ruse of representable representation. The return "home," after an absence of twenty years, is, in the first instance, a return back to a memorized place. To a degree, the photo is also representative of my desire to memorialize Spilinga—in the face of dispersion and loss. As such, it is also a site inscribed with desire—an aching desire which is animated daily by the unbridgeable difference between the physicality of my contemporary location in Sydney, Australia, and my memorialized visions of Spilinga, which I carry daily with me, even as I live in another time and place, far removed from Spilinga's materiality and its geophysical existence.

It is in this sense that my return journey operates on two simultaneous levels. I return to Spilinga, boarding and disembarking modes of transport that enable the possibility of return. However, this return is itself structured by the daily turn, my imagined transportation *within* the practices of my everyday life, to Spilinga: as place, as faces, rooms, and as a cluster of fragrances and smells—the unmistakable fragrance of warm dough, the dank smell of rising damp in *Zia* Iris's dark dining room, and the smoke of burning wood out in the field—which transport me with a force back to Spilinga precisely when I am most physically removed from the place, when I have forgotten to remember the village and it has ceased to exist. In this series of sensory provocations-as-returns, the physical signs of Spilinga are displaced and transmuted into so many tropes that daily structure and (dis)order my existence. The smell of rising damp metonymically establishes my aunt's room as it calls into existence her defiant laugh; the fragrance of wild oregano metaphorizes the village's pastoralism as it provokes desire and longing.

This essay is a meditation on the asynchronous and stratified structures of return that mark the relation to my birthplace. The asynchronous nature of time as lived experienced is represented in this essay by my shifting and abruptly alternating use of tenses. In attempting to articulate the complex layers that inscribe this relation, I will negotiate a cluster of seemingly disparate categories that constitute it. Questions concerned with macro configurations—for example, nation and historical events of great magnitude such as mass migration—will be intertwined with those micro figures of desire and loss which trace the affective tropics of the diaspora.

This essay on exile and return is not an attempt to find a resolution to these complex relations. Neither is it an effort at self-diagnosis which, in mapping the symptomatology of the migrant as displaced subject, will strive to cure the pathology of loss, multiple returns, and spatio-temporal disorders. Rather, this essay situates itself at the level of translation: How can I begin, as diasporic subject, to convert the flux of everyday life—as stratified by spatio-temporal disjunctions and contradictory affects—into language, into an embodied representation that will strive not for mimesis but for truth-in-desire, as that which "is" simultaneously here and elsewhere? I place "is" under interrogation, as truth-in-desire is what disrupts the possibility of a pure ontology which is complacently self-identical and securely self-present to oneself. The exile, by definition, is already fractured by a violent transportation from oneself: oneself as here and elsewhere, as self and other. This essay, then, attempts to delineate the contours of these fractures by deploying the paradoxical logic of language. Language will order, incarnate, and make intelligible the complex economies that drive the diaspora, even as its constituent tropes (so many metaphors and metonyms) will silently mock mimesis through a process of figuration that always exceeds the parameters of all realisms and carries with it, and before it, all those incommunicable traces of the past that haunt the practices of representation and always already defer the possibility of an untrammeled self-presence.

My use of the trope of translation is not fortuitous. Is it not precisely translation that embodies the practices of everyday life for the migrant—from one nation to another, from one language to another, from one gesture to another? Translation is the process that already articulates this relation of the self to the other. Translation also encompasses the desire to be transported from one to the other without the violence of assimilation or the obliteration of difference—even if the reality of transportation too often serves, on arrival, to augment, at other levels and in unexpected forms, the very violence one had hoped to escape.

Anachronic Returns

My flight from Rome to Calabria's Lamezia airport was shorter than I had remembered. As the plane began its descent over the mountains of the Aspromonte, I experienced a sense of visceral anxiety that intertwined with the air turbulence that was affecting the plane. With me, everything quickly becomes hopelessly corporealized. My thinking, system of conceptuality, and affects—all are generated by my physiological ensemble in its relation to the metaphoricity of language. Nietzsche captures the logic of this physio-semiotic chain: "A nerve stimulus, first transposed into an image—first metaphor. The image, in turn, imitated by a sound—second metaphor..." (46). The fabled disjunction between body and mind has always remained outside my purview.

Twenty years was an unthinkable absence that I could not afford to dwell on, and the momentum of arrival precluded the possibility of dwelling on this. My relations were all clustered at the exit of the arrival gate. My cousins were largely unrecognizable, my nieces and nephews strangers; only my uncles and aunts were identifiable—their lined features signified a point of recognition and contact in the emotional blur of arrival. The term *arrival,* in fact, fails to convey the sense of controlled upheaval that scripts the moment of return. Paradoxically, at the point of arrival and contact everything becomes momentarily suspended and any sense of grounding is temporarily liquidated. I move in a fluid medium in which my anchors have been cut loose. The arrival unfolds in a sequence of slow-motion shocks: a choreography of gestures, embraces, and kisses organizes the disposition of bodies as they come together, part, and accidentally collide in the crush. The moment of arrival is structured by the failure of synchrony: you, whose visage I've carried for so long in my memory, are no longer "you"; my act of superimposition—memorized image superimposed onto the face before me— creates the haunting effect of a mismatch; the blurred double-contours of this mismatch signify the temporal distance between my past and this present; so many physiognomical features—the shape of the lips, the thickness of the nose— have been realigned in the diachrony of my absence. The exposition of your differences, as a manifestation of the labor of time, is what hollows out the comfort of your welcome. Even as we embrace, you are already elsewhere, and my joy is tempered by this asynchronous distance that will stay silently unbridgeable because it resides in the totality of a past that will remain, in all its significant minutiae, largely unknowable. The physicality of our words and the metaphors of caress and embrace will attempt to transcend this partition.

The drive into Spilinga was chaotic. The entire countryside was shrouded in an unseasonable fog. Even though it was one o'clock in the afternoon, and the weather was warm and humid, a thick mist hung over the landscape, and I could recognize nothing. The convoy of cars that left the airport soon broke into so many parts, some getting lost in the fog, some taking unplanned alternative routes, some speeding recklessly ahead, whilst others trailed slowly and cautiously through the fog. After innumerable stops and starts we entered the mist-covered main street of Spilinga.

If the first day of my arrival had mobilized the weather, with its mists and fog, in order to enhance the occultation of the return to my native village, the following morning staged a graphic reversal. I awoke in the darkened bedroom of my uncle's house and proceeded to open the doors and shutters of the balcony. Before me lay the dazzling blue of the Mediterranean, and sitting on the horizon, directly in my line of sight, was Stromboli, the active volcano rising out of the ocean in the light of the sun, a plume of smoke trailing from its crater. The beauty of the scene was acute. Perched high on the shoulder of Monte Poro, my uncle's house has an overview of the entire village. Spilinga, from this height, is a configuration of terracotta tiles from which rises the bell tower. From Spilinga, the landscape rolls precipitously down to the granite cliffs of Capo Vaticano. Unaccountably, I was unprepared for this. As a vision without the normative mediation of memory, it struck a body blow. This is what I have lost. I have lived all these years without this. This is what has endured in my absence. This is what predates me and what will survive my departure. Inscribed in this moment is an experience that must be peculiarly conditional to the diasporic subject: the experience of a sense of loss and bereavement for what one never possessed. This is the loss of that which has existed entirely on the hither side of memory and consciousness. Irrecuperable precisely because it has never been possessed, it still provokes mourning as it underscores another form of exile.

In this instant of visual absorption, the scene before me becomes my brief duration. It temporizes my existence. Here on the edge of this balcony, on the side of this mountain, on the shore of the Mediterranean, I experience a brief reprieve. This is not, however, a triumphant moment of reclamation. Rather, it is a moment marked by the upsurge of a generosity that disrupts the circuit of reciprocity and repossession as it overflows the demands of exchange economy. Indeed, my return as diasporic subject is predicated on a logic that guarantees the failure of my re-turn as such: My re-turn is, by definition, always already anachronic and dislocated in my relation to the desired point of origin. Levinas articulates the logic of this relation: "A work conceived radically is a movement of the same unto the other which never returns to the same" ("The Trace" 348). The radicality of exile, the force of its multiple trajectories, lies in the law, almost avowed and largely undisguised, that guarantees the failure of the same, in its return, ever to coincide with the other.

In this moment of temporary proximity, in which I can never aspire to the rootedness of habituated belonging or effective reinstatement, Calabria exceeds itself in its evanescence: It shimmers with ingratitude in the face of my affection. Levinas offers a profound meditation on this paradox: "A work conceived in its ultimate nature requires a radical generosity of the same who in the work goes unto the other. It then requires an *ingratitude* of the other. Gratitude would in fact be the *return* of the movement to its origin" ("The Trace" 349).

The modality of my relation to Calabria is structured by ellipsis, the rhetorical figure that so readily implies a particular absence and omission by the context. My ellipsis is punctuated by insurgent but always displaced returns. Every departure, every separation, is animated by a recursive movement. My returns are underwritten by an "inaugural" dislocation that has a serial-like quality: Every return reinaugurates that *indivisible* act of departure and dislocation. I say "indivisible" because one can never hope to locate definitively "the point" of departure as a singular act of scission. The point of departure is in fact constituted by an ensemble of events that refuse separation—even if, collectively, they serve to enable the rupture of separation as such. The structure of this ellipsis, as dispersion and absence, is what enables the generosity of this gift founded on loss and difference. My return to you is only made possible by the impossibility of ever coinciding with you. The possibility of every return to you is predicated on this very difference, on this ingratitude, on the necessity of my exile.

In the Ruins of Diaspora

The necessity of exile in Calabria is brutally historical, political, and economic. The material fabric of Spilinga, its people and houses, all bear witness to the violent effects of this necessity. I draw on Walter Benjamin's "angel of history" in order to make sense of this violence:

an angel looking as though he is about to move away from something he is fixedly contemplating. His eyes are staring, his mouth is open, his wings are spread. This is how one pictures the angel of history. His face is turned toward the past. Where we perceive a chain of events, he sees one single catastrophe which keeps piling wreckage upon wreckage and hurls it in front of his feet. The angel would like to stay, awaken the dead, and make whole what has been smashed. But a storm is blowing from Paradise; it has got caught in his wings with such violence that the angel can no longer close them. This storm irresistibly propels him into the future to which his back is turned, while the pile of debris before him grows skyward. This storm is what we call progress. (257–58)

The angel of history has passed through Spilinga. It has emptied the village of two-thirds of its inhabitants, dispersed across the globe by the necessity of immigration. For over a century, Calabria's greatest export has been its human population. In the words of Pasquino Crupi, Calabria's export of people must be viewed in terms of *tonnellata umana* ("human tonnage") (*Tonnellata* i). Spilinga bears witness to the passage of the angel of history. The village appears as though it has been hit by a large-scale catastrophe, when in fact it stands victim to the soft tread of the angel of history. The evisceration of the village never occurred in terms of a grand exile *en masse*. Rather, the process was constituted by the relentless trickle of so many small-scale departures—an uncle, a father, a sister. Every silent yet anguished departure served to tear away at the sociophysical fabric of the village. The sum of all these singular flights functioned to produce the overwhelming drama of dereliction and decay that now governs Spilinga's fate.

As the angel is propelled into the future, the pile of debris grows skyward. With only every third house still inhabited in the old quarter, every other house is in a state of dereliction. A few of the vacant houses are boarded up, the doors and windows nailed shut. They have been shored up against the violence of history—the power of the storm is inexorable. Even the boarded-up doors and windows are in varying stages of collapse. These houses all manifest the signs of structural fatigue and profound traumatism: They have been waiting too long for the return of their exiled inhabitants, who have now been swept up into other lives, cleaning and maintaining other houses in other countries. These houses have now submitted, with varying degrees of passivity and half-hearted resistance, to the forces of decay. Some of the houses are in a state of utter collapse; they look as though a bomb has exploded in their very core, tearing the heart out of them.

To a degree, humans have become ancillary to the old quarter of the village. Indeed, the remnant population of Spilinga has moved to the outskirts of the village where they have bravely established a new quarter: *Spilinga Nuova* ("New Spilinga"). Most of the houses in Spilinga Nuova are, however, in varying states of incompletion and have been, my relatives tell me, in this state for years. Most of the houses in the new quarter are uninhabited. Many of the remaining

Spilingoti families have in fact been forced to live permanently in their farm-houses in order to guard their livestock from the endemic cattle rustling that afflicts the countryside. These same families have initiated, over the years, the construction of new houses in Spilinga Nuova. These new houses have rapidly become superfluous to the exigencies of their lives. Some of these houses-in-progress, on close examination, already show signs of incipient decay. The very act of defiance, in attempting to arrest the violence of history by founding a new village on the margins of the old, has already been contaminated and disabled. Spilinga Nuova has already assumed the disquieting air of an abandoned place.

New Spilinga signifies for me the topos of historical repetition, inscribed by the figure of the chiasmus. The old quarter of Spilinga divides into two unequal parts: Spilinga proper and Carciadi. There is no visible line that divides Spilinga from Carciadi. To an outsider, there is no difference or structural demarcation announcing the fact, as one walks the streets of the village, that one has moved from Spilinga into Carciadi. One can catch a glimpse of this difference, how-ever, from the aerial view of Spilinga that is offered from the top of Monte Poro. From this position, Carciadi appears as an irregular outgrowth attached to Spil-inga proper.

The history of Spilinga's relation to Carciadi is located in the genealogy of invasions that have convulsed this region. At one time or another, this region has been invaded by Carthaginians, Greeks, Romans, Arabs ("Saracens"), Normans, Swedes, Turks, Spanish, and French. In the ninth century, the Arabs colonized the region and established an emirate at Tropea. The necropolis of the emirate was located in what are now the fields of my late grandfather's farm at Aramoni, just outside Spilinga. In their lengthy occupation of the region, the Arabs con-solidated their hold by intermarrying with the local population. Thus, in the first century of the new millennium (1048), when the Arabs themselves where placed under notice of eviction by the incoming Normans, the ethno-cultural mix of Spilinga precluded the possibility of simply deporting the Arab population. Spi-linga's solution to the problem, according to the legends handed down over the generations and related to me by my father, was to establish a type of internal exile: The Arab-Calabrese population was relocated to the edge of the village, in a separate quarter known as *Carciadi*—"the Outcasts."

On the cusp of another millennium, one thousand years after the establish-ment of Carciadi, Spilinga is constructing another quarter for outcasts. Only, in this instance, the outcasts are the Spilingoti themselves. Spilinga Nuova is the locus of another internal exile. It completes the chiastic structure of a history predicated on repetition-as-inversion: Between Carciadi and Spilinga Nuova, the heart of Spilinga's old quarter is cut by this diagonal cross.

Spilinga Nuova owes its existence to the violent forces of immigration. It has been secreted out of the cultural fabric of the old quarter as a type of defiant gesture against the angel of history and the scandal of decay and dereliction that laps at its freshly laid concrete and steel foundations. Even as Spilinga Nuova rises above the wreckage that piles up at its feet, the animus of the old village, formed out of a history of violent invasions and expulsions, inscribes itself on the freshly constituted fabric of the new—on the concrete pillars of the new houses already blistering and flaking in their exposure to the elements, on the steel frames striated by the bloody rivulets of oxidization. The old quarter has become the crypt and repository of a violent history that refuses to be isolated or quarantined from any defiant gesture of the new. This old violence interlaces with the new and silently founds it—founds it as an ironic but bitter act of repetition and undermining. In this village, the angel of history moves between millennial acts punctuated by so many minor dramas of exile and return, decay and renewal.

As I move from empty building to empty building, photographing and composing the decomposition of the old quarter, a peal of laughter behind me compels me to turn around and face two young girls who, assuming I'm a foreign tourist, sarcastically remark in the Calabrian dialect: "Ma guarda stu sciemu, sta fotografandu i monumenti!" ("Just look at this fool photographing the monuments!").

On the Failure of Criminal Anthropology

Prior to my arrival in Spilinga, I spent three days in the Biblioteca Nazionale and the Biblioteca Universitaria Allessandrina in Rome reading a selection of the works of the nineteenth-century, Northern Italian criminal anthropologist Cesare Lombroso. Lombroso wrote extensively on Southern Italians. Calabrians in particular were objects of academic study and fascination for him, specifically in the context of Lombroso's racist theories on the biological determination of race. *In Calabria,* first published in 1862 and subsequently reissued in 1898, offers a detailed mapping of the psycho-congenital characteristics of Calabrians, simultaneously elaborating the sociocultural context that they inhabit and within which they operate. Lombroso's psycho-congenital profiles of Calabrians already bristle with a cluster of stereotypes that quickly congeal into ontological attributes: lascivious, thieving, backward, violent, and dirty. For Calabrians, "To kill someone with a gun, or with a knife, is a joke performed with little or no inconvenience" (95). Sitting in the library reading Lombroso's text, I would often break into laughter because of the abundant absurdities or contradictions: "The Calabrians of bilious temperament, and they are the majority, are particularly susceptible to haemorrhoids" (132). Lombroso, amongst a host of other maladies, found cretinism to be so widespread in Calabria "even the dogs were afflicted by it" (129).

Lombroso's travelogue-psycho-anthropological work on Calabrians reads like a treatise written in hell. His catalogue of congenital diseases and deformities (including "obstinate constipation" and elephantiasis) are situated in a context of filth and appalling hygiene. The clinical concern with hygiene, however, is contaminated by a moralizing strain that repeatedly suggests the biological link between physical and moral degeneration:

> The houses of the poor are everywhere lurid, particularly those beneath street-level; the ground-floor is of naked, humid earth; the stairs are ladders; the other floors are scaffolding of beams and straw where, in the succeeding levels, are lodged entire families…and it's worth noting, moreover, that the household animals—the pig, the chicken and the donkey, whoever is lucky actually to own such animals—occupy the best possible spaces. (103)

Perversely, I think here of my maternal grandmother, *Nonna* Augusta, and her pride and joy, the chicken Teresina that would follow her everywhere, and with whom my *nonna* would have animated conversations. Moreover, every morning, there would be a fresh egg. On one occasion, Teresina disappeared and my distraught *nonna* searched the entire village but failed to find her. For months she went missing; then one day *Nonna* Augusta heard Teresina's distinctive clucking as the chicken made her way excitedly down Via Carducci toward her, with a woman in hot pursuit. *Nonna* Augusta swiftly grabbed Teresina and folded her under her arm, as the unknown woman proceeded to argue that the chicken was hers. With immovable dignity, *Nonna* Augusta pointed to Teresina's red crest and said: "There is only one Teresina: This is Teresina of the *gagja a fiuri* (flowered crest)." With this, the thief was vanquished.

Walking the streets of the old quarter of Spilinga, I meditate on the violence of anthropology, criminal or otherwise: on its blindness to the very practices of everyday life that it assumes to record and analyze, on its obtuseness to the fragile systems of value that orient even the most seemingly banal practices and relations. In winter, the household animals that would sleep in the *catoio* ("ground-floor room"), so luridly described by Lombroso, would give a family, fortunate enough to own livestock, warmth and the comfort of companionship.

I try to enter through the entrance of an abandoned *catoio* that has lost its front door, and I'm struck by the lack of height. The Spilingoti prior to my generation were all relatively short because of severe malnutrition. The transgenerational effects of famine ensured the reproduction of this epigenetic inheritance. My octogenarian relative, *Compare* 'Ntoni, reminds me that questions of hygiene were not a priority in a context where so many Spilingoti didn't have the money to buy salt to flavor their meals, usually a plate of wild greens gathered in the surrounding fields. For many, bread was a seasonal food made from ground chestnuts harvested in the ravine of Livasi that borders Spilinga. *Comare* 'Ntonuzza speaks to me of the night she so craved some flavorsome dressing that she used the lamp-oil that she had saved for emergencies as a condiment to dress her dish of wild greens.

In *In Calabria,* Lombroso's intertwining of the discourse of clinical anthropology with that of morality finally gives birth to the monstrosity of Social Darwinism:

> This example of the degeneration of a race because of the neglect of the selection of the species confirms Darwin's theory as outlined in his *On the Origin of the Species,* where he tells us that a species lives and perfects itself when it is given the opportunity, both through the artifice of man (sic) and through spontaneous pre-selection, to breed with the best examples of the species; a species becomes extinct or degenerates when this spontaneous or artificial process of selection ceases. (106–7)

In the face of the squalor and poverty that affronts the sensibility of the criminal anthropologist, Lombroso fails to see the historico-political structures of entrenched exploitation and brutal expropriation that serve so effectively to reproduce the appalling conditions that disgust him. With a moralizing complacency, Darwin's theory conveniently allows him to locate the causes of poverty and misery in the breeding practices of animals.

The Camel of Fire

The close of every *festa* in Spilinga is marked by the dance of the *cameju i focu* (the "camel of fire"). Prior to the feast, canes are assembled into the skeletal structure of a camel. The hollow canes are filled with gunpowder and firecrackers. The flesh of the camel is made of brilliantly colored papier-mâché. Its head is carved from the soft wood of the fig tree. A tongue of flame gives the face a defiant grimace. At midnight, a man places the frame on his shoulders and the camel of fire enters the crowd-filled square to the beat of drums. The camel is said to represent the expulsion of the Arabs who, during the period of the emirate at Tropea, traveled across the countryside on their camels in order to extract their dues from the local people. The camel of fire is also said to symbolize the burning of Arab ships in the port of Tropea at the time of the Norman Conquest.

Having entered the square, the beat of the drums becomes louder and the dance of the camel becomes more frenetic as it emits sulphurous fumes and intermittent explosions. The camel trembles and shakes with the force of the exploding fire-crackers; the figure of the man bearing the frame disappears in the smoke and the camel assumes a life of its own.

At this point in the spectacle, this camel of fire no longer works for me in terms of folk allegory, ethnographic anecdote, or political metonym signifying the expulsion of the Arab conquerors. In its writhing pain and sheer incendiary beauty, the camel becomes something else altogether. Its signifying status is transmuted into the figure of sacrificial animal caught in the impersonal relations of force and violence that constitute Calabria's history of invasions and expulsions. This moment of triumphant vengeance and overthrow is, for me, marked by a painful ambivalence which is always reanimated when I witness this spectacle of expulsion.

Calabria's convulsive genealogy of invasions and expulsions, rhythmically underscored by the extraction of expropriative tolls and the outright decimation of the local people, culminated in one of the largest mass expulsions of modern times with the enforced exile of Calabria's own: Between 1951 and 1971, 700,000 emigrated from Calabria; over the last one hundred years, the total is 2 million (Crupi, *Tonnellata* 251). Crupi names this mass migration and dispersion "the white genocide of the Calabrian people" (*Tonnellata* 137). Crupi is, however, singularly unreflexive of the ideological load that the racial marker "white" brings to bear in his use of the term "genocide." His use of "white" situates his discourse in the hierarchized and racist binaries of eurocentrism, where "white" serves to signify in contradistinction to the more barbaric atrocities naturally perpetrated in instances of "black" genocide. Situated in the Italian context, the qualifier "white" assumes the dimensions of dramatic irony: The South has, over the centuries, served as Northern Italy's racial other. In the words of the popular Northern Italian aphorism, "Africa begins south of Rome." In the North's desire to be viewed as "European," it has constructed the South as the repository of an altogether primitive and backward race, the *Terroni* (literally, people who eat earth/soil), contaminated by African and Oriental blood (see, for example, Lombroso, *L'uomo* 234). Saverio Strati has eloquently articulated the dimensions of this racism: "Overseas, we are the dirty Italians; for the petit bourgeois of Turin and Milan, we are an inferior race. Famished, uncultured, illiterate and pre-medieval. Used and exploited and always placed apart like the Blacks of America...I find it impossible to retell certain experiences. My tongue becomes stuck and my hair stands on end" (182). In a gesture of defiance, the painter Enotrio Pugliese has reclaimed this racist history in his affirmative celebration of *Calabresità come Negritudine* ["Calabrianness as Negritude"] (qtd. in Baldini 30).

The polar axis that divides the Italian peninsula is constituted by a system of differential relations: The North needs the South, and vice versa, if it is to maintain its own sense of identity. In other words, and in Derridean terms, the South is already internal to the North's self-identity: Its exteriority is already inside the North. The stereotypical series of Southern attributes—backwardness, criminality, and barbarism—function to supplement the inverse Northern series: progressiveness, the rule of law, and civility. These polarized series, which could be expanded indefinitely, are differentially dependent upon one another, and thus their exteriority is already inscribed within the self-identity of the other: The one supplements the other. This supplementary logic simultaneously overturns the very polarity it establishes, as it generates the following (impossible) configuration: "[T]he north amounts to the south of the south, which puts the south to the north of the north" ("Grammatology" Derrida 218). This deconstructive move, however, does not do away with geopolitical effects that continue to situate and inscribe the bodies of Southern Italian subjects. Rather, I'm interested in mapping the continuation of these effects outside the parameters of the Italian state.

The history of the racism internal to the Italian state has produced, for the Calabrian diaspora, a peculiar doubling effect that requires comment. If, in the context of the Italian peninsula, the Calabrian is already positioned as other to the Northern Italian, then this effect can be seen to be duplicated and amplified in the country of exile. I wish to trace this unsettling process of doubling, with all its peculiar convolutions, in the context of my own experience.

Having undergone during the decade of the 1960s, in the Australian context, the regime of assimilation, with its insistent demand that the migrant erase all the markers of cultural difference that deviated from the dominant Anglocentric norm, the 1970s were characterized for me as period of increasing politicization about the assimilationist processes that I had undergone. I set out to reclaim my Italianness. It is at this point, however, that a series of peculiar contortions and doublings must be seen as having come into play.

The process of publicly reclaiming an Italian identity entailed embracing and affirming the dominant and stereotypic signifiers of Northern Italian high culture—its literature, music, art, fashion, design, and so on—through which Italianness largely signified, and continues to signify, in an international context. This act of reclamation was internally fraught for me, as Northern Italian high culture was not only remote and alien to me, it was simultaneously marked as other—in certain ways that were, in the context of the racism against non-Anglo migrants in which I lived, unspeakable. As Strati remarks in his analysis of the North/South divide, "One always has the sense that the South is not Italy" (13). To assume, then, an Italian identity in the context that I am describing produced the effect of feeling oneself to be an impostor—a fraud who mouthed an identity that was substantially as alien as Anglo-Australianness.

In the Australian context, Calabrians experienced a double racism: They were discriminated against by the dominant Anglocentric policies of the Australian state (see Pugliese) and, simultaneously, they were discriminated against—on the factory floor or in the context of the Italian embassies and consulates—by many of the Northern Italians who had also emigrated to Australia and who continued to treat Southerners as people of an inferior race. Consequently, my celebration of Italianness was short-lived, as it became impossible to affirm an Italian identity that not only erased its other half but that, in multiple ways, systemically discriminated against it. My use of Italianicity was tactical and contingent on a particular political context. It was also a relief to discard its painful torsions and contradictions. I inhabited Italianicity-as-cultural-identity in a relation of misrecognition and fraudulent approximation. This was a position that had already been articulated in my relation to Australianness. What was different and unbearable about it was the fact that it was supposed to signify "home"—in the sense of "place of origin" and refuge in the face of racist discrimination and non-belonging. Unsettled, unhoused, unhinged—diasporic subjects are always incommensurate to all the configurations of grounded identities that are complacently at home. This paradoxical essentialization that attempts, through a sleight of hand, to construct another trope of belonging ("home" as constituted by a permanent state of exile) is too facile. The movement, rather, must be seen as structured by the desire to take up a position of belonging in the face of an externality already prior and anachronous to that desire. It is this very *apriority* that provokes desire. Levinas, characteristically, identifies its traces: "Incommensurable with the present, unassemblable in it, it is always 'already in the past' behind which the present delays, over and beyond the 'now' which this exteriority disturbs or obsesses" (*Otherwise* 100).

In the conclusion to his invaluable analysis of the history of Calabrian migration, Crupi writes that "There is an appalling historical continuity which pervades Calabria: the state of permanent misery and backwardness. Against this [historical continuity], two safety valves have operated: brigandage and emigration" (*Tonnellata* 138). "Backwardness" is the one term that is firmly entrenched in any lexicon on Calabria, "brigandage" surfacing, in comparison, with a tolerable periodicity. "Backwardness" is a term that resonates with teleological pretensions and ethnocentric demands, and Crupi falls into the trap of reproducing this order. "Backwardness" has, through the process of repetition, achieved a type of naturalized status that effaces the structural conditions productive of poverty and misery. In the Orientalist discourses on Calabria, in innumerable anthropological and ethnographic studies, in history books and travelogues, "backwardness" is represented as, quite simply, the congenital condition of Calabrians. In the grandiloquent words of one Italian politician, Calabrian misery and backwardness can only be overcome through the process of expulsion and dispersion, here euphemistically termed "migration":

> Migration is a necessity; necessity not in a fatalistic or resigned sense of an incurable sickness or of a cruel destiny, but of historical necessity, in that it corresponds with a new and orderly plan of the State in the context of the international community and the actual process of economic and social progress in the world. (qtd. in Crupi, *Tonnellata* 132–33)

In this grand schema, the telos of progress, as that which will finally overcome backwardness, is driven and enabled by the beneficence of historical necessity, an anonymous yet providential historical necessity comfortably articulated from a financial position that insulates the politician from the self-same forces that arbitrarily compel some but not others to emigrate. The history of the Italian state's relation to Calabrian migration has been one of posturing concern and fundamental neglect.

As an afterthought to the centenary celebrations of Italian unification, the president of the Republic, Fanfani, deigned in 1961 to descend into the nether regions of the Italian peninsula. He spent five days touring Calabria, with an entourage of Northern Italian journalists, each recording the spectacle of destitution and chronic poverty that confronted them, each horrified by conditions unanimously condemned with moral outrage (see Greco-Naccarato's *Calabria Oggi,* an extraordinary anthology of the reportage generated by this official journey into Calabria). The repeated demands from the Calabrians who spoke to Fanfani centered on the desperate need for basic infrastructure—such as running water, sewerage, electricity, roads—and jobs. The days spent by the president in Calabria were characterized by the journalist Michele Tito as "five days of protests and denunciations" (qtd. in Greco-Naccarato 33). The five days of "inspection" completed, the president and the journalists returned North, and the exodus from Calabria continued unabated.

Watching the spectacle of the camel of fire in the village square, the sacrificial animal assumes for me an emblematic status. I think of the shiploads of Calabrian migrants who never made it to their destination because they died at sea. Crupi offers, in a footnote, an incomplete catalogue of the thousands of deaths at sea due to overcrowding, famine, and disease (*Letteratura* footnote 9, 48). One disaster, in particular, haunts me: the *Matteo Bruzzo,* with 1333 passengers, bombarded with canon-fire as it attempted to enter the port of Montevideo because of the fear of importing the cholera epidemic that was raging on board ship. The ship was subsequently refused entry to a number of ports, and the majority of its passengers died on board, their corpses unceremoniously dumped at sea.

As the dance of the camel of fire nears closure, the animal catches fully alight and, after a series of wrenching motions, it is thrown over the ramparts of the village square into the ravine of Livasi. In its flight of immolation, it traces a fiery arc into the void. Its incandescent form tumbles toward the *fiumara* below. The *fiumara* will douse its flames and carry its smoldering remains out to sea.

The Topography of Displacement

In his landmark essay, "Calabria in Idea," Augusto Placanica traces the various topoi that function repeatedly to constitute the concept of Calabria across a heterogeneous body of texts. Among the most enduring topoi, Placanica draws attention to those that represent Calabria in terms of "archaic myth" ("Garden of Eden" and "Magna Grecia") and Calabresità in terms of "reliability, tenacity and even susceptibility, reserve and shadowiness" (587 and 649). Concluding his essay by bringing into focus the impact of migration on this semiotic construction of Calabria, Placanica suggests that the concept of Calabria is "never as powerful in itself as it is in the thoughts of those who have left it" (649).

To me, a Calabrian of the diaspora, the constellation of topoi that Placanica articulates is meaningless; this essentialized configuration of characteristics is alien. In fact, my own experience as a migrant has compelled me to treat with suspicion all essentialized configurations of national or regional character traits (see Pugliese 232–51). When I think of Calabria, I think topography rather than topoi—specifically a topography of exile and lines of flight. Calabria, for me, is modeled, as a semiotic construct on the screen of my computer, in terms of a region whose coastal contours, mountain elevations, and precipitous ravines are constituted by myriad lines of flight. Each line of flight represents the journey of one of its immigrants; irregularly, select lines trace the loops of intermittent returns. Over the years, each line of flight overlaps and begins to shape the grid-lines of a topographic map, building up the details of topological relief. Each grid-line is a lifeline of one its immigrants; together they elaborate so many historical folds and substrata. So many of these lifelines will remain mute and occluded in the face of those historical surges that provoke another mass exodus and thereby deposit another thick layer onto the topographic map of the region. These lines of flight signify so many anonymous histories that serve to fabricate the text of a Calabria that now fails to coincide with itself, with that self-image figured by the attributes of its traditional topoi. My simulated model of the region, with its topography of dislocations and displacements, serves to wrench Calabria irrevocably from its fateful history of archaisms, from the deadweight of topoi that can only signify in terms of the past. This simulacrum of Calabria, with its anguished yet liberating lines of flight, is an other Calabria altogether to that physical space inhabited by those who never left. It is a cyber-Calabria characterized by the fact that it exists altogether elsewhere: atomized and dispersed yet cohering along those lines of force that compelled the mass movement of so many millions of its subjects.

Note

All translations from the Calabrese and the Italian are mine.

Works Cited

Baldini, Jolena. "Enotrio: Calabresità come Negritudine." *La Regione Calabria: Emigrazione* 9–10 (December 1996): 30–37.

Benjamin, Walter. *Illuminations.* Trans. Harry Zohn. Ed. Hanna Arendt. New York: Schocken Books, 1989.

Crupi, Pasquino. *La Tonnellata Umana.* San Giovanni in Persiceto: Barbaro, 1994.

———. *Letteratura ed Immigrazione.* Reggio Calabria: Casa del Libro Editrice, 1979.

Derrida, Jacques. *Of Grammatology.* Trans. Gayatri Spivak. Baltimore: Johns Hopkins UP, 1976.

————. *The Truth in Painting.* Trans. Geoff Bennington and Ian McLeod. Chicago: U of Chicago P, 1987.

Greco-Naccarato, Gaetano. *Calabria Oggi.* Milano: Rizzoli, 1962.

Levinas, Emmanuel. *Otherwise Than Being or Beyond Essence.* Trans. Alphonso Lingis. Dordrecht: Kluwer Academic, 1991.

————. "The Trace of the Other." Trans. Alphonso Lingis. *Deconstruction in Context: Literature and Philosophy.* Ed. Mark C. Taylor. Chicago: U of Chicago P, 1986. 345–59.

Lombroso, Cesare. *In Calabria.* 1862. Catania: Cav. Niccolò Giannotta, 1898.

————. *L'uomo deliquente in rapporto all' antropologia, alla giurisprudenza ed alle discipline carcerie. Vol. I: Deliquente—Nato e pazzo morale.* Torino: Fratelli Bocca, 1889.

Nietzsche, Friedrich. *Friedrich Nietzsche on Rhetoric and Language.* Trans. and eds. Sander L. Gilman, Carole Blair, and David J. Parent. New York: Oxford UP, 1989.

Placanica, Augusto. "Calabria in Idea." Storia d'Italia. *Le reggioni dall'Unità a oggi: La Calabria.* Eds. Piero Bevilacqua e Augusto Placanica. Milano: Giulio Einaudi, 1985. 587–650.

Pugliese, Joseph. "Assimilation, Unspeakable Traces and the Ontologies of Nation." *Asian and Pacific Inscriptions: Identities, Ethnicities, Nationalities.* Ed. Suvendrini Perera. Melbourne: Meridian, 1995. 229–54.

Strati, Saverio. *Noi lazzaroni.* Milano: Arnoldo Mondadori, 1972.

❖ Chapter 15

(Re)-Visiting Der Heim: *The Amazing Return to the Place You've Never Been Which Isn't There*

Andrew Palmer

All immigrant communities retain nostalgia for their place of origin, and later generations develop a desire to revisit the home they have never seen. This provides the occasion for a particular type of travel narrative, a thriving subgenre: the narrative of return. Perhaps the most famous example is Alex Haley's *Roots* in which an African-American author traces an ancestry and journeys to Gambia. Narratives of return by Jewish writers are legion, each one in search of the Old Country or, in the Yiddish phrase, *der heim*—the Home. Two recent examples are *Roots Schmoots* (1993) in which Howard Jacobson returns to Serhai in Lithuania, from where his great-grandparents emigrated to Britain in 1899, and *Konin: A Quest* (1995), in which Theo Richmond travels back to the Polish town of Konin, which his parents left just before World War One.

Both narratives follow the same circuitous route to Eastern Europe from England, via the United States and Israel, so their route "back" embraces the new Jewish communities that resulted from the dissolution of the old, before returning to the site of the lost and unregainable prewar communities in Eastern Europe. However, Jacobson and Richmond follow this common route, ostensibly at least, for different reasons. Richmond travels to America and Israel first in order to interview the dispersed and elderly survivors of Konin's prewar Jewish community, to ransack their memories before they die and the information is lost forever. Jacobson's motives are less clear: He subtitles his travelogue "Journeys among Jews" and, in describing his encounters with Jews of all descriptions—from Hassidic New Yorkers to Israeli atheists—he seems to be searching for a Jewish identity he *likes*. Between them, these journeys problematize Jewish identity, expressing anxiety over its protean nature, its lack of fixity, but ultimately recognizing that this element of indeterminacy in Jewish identity is an essential constituent characteristic of it.

The difficulty with Jewish narratives of return is that there is no Old Country left to visit—the communities in Eastern Europe from where Richmond's and Jacobson's forebears emigrated were destroyed by the Nazis. So what do these writers hope to find? What are they going to see? Richmond comments that most of the elderly survivors of Konin's prewar Jewish community he meets have no desire to revisit the town (411). Those few who did go back did so either just after the war, when they found their homes destroyed or occupied by Poles, the synagogue ransacked (233–44), or later in life when there was even less evidence that the community had ever existed.[1] If actual emigrants either refuse to return, or return to find nothing, why does Richmond desire to narrate a journey there? It is not as if the Jewish experience of Eastern Europe was a good one, as Jacobson points out: "Something is wrong with the way we modern Jews idealize a past we wouldn't touch with a barge-pole if it were offered us again" (192).

Both books climax with the writer's arrival in the Old Country and a description of his search for any evidence that a Jewish community once existed there. The last resort for both Richmond and Jacobson is to seek out the Jewish cemetery. Richmond describes a long and frustrating search through undergrowth that culminates in the discovery of nothing but "three shallow depressions in the ground, rectangular in shape, side by side in a row: unmistakably graves. And…one slender strip of stone hidden in the grass, the foot of a memorial snapped off at its base" (428). Similarly, Jacobson is assured that a Jewish cemetery exists, but searches in vain. Finally, one of his guides calls out that he has found it: "We wind down…to where the cultivated land gives out to overgrown but winter-dead grass, to what looks like waste land, and there, sticking up at odd angles, twisted, chipped, faded, broken, mis-shaped, discoloured and utterly, utterly ignored, are the gravestones" (499). These scenes form the climax, or anticlimax, of each narrative. Both writers arrive to find nothing, or almost nothing. Richmond puts it succinctly: "Every trace of Jewish life had been expunged, and only in the mind could that life be resurrected, perhaps more easily at a distance from this dismal place, which only seemed to deny its past" (426). A fair point. So why go there? Alex Haley was able to find codescendents—to find the community he would have belonged to had his ancestors not been enslaved. No such resolution is possible for Richmond or Jacobson. The explanation for their attempt to accomplish an impossible "return" lies in the unstable, protean nature of Jewish identity.

The Jew has been placeless and unplaceable by Europe. As Jean-François Lyotard comments in *Heidegger and "The Jews"*: "What is most real about real Jews is that Europe…does not know what to do with them: Christians demand their conversion; monarchs expel them; republics assimilate them; Nazis exterminate them" (3). In different contexts, then, European Jews have been perceived as a race, as a religion, and as a nation. However, there are white, black, and brown Jews—it is not a race. There are atheist Jews—it is not a religion. There are anti-Zionist Jews—it is not a nation. Jewishness is caught somewhere between the categories of identity constructed by liberal ideology. As Daniel and Jonathan Boyarin put it: "Jewishness disrupts the very categories of identity because it is not national, not genealogical, not religious, but all of these in dialectical tension with one another" (721). Bryan Cheyette notes Zygmunt Bauman's argument that it is this uncategorizability which worries dominant culture and leads to the construction of "the Jew" as Other. In other words, the allegorized "Jew," representing alterity, stems not from "heterophobia" (resentment of the different) but rather from "proteophobia" (apprehension caused by those who do not fall into established categories). Bauman argues that "given the ordering, classifying nature of modernity—signified, above all, by the rise of the nation-state—the ambivalent 'Jew' was particularly threatening because s/he made light of all modern social, political and cultural distinctions" (Cheyette, "Ineffable" 297).

If the dominant culture's attitude to Jewry is proteophobic, so too is British Jewry's attitude to itself. Writers who consider themselves both British and Jewish find their uncategorizability a source of anxiety which they seek to resolve. One way of doing so is to identify strongly with Englishness. This method, though, can be problematic because, in English discourses, Jewishness has been antithetical to Englishness and, as Cheyette argues, the allegorized "Jew" has been used to shape modern Englishness. It has been, he says, "a key touchstone for the racial boundaries of European 'culture' and the 'Englishness' of modern English literature" (*Constructions* 12). In this context, it is hard to identify as both Jewish and English.

Richmond, on the one hand, confesses "a secret longing to be buried by a yew tree in an English Country Churchyard" (358) and yet, on the other, amongst elderly Jews in New York who have emigrated or escaped from *der heim,* he laments his Englishness which prevents him communicating with them: "I come away despondent, feeling trapped in my Englishness, an outsider, an alien, denied yet again the elusive joy of belonging" (148).

Similarly, when asked in Lithuania if there are oak trees in England, Jacobson replies incredulously: "Oaks? In England? We invented oaks. We *are* oaks" (494). However, when he is in Israel he is a Semite, seeing himself as having more in common with the Palestinians than non-Jewish English visitors: "With [the Palestinians] we are just having a family quarrel. The enemies of my soul come from Tunbridge Wells" (339). Jacobson, like Richmond, is English if he is anything, and nothing if not a Jew.

The relationship with Englishness, then, is deeply ambivalent. Anxiety over the indeterminacy of their identity leads these writers to desire a strong identification with England but, in certain contexts, it just will not wash. Their desire to write travel books narrating a "return" to *der heim* can be understood in this context. The Old Country is mourned, remembered, sentimentalized, because when it was destroyed, what was taken away was a fixed Jewish identity. In *der heim,* a concentration of Jews lived specifically Jewish cultural and political lives, before emancipation and dispersal blurred the distinctions that set them apart. We desire this fixity and seek to regain it.

In this desire, Richmond is obsessed with prewar Konin—that is, both a time (prewar) and a place (Konin). He attempts to regain it by combining a temporal journey with a spatial journey. The temporal journey is conducted via accounts in documents and memories gathered in Britain, America, and Israel. When he comes to narrate his own spatial journey to modern-day Konin, he repeatedly compares the place before his eyes with the information he has collected in an attempt to link the two and so regain *der heim.* For example, the first Nazi execution in Konin in 1939 is described twice in the book: The first account is reconstructed from texts gathered and memories plundered in Britain, America, and Israel (75–77), the second occurs as Richmond narrates his own arrival at, and recognition of, the place where the event happened (422). Ultimately, though, the attempt to link the temporal and the spatial (and so regain *der heim*) fails. He locates buildings that once held Jewish homes or businesses, but he can find no evidence before his eyes that they ever did. So he says: "[H]ere is where Fordoynski sold ropes, Strykowski iron goods, Bonzdrow herrings, Krauser cloth, Walkowicz gramophones, Rachwalski dishes; where Cukier made wire fencing, Ancer kept his horses, Kleczewski had his tinsmith's yard, Monczka his timber yard" (425). However, when he searches each building for a *mezuzah,* i.e., the small container attached by Jews to their doorposts which holds a parchment inscribed with scriptural passages, he finds nothing: "[M]y *mezuzah* hunt...yielded not a single trophy, not even a trace of the nail holes where the *mezuzahs* were once fixed to the doorposts" (426).

The tone is overwhelmingly one of loss. Prewar Konin is unrecoverable. The book ends with Richmond, sitting in a Polish bus shelter on the day of his departure, feeling no regret at leaving. He concludes: "I knew now that it was not the place that held meaning for me but the people who once lived there" (466).

Jacobson's strategy is different. He embraces the "lostness" of *der heim* and seeks to get beyond the desire for a fixed, categorizable identity by encountering a bewildering panoply of Jewish identities. Richmond is motivated by a desire to salvage what can be salvaged; he arrives wanting to find something. Jacobson, contrarily, is on a "Jewish journey in pursuit of loss" (7). His focus is not the past, but the *lostness* of the past. He says he travels "not with the ambition of repossessing the sensation of belonging, but rather with the much more voluptuous expectation of repossessing nothing" (7). On reaching *der heim,* he tries to summon up a sense of homecoming and fails:

> Do I feel anything? I look around. Between the wooden houses you can see ploughed fields, gentle valleys, water, smallholdings, modest raids on the earth. People are inside their houses. You can taste their warmth. It *almost* gets me, it's

almost something I remember, from somewhere, but it isn't quite, it isn't truly, it isn't in *fact*. (495)

His attempt to overleap the desire for the unregainable past leads him into an engagement with all kinds of Jewishness which offer alternative loci for identity. He meets Jews of various denominations (Orthodox, Reform, Conservative, Reconstructionist); he meets Jews for Jesus; he meets secular Russian-Jewish immigrants. He considers Jewish food as a locus for identity. In Los Angeles, he visits a gay synagogue and, having shunned religious services all his life, is provided with an experience he unexpectedly enjoys and understands (206). His journeys to America and Israel enable him to explore all these identity options en route to *der heim*. The final arrival in Lithuania brings him to the only option not available: *Der heim* is unrecoverable.

In Israel, Jacobson experiences an epiphany at the realization of an alternative oriental identity. On seeing, in an Israeli shop window, a pair of tennis shoes decorated with sequins and seed-pearls, he expresses his embarrassment over a perceived Jewish taste for garish clothes, but his wife Ros suggests that, in a Middle-Eastern context ("a place which is so brightly coloured"), tastes which appear garish or kitsch back in Manchester are "vibrant and lustrous." Jacobson concludes that the self-consciousness European Jews feel about their own taste arises from "a fundamental geographical error":

> We have forgotten where we come from and what made us, what climatic conditions shaped us and gave us our love of hot colours and bright lights....We are not, then, aberrant Europeans. We are not freakish Litvaks. We are normal, regular, displaced Middle Easterners....
>
> I look around. The sky is no blue you ever see in northern Europe. The hills of Jordan are shocking pink. The Negev is three shades of purple....Forget Poland and Russia and Lithuania and the ghetto and Yiddish. We are Bedouins. Tent- and oasis- dwellers, who like to festoon our pavilions with cloths that sparkle. (300–1)

In Israel, then, Jacobson discovers an oriental, Bedouin identity he did not know he had. This "return" to a distant ethnicity appears to make the planned trip to *der heim* redundant, but Jacobson resists the temptation to embrace a fixed identity. The Israel section of his book is characterized by an ambivalence which is never resolved. On the one hand, he is moved by a completely unexpected sense of return. On the other hand, he is dismayed by the Israeli taste for discos, tacky music, self-assurance, and machismo. All these things seem un-Jewish to him, and in Israel, where there is no sense that exile is home, where there is no projection of Jews as an allegorized other, where the diasporic mentality has evaporated in the heat, what need have Jews for those characteristics which, in the diaspora, constitute Jewish identity?

Cheyette notes how "virtually every post-war British-Jewish writer has located a good deal of their fiction or drama either on the Continent of Europe or in Israel or America" ("Ineffable" 308). Both Richmond and Jacobson bring all these locations into one travel narrative, but they also include England as their starting point and, although they view the identities offered elsewhere, each narrative ends with the return to England imminent.

Curiously, neither narrative actually describes the return to England at the end, despite its inevitability (there is nowhere else for them to return *to*). The absence of the final leg of the round-trip indicates a resistance to closure. This is not a touch of postmodernism, but rather an old-fashioned Jewish incapacity to fix identity. These British-Jewish writers have enacted anxieties over their own uncategorizability and have sought to resolve this problem by attempting to "return" elsewhere. The realization that the only home-exile acceptable to them is the one they left at the start of the narrative is a source of anxiety but also relief. Hence, the return home from the "return" to *der heim* is both imminent and nonnarratable.

Richmond accepts, in his closing paragraph, that his journey was in some senses futile ("I knew now that it was not the place that held meaning for me" 466) while *Roots Schmoots* closes with Jacobson watching the modern inhabitants of Serhai coming out of church. They both end, then, with the momentary insight that *der heim* is not home to anyone or anything connected with their Jewish identity.

Both *Roots Schmoots* and *Konin: A Quest* seek a "return" but find they have nowhere to return other than a home which is an exile. This paradox is central to their sense of identity. They both write from and into their Englishness. Having begun by wanting to settle a problem of identity, they end by affirming the problematization of modern identities based on race, religion, and the nation-state—and embrace the protean nature of Jewish identity as its defining characteristic.

Note

1   For example, see the narrated returns of Leopold Infeld, headmaster of the Jewish School, who returned in 1963 (117), Mendel Leben (208), Henry Kawalek (239), Mike Jacobs (299–301), and Rivka Klapstein (378).

Works Cited

Boyarin, Daniel, and Jonathan Boyarin. "Diaspora: Generation and the Ground of Jewish Identity." *Critical Identity* 19 (1993): 693–725.

Cheyette, Bryan. *Constructions of "the Jew" in English Literature and Society: Racial Representations 1875–1945*. Cambridge: Cambridge UP, 1993.

———. "'Ineffable and Usable': Towards a Diasporic British-Jewish Writing." *Textual Practice* 10 (1996): 295–313.

Jacobson, Howard. *Roots Schmoots: Journeys among Jews*. London: Penguin, 1993.

Lyotard, Jean-François. *Heidegger and "The Jews."* Trans. Andreas Michel and Mark Roberts. Minneapolis: U of Minnesota P, 1990.

Richmond, Theo. *Konin: A Quest*. London: Cape, 1995.

✲ Chapter 16

Australian Muslim Experiences of the Meccan Pilgrimage or Hajj

Katy Nebhan

Except on the Hajj itself we do not find together in one place so many Muslims from different parts of the world, all with their little peculiarities. Turkish, Arab, Malay, Bosnian, sub-continent (India, Pakistan, and Bangladesh) and African Muslims predominate but altogether we have Muslims from 68 different ethnic and linguistic groups. That we get along at all, is one of the miracles of Islam.

—Bilal Cleland, *On Becoming a Muslim*

In July 1998, what was believed to be the first Australian Muslim Youth Art Exhibition was held in the hall of the Islamic Council of New South Wales, located within the grounds of the Malek Fahd Islamic School in the western Sydney industrial suburb of Chullora. Sponsored and organized by the Muslim Welfare Association School Scripture Program, this exhibition involved Australian Muslim youths ranging in age from five to seventeen, from both state and private Islamic schools across New South Wales. In asking these youths to articulate visually the role Islam plays in their lives, the organizers sought to provide a public forum in which their understandings could be shared with members of the broader Australian Muslim community.

With varying degrees of sophistication, the majority of the hundreds of images, models, and picture books on display were preoccupied with the standard image of the Great Mosque dominating the Holy City of Mecca. Particularly striking were the few images that took the holy precincts of Mecca and colored them with images of national flags, which, through their imminent association with nationalism, are regarded by many Australian Muslims as non-Islamic. One drawing had an Australian and an Iraqi flag emerging from the *Ka'ba* (the large cube-shaped structure standing in the center of the Great Mosque), and another depicted Lebanese flags encircling the minarets of the Mosque. These images, with their innocent juxtapositions of the ideal sacred space with particular manifestations of the secular present, created a sense of anxiety among organizers. When the time came for the distribution of the prizes, one of the conveners asked parents to discourage their children from engaging in these types of representations in the future. For the organizers and many of the observers, these works were seen as usurpations of an image they thought should remain "unmarked" by any nationalistic impositions. In these works, it was as if the "sacred" had been desecrated, threatened by the complexities of contradictory images, and the layers of identification surrounding it exposed.

An interesting comparison can be seen in a comment made by a critic of the War Memorial in Canberra in 1928, stating that "it requires some alteration in the windows and doors to make a typical eastern Mosque" (qtd. in Kapferer 139). What this critic saw in the architectural elements of the War Memorial were marks of an "external" force which, for him, threatened the carefully constructed sacredness of this national monument, the "temple of the people" (151). That Mecca be shrouded in the costumes of various nationalisms was similarly seen to be entirely inappropriate. Though very different, both the War Memorial and Mecca, the Islamic "center" seen to unite the *ummah* (the Islamic community of faith), are invested with certain meanings that are essential to the ways in which they have been located within a collective consciousness.

Drawing on the problematic socio-religious "visions" of an uncontested Australian Muslim *ummah* emerging from it, this chapter will enter into the broader questions of the relationship between multicultural politics and the structure of the Australian Muslim community, as they have been articulated through the experience of the *hajj,* or pilgrimage to Mecca. Two critical issues permeate the dynamics of the Australian Muslim *hajj* experience: the attempts to understand the many cultures that make up Australia's Muslim population, and the desire to access and articulate the diversity these present into a sense of a unified *ummah*. Both of these issues call upon a recognition of an overriding "Australian" national experience.

Unity in Diversity: The Struggle for "*Ummah* Consciousness"

Making up the one percent of Australians who profess the Islamic faith are sixty-eight distinct ethnic groups including Turkish, Lebanese, Croatians, Egyptians, South Africans, Indians, Bosnians, and Indonesians, speaking over fifty-five different languages. As a multicultural group within a larger multicultural nation, Australian Muslims can see mirrored within their own community the diversity and cultures, meanings, and identifications of the growing population of Australia. They also see and experience the complexities and tensions that exist within.

For its adherents Islam can, and often does, provide a strong sense of belonging to a Muslim *ummah* or community. However, in western nations like Australia, the level and intensity of the immigrant Muslim community's sense of solidarity is often shaped by the ethnic, cultural, and sectarian makeup of its population. As Cleland's introductory statement suggests, these divisions, along with linguistic and generational differences, have made the struggle for a cohesive Australian Muslim communal sense of identification an abstract hope which has yet to be fully realized (43). Up to the 1960s the flow of Muslim immigrants to Australia was sporadic. Following the period of mass migration of Muslims to Australia in the 1970s, an increasing number of associations and mosques were built around Australia, particularly in Sydney and Melbourne, including the Albanian Mosque, and the Lakemba Mosque built by the Lebanese Muslim Association in Sydney, the Bangladesh Islamic Centre, the Croatian Islamic Centre, and the Sydney Turkish Islamic Culture and Mosque Centre.

The designated names of these and many other associations and mosques suggest that religious identification, though important, has not generally acted as the socially or organizationally cohesive agent through which an Australian Muslim *ummah* can be sustained. In offering social services like nursing homes for the elderly, recreational facilities and weekend language schools for young Muslims, and other community services, these institutions set up security and social networks for members of their own ethnic communities. By the very nature of their ethnic, cultural, and linguistic distinctiveness, these networks are largely exclusive, and stand in stark contrast to the idea of a socially and religiously united Australian Muslim *ummah*. In an edition of the Australian Muslim magazine *Insight,* entirely devoted to placing Islam within a contemporary global perspective, Abden referred to the importance of "*Ummah* consciousness" as a "consciousness of community; that Muslims develop a source of belongingness with other believers in the same faith. This mutual belongingness among Muslims, enshrined in the Muslim's mind and experienced by the Muslim's heart is a characteristic feature of the Muslim community world wide..." (9). Similar references to the need to perceive the Muslim *ummah* as being "under one banner—the banner of Islam" (Matthews 4), and the desire to improve the "collective voice and influence of the Muslim community" in Australia, document the persistent struggle Australians Muslims have undergone, and continue to experience, in their search for unity on a national as well as international scale ("Islam" Ahmad 317).

At the center of this struggle are questions relating to the form and agency through which this Australian Muslim *ummah* will take shape. In their attempts to establish a collective intercultural and intercommunal dialogue, Australian Muslims have needed to confront the question of locating their diversity within a form of community that, as Ziaul Ahmad points out, recognizes the existence of "Multiculturalism in Islam" and the Islamic "principles of unity in diversity" (2). For some this has meant removing the marks of ethnicity from those structures, namely mosques [being one of the most critical physical manifestations of the idea of a universal Muslim *ummah* amongst Muslims], and replacing them with a unifying "Australian" one: "A small step towards establishing an Australian

Muslim *Ummah* could be to erase the ethnic graffiti from our mosques and rename them according to the area they are built in. No more Bengali, Turkish, Lebanese etc." (Samnakay 6).

Some of the earliest institutions to promote the centrality of this idea of an Australian Muslim *ummah* include the Federation of Australian Muslim Students and Youth (est. 1967), the Muslim Women's National Network of Australia (est. 1980s), and the Muslim Community Cooperative Australia (est. 1989). In the last decade, there has also been a marked increase in the number of nonethnic-based suburban institutions like the Islamic Cultural and Information Network, the Islamic Welfare Centre, and the Newcastle Muslim Association. In their attempts to place emphasis on the importance of assuming an Islamic identity before any other, the communal structures of these institutions are largely based on an ideological rather than an ethnic foundation.

One of the most influential examples is the Multicultural Eid Festival and Fair (MEFF), established through the Australian MEFF Consortium in 1987, and held annually at the end of the fasting month of Ramadan in Sydney. From 800 participants in 1987 to over 30,000 in 1999, the festival has used lively multicultural dress parades, songs, and cuisine "from different corners of the world" to fuse a harmonious, efficient, and ordered flow of socio-religious activity embracing a "recognition of the fact that there is a lack of tolerance and acceptance among people of different ethnic, cultural and linguistic backgrounds within the Australian Muslim community" ("Mission Statement" 2). The main thrust of the event is geared more toward helping Australian Muslims "adopt and thrive" as a unified Muslim community, but also as an Australian one. The rich blend of religion and culture the festival has inspired led the president of the Islamic Circle of North America to state on his visit to Australia in 1997 that he would recommend that all American Muslims visit Australia to attend the festival.

Although these institutions have been able to provide a sense of unity among many Australian Muslims, the sphere of their influence and participation remains governed by the physical barriers of geographic location. The Multicultural Eid Festival and Fair is not accessible to those who live outside of the suburbs of Sydney unless they are willing to travel some distance for a one-day event. Further, the viability of large institutions like the MEFF Consortium and the Australian Federation of Islamic Councils (AFIC) is also bound by cultural politics founded upon exclusions. Though consisting of office bearers from various ethnic backgrounds, the inevitable use of English as the universal language of communication means that a significant proportion of non-English speaking migrants cannot actively participate in many of the events they organize. Other exclusions may be seen in the absence of women holding office in many institutions as well as the tendency to select educated middle-class office bearers. In the process of drawing on a unifying Australianism in order to eliminate ethnic differences, many of these Australian Muslim institutions have tended to overlook regional, educational, class, and gender differences.

The *Hajj* and the Mapping of Meaning

It was in 1986 when Imam Al-Hilaly made a request to the Minister of *Hajj* asking that Australian Muslim pilgrims be recognized as independent of those from Europe and America, that the *hajj* was officially born as the temporal and multi-dimensional space through which this dialogue and an Australian Muslim *ummah* could be actively experienced:

> I said we from the Australian continent and an independent nation and we should not be aligned with the other countries. Australian pilgrims now have their own name [Australians] placed on their cards and identification, we have our own *mutawif* [pilgrimage guide] and offices where we are officially welcomed. We go there as Muslims, however we go with an Australian identity…each Muslim is proud to say that I am from Australia. I am an Australian Muslim. (Al-Hilaly)

In identifying the pilgrimage to Mecca as an agent capable of maintaining a potent sense of a distinctly Australian Muslim *ummah,* a number of questions need to be considered. How has the *hajj* been organized, involving as it does socio-religious and potentially sensitive ways of transcending cultural and class divisions? How have Australian Muslims used this journey to reconcile their multi-cultural, and thus intrinsically diverse community, with the unity they seek through the experience of the *hajj*? What makes Mecca a privileged site for the appropriation of the "'soft' borders" (Johnson and Michaelsen 1) of benevolent nationalisms, cultural essentialisms, and the multicultural character of the Australian Muslim population?

In the January 1999 edition of the *Australian Muslim News,* the Australian Federation of Islamic Councils (AFIC), the peak Islamic organizational body in Australia and the Pacific, declared that after sixteen years it would no longer be making *hajj,* or pilgrimage, arrangements for Australian Muslims. The reason given was the "growing number and variety of packages that are available nowadays" (3). The newspaper exulted in the growing network of Muslim communities who now offer "numerous packages" to those members who wished to perform the *hajj,* and followed this news with other pieces of "AFIC News" that spoke of its successes and growing public profile and activism (AFIC 3).

It serves to remind the reader of the commitment which AFIC has made in providing the Muslims of Australia, Fiji, and New Zealand with *hajj* packages for so many years. By officially acknowledging the growing role of its member organizations in assisting Australian Muslim pilgrims, AFIC attempts to position itself as the vantage point from which everything coheres; from the lowest levels of organizational imitation, to the norms and patterns of Islamic life in Australia where the *hajj* plays a vital part, and from where all elements of socio-religious unity emanate.

Underlying AFIC's claim to establishing communal unity on a structural level is an appeal to the ideological stream of consciousness surrounding the *hajj* with which readers are familiar. The last few decades have seen an increase in the numbers of Australian Muslim pilgrims from one in 1975 to over three thousand in 1999. In *Consuming Places* John Urry refers to the relationship between consumption and the environmental, visual, and literal significance of place (1–2). With the increase in the number of Australian pilgrims, Mecca has come to stand as a site of socio-religious "consumption" born from both the experience of the pilgrimage to Mecca and the universal Muslim perceptions of its significance, but more critically and as Campo suggests, from the understandings of the *hajj* as constructed away from Mecca, in the milieu of the pilgrim's homeland (147).

As the fifth and final pillar of the Islamic faith, the *hajj* is obligatory for every Muslim physically and financially able to make the journey to Mecca. As a single event, the *hajj* brings together over three million pilgrims from one hundred fifty nations across the globe to one place, the city of Mecca, and at one point in time between the eighth and the thirteenth day of the twelfth month of the Muslim lunar year. The complexities arising from the dynamic interaction between Australian pilgrims and their fellow Australian Muslims on the one hand, and the pilgrims's experience of being part of a wider Muslim *ummah* on the other, are forged in the juxtapositions between the universal perceptions of Mecca, and the mosaic of associations that translate the needs and desires of their local context.

The strength of the conceptions of history and time, of the social and the spiritual, embedded in the rites and the roles surrounding the experience of the *hajj*, rests on the universal perceptions that Muslims worldwide have of the *hajj* and the city of Mecca. For Muslims today, as in the past, the very essence of the *hajj* pertains to an experience that is largely social. This reality is reflected in the rites of the *hajj* that are essentially a demonstration and practical application of all the pillars of Islam. As the pilgrims pray together, the complete awareness of themselves in the presence of God is a continuation of the spiritual state manifested in the obligatory daily prayers. The act of sacrificing a sheep at Mina embodies certain characteristics of alms-tax, part of which must be given to the poor and needy, and is the third pillar of Islam. In restraining from sexual activities and avoiding every degrading act, the *hajj* also contains some aspects of the fourth pillar of Islam, fasting. Further, the *hajj* demonstrates a profound visual and practical attestation of Islam's abhorrence of all forms of social distinctions. All the male pilgrims wear the seamless white garb (the *ihram*), demonstrating the equality of all humankind before God and to each other with no regard to position, race, wealth, or power. Only the women may wear ordinary clothing provided that all is covered except the face and hands. Finally, the *hajj* is a manifestation of the belief in the unity of God—all the pilgrims worship and obey the commands of the One God.

Although many of these personal acts of worship may be seen in the pilgrims's homelands, the *hajj* reinforces the significant collective aspects of these pillars more dramatically by placing them within a universal framework and an articulated socio-religious context. The strong emphasis on universality throughout the *hajj* and the great respect throughout the Muslim world for its religious significance has both made preserving the religious atmosphere of the event easier, and the pilgrims more receptive to other ideas despite existing global and local tensions and divisions (Long 106). The defining lines of this universality are drawn through the reconstructed geographic presence the pilgrims impose on the city of Mecca on their arrival. Unlike the Australian Muslim pilgrims, the vast majority of pilgrims to Mecca come from regions made up of a dominant ethnic group, language, and culture, and where Islam is the predominant faith. For many of these pilgrims, the *hajj* is performed against a background defined by long established and shared religious traditions and social expectations. Whereas in Australia the presence of Islamic institutions and networks has been based upon various ethnic, regional, and cultural differences, those found throughout the Middle East, Southeast Asia, and Africa have tended to have a more solidifying effect on their Muslim populations. As such, the pilgrims in the majority of these societies are generally not relied upon to inspire the sense of "communitas" so critical to Victor Turner's pilgrimage model (*Image* 250–51).

While the social and physical landscapes of Mecca do not erase the differences in culture, language, and ethnicity each of these pilgrims bring, the ideals with which they are associated translate their differing viewpoints into a discourse understood by all. Performed as an annual Islamic "congregation" bound together in a "visual sacrament of unity, geographically realized from the ends of the earth," the idea of "communitas" is not spontaneous, but rather expected during pilgrimage experience (Pearson, *Pious Passengers* 67). As Pearson states in his "Travellers, Journeys, Tourists: The Meaning of Journeys":

> The *hajj* is central and orthodox; indeed, it exemplifies orthodoxy and what is done is dictated by orthodox texts and guides. Certainly there is *communitas*, but all constraint and control is not lost. Certainly, it is an overwhelming experience, but within tightly circumscribed bounds. Those on the *hajj* were not free-floating, unbounded by any social norms; quite the reverse, for usual social structures were replaced by others which often were stricter than those of everyday life....(130)

Although the pilgrims's search for unity is realized through tight socio-religious structures, they are not necessarily those of *ihram* as Pearson suggests. It may be argued that it is the pilgrims who (though performing full the rites of the *hajj*), in response to the expectations of their fellow Australian Muslims back home and their own role as representatives who seek to fulfill these expectations, impose rigid structures of their own.

For the Australian Muslim population whose institutions represent the "full gamut of cultural, traditional and individual expressions of Islam," (Mustapha 18) the expectations they weave around the *hajj* are inspired by the richly cosmopolitan city that Mecca becomes during the pilgrimage season, as it is one within which their own multicultural makeup can be contexualized and explored. The ideological structures the pilgrims carry with them to Mecca are those that mirror the ideals that help set up the frameworks of their own experiences of the *hajj,* and the accounts with which they return to their communities in Australia. They recognize the importance of spiritual enlightenment despite physical hardship, greater religious self-understanding, and the effort to assimilate the self with the will of God. However, the Australian Muslim experience of the *hajj* centers on the importance of Islamic unity on a universal scale as well as a local one, and the ideals of equality and the sense of belonging associated with them.

Within this context, Australian Muslims have used the *hajj* as a dynamic agent for articulating a sense of communal unity and a distinct Australian Muslim identity. Drawing on primary material and a series of interviews conducted with Australian pilgrims representing both genders, as well as various ethnic and age groups between January and July 1997 (Nebhan 1997), the next section will examine this use through local verbal and visual discourses.

Mecca: Experiences of the Multicultural and the Religious

When Malcolm X made his journey to Mecca in 1964, he stated that in his "thirty-nine years on this earth, the Holy City of Mecca had been the first time I had ever stood before the Creator of All and felt like a complete human being" (Haley 482). The echoes of his moving comment on the "overwhelming spirit of true brotherhood as is practiced by people of all colors and races in this ancient Holy Land" (454) continue to mark the pages of the numerous accounts of the *hajj* experience since. His words have left not only a powerful exposition of the transformative influence of the *hajj*—the influential black activist adjusted his thinking to the point where he believed that whites were human beings—but also an account of an experience which has been actively consumed by those Muslims who are "seekers for the truth" (Cleland, "The Great" 3).

In his discussion of the levels of entry experienced through travel, Eric Leed refers to the importance of the "process of 'identification'" (85). The sentiment of coherence this process develops between person and place is reflected in the use of Mecca and the *hajj* experience as sites of consumption by Australian Muslims. The idea of "Mecca," even in the secular West, provides a metaphor for the fulfillment of personal and communal aspirations. For Australian Muslims who are particularly aware of the fact that this sacred space is reserved purely for members of the Muslim *ummah,* the geography of this metaphor is carefully mapped out before the pilgrims's arrival in the Holy City. All members of the Australian Muslim population, on differing levels, use verbal and visual discourses to represent a dynamic interdependence between the participant, their community, and the spatial aspects of their liminality.

First, these complex relationships have been translated into a local pilgrimage culture that adapts and changes according to personal and communal needs.

In the verbal articulations of this pilgrimage culture, history and memory are turned into icons ready for local consumption. Most Australian Muslims are familiar with the texts put together by popular orthodox scholars including Al-Bukhari (A.D. 810–70) and Al-Ghazali (A.D. 1058–1111) because they "spiritually prepare you how to make the *hajj* and how to do it in the proper way" as one pilgrim put it (Yucel). Australian Muslim literature, including the *Australian Muslim News, Insight,* the *Australian Minaret,* and the *Australian Islamic Review* has proved to be more influential in its use of the underlying messages of these religious narratives to suit the local context.

The most popular style of documentation used in this literature is exhibitive. Drawing on the spirituality of the event, it reveals those characteristics that render the experience of the *hajj* suitable for the reader and their expectations: "*Hajj* is neither ritual nor rite nor prayer. *Hajj* is a vivid, living pulsating lesson....A lesson of Signs and Symbols, painted in colours of a universal clarity so that all who behold may understand...Sacrifice, sacrifice of oneself; Gratitude; Fear of Allah; Struggle; Preparedness; *Jihad* against Evil; Unity and Discipline...This is the lesson of Hajj" (Sunback 24). It is a style that reveals little of the way the *hajj* is experienced by its participants, concentrating instead on the "mental preparation" for the event which should not be limited to the individual, but "encompass how that individual, as a returnee, can benefit the community" ("The *Hajj*"). The Quranic lines speaking of the religious "unity that has taken away the differences" (49:10) and the establishment of Mecca as the center "Full of blessing / And of Guidance / For all kinds of beings" (3:96), are worked into the front-page reports of the *hajj* in the various Australian Muslim newspapers and magazines each year. In almost all cases, these reports are accompanied by a standard image of the Holy Center where the prominent Great Mosque is surrounded by a few modest buildings, and where imageless "dots" representing the pilgrims stand in concentric circles around the *Ka'ba.*

It comes as no surprise that this exhibitive use of the spiritual and the unifying is transplanted with faithful zeal into the literature covering the personal experiences of Australian Muslim pilgrims. As well as providing them with guidance, references to the theological significance of the *hajj* are perceived as active metaphors that seek to contextualize the relationship between the pilgrims themselves and Mecca. As such, they leave no room for what Michel de Certeau would refer to as the "legendary or ritual space that would be merely ritual" (24). A close look at the personal accounts of Australian pilgrims reveals the ways in which these metaphors are encoded in the *habitus* of the Australian Muslim community, through their presence in social expectations and socio-religious obligations. The earlier reference to the expectation that pilgrims will return with something to offer the community is clearly drawn in the numerous references to the significance of *hijrah* (leaving one's homeland for the sake of Islam) for the Australian Muslim population. In an edition of *Insight* devoted entirely to exploring issues surrounding Muslim migrants to Australia, references to *hijrah* sought to inculcate its spirit within the community, and awaken in Muslims their responsibility to its social and moral growth as well as that of the broader Australian one: "We as Muslims in Australia have a novel experience of Muslim multicul-turalism and *Shari'ah* differences which provides us with the major motivating factor in compelling us to think more deeply and behave more cautiously within the Muslim community. It will be traumatic if Muslims cannot utilize the same sense of diplomacy in their dealings with non-Muslims" (Editorial 3). Although the journey to Mecca is not by definition a *hijrah* as the pilgrims return to their homeland after completing the *hajj*, the opportunity it provides Muslims from different regions and with different political and socio-religious ideas to both spread and absorb these ideas and transmit them to various areas around the world has been particularly significant for Australian Muslims (Netton 31–32).

Coming from a nation where the viability of multiculturalism remains a con-tentious issue (Jupp 176–87), Australian Muslim pilgrims have, as both partici-pants and observers, sought actively to consume the sense of equality, toleration, and unity inspired by the religious obligations set throughout the *hajj*, and through them, explore the complexity of their own multicultural community. Pilgrims refer to "that brotherhood, that sisterhood" existing in the "one huge community" which the *hajj* creates. Subtle reminders of the nature of "true mul-ticulturalism" are also offered: "You meet people from Canada, from America, from Finland, from South Africa, from all over the world....Over there multicul-turalism is practiced in the fullest sense, not as political correctness. Multicultur-alism is practiced within Islam. Status does not matter, national identity has no significance whatsoever because when you meet someone you say 'peace be upon you.' We are all Muslim. That is all" (Abdo). Identifying bonds that rise above controversial differences like sect, class, and more common ones including ethnicity and culture, Australian pilgrims have been able to use the multidimen-sional space of Mecca to "communicate and find out what is happening to Mus-lims in all the countries" (Chami), and to explore the workings of multiculturalism in a securely "educational" and "tolerant" environment: "You meet people from all over the world, from countries that you have never heard about. It [*hajj*] really broadens your thoughts and experiences, your opinions, everything. You see different people, different cultures and dress...it is like you have traveled the world in a couple of days" (Abdullah). These pilgrims's ac-counts present a unity of expression in the "difference" they celebrate and ab-sorb into their memories of the *hajj*. These memories are critical to the role Australian pilgrims perform as mediators between the ideals the *hajj* represents, and the aspirations of the local Australian Muslim population.

Like all modern travelers, pilgrims also articulate their experiences of place through images and photography. The visual version of *communitas* Australian Muslim pilgrims present has also been critical in perpetuating their role as wor-thy negotiators between the religious epicenter, Mecca, and the local Australian Muslim *habitus* where the pilgrimage culture is constructed. These visual expressions of the *hajj* also reflect more powerfully the tenuous negotiations between an appreciation of diversity and the struggle to uphold a cohesive model through which a sense of unity can be created and experienced. In his comment on the idea of "visual editing," John Szarkowski defined one's selection of an image as a "matter of surrounding with a frame the portion of one's cone of vision" (qtd. in Sontag 192). In their efforts to strike a balance between their vision of an all-embracing "Australian" Muslim multiculturalism and an *ummah* consciousness, Australian pilgrims have been selective in their visual representations.

The vision these pilgrims have come to create is meticulously structured around the rich mixture of "material residue" from the *hajj* experience, and personal photography. Mass production and technological innovations have allowed widespread circulation of the images of Mecca and its Great Mosque. These images are a feature of many Muslim homes and institutions in Australia. Wall and prayer rugs, key rings and greeting cards, models and jewelry depicting Mecca and the surrounding area are all brought back by pilgrims as souvenirs. What stands out in all these is the standard image of the Holy City referred to earlier. The modern city Mecca is today is eclipsed by the emphasis on the Great Mosque and the figures of pilgrims who are represented as an endless group of worshippers with no apparent cultural, ethnic, or linguistic "face." There are no competing images, nor any trace of the diversity celebrated in the verbal accounts. Rather, the image presented is almost clinical in the ways any signs, no matter how slight, of the racial distinctions and "national ethnocentralism" which are regarded as a "threat to the unity of our Muslim *Ummah*," are "edited" out (Hasan 12).

On an ideological level, this editing of what is celebrated in the verbal expressions of the *hajj* experience may be attributed to the fact that the pilgrims, the recipients of their gifts, and the Australian Muslim population at large are only willing to acknowledge and explore the active consumption of the diversity in Mecca within certain limits. Understanding the multicultural nature and complexities of their community operates alongside the desire for a unity that can override them. They may practice and experience the joys of multiculturalism in an environment free from the structured institutions and cultures from which they came, but at the end of the day, the images they want to hang on their walls are those depicting their journey for equality, sincerity, and unity. Unlike the literature and the oral accounts, this image is not exclusive. Any Australian Muslim can look and imagine himself or herself as one of the figures standing before Mecca, and through this process visually consume an element of the *hajj* experience and the *communitas* it inspires.

In the standard images of Mecca the surrounding "modern reality" is not so much denied as it is put aside. The pilgrimage narratives reflect on the contradictions between these images and the scene the pilgrims encounter: "we thought when we get to Mecca that we will see this big towering Ka'ba, but it's not like that. We thought it would be bigger" (Issa). However, these contradictions are dismissed as irrelevant. In accordance with religious teaching and the pilgrimage culture in the case of Australian pilgrims, it is the fulfilling of this religious obligation, and taking heed of the ideals they have constructed around the *hajj* experience which is significant. The core of their experience focuses on the image of their dream—a dream that is "timeless." One may see in this image the concentric circle of millions which the pilgrims form as they surround the *Ka'ba,* thus placing emphasis on the unity it inspires. However, it also points to what remains the most visible display of Muslim unity—what Schimmel has described as the "spacialization of their belief in one, and only one God" (164). It is this unity the pilgrims seek to bring with them through their gifts, forming a bond or a shared experience between the pilgrims and their community, a reminder of the ideals this experience seeks to create.

One can argue that Australian Muslim pilgrims conform to this representation of Mecca as a result of the ways in which it has been marketed through the various forms of mass-produced images and objects. I would suggest, however, that the pilgrims's interpretation and reworking of this image reveals a more complex situation. Although personal photography has been limited by the Saudi ban on cameras in the Holy Land, those photographs that have been taken by Australian pilgrims reflect on two critical uses of visual politics. Whereas the standard image is reproduced in things like local calendars and greeting cards, a number of personal photographs point to a confident move away from the standard depiction of the Meccan space. Unlike the imageless dots symbolizing the pilgrims in the popular representations of Mecca, a number of these photographs focus on the pilgrims who have a face, an identity, rather than places. A photograph published in the *Australian Muslim Times* in 1991, for instance, depicts three "Australian converts departing for the *hajj*....Prominent Aboriginal leader, Mohommed Ishaq (formerly, Clarrie Isaacs), President of Islamic Council of WA, Ibrahim Abdullah and Imam of Alice Springs Mosque, Iman Adams" (Young). The image of these converts reflects on the regional unity the *hajj* inspires as each of the figures is representative of a different Australian state. This photograph also provides an unmistakable Australian flavor by making a connection to a distinctly nationalistic appropriation of Aborigines by Australian Muslims.

It is possible to view this image as an extension of the popular and more universally focused image of Mecca's pilgrims; a powerful display of unity before the experience of the *hajj.* Here it is the body that seeks to initiate the viewer into the ideals the *hajj* represents and which the pilgrimage culture seeks to uphold and promote. However, the body in these personal photographs is almost never singularly defined, but cast against "other" bodies that share a common faith. In a personal photograph taken by a pilgrim in 1986, Australian pilgrims stand on Mount Arafat, where some three million pilgrims pray on one designated day (Nebhan 86). Here the gaze is drawn to the pilgrims, not the mountain, and the fact that the Australian pilgrims, unless one knew them personally, cannot be distinguished from those others around them. The strength of such photographs lies in their ability to transmute the ideals and the literary and visual aspects of the pilgrimage culture into a visual journey. They give Australian Muslims a visual narrative with which they can identify, by endowing Australian pilgrims with the symbols of their own local and personal quests. This is a role that the standard images of Mecca can only partially fulfill. Whereas Mecca provides the universal fabric for the pilgrims, it is these pilgrims who project their own local "centers" onto the ancient rites, history, and stones that make it.

Mecca stands as a center to which a journey is seen by many as the fulfillment of a dream. Those who seek it come from societies that are "worlds apart in perception and motivation" (Coleman and Elsner 64). The form of the *hajj* is one they all share. The thoughts and aspirations they carry with them are those formed in their homelands. In many ways, Mecca is a name with many meanings, and the *hajj,* an agent through which they may be explored and perhaps even realized.

For Australian Muslims, the *hajj* involves the struggle for a sense of unity within the multicultural, in relationship to the changing socio-religious space of the local. The verbal and visual representations they employ suggest the possibility of multiple understandings of this struggle within different temporal and power relations. As the distinctions between the secular and the sacred are not separate entities in Islam but have, as Carol Delaney argues, more to do with western categories than Muslim ones, the ideals surrounding the *hajj* provide a stable reference point and neutral channel through which pilgrims (within the limits of the *hajj* ideals they impose) can articulate and critique local issues (513–30).

In their role as active negotiators between an ideal religious and enlightened experience, and a set of local expectations, these pilgrims stand, in the metaphoric sense, on what Victor Turner refers to as the "threshold," a place and moment "in and out of time" (*Drama* 197). In providing a detached meeting point between their local context and the stimulating space of Mecca, these pilgrims disseminate a specific type of knowledge relating to the workings of multiculturalism, one sustained and determined by the role of the pilgrimage culture which increasing numbers of Australian pilgrims regenerate annually. It is through this process that what are, at the local level, often seen as divisive cultural and ethnic tensions, come to be celebrated as the diversity of an international Islamic community. However, as the many national identifications which make up the Australian Muslim population get absorbed into the pilgrims's experiences of unity through the *hajj,* they remain distinct in their use of an "Australian" Muslim identity. These multiple nationalities are embraced by the international character of Mecca during *hajj* season, only to reappear as a new and distinct form of Australian nationalism.

Note

I would like to thank Richard White from the Department of History at the University of Sydney for his reading this chapter and for his helpful suggestions.

Works Cited

Abden, Syed Zainul. "Ummah Consciousness and its Global Obligations." *Insight* 5 (1990): 9–10.

Abdo, Maha. Personal interview. 1 March 1997.

Abdullah, Amatullah. Personal interview. 12 March and 18 June 1997.

"AFIC News." *Australian Muslim News.* Jan. 1999: 3.

Ahmad, Qazi Ashfaq. "Islam and Muslims in Australia." *Islam, Muslims and the Modern State: Case Studies of Muslims in Thirteen Countries.* Ed. Hussin Mutalib and Taj ul-Islam Hashmi. New York: St. Martin's, 1994. 317–38.

Ahmad, Ziaul Islam. "Sydney Eid Festival Attracts Tens of Thousands." *Australian Muslim News* Feb. 1999: 1–2.

Al-Hilaly, T. Personal interview. 27 February 1997.

Campo, Juan Eduardo. "The Mecca Pilgrimage in the Formation of Islam in Modern Egypt." *Sacred Places and Profane Spaces: Essays in the Geographics of Judaism, Christianity, and Islam.* Eds. Jamie Scott and Paul Simpson-Housley. New York: Greenwood, 1991. 145–61.

Certeau, Michel de. *The Practice of Everyday Life.* Trans. Steven Rendall. Berkeley: U of California P, 1984.

Chami, Khalil. Personal interview. 26 February 1997.

Cleland, Bilal. "The Great Gathering." Editorial. *Australian Muslim News* Apr. 1998: 3.

———. "On Becoming a Muslim." *Al-Nahda* Jan.–Jun. 1997: 41–46.

Delaney, Carol. "The Hajj: Sacred and Secular." *American Ethnologist* 17 (1990): 513–30.

Editorial. *Insight* 2 (1987): 3.

Elser, John and Simon Coleman. *Pilgrimage: Past and Present.* London: British Museum Press, 1995.

Haley, Alex. *The Autobiography of Malcolm X.* London: Penguin Books, 1965.

Hasan Ibn. "Facing the Challenge." *Insight* 2 (1987): 11–12.

Issa, Sarah. Personal interview. 1 February 1997.

Johnson, David, and Scott Michaelsen. Introduction. *Border Theory: The Limits of Cultural Politics.* Ed. David Johnson and Scott Michaelsen. Minneapolis: Minnesota UP, 1997. 1–39.

Jupp, James. *Immigration.* 2nd ed. Melbourne: Oxford UP, 1998.

Kapferer, Bruce. *Legends of People–Myth of State: Violence, Intolerance and Political Culture in Sri Lanka and Australia.* Washington: Smithsonian Institution Press, 1988.

Leed, Eric. *The Mind of the Traveler: From Gilgamesh to Global Tourism.* New York: Basic Books, 1991.

Long, David. *The Hajj Today: A Survey of the Contemporary Makkah Pilgrimage.* Albany: State U of New York P, 1979.

Matthews, Zachariah. "United We Stand, Divided We Fall." Editorial. *Salam* Jan.–Feb. 1998: 4.

"Mission Statement." *Multicultural Eid Festival and Fair 1997 Annual Report.* Sydney: Australian MEFF Consortium, 1997. 2.

Mustapha, S. "Visit to the Eid Festival." *Insight* May 1993:18.

Nebhan, Katy. "The Meccan Pilgrimage: An Australian Experience." Diss. The University of Sydney, 1997.

Netton, Ian. *Seek Knowledge: Thought and Travel in the House of Islam.* Surrey: Curzon Press, 1996.

Pearson, Michael. *Pious Passengers.* London: Hurst, 1994.

———. "Travellers, Journeys, Tourists: The Meanings of Journeys." *Australian Cultural History.* 10 (1991): 125–34.

Samnakay, Rashid A. "Australian Muslim Identity." *Australian Muslim News.* Apr. 1999: 6.

Schimmel, Annemarie. "Sacred Geography in Islam." *Sacred Places and Profane Spaces: Essays in the Geographics of Judaism, Christianity, and Islam.* Eds. Jamie Scott and Paul Simpson-Housley. New York: Greenwood, 1991. 163–75.

Sontag, Susan. *On Photography.* London: Allen Lane, 1978.

Sunback, Sadiiq. "Hajj: The Pilgrimage to Makkah." *Insight* 9 (1994): 21–24.

"The *Hajj* and the Individual." *Australian Muslim Times* Jun. 1992: 1.

The Holy Quran. Trans. A. Yusuf Ali. Beirut: Dar Al-Arabia, 1934.

Turner, Victor. *Dramas, Fields and Metaphors.* London: Cornell UP, 1974.

———. *Image and Pilgrimage in Christian Culture Anthropological Perspectives.* New York: Columbia UP, 1978.

Urry, John. *Consuming Places.* London: Routledge, 1995.

"Young and Old Depart for Hajj." *Australian Muslim Times.* Jun. 1991: 1.

Yucel, Salih. Personal interview. 6 March 1997.

Chapter 17

A Million Enigmas Now: V. S. Naipaul's Use of Landscape in the Construction of the "English" Self

Pallavi Rastogi

Vidiadhar Surajprasad Naipaul's carefully constructed narrative identity marks a constant tension in his relationship with both East and West. This is manifested in his deliberate crafting of landscape[1] and locale through which the narrating self is repeatedly built and rebuilt. Written between 1984 and 1986, his autobiographical "novelogue," *The Enigma of Arrival,* creates a world in which the weary itinerant (Naipaul himself) is brought back to intellectual life by the regenerative powers of the quintessentially English landscape. That such a landscape is a fictional creation is important in understanding this memoir as a meditation on a journey of flight. Because Naipaul "escapes" from the stifling confines of his Asiatic Caribbean community, England becomes a sustaining space that needs to be created as absolutely antithetical to his homeland. Given that the England in which Naipaul arrives is awash with corruption and decay, the England that Naipaul recreates is instantly idealized, especially in terms of its physical landscape, which is frequently contrasted with the stench and squalor of his own country. However, the narrator is well aware that this is a willed creation of a romanticized landscape and mourns for the passing of a certain way of life. The sustaining fantasy is enacted during the course of the novel primarily to insert Naipaul (or the narrator) within the dominant mode of traditional English narrative discourse, namely the high romantic manner of Wordsworth. Naipaul then establishes himself, the alien, as a firm part of the canonical English literary tradition rendering his migration not so much multicultural as much as monocultural. Paradoxically, Naipaul never abandons his "Third World" identity, because it becomes a convenient garb to don, well in accordance with the fashioning of the narrating self as the eternal voyager.

India: A Million Mutinies Now was begun almost a year after the completion of *The Enigma of Arrival.* Critics have seen this as the emerging of a "kinder" and "gentler" travelogue, lacking the vituperative bite of *An Area of Darkness* (1962). However, even here, landscape and locale are tied into the construction of a particular sort of narrating self. India is still all "heat, fumes and din," a description that jars on the exquisite sensibilities of Naipaul, coming as he is from the idealized England of *The Enigma of Arrival.* The many realities of India cannot sustain the fantasies. England is significant as it allows Naipaul to project India as the stranglehold of creative prowess, similar perhaps to representations of the Caribbean in the earlier memoir. Using the discursive paradigms of the West/First World, Naipaul also simultaneously fashions himself as the authentic voice of the Third World. This position is connected to the constructions of the narrating self in the earlier book for it is this more-British-than-thou Naipaul/narrator seen in *The Enigma of Arrival* who can project himself as the native informant precisely because of his literary canonization by British society.

This essay will engage in a critical analysis of these works, keeping in mind Naipaul's deliberate creation of a fictional (English) self in two texts proclaiming themselves to be either semi-fiction or nonfiction. It will emphasize that in both texts, Naipaul's creation of an English self is strongly tied into his construction of and reaction to landscape, where in one work, landscape is idealized and in the other, orientalized. It will develop the many complicated links between the narrating selves in the two works and will finally make the claim that even though the structure of the two texts lends themselves to multicultural migrations and the democratization of travel writing, such a moment is endlessly deferred. This is primarily because Naipaul is writing in the discursive paradigms of the Imperial West in both novels and thus nullifying any subversive potential inherent in such writings, narrated as they are by a persona who sees himself as more British than the stiff upper lip.

***

The Enigma of Arrival is Naipaul's first work devoted (pun intended) to England. Set in a little cottage in Wiltshire, where Naipaul/the narrator[2] has located himself to recuperate from mental fatigue coupled with some mysterious illness, much of the novel is preoccupied with lingering descriptions of the narrator's surroundings. Indeed, the novel opens with an oh-so-ever British description of the weather: "For the first four days it rained. I could hardly see where I was" (5). The novel's opening lines establish the central structuring thematics of this tale: the landscape, the I, and the overwhelming link between the two. This becomes more clearly defined as the novel progresses, reflecting all the while Naipaul's particular and peculiar postcolonial tension with England and Englishness.[3] Since landscape is firmly anchored to identity construction, the people in this novel are assimilated within and into the broader confines of landscape.

Here is Naipaul on Jack, one of the inhabitants of the many derelict cottages dotting the Wiltshire countryside: "Jack himself, however, I considered to be part of the view. I saw his life as genuine, rotted, fitting: man fitting the landscape" (15). Since Jack belongs, simply by virtue of his Englishness, the narrator is all too acutely aware that his presence is intrusive in this close, cloistered community: "a change in the course of the history of the country" (15). This is a potentially subversive moment in the novel. However, as I shall demonstrate later, it is a subversion that is never brought to life. Even though the narrator's racial presence is an infringement on the whiteness of the landscape, he will, through the course of the novel, model himself into precisely that pristine paradigm of validated antiquity that his presence seems to disrupt.

This un/belonging is anchored to an almost paradoxically proprietorial sense of ownership of language and literature. While Naipaul makes "the canon of Western literature an implicated witness to his mapping of the moment of postcolonial arrival" (Suleri 155), the English language and its literature also gives him the power to admit fantasy into the creative regions of his mind. Naipaul acknowledges his debt to the English language by using it to create an England imagined through the fantastical prism of English literature. Jack's father-in-law is a markedly Romantic creation: "He seemed a Wordsworthian figure: bent, exaggeratedly bent, going gravely about his peasant tasks, as if in an immense Lake District solitude" (*Enigma* 16). While the narrator is eager to impose notions of authenticity and belonging onto Jack and Jack's father-in-law, that he chooses English literature to do so leads to the construction of a self whose understanding and appropriation of English literature makes him supremely English. Judith Levy makes the case for Naipaul as a postcolonial and emphasizes, "his rejection of the given tradition of English literature in the process of finding the appropriate expression for his particular brand of self-hood. *The Enigma of Arrival* also demonstrates how much Naipaul owes to the intellectual climate in which he has spent the past thirty years or more" (119). While it is difficult to see this novel as rejecting the great tradition of English literature, it can be conceded that Naipaul is using English literary traditions to determine his particular brand of self-hood. However, it is ironic that his self-hood, as particular as it may be, is also so quintessentially English. Ambalavaner Sivanandan asserts that Naipaul's sensibilities are uniquely English, a statement which is repeatedly corroborated in this memoir. Naipaul is "an Englishman from the beginning—not British, English—wholly, uniquely English because his imagination is English, of England—of its woods, trees, birds, seas, seasons, stories, live, loves, poets, kings...and his reality is an imagined reality" (34). Naipaul's narrative self is thus strongly fixed/fixated in the English imagination, which is itself, following Wordsworth, strongly moored to the landscape of England.

As the novel progresses, the narrator's frayed nerves are miraculously soothed by the regenerative powers of the landscape: "Living in the grounds of this shrunken estate, going out for my walks, those nerves were soothed, and in the wild garden and orchard besides the water meadows, I found a physical beauty perfectly suited to my temperament...." (*Enigma* 53). For Naipaul, England becomes a site which both generates and alleviates anxiety. This paradox is sustained through the production of a binary between town and city, in itself an ancient literary device, harking back to the grand pastoral tradition of Milton and Wordsworth. It is the quintessentially English countryside that restores the narrator back to literary vigor while the city, with all its teeming immigrants, only serves to enhance the narrator's sense of fatigue and claustrophobia. Ultimately, it is the countryside that fulfills the narrator's childhood fantasies of England. Even so, it is significant that such wish-fulfillment is not steeped in actuality but rather comes about only through the vitality of the narrator's imaginative powers which have been restored to him by the English countryside [in] "a place where I was truly an alien, I found I was given a second chance, a new life, richer and fuller than I had had anywhere else. And in that place...I did some of my best work" (103). Here, the narrator constructs himself as a poet steeped in the high Romantic tradition. The mind of the genius requires solitary confinement to be able to create and only the English countryside, albeit in decay, can produce this state of mind. While Naipaul recognizes that the country is in a state of collapse, this sense of ruin further intensifies his construction of English glory—"decay implied an ideal, a perfection in the past" (210)—and deeply regrets that he came in too late to fully participate in the splendor of the British Empire: "...I had come too late to find England, the heart of Empire" (130). As Sara Suleri says: "Naipaul records a perspective that knows its time is done even before it has had the chance to be fully articulated" (150). Rob Nixon agrees but places Naipaul in the context of his colonial upbringing: "[E]motionally and culturally, Naipaul's childhood had prepared him for a Victorian Britain that had long since passed. He never fully recovered from that chimera" (46). The narrator tries to plug this lacuna between sense and reality by keeping England's hierarchy intact in the grand Naipaulian scheme of things.

It is interesting that Naipaul's sense of fragmentation in both Trinidad and England is largely due to his position as a colonial subject because of which ideas, such as the innate supremacy of English literature, have filtered to the very center of his consciousness. It is then only apposite that he finds fulfillment only in and through England. Sivanandan's comments, although acid, are appropriate: "That which makes the colonial unmakes him, and he remakes himself in the image of that which has unmade him" (38). To make himself in the image of his "deracinator," he also needs to unmake his past. Trinidad with its stench and squalor and "colonial smallness" cannot consort with "the grandeur of his ambition" (*Enigma* 92). With the death of Jack, Naipaul comes to terms with the fragility of the local's hold over his land and realizes that the land (and by extension, Englishness) itself is also up for grabs. To seize the English land and Englishness, Naipaul needs to negate his colonial background selectively. In *The Enigma of Arrival* there is a careful surfacing/concealing of the Colonial/Hindu self, which appears/disappears as and when Naipaul emphasizes his sense of alienation or projects himself as the native informant on the Third World.[4]

Naipaul's relationship with Trinidad has always been inherently and fundamentally vexed. That Port of Spain could actually suggest antiquity comes as a revelation to him. Moreover, his earlier denial of any sort of validated antiquity for the land of his birth is strongly moored to his sense of its landscape. The narrator comments wonderingly: "The squalor and pettiness and dinginess—the fowl coops and backyards and servant rooms and the many little houses on one small plot and the cesspits—seemed too new" (*Enigma* 157). Experiential knowledge brings with it the hint of a possible past to Trinidad—yet Naipaul does not desist from continuing to describe it in the stereotypes provided by the West. Trinidad is a cesspit, the rot of which contrasts essentially to the grandness of the decay of Wiltshire. Thus, by associating his sensibilities, which firmly favor antiquity, tradition, and class, with rural England, Naipaul establishes himself as canonically English. In a more charitable reading, Judith Levy argues that "Colonialism did not cut him off from an origin but from a myth of origin, and that is his recognition of his inability to make any collective myth (whether Hindu, Trinidadian—which he claims did not exist—or English) his own that has served as the basis for the autobiography that is titled *A Novel in Five Sections*" (114). However, it is still deeply troubling that Naipaul turns to that which denied him the myth of origin in the first place to try and create a myth of origin which is uniquely English. Thus when Naipaul makes the claim that he had discovered in himself a "deep interest in others, a wish to visualize the details and routine of their lives, to see through their eyes" (244), it is not surprising that this cast of characters (the "Others") is purely British: Alan, Bray, Jack, The Landlord, and so forth.

India, the source of Naipaul's actual origin, emerges as a complicated "subject full of nerves" (Naipaul qtd. in Theroux 321): "I didn't look back to India, couldn't do so; my ambition caused me to look ahead and outwards to England" (*Enigma* 130). Even though Naipaul never looked *back* at India, he has almost always looked forward to India, i.e., India has provided him with considerable fodder for writing.[5] Additionally, Naipaul's comments on his English landlord's Orientalist poems on India could be well read as a comment on Naipaul's work and the space that India occupies in his literary life: "Ruskinism, a turning away from the coarseness of industrialism, upper-class or cultivated sensibilities...my landlord's Indian romance partook of all those impulses and was rooted in England, wealth, empire, the idea of glory, material satiety, a very great security" (212). The narrative tone here is awestruck, although it is also possibly tinged with irony. Naipaul establishes an implicit comparison between his writing and the writing of his landlord. Like his landlord, there is nothing of "contemporary cult" or "fashion" in this book. However, unlike Naipaul, the landlord has inherited his art from the days of imperial glory. Nevertheless, in implying a comparison between his landlord and himself, Naipaul is also claiming his own place in the western canon. Like his landlord, Naipaul too shies away from much of the coarseness of industrialization by cloistering himself in the woods of Wiltshire. Thus the narrator's disclaimer that the landlord's poetry has very little to do with his (the narrator's) past life or ambitions rings false. It may not have anything to do with Naipaul on a strict level of plotline, but the similarity of the thematics and structural methodology are telling. Landlord and tenant are deeply invested in India, but it is an investment "rooted in England" or, more appropriately, in the English land. The landlord's inherited sense of Englishness is closely allied to his perception of the pristine value of the country. Perhaps Naipaul himself best gives a sense of closure to his special relationship to landscape in this novel: *Land partakes of what we breathe into it. It is touched by our moods and memories* (emphasis added, 335).

***

Naipaul began *India: A Million Mutinies Now* soon after completing *The Enigma of Arrival.* This travelogue is Naipaul's longest work in any genre. Fawzia Mustafa explains, "the scale of the book more or less meets the agenda of Naipaul's introductory explanation of the fruition of the nation's secular-democratic experiment" (186). It is generally conceded by critics that the earlier two travelogues[6] were much more vitriolic for reasons as varied as Naipaul's relative youth at the time of writing *An Area of Darkness* and the shock of encountering an India vastly different from the one created by his imagination. While Rob Nixon sees a "kinder, gentler Naipaul" (159) emerging in his later narratives, even in this travelogue, stereotypical descriptions of landscape are still tied into Naipaul's construction of the English identity. Mustafa claims that "the book's physical density matches in degree the density of *The Enigma of Arrival,* where description crossed the line between background and foreground; it lends *A Million Mutinies Now* an evocative visual appeal that is calibrated with the novel's auditory tone" (187). While Mustafa agrees that Naipaul recycles his old prejudices, she does not link this to its "evocative visual appeal" which is presented only through one of two stereotypes. Predictably, the first line of the travelogue is: "Bombay is a crowd." The next few lines proceed as follows: "With me in the taxi, were fumes and heat and din. The sun burned; there was little air; the grit from the bus exhausts began to stick to my skin….concrete buildings mildewed at their upper levels by Bombay weather, excessive sun, excessive rain, excessive heat…" (*Mutinies* 1). This seems to be a statement made by a man who has never visited a warm country, but it must be remembered that this is Naipaul's third visit to India. That Naipaul actually lived the first eighteen years of his life in the Caribbean but gazes at India through the eyes of a Westerner is significant. This allows him to construct himself as English through his reaction to the obtrusive physicality of India. Although he rarely makes contrasts with Trinidad, our prior knowledge of *The Enigma of Arrival* reveals some astonishing similarities: "A general impression of blackness and greyness and mud, narrow ragged lanes curving out of view; then a side of the main road dug up; then black mud, with men and women defecating on the edge of a black lake, swamp and sewage, with a hellish oily iridescence. The stench was barely supportable" (58). Naipaul here is talking about the Bombay slums, easily the poorest area in the city. His vision of India, however true it may be, is tarred by the language he uses, mired, as it is, in the Orientalist discourse of the West, which views the Third World only through the polarizing stereotypes of extreme exotica or extreme poverty.

Naipaul's description of Goa, which he describes as crowded, noisy, and teeming with "threat" and "urgency," is a case in point (136). However, when he sees Old Goa, Naipaul is both awestruck and condescending. While giving to Goa the antiquity he denies to Trinidad in *The Enigma of Arrival,* he does not give it the *validation* of antiquity that he gives to England. "Old Goa was very old. Almost as many years separated it from the present as separated the final Roman defeat of Carthage from the fall of Rome itself" (143). Interestingly, the touchstone for validation is ancient Rome/Greece, even now considered to be the crucible of all civilization. Unlike other western travelers who did not have any other comparisons except those of the West to draw on and draw out, Naipaul does have Trinidad to compare with India. His encounter with the antiquity of Trinidad leaves him cold. India has some antiquity yet it is only comparable to the West and even then it falls short. This allows Naipaul to construct himself as historian and chronicler of not only the Indian past and present but also of the western tradition.

Lucknow receives similar treatment. Naipaul has always critiqued the Third World habit of mimicry[7] while neglecting to observe the mimicry manifest in his own writings. His writings mimic Englishness to such an extent that they eventually become more English than the English canons themselves. However, he continues to run down India as a nation of mimics. At the Residency, in Lucknow, he describes the Mutiny of 1857 as "a kind of mimicry, seeking to give old India something of the socialist dynamism the Russians found in their own history" (351). That this socialist dynamism reached its peak in Russia in 1919, sixty-two years after the Mutiny, is something Naipaul willfully misrepresents, for he cannot even begin to fathom that the Third World could develop something that is unique and original and not a mimicry of the West. Correspondingly, Naipaul continues to glorify the British through his adulation of the buildings that speck the landscape: "The damaged buildings of the besieged Residency were preserved as a monument of *British* courage" (emphasis added, 352). This is completely in keeping with the British point of view that denounced the native insurgents as barbarians who mercilessly slaughtered the innocent, courageous British. Naipaul makes no effort to subvert the power structures built into this sort of travel writing. Instead, he continues to reify the British point of view, which is further validated by his positioning of himself as the native informant.

Therefore, these monuments, according to Naipaul, are an enduring testimony to the eternality of the British presence in India, even, especially after the exit of the colonizer. Remarking on a pillar near the residency, Naipaul says: "Independent India had put that monument up, to counter the British Raj's monument to itself. It was a feeble thing..." (353). Clearly, Naipaul is establishing himself as quintessentially British by identifying his emotions with the British part of the monuments and landscape.

Moreover, Naipaul sees India's present predicament to be a failure on its part: a failure to allow itself to flourish individually and instead be trampled on by others. Chandigarh, which could have been redeemed by Le Corbusier's architecture, is instead stained and diseased by hostile weather. While Naipaul concedes that this architecture is at variance with the landscape, he pins the blame squarely on the helpless colonized rather than the colonizer: "India had encouraged yet another outsider to build a monument to himself" (351). Ironically, Naipaul's travelogues perfectly describe the unequal power relations inscribed in such a statement where the outsider rides roughshod over the indigenous. Naipaul's three Indian travelogues then become monuments to not only himself but also, especially, to the English and Englishness:

> The most attractive and immoral move, however, has been Naipaul's, who allowed himself quite consciously to be turned into a witness for the Western prosecution. There are others like him who specialize in the thesis of what one of them has called self-inflicted wounds, which is to say that we non-whites are the cause of all our problems, not the overly-maligned imperialists. Naipaul's accounts of the Islamic, Latin American, African, Indian and Caribbean worlds totally ignore a massive infusion of critical scholarship about those regions in favor of the tritest, the cheapest and the easiest of colonial mythologies about wogs and darkies. (Edward Said qtd. in Mustafa 166)

Said's complaint that Naipaul uses only the over-determined discourse of the West to define the Non-West is thus validated by Naipaul's writing itself. As Nixon repeatedly asserts:

> When Naipaul enunciates his I, his voice is not that of a polymorphous indigenous authority assured of some common experience with sundry non-Western nations or communities. Rather he speaks a language that resonates with traditions of discursive power that assert the visual and political ascendancy of metropolitan knowers over the peripheral and underrepresented known. (80)

As indicated by my analysis of Naipaul's commentary on Bombay, Goa, Lucknow, and Chandigarh, Naipaul enunciates his "I," politically loaded, as it is, by reactions and responses to the physical, geographical, and historical landscape.

Even so, it needs to be admitted that there has been a self-conceded change in Naipaul's manner since he wrote *A Million Mutinies Now.* Naipaul acknowledges that his earlier visits to India and his accounts thereof were based on a sense of exclusion implied paradoxically through familiarity: "I knew the rituals but couldn't participate in them; I heard the language, but followed only the simpler words. But I was near enough to understand the passions...the India of my fantasy and heart was something lost and irrecoverable" (*Mutinies* 491). This posits an interesting contrast to his relationship with England as seen in *The Enigma of Arrival*. In India, Naipaul feels like a stranger only able to half-participate in its arcane rituals. In England, however, he finds it easier to assimilate. He can imagine a reality at harmony with the world of English literature and by writing such a reality he can also place himself at the fount of that reality. India does not encourage fantasy, unlike England, where fantasy comes to full flower. India seems to make Naipaul more aware of his very alien-ness and therefore more eager to assert his Englishness. Hence his optimistic conclusion becomes troubling. At the end of *A Million Mutinies Now,* Naipaul reviews *An Area of Darkness,* his vitriolic diatribe of 1962, and rationalizes it thus: "India was now a country of a million little mutinies. A million mutinies, supported by...twenty kinds of group excess, sectarian excess, religious excess, regional excess...what the mutinies were also helping to define was the strength of the *general intellectual life* and the wholeness and humanism of the value to which all Indians now felt they could appeal" (518, emphasis added). I quote this at length as it is important in understanding Nixon's "kinder, gentler Naipaul" (159). Here, Naipaul realizes that his earlier perceptions were erroneous. However, those very perceptions, India as an area of darkness and/or a wounded civilization, also are harnessed in *A Million Mutinies Now*. Admittedly, not to the extent as in the other two novels, but the same stereotypes still prevail. Moreover, in this statement, Naipaul reveals his innate elitism (called his Brahminism by some) by elevating the beginnings of an intellectual life as the road to redemption. That he can make such a statement after visiting the slums of Bombay (and being appalled by the hellishness there) is significant. The mere presence of slums seems to contradict Naipaul's notion of an all-pervasive, albeit general, intellectual life. Commenting on his travelogues, Naipaul has said: "Nerves was the subject of the first book. The second was more analytical, in the third book, I had arrived at this new way of writing, exploring civilizations not through what one thought of them *but through what the people had lived through and making a pattern of that*" (qtd. in Theroux 329, emphasis added). Naipaul's analysis only makes sense if we realize that he is using the middle class/aristocracy to make a pattern of India as a whole. It is true that in the thirty-odd years between *An Area of Darkness* and *A Million Mutinies Now* there has been the development of an educated, somewhat liberal, middle class who knows what it wants. It is perhaps this change that most surprised Naipaul, and it is faithfully recorded through his interviews. However, while he claims to have interviewed sections across Indian society, most of his interviewees range from upper/lower middle class to the former aristocracy. Predictably, Naipaul is fascinated with "glorious decay" and spends long hours (and longer pages) talking to/about the former aristocracy of Lucknow and Kashmir. This decay, a justifiable decay as it represents a former glory now lost by the vagaries of time, reflects back with startling similarity to *The Enigma of Arrival.*

Thus, in our efforts to admire Naipaul's rare compassion in *A Million Mutinies Now*, we must also be careful to notice his complicity in perpetuating the discourse of hegemony. Significantly, Naipaul retains the term "mutiny," [8] loaded with all its colonial currency, thus continuously reaffirming the omnipotence/presence of the British in everyday Indian life and also establishing his perspective as uniquely British. In his travel narratives, Naipaul creates a situation in which the Third-World intellectual gives sanction to the Master's discourse. This stamp of approval is accepted as authentic not only because it is from a Third-World intellectual but also because it is reinforcing First-World hegemony, which Naipaul further perpetuates by using the discursive paradigms provided by the First World.

***

In both texts there is a willed creation of a self that is uniquely English; this is more latent in the travelogue than in the novel. There is also, however, a paradoxical staging of Naipaul's presence as someone different from anyone else. It is no contradiction that this self-constructed persona, so different from anyone else, is also more English than the English themselves; for as Naipaul sets about demonstrating in *The Enigma of Arrival,* no one but him has the right to the quintessentially English landscape that he has willed into creation. That this is potentially subversive is without doubt. However, its subversive momentum is never fully drawn out as Naipaul only fits into the landscape he has created by virtue of his aesthetic sensibilities, which are purely and canonically English. This sensibility also finds its way into his writings about the Third World. It is interesting to analyze the first-person narrator in a travelogue, especially because travelogues claim themselves to be works of nonfiction, underlining the presumption that the "I" is therefore objective. It is thus crucial to see the "I" in Naipaul's travelogues to be as carefully constructed as the fictional narrator in *The Enigma of Arrival.* As Fawzia Mustafa says: "Naipaul's use of his own writing persona, mainly as a traveler in his non-fiction and in most of his fiction as narrators or characters whose backgrounds reflect colonial and postcolonial compositions similar to his own, has allowed him to invest the public expression of his works with the aura of a private, personalized, somewhat self-critical subjective presence" (167). Naipaul's travelogues then are imbued with subjectivity. How self-critical his persona is, is an altogether controversial question. This is further complicated by Naipaul's narrative style. His self-obsessed ruminations continue to intrude even in his travelogues. His fixation with India is similar to his fixation with England as both have what Naipaul values above all: classical antiquity. By resorting to

Hinduism and Brahminism, Naipaul combats a culture that has denied him access; yet it is only a selective imbibing of Hinduism and Hindu culture, which is separate and distinct from India, and Indian culture(s). As Theroux says: "Vidia denied being Indian. He saw himself as a new man. But he behaved like an upper-class Indian caste conscious, race conscious, a food fanatic, precious in his fears from worrying about his body being tainted" (344). There is perhaps not such a difference between High Brahminism and High Englishness[9] and both collapse into Naipaul's many narratorial selves. It is disturbing that Trinidad comes out last and lowest in such an analysis whichever text we consider. Naipaul is thus at pains to project his identity as an expediently selective assortment of Trinidadian, Indian, and English. That his intellect and imagination are uniquely English prove themselves repeatedly, through very different modes, in both *The Enigma of Arrival* and *India: A Million Mutinies Now*. Ultimately, it is the landscape of the imagination that seizes upon externalities to claim those for the self. That this self is more English rather than Indo-Caribbean remains the enigma of Naipaul's particular mutiny.

Notes

1   Because I use *landscape* in a very broad sense, its referents include the physical, geographical, and architectural landscape.

2   Given that *The Enigma of Arrival* is so deeply autobiographical, I consider "Naipaul" and the "narrator" to be interchangeable.

3   I am aware that I often conflate Britishness with Englishness in this essay, but, Englishness is still considered to be the heart of Britishness. While the discourse of national identity altered from Englishness to Britishness (encompassing the Irish, Scots, and Welsh) in the twentieth century, most colonial subjects, especially those of Anglophilic orientation like Naipaul, would identify England with Britain. For more on the politics of Englishness versus Britishness see Ian Baucom's *Out of Place: Englishness, Empire and the Locations of Identity* (Princeton: Princeton University Press, 1999)

4   I will discuss this in greater detail in my analysis of *A Million Mutinies Now*.

5   This preoccupation with India manifests itself most noticeably in his three travelogues on India.

6   *An Area of Darkness* (1964), *India: A Wounded Civilization* (1977)

7   See for example *The Mimic Men* (1967).

8   This is a highly politicized issue of nomenclature. The British insisted on calling the uprising of 1857 a "mutiny" while Indian nationalists called it "the Revolt of 1857" or "the First War of Independence." Also, see Nixon, *London Calling*.

9   Nirad C. Chaudhuri, author of the highly anglophilic *A Passage to England*, is a foremost example.

Works Cited

Baucom, Ian. *Out of Place: Englishness, Empire and the Locations of Identity*. Princeton: Princeton UP, 1999.

Chaudhuri, Nirad C. *A Passage to India*. New York: St. Martin's Press, 1959.

Levy, Judith. *V.S. Naipaul: Displacement and Autobiography*. New York: Garland, 1995.

Mustafa, Fawzia. *V.S. Naipaul*. Series: Cambridge Studies in African and Caribbean Literature. Cambridge: Cambridge UP, 1995.

Naipaul, V.S. *An Area of Darkness*. Harmondsworth, Penguin, 1968.

———. *The Enigma of Arrival*. New York: Vintage Books, 1988.

———. *India: A Million Mutinies Now*. London: Minerva, 1990.

———. *India: A Wounded Civilization*. New York: Knopf, 1977.

———. *The Mimic Men*. New York: Penguin, 1967.

Nixon, Rob. *London Calling. V.S. Naipaul: Postcolonial Mandarin*. New York: Oxford UP, 1992.

Sivanandan, Ambalavaner. "The Enigma of the Colonised: Reflections on Naipaul's Arrival." *Race & Class: A Journal for Black and Third World Liberation*. 32:1 (July–September 1990): 33–34.

Suleri, Sara. "Naipaul's Arrival." *The Rhetoric of English India*. Chicago: U of Chicago P, 1993.

Theroux, Paul. *Sir Vidia's Shadow: A Friendship Across Five Continents*. Boston: Houghton and Mifflin, 1998.

Chapter 18

Jonathan Raban's Coasting *and Literary Strategies in Contemporary British Travel Writing*

Jan Borm

"Travelling is no longer that much of a problem of distances, discoveries, privileges or heroism, but a matter of imagination," Jean-Didier Urbain notes in his study *Secrets de voyage*[1]; "the truth of the journey is to be found in the ties that the imagination establishes between the traveller and his journey" (351). Such mediating of imagination is one of the key characteristics of contemporary British travel writing. One of the most imaginative contemporary authors is undoubtedly Jonathan Raban, whose journey home, *Coasting* (1986), will be explored in some detail below. In his preface to the Picador Travel Classics edition of *Coasting* (1995), Raban explains how his travel book came to be written only after he had finished a novel on the same subject, stressing how *Coasting* was to "...have the improvised, imaginative structure of a work of fiction, rather than the Gradgrindish, topographical procession from A to B of the conventional travel book" (xviii).

The question is how contemporary British travel writing circumvents the conventional travel book and in what way imagination can be seen at work both in the structure of contemporary books and possibly in the inventiveness of the writing. Do these narrative strategies, that are in fact literary, allow contemporary authors to leave the circle of the conventional? If so, does their wish to leave the center not show to what extent contemporary authors are concerned with their own relation to the center? To find some answers to these questions, I will move from an analysis of the opening section of *Coasting* and the book's structure to more general questions concerning the notion of *circling* in contemporary British travel writing and the idea of the *center*.

Coasting, or How to Avoid the Conventional in *Style*

It seems useful to remember first of all what one may understand by *Style* in literary studies. As Michel Morel puts it: "the style is the textual witness of the meeting between the individual and the generic dimension...the term stands both for the individual inventiveness of an original discourse and the simple re-producing by this discourse of predominant linguistic models" (Morel 325–26). What I would like to point out is how *Coasting* deals with a conventional theme in travel writing, "the journey home," in a strikingly dynamic way.

The opening section of *Coasting* makes the point. At first glance, it deals with what one would expect it to deal: approaching Britain, i.e., the beginning of the journey, or Britain seen from mid-distance. Not surprisingly, the British coast and sky seemed rather gray on Raban's first day of observations, and the warn-ings concerning the danger of *coasting* in the British Isles may confirm the im-pression that one is reading a text attempting to represent the real in a largely referential, or documentary way.

Nonetheless, certain sentences, or rather, certain phrasings attract attention: "The engine, the engine" (11). Why does the narrator repeat the expression? One learns thereafter that the sea is "so regular and monotonous that you keep on hearing voices in it" (11). The repetition may therefore allude to the sea but still one wonders what voices the narrator hears? The narrator continues: "Sometimes, when the revs are low, there's a man under the boards reciting poems that you vaguely remember..." (11). By this stage one wonders not only about the man but also about the poem and what all this has to do with a de-scription of Britain seen from the sea. Raban's phrase "the engine, the engine" appears to echo one of the most famous French lines on the sea, Paul Valéry's "La mer, la mer, toujours recommencée!"[2] If this may be granted, quite a few possibilities offer themselves to read between Raban's lines. There is the irony that Valéry's verse is part of a poem called "Le cimetière marin." Thus, the dan-gers of sailing are hinted at via the implicit reference to Valéry's cemetery of sailors. Such a *Valerian* reading of Raban can alert the reader about other sen-tences that may express more than meets the eye.

This opening can therefore be read both as a view of the British coast and the state of Britain, or better, the state Britain is in. To give only one or two ex-amples, one can look at the expression "the wavelets peak and dribble dully down their fronts" (11). If one replaces "wavelets" with "Britain" one reads that the latter was "dribbling dully down"; in other words, that Britain was going "down the drain." Let's not forget that Raban is writing about Britain at war with Argentina over the Falklands. The sentence "Sails hang in loose bundles from their spars" can suggest that Britain is running out of steam.

That the theme of the state of Britain during the Falklands War is raised here can be seen in the sentence, "We're crossing into the cold fifties of latitude, as far from the warm middle of the world as Labrador at one end of it and the Falklands at the other" (12). Labradors are undoubtedly among the most popular dogs in Britain and the region thus named brings us back once again to the theme of Britain: a cold place at war. One could go on for quite a while to establish such links, but these examples sufficiently show that the reader is dealing here with a text that offers various ways of reading and bears witness to the author's use of imagination.

I have already noted how Raban intended to give *Coasting* the "improvised, imaginative structure of a work of fiction" (Preface xviii). In the same section, Raban explains what particular characteristic of some kind of travel writing he tried to move away from: "I began to hate the *and then, and then, and then* form of the conventional travel book" (xvi). Additionally, this leaving behind of chronology in strict order is echoed by a discontinuous itinerary. Raban goes as far as proposing a summary of his journey fairly early on in the book for those who only want to know what happened next, a sort of *digest* for busy readers: "I got drunk in Torquay, had a fit of memoirs in Portsmouth, turned lyrical in Brighton...was at my wits' end in Dublin...lost my temper off Land's End and summed things up pretty neatly in Falmouth. *The End*" (50). One may note in passing the punning or rearranging of expressions that illustrate the author's inventiveness once again. Thus, the narrator's "wits' end" may possibly be associated with Land's End (in Cornwall) and a land that is at its wits's end. Similarly, one is weary of a narrator summing up things in Falmouth—with a foul mouth, so to speak. Of more interest, however, is the idea that Raban decided to cut up the order of sequences. The nonsequential chronology serves two purposes. One is the idea, alluded to by Raban in his preface, of breaking away from the overpowering *diktat* of the linear. The other is to make the book's theme, coasting, match with the very structure of the book. As Raban explains just before the *digest* quoted above: "The difficulty with a circular voyage is that, once you have gone on past your original point of departure...it has no destination and no ending..." (50). This kind of voyage is endless by definition and may thus be taken to represent a circle. This is in fact where the continuity in Raban's narrative is to be found, the missing link, as it were, which is literally illustrated by the dash ending the narrative. Not only is this a tribute to Sterne's *Sentimental Journey,* but a reminder that literature and life are (intimately) linked: "The long dash perfectly symbolizes the threadline separation between the world of the book and the continuing real life outside it" (Preface xx). It is less the journey that represents the stuff dreams are made of here but the book that makes one *dream on,* if one can accept that expression.

Circling around the Center

It is precisely the desire to reinforce the role of imagination in representing travel that is one of the driving forces of contemporary British travel writing. Bruce Chatwin made this one of his foremost aims in *In Patagonia,* the quest for a substitute for a piece of skin being but the substitute for another quest consisting partly in trying to reach back to his earliest memories and his Patagonia of the mind. However, this enterprise is not a question of (long) distance. Whether one travels to the *uttermost part of the earth*[3] or back home does not determine to what extent one has managed to leave the center that home represents. As Jonathan Raban notes: "Finding yourself to be a foreigner, abroad in an alien place, whether it's Wigan or Patagonia, is at the heart of every classic book of travel....Place by itself is not the important thing" (Preface x). Similarly, Jean-Didier Urbain suggests: "The destination seems secondary: just a pretext in the strong sense of the term. The essential thing is the challenge, unique, and then the exclusive narrative one will write about it" (130).

How then, do contemporary authors manage to reinforce the role of imagination? A particularly striking way of doing so is the use of certain literary strategies. Indeed, a number of contemporary travel books are written, in part, as though they were novels, or "non-fiction novels," as David Lodge has noted: "There has been in Britain in recent years, however, something of a renaissance of literary travel writing, much of which perhaps belongs in this category of the non-fiction novel" (8). First of all, the narrator no longer functions as the reader's "yours faithfully, epic self." In Chatwin's *In Patagonia* the narrator is elliptical about his own itinerary up to a point that exasperated Theroux to the extent of publishing a rather critical article on Chatwin's strategies after the latter's death.[4] Raban is, if not elliptical, at least *discontinuous* about his itinerary in *Coasting,* and literally becomes another U.S. citizen during one afternoon in Guntersville in *Hunting Mr. Heartbreak,* and his fictional, "third-person self" in Seattle, represented by a character named "Rainbird," the traveler's alter ego. Other contemporary British authors, such as Colin Thubron or William Dalrymple also tend to be rather discreet about their everyday life as travelers, whereas Redmond O'Hanlon goes to the other extreme of detailing the pains of his quotidian efforts when hacking his way through the jungle.

Furthermore, one may look at the considerable size or length of dialogues in contemporary travel writing. To take O'Hanlon as an example, his travel books feature whole casts of characters that have or, to be more precise, are given the hair-raising quality of answering back in English to the narrator, a technique that allows O'Hanlon to raise the question of the role of the white traveler/anthropologist when visiting/describing natives. Linked to this aspect, one will find that a number of contemporary narrators refrain from commenting upon events, another way, so-to-speak, of *circling the center* of convention. One cannot possibly explain everything one sees on the road, and it is not one's job as a narrator to do so. In this sense contemporary travel books may for instance be seen to differ from *reportage.* To give only one example, Chatwin rarely mentions the tragic destiny of Patagonian and Fuegian natives explicitly, but via a whole system of metaphors ("Songlines" 8), or what David Lodge calls "iterative symbolism," that the reader is invited to "reactualize," to use a term of Umberto

Eco's. We have seen a similar strategy at work in Raban's *Coasting*, and such metaphorical use of language may be observed in numerous other contemporary works. Finally, one could look at the function of intertexts in contemporary travel writing, but this would lead us too far.

To come back to the notion of the circle, one may wonder then how a certain unity of the text is maintained in contemporary travel writing despite its extensive use of *discontinuous* strategies.[5] After all, *In Patagonia* ends out at sea without any hint as to the boat's destination. Even so, someone plays Debussy's "La Mer" aboard the ferry and the pun does not only play on the notion of the "sea" but also that of the "mother." Thus, one can read Chatwin's ending as echoing Robert Byron's return to a rather dreary England at the end of *The Road to Oxiana*, in that Byron returns home to present his travel narrative to his mother. What is at stake here is the idea of some kind of return. Even if contemporary authors abandon linear narrative strategies, the return, another fundamental element of any quest story (incidentally, any travel book seems by definition a quest), surfaces predominantly in contemporary travel books. I obviously do not mean "return" in a literal sense. Indeed, contemporary British travel books that end at the narrator's home or starting point seem so rare that it is worthwhile to point out one of the few examples one can think of, Peter Levi's *A Bottle in the Shade* (1996).

The kind of return, then, that seems predominant in contemporary travel books is a form of what Jean-Didier Urbain calls "pastoral nostalgia" (209). The author's childhood thus functions as a mediator, as one can note in the works of Chatwin, O'Hanlon, and Raban, among others. David Espey has analyzed the childhood trope in travel writing and cites Raban's *Old Glory* as one of his examples: "Raban's adventure epitomizes Freud's notion of travel as escape from the father" (52). Additionally, Raban's escape also concerns the fatherland, not exactly a *bad land*,[6] but a place to distance oneself from, or a place to look at from some distance, as Raban does in *Coasting*. Thus Espey notes: "Childhood affects travel literature precisely in this way; it is a palimpsest of memory, desire, and impression—an earlier manuscript which lies beneath the travel narrative and guides it" (57). The childhood "text" would therefore be one of the aspects of the traveler, of the *viator in fabula*, as Jean-Didier Urbain notes: "This is how one becomes a *viator in fabula*, a traveller travelling inside a story: a biography, a novel or a tale...." (362)—an autobiography, one could also add.

The childhood trope functions as a framework to *In Patagonia,* and is present in all of Redmond O'Hanlon's travelogues, and working in a slightly different way in Raban's *Coasting*. In other words, the pastoral nostalgia of contemporary travelers works as a substitute for the voluntary abandoning of the "beaten" epic track. It takes the form of a "...quest for the pastoral ideal of an illusory golden age," as David Espey puts it (53), in Chatwin's first book and in O'Hanlon's narratives, and it works as a kind of catharsis in Raban's *Coasting*. To give only one example from *Coasting,* the narrator visits his parents and pre-

sents an image of himself and his father in which the narrator has trouble deciding who is more of a youngster: "Squaring up to each other with lopsided,
smoker's smiles, we bobbed and weaved like image and essence in a looking-
glass. Father and son, definitely. But an outsider might have found it difficult to
tell who was which and which was who" (171). Looking at his father as a
stranger, the narrator seems to be struck by the likeness of father and son, suggesting that the latter is as strange as the former, if not stranger. Perhaps, as
Chatwin's laconic narrator might be tempted to put it, it's a question of *Style*.

(Re-)placing the Center

If the childhood trope is as present as we have suggested above, one may wonder
to what extent contemporary British travelers really turn their back on where
they once seem to have belonged. Leaving the center that Britain can be seen to
represent, if only to look at the country from out at sea, does not necessarily suggest that one is no longer part of it or concerned by it. In a recent essay, Tim
Youngs has raised the question of home as an "absent presence" in travel writing
(75). On the one hand, he notes, "The willed (which is not to say actual) removal
of oneself from the center...helps explain the high profile of writers like Chatwin
and Theroux" (75). According to Tim Youngs, one of the reasons for this "willed
removal" is the following: "[F]or Theroux and Chatwin the wish for apparent
dissociation from national loyalties may be a response to political antagonisms,
especially as manifested in and after the Second World War" (78). Conversely, as
Youngs points out, "Writing one's way out of position becomes the very marker
of one's place" (80). It can be thus suggested that the childhood trope is one of
the ways in which that otherwise "absent presence" of the center is referred to in
some of the works mentioned above.

The issue at stake here is to know to what extent the process of writing one's
way out of the center might be seen as yet another form of the *ethnocentric*. To
take one example, Paul Fussell mentions a whole series of British narratives from
between the wars that he groups together in the following way: "An insistent
leitmotif of writing between the wars, for both successful and would-be escapees,
is *I Hate It Here*" (16). If "Here" is the center that Britain represents to these
authors, their wish to foreground their "hate" for the center might be seen as
another way of focusing primarily on the center, and even a "willed removal"
may be just another form of the *ethnocentric,* as suggested above.

How can one get out of this seemingly vicious circle? If one can conceive of
the *ethnocentric,* one can possibly also speak of the *ethno-eccentric*. The latter
would stand for something that is not primarily concerned with the center, or
rather differently so. Jean-Didier Urbain's definition of an *eccentric* seems particularly helpful in this context: "Exceptions set apart, an eccentric is neither a
madman nor a rebel wanting to cut himself off from his own society. It is the
latter that inspires him, that makes him possible and live" (141). My comments

on *Coasting* have shown how Raban might be considered to be an *eccentric* in this sense. While "eccentring" himself in *Coasting,* his discourse is inspired by, or reacts quite considerably to, British society. This strategy corresponds to another characteristic of the eccentric, according to Urbain: "An eccentric does not rise up against society but against its lack of clearsightedness, imagination and projects, its loss of meaning and its monotony, its absurdities or boredom. Moving away from its conventions, eccentring himself from the centre and its habits, preconceived views and commonplaces, he only moves away from it" (141). Thus, *eccentring* oneself would be, according to Jacques Meunier, "a way of social experimenting" (qtd. in Urbain 142). After all, Jonathan Raban points out implicitly that the aim in travel writing, or at least his aim, is "to tell true stories about society" (Preface xxi). If that is the aim, then, as Urbain puts it when speaking about ethnography of the near, "what one needs to do is to defamiliarize oneself with one's own world" (248).

To Come Full Circle, or "Eccentric" as in "Ethno-eccentric"

Such defamiliarizing is more or less what Jonathan Raban does in a particularly dynamic way in *Coasting,* even if his journey home may not strike one offhand as one of the most eccentric of destinations (but then again…). Whatever the case may be, it seems to me that authors of Chatwin's generation and also those who have been publishing since the 1950s, such as Patrick Leigh Fermor or Norman Lewis, set out to rediscover—if not the world—at least what may seem extraordinary in it (whether at home or abroad) by *eccentring* themselves. To what degree they may have done so remains evidently a matter of debate. Indeed, it seems feasible to speak of ethno-centric and ethno-eccentric elements within one given text. One could conceive of them as two binary poles between which the traveler negotiates her or his "journey and the book," to refer to Raban's article on the writing of travel.

Eccentring oneself has thus been one way of renewing the tradition of travel writing and possibly one of the ways in which to explain the travel book's recent "renaissance" (to borrow Lodge's term). If one has to be aware of possible ambiguities in such a project, one also needs to point out the literary energy thereby set free in contemporary travelogues. In other words, the *ethnocentric* and *ethno-eccentric* as I would suggest to call the *eccentric* here, (as we are concerned with individuals and societies), are not mutually exclusive worlds or stances. If the *ethnocentric* may be spotted in contemporary British travel writing, one also has to underline the idea that the *other* can be met with and presented in a supple, open, or "nomadic" way, (to borrow the term introduced by Syed Manzurul Islam). As we have seen, one of the characteristic strategies of contemporary authors consists in trying to account for the *other*—if the term may be granted—in *Style.* Raban's engine may echo Valéry's sea and Chatwin's "La Mer" and Byron's mother. Such intertextual "repetitions" are just one way contemporary authors have found to get back at the conventions of the travel book. Using style to establish differences and repetition, they have both maintained the tradition and renewed the genre. As the dash at Raban's journey home suggests, there is no end to this form of coasting. This, in turn, leads us back, one more time, to Valéry's memorable line: "La mer, la mer, toujours recommencé!"

Notes

1   Jean-Didier Urbain. *Secrets de voyage—Menteurs, imposteurs et autres voyageurs invisibles.* Paris: Payot, 1998 (American edition forthcoming at Notre Dame); N.B.: all passages quoted from Urbain's study have been translated by myself.
2   Paul Valéry. "Le cimetière marin" in *Poésies* (1929. Paris: Gallimard, 1958).
3   In reference to Lucas Bridges's memoir of Fireland *Uttermost Part of the Earth* (1948).
4   Paul Theroux. "Chatwin Revisited" in *Granta* N°44. (London: King, Sell, & Railtor, Ltd. 1993, 213–21).
5   For a discussion of this term see Roland Barthes, "Littérature et discontinu" in his *Essais critiques* (Paris: Seuil, 1964).
6   *Bad Land* is the title of one of Jonathan Raban's recent books, set mostly in eastern Montana (London: Picador, 1996).

Works Cited

Barthes, Roland. "Littérature et discontinu." *Essais critiques.* 1962. Paris: Editions du Seuil, 1964. 175–87.

Bridges, Lucas. *Uttermost Part of the Earth.* London: Hodder & Stoughton, 1948.

Byron, Robert. *The Road to Oxiana.* London: Macmillan, 1937

Chatwin, Bruce. *In Patagonia.* 1977. London: Picador, 1979.

———. *The Songlines.* 1987. London: Picador, 1988.

Eco, Umberto. *Lector in fabula.* Paris: Grasset, 1985.

Espey, David. "Childhood and Travel Literature." *Travel Culture: Essays on What Makes Us Go.* Ed. Carol Traynor Williams. Westport: Praeger Publishers, 1998. 51–57.

Fussell, Paul. *Abroad: British Literary Traveling Between the Wars.* Oxford: Oxford UP, 1980.

Islam, Syed Manzurul. *The Ethics of Travel: From Marco Polo to Kafka.* Manchester: Manchester UP, 1996.

Levi, Peter. *A Bottle in the Shade: A Journey in the Western Peloponnese.* London: Sinclair & Stevenson, 1996.

Lodge, David. "The Novelist Today: Still at the Crossroads?" *The Practice of Writing*. 1992. 1996. London: Penguin, 1997.

Morel, Michel. "*Praxis de la lecture*." Diss. Paris: Université de la Sorbonne Nouvelle—Paris III, 1989.

O'Hanlon, Redmond. *Into the Heart of Borneo: An Account of a Journey Made in 1983 to the Mountains of Batu Tiban with James Fenton*. 1984. London: Penguin, 1985.

———. *In Trouble Again: A Journey Between the Orinoco and the Amazon*. 1988. London: Penguin, 1989.

———. *Congo Journey*. London: Hamish Hamilton, 1996.

Raban, Jonathan. *Old Glory*. 1981. London: Picador, 1986.

———. *Coasting*. 1986. London: Picador, 1987.

———. "The Journey and the Book." In *For Love & Money*. 1981. 1987. London: Picador, 1988.

———. *Hunting Mr. Heartbreak*. 1990. London: Picador, 1991.

———. Preface. In *Coasting*. 1986. London: Picador, "Picador Travel Classics," 1995.

———. *Bad Land: An American Romance*. London: Picador, 1996.

Sterne, Laurence. *A Sentimental Journey*. 1768. Ed. Graham Petrie. London: Penguin, 1967.

Theroux, Paul. "Chatwin Revisited." *Granta N°44: "The Last Place on Earth."* London: Granta, 1993. 213–21.

Urbain, Jean-Didier. *Secrets de voyage: Menteurs, imposteurs et autres voyageurs invisibles*. Paris: Payot, 1998.

Valéry, Paul. "Le cimetière marin." *Poésies*. 1929. Paris: Gallimard, 1958. 100–5.

Youngs, Tim. "Punctuating Travel: Paul Theroux and Bruce Chatwin." *Literature and History* 3rd Series 6:2 (Autumn 1997): 73–88.

Notes on Contributors

JAN BORM is a member of the research center "Suds d'Amériques" and Associate Professor in English at the University of Versailles at Saint-Quentin-en-Yvelines. He co-edited (with Matthew Graves) Bruce Chatwin's posthumous collection, *Anatomy of Restlessness: Selected Writings 1969–1989.* He has written on the contemporary British travel book in his doctoral thesis (University of Paris 7) and in a number of published articles.

MARCO DIANI is Senior Research Fellow at the Centre National de la Recherche Scientifique (CNRS) and Research Director of the "Institut de Recherches sur le Moderne," an international multidisciplinary research center on Comparative Modernities. He has published several books, and over seventy scholarly articles in his areas of interest, that include new technologies and organizational change, urban sociology, sociology of work, sociological theory, and the social study of literature.

MARÍA FRANCISCA LLANTADA DÍAZ is Assistant Professor in the Department of English Philology at the University of Santiago de Compostela in Spain. She has written several articles and reviews on Dorothy Richardson and Modernism.

ANDREA FEESER is Associate Professor of Modern and Contemporary Art and Theory at Clemson University in South Carolina, and earned her Ph.D. in Art History at the City University of New York Graduate Center. She has received grants from the Samuel H. Kress Foundation and the National Endowment for the Humanities, has published various articles on modern and contemporary art, and produced the public art project *Historic Waikiki* with Gaye Chan.

DONNA FORAN is a Lecturer at Marquette University and Mount Mary College, Milwaukee, Wisconsin. She earned her Ph.D. in English, specializing in nineteenth-century British literature, at Marquette University.

CYNTHIA HO is Associate Professor and Chair of the Literature Department at the University of North Carolina, Asheville. She earned her Ph.D. in Medieval Literature from the University of Maryland. She has edited *Crossing the Bridge: Comparative Essays on Heian Japanese and Medieval European Women Writers* and written articles on women and didactic literature from the Middle Ages.

THEODORE C. HUMPHREY is now Professor of English (Emeritus) at California State Polytechnic University, Pomona, where he has taught since 1968. He earned his Ph.D. in English literature of the Eighteenth century from the University of Arkansas. He has published numerous critical essays on contemporary novels and nonfiction in encyclopedias and other reference works as well as articles on folklore.

MELANIE R. HUNTER is Instructor of English at Tulsa Community College in Tulsa, Oklahoma. She earned her M.A. degree at the University of Tulsa and is currently completing her Ph.D. from the University of Arizona. She has presented papers and published several articles and a book review on the work of Doris Lessing, V.S. Naipaul, travel writing, science writing, and Salman Rushdie and the Booker Prize.

KATY NEBHAN is completing her Ph.D. at the University of Sydney and is writing her thesis on Australian Muslim Nationalism. She has published various pieces on representations of Muslim fundamentalism and the anatomies of violence, the role of the Afghan cameleers in Australia's pioneering history, pilgrimage, and expressions of time in modernist art movements.

CECILIA NOVERO is Assistant Professor of German Studies at Pennsylvania State University. She works on avant-garde aesthetics and politics as well as neo-avant-garde artists, in particular Eat Art. She has written a dissertation on the Metaphors of Incorporation and Consumption in Walter Benjamin, Dada, and Futurism. She has published articles on cookery texts in the thirties, Dada and artist Daniel Spoerri in a variety of journals and one exhibition catalog, as well as encyclopaedia entries on German gastronomy, feminism, and women writers. She is currently writing a book on avant-garde/neo-avant-garde relations from the perspective of their rhetorical and "material" uses of foods.

ANDREW PALMER is Senior Lecturer in English at Christ Church University College in Canterbury, England. He received his doctorate from the University of Sussex and has published fiction and various articles on modern English literature including figures such as Alan Sillitoe, Bruce Chatwin, George Orwell and Howard Jacobson.

ADAM PIETTE is the author of *Remembering and the Sound of Words: Mallarmé, Proust, Joyce, Beckett* and *Imagination at War: British Fiction and Poetry, 1939–1945.* He is currently Reader at the University of Glasgow. He worked in Swiss universities for ten years previously. He also helps run the Edwin Morgan Centre for Creative Writing (Glasgow/Strathclyde).

JOSEPH PUGLIESE is Lecturer in Critical and Cultural Studies at Macquarie University, Sydney, Australia. He earned his Ph.D. from the University of Sydney. He has published widely in books and journals on issues of race, ethnicity, diaspora, and colonialism.

PALLAVI RASTOGI is Assistant Professor of English at Utah State University. She is currently working on a manuscript on "cosmopolitanism" in colonial and postcolonial travel narratives from India. She has published critical essays on South Asian life-writing and fiction from the subcontinent.

KRISTI SIEGEL is Associate Professor of English at Mount Mary College in Wisconsin and earned her Ph.D. in Modern Studies from the University of Wisconsin-Milwaukee. She published *Women's Autobiographies, Culture, Feminism* (Peter Lang, 1999, 2001), is editing another collection of essays, this one treating women's travel writing, *Gender, Genre, and Identity in Women's Travel Writing* (Peter Lang, forthcoming 2003), serves as General Editor for the book series *Travel Writing Across the Disciplines* (Peter Lang), and has published various articles on postmodern, feminist, cultural, and autobiographical theory.

HEIDI N. SJOSTROM earned an M.A. in English/Creative Writing from the University of Wisconsin-Milwaukee where she is currently finishing her Ph.D. She has been an Instructor, teaching mainly writing courses, at Mount Mary College in Milwaukee, and is now a Lecturer, teaching writing and British literature courses, at Marquette University. Sjostrom has published reviews, articles, and a scholarly article on Frederick Buechner. At present, her area of specialization is transgressive and subversive women in twentieth-century fiction, a topic she is also using for a novel she is completing.

GARY TOTTEN is Assistant Professor of English at Concordia College in Moorhead, Minnesota, and earned his Ph.D. from Ball State University. His teaching and research focuses on late nineteenth- and early twentieth-century American literature and culture, travel literature, and critical theory. He has published articles on Edith Wharton's fiction, Theodore Dreiser's travel narratives, and Charlotte Perkins Gilman's short fiction.

EDWARD WHITLEY is a Ph.D. candidate in American literature at the University of Maryland, College Park, and is currently completing a dissertation on Walt Whitman and other nineteenth-century American poets.

TONI B. WULFF is Associate Professor of French and Dean of Faculty at Mount Mary College in Wisconsin. She received her Ph.D. from Syracuse University after spending two years teaching in France with a Fulbright French

Government Assistantship. She has published and presented various articles on French medieval theatre, issues in intercultural communication, and French Caribbean women writers.

�֍ Index